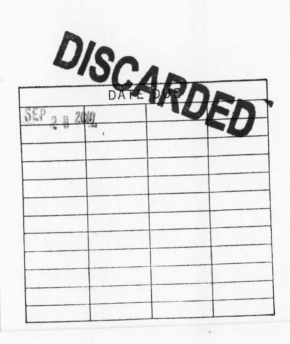

A Theory of
Argumentation

STUDIES IN RHETORIC AND COMMUNICATION
General Editors
E. Culpepper Clark
Raymie E. McKerrow
David Zarefsky

"Hear O Israel":
The History of American Jewish Preaching, 1654–1970
Robert V. Friedenberg

A Theory of Argumentation
Charles Arthur Willard

Charles Arthur Willard

A Theory
of Argumentation

The University of Alabama Press   Tuscaloosa and London

Copyright © 1989 by
The University of Alabama Press
Tuscaloosa, Alabama 35487–0380
All rights reserved
Manufactured in the United States of America

Library of Congress Cataloging-in-Publication Data

Willard, Charles Arthur.
  A theory of argumentation / Charles Arthur Willard.
    p. cm. — (Studies in rhetoric and communication)
  Bibliography: p.
  Includes index.
  ISBN 0-8173-0427-4
  1. Reasoning. I. Title. II. Series.
BC177.W544 1989
168—dc19   88-27742
                                                    CIP

British Library Cataloguing-in-Publication Data available

To My Parents
Herbert C. Willard
and
Christine S. Willard

Contents

Preface

This book attempts to make good on two promises implicit in *Argumentation and the Social Grounds of Knowledge* (Willard, 1983, hereafter *ASGK*). These debts arose with *ASGK*'s strategy of linking knowledge to argument *assuming* the viability of the interactional view of argument and with *ASGK*'s claim that argument must not be isolated from the empirical facts of communication and persuasion. Both moves asked the reader provisionally to grant that arguments are social processes central to the creation, maintenance, and use of knowledge and that a communication theory is the optimum context for a theory of argument. Thus capitalized by the reader's indulgence, *ASGK* was a heavily mortgaged venture.

To redeem these debts I will draw once again on the reader's indulgence. The viability of the argument field as a unit of analysis is presumed here but not explicitly defended. And though I have elsewhere defended the idea that opposition should be valued as an end in itself (Willard, 1987a), the exposition in these pages is so dependent on the presumed value of opposition that a full-blown defense buttressed by case studies is needed. So this book should be seen as a stage in an exposition stretching over three subsequent works. "The Balkanization of Knowledge and the Problem of the Public Sphere" (Willard, 1988) defends the argument field as a unit of analysis and as a way of defining the problem of the public sphere. The central claim is that organizational structure disprefers conflict. Thus "Valuing Dissensus" (Willard and Hynes, 1988) combats the mystique of consensus by defending dissensus as an end in itself. Drawing upon these works—repaying the debts *they* incur—is a work that exists now only in sketches. "The Prospects of Criticism in a Relativized World" will deal with the problems of critical discourse posed by the pluralism of the modern world and the possible grounds for a philosophy of the public sphere.

The theory presented here is a hopeless mutt with a family history of indifference to breed. The reader will note debts to Illinois School Constructivism, Chicago School Symbolic Interactionism, and to Barbara J. O'Keefe's distinctions among message design logics. My corridor colleagues, Anne Holmquest, Shirley Willihnganz, and especially Thomas J. Hynes have contributed many ideas and suggestions. I have also borrowed ideas from J. Anthony Blair, Frans van Eemeren, Walter Fisher, Michel Foucault, Steve Fuller, G. Thomas Goodnight, Rob Grootendorst, Sally Jackson, Scott Jacobs, Ralph Johnson, Larry Larmer, Daniel O'Keefe, Nicholas Rescher, Stephen Toulmin, Walter Weimer, Joseph Wenzel, and David Zarefsky. I doubtless owe some of these people a greater debt than citations of their published work betray. On countless evenings, fighting our way through a scotch mist, we have hashed out many of the positions taken here. For instance, the idea (Chapter 12) that communication does not require common ground is Barbara O'Keefe's. If I have appropriated their ideas without crediting them, I hope they will understand—or not remember.

Whatever its merits now, this manuscript was once a less disciplined, more carelessly argued exposition—not your well-wrought urn. Its improvement is largely owed to the good ideas and surgical skills of the readers for the University of Alabama Press.

I thank Ray McKerrow, editor of the *Journal of the American Forensic Association*, for permission to lift several large chunks from essays I have published there, especially "A Reformulation of the Concept of Argument" (Willard, 1978a). Readers familiar with that essay will notice changes here. I have also used substantial portions of essays originally published in the *Proceedings* of the biannual SCA/AFA Conference on Argumentation. This conference has been my best opportunity for trying ideas out, so I owe a considerable debt to Malcolm O. Sillars and his colleagues at the University of Utah who have made the conference possible.

C.A.W.

A Theory of
Argumentation

General Introduction:
Argument and Opposition

The burden of this book is to establish a theoretical context for, and to elaborate the implications of, the following claim: *Argument* is a form of interaction in which two or more people maintain what they construe to be incompatible positions. The theoretical context is a communication theory. Seeing argument as a form of communication has consequences for epistemic/political matters as well as for such constructs as rationality, freedom, and the theory of fallacies. This introduction speaks first to the importance of the subject and second to some advantages of the definition.

Importance of the Topic

An interest in argument comes readily to those who care deeply about politics. This interest arises in one's recognition of the importance and urgency of the public agenda. It crystallizes with one's appreciation of the obstacles to good decision making—interests and ideologies—and of human frailties (sloth, fanaticism, greed, stupidity) writ large in public life. The interest in argument becomes paramount for those who believe that a political culture is a legacy of means (Hanson, 1985), that it very much matters how decisions are made.

Our interest in argument intensifies when we appreciate the fragility of the institutions and folkways that nurture debate. Free debate is more expensive than its alternatives and too easily mistaken for an expendable luxury or rhetorical trapping in the world of *realpolitik*. And the process itself is more delicate and precarious than the institutions and customs that promote it. Just as we prize porcelain for its fragility and flowers for their brevity, we admire argumentation for its frangibility, the vulnerability inherent to its use. Argument is easily subverted, its counterfeit not easily unmasked. Dialectic cannot ensure the participants' good will, without which decision making becomes pathological (Hogwood and Peters, 1985), a sham ritual stamping the imprimatur of a veridical procedure on prearranged results—perhaps what Mencken had in mind in calling democracy "the most expensive and nefarious kind of government."

In tandem with these political realizations, we are drawn to the subject of argument by our scientific curiosity about how ordinary folk argue. Argument is a ubiquitous communication process whose study may illuminate the structures of our conversational system, social life, and public knowledge. We may learn how deliberative theories filter out of the academy into the public domain or how folk wisdom and ordinary practices are unequal to the task of using opposition to test ideas.

An interest in and ambivalence toward opposition heightens our fascination with argument. One might loathe argument and opposition in personal matters (Benoit, 1982) but insist on it in public affairs—rather as if one distinguishes the private from the public on the basis of the former's morality and the latter's corruption. The separation-of-powers doctrine is emblematic of a deeper hope that overt opposition is an antidote to public corruption—the only reason democracy is feasible. Democracy, Dewey says, is more than a form of government; it is "a mode of associated living, of conjoint communicated experience." Its foundational processes are competition and accommodation; its tool for achieving accommodation and reconciliation is argument. Just as human activities breathe life into public affairs, public values radiate to more intimate domains. Opposition may thus be as central to private affairs as it is to public life.

Coincidentally, there is our professional commitment to refine and strengthen the dialectical methods of intellectuals. Argument is the organizing process of disciplined thought (Rescher, 1977a, 1977b; Toulmin, 1972, 1976; Weimer, 1979; Johnstone, 1959, 1978; Latour and Woolgar, 1979). We expect professionals to be committed to a free intellectual marketplace fully as much as we expect them to be honest and tolerant. We are curious about the epistemic practices of expert fields because they license knowledge claims—the epistemic stature of a claim being proportional to the epistemic standing of the processes that authorize it—and because we suspect that disciplined deliberative practices may be worthy of emulation in public discourse. The study of such practices may thereby enhance our prospects for improving the public procedures central to intellectual life.

Notice the Hobbesian leitmotif uniting these interests, a view of argument as a *technique*. The move from theory to practice is all too easily expressed as a technical problem of defining impersonal roles, rules, and boundaries of sound argumentation with an eye to guaranteeing rational and prudent decisions whether or not people themselves are rational or prudent (Hoaglund, 1987). This is a flawed scenario—and not just because Hobbes's jaundiced view of human nature is a caricature. The deeper flaw is that a preoccupation with technique obscures vital personal commitments, interpersonal perceptions and strategies, and organizational variables. If one seeks procedures and techniques that will succeed despite human frailties, one risks ignoring the organizational and interpersonal conditions that encourage good will—the personal beliefs, disciplines, and commitments, the conversational conditions, and the institutional mores and practices that allow arguers to use deliberative techniques to best advantage.

The language of technique does allow us to see argument as a modifiable tool rather than a natural given. Just as tools extend our hands, techniques broaden our expectations. In studying public discourse, in understanding its inner workings, we create possibilities for changing it. Our current vision of public discourse is an engine designed in the eighteenth century—perhaps not the most efficient or powerful engine available. Since its functions are vital to the accomplishment of goals we care about, we should be puzzled by its failures and curious about tinkering with it.

Quite apart from these political and empirical interests, argument seems to be an idea of metatheoretical and heuristic power. Though it is dubious to hold that an argument theory can surmount relativity by becoming a privileged discourse overarching interfield differences, achieving a grand synthesis of divergent strands of thought, argument has certainly become an interdisciplinary concept. Argument has figured prominently since antiquity in communication theory, but it has lately acquired importance in such otherwise divergent fields as the Philosophy and Sociology of Science, Sociology of Knowledge, Informal Logic, Epistemology, Ethics, Political Science, and Criticism. (I am capitalizing to name disciplines—Argumentation, Logic, etc.—and using lower case for subject matters—argumentation, logic, etc.)

Advantages of the Definition

No subject is so great that one can't say banal things about it. In conceding the importance of argument, the reader grants nothing about the theory presented here. Nor does the reader's fascination with the subject imply a commitment to generosity or partisanship. One may be satisfied that important matters are afoot yet wonder whether anything consequential is likely to be said about them.

Nonetheless the weighing of this theory may be a rewarding entertainment. To consider its details—even remaining unconvinced of its merits—has valuable side effects: a useful skepticism about argument's epistemic effects, a clear view of argument's nature, and a basis for reconstructing the Argumentation discipline. These advantages coalesce to yield a fourth, an understanding of the relations between our knowledge of argument and the epistemic needs of the public sphere.

I.1. Useful Skepticism

Theories should begin in skepticism or not at all. A theory that makes argument central to decision making must confront the possibility that it is trafficking in myth. This doubt arises if we acknowledge the hollow ring Jeffersonian proclamations sometimes have. It is one thing to proclaim that debate is the cornerstone of democracy and quite another to believe it. The disciplines concerned with argument, decision making, rationality, critical thinking, and debate put a premium on the proclamation. Their common rationale is a rhetoric of rationality which underwrites an explicit pedagogical path—seeing rationality as a coherent package of skills and techniques—and an implicit theory of knowledge, the belief that rationality so packaged is a prerequisite to the attainment of higher intellectual understanding and control of events. This rhetoric paints a comforting picture of rational decision makers confronting thesis with antithesis, claim versus claim, thus transcending the passivity and powerlessness to which they might otherwise be condemned. It assumes that people can influence events, that their rational processes count for something. It suggests that received knowledge really is knowledge—that it is dialectically acquired, tested by argumentative give and take.

"A wise man," Hume says, "proportions his belief to the evidence." Whether the rhetoric of rationality can survive a confrontation with *any* evidence is doubtful. Evidence from organizational studies, information theory, and policy science suggests not merely that the rhetoric of rationality is exaggerated but that it is false.

Bureaucracies, Balzac said in a simpler time than our own, are giant mechanisms run by pygmies. Certainly we must acknowledge the incorrigible bigness of things: big government, big rule structures, big science, and big corporations (Dye, 1976; Ermann and Lundman, 1978; Ewen, 1976; Galbraith, 1973; Green, 1972; Kolko, 1962; Lenski, 1966; Mills, 1956; Nadal, 1976; and Sampson, 1973). The inertia of such bigness, the way great monoliths grind their way across increments of change, their interlocking directorates and elite power structures (Aron, 1950; Domhoff, 1967, 1970, 1972, 1978; Dye and Zeigler, 1975; Hunter, 1959; Keller, 1963; Putnam, 1976; Prewitt and Stone, 1973; Rose, 1967), are intimidating checks on a rhetoric of rationality. A modest reading of the evidence is that contemporary decisions are often so complex that decision makers cannot be competently rational (Janis, 1982; Neustadt and May, 1986; Vertzberger, 1986). Certainly incrementalism, "muddling through," and "the bureaucratization of decision-making" (Perrow, 1979) are less romantic portraits than Jefferson's heirs often paint. At worst, we might have to live with the conclusion that argument and decision making are comforting rhetorical myths contrived to shield us from having to admit our powerlessness (March and Olsen, 1976; March and Simon, 1958, 1965).

When environmentalists *apparently* engage their opponents in free and open dispute, when deliberative formalisms and language prevent them from saying what they really mean (Tribe, Schelling, and Voss, 1976), they are doomed to lose—and perhaps to blame themselves for arguing in bad faith. Cox (1987:8) recalls his congressional testimony: "For all that I was (and am) moved by aesthetics of wild streams and forest or concern for endangered species, my testimony, of necessity, spoke in a different voice. I spoke of discounted values of timber harvest, of management indicator species, and maximizing present net value. I did not speak about what I most valued."

As we look at the world we really live in, it is sometimes hard to believe that decision making and rational deliberation are anything more than the dated argot of a credulous age, like heraldry and chivalry. The language of argument seems anachronistic—not merely passé, like snuff boxes and powdered wigs, but unfit and incompetent. Argumentation books seem to belong on the Fantasy or Gothic Romance shelves. But where Don Quixote evokes nostalgic sympathy, the anachronisms of rationality provoke incredulity and frustration. We summon a computer expert but D'Artagnan shows up. If decision making is little but post facto rationalization, rationality a whore's rouge for touching up institutional excrement, and debate a legitimizing morality play for cloaking greed, corruption, and inertia in a mantle of respectability—in sum, a cynical, empty, false consciousness made all the worse because we sustain it to fool ourselves—then things *are* beyond control; alienation is the stance of prudence. When public rationales differ substantively and substantially from the pragmatic genesis of decisions, the public forum becomes an empty shell, a theatrical stage, or a stylized ritual—prized for its entertainment value but empty and valueless except as fuel for cynics. A wish and a pinch of pixie dust won't make debate and critical thinking real possibilities in our world.

We should acknowledge the same possibilities in our rational enterprises. Big Science bashing is perhaps a more robust industry than is warranted (Kenny, 1986; Kohn, 1987; Taub, 1986; Redner, 1987), but even in resisting the hyperbole (Willard, 1987), we are obliged to appreciate how fragile the intellectual honesty of consensus may be. If decision making is a myth in the public sphere, it is prudent to wonder whether the disease has spread.

To acknowledge these possibilities is not to wallow in cynicism. Perhaps the world does not work like Athenian democracy. Neither did Athens. Even the gloomiest empirical scenario does not make theorizing about argument an exercise in futility. An appreciation of our powerlessness does not undercut the theory or its claims on our interest—though it inhibits naive idealism. The rationale for argument does not rest on the fact that anyone does it well.

Conceding the strongest skeptical case, we need not admit that argument will go the way of the unicorn. The difference between argument and the unicorn is that argument is an uncontestedly real phenomenon in daily life. Incrementalism and bureaucratic inertia are facts. But the cynic who would conclude too much from them has to get around our fact: people do argue—often, heatedly, about many things. Before we become hypnotized by the grinding wheels of big institutions, we should remember that nothing grinds smoothly. Opposition, controversy, and conflict everywhere throw sand in the gears. The view of huge, grinding monoliths is as apt to be a superficial impression as the idealism we have set aside. Bewailing powerlessness is not just bad for morale or a maladaptive ideology, it is an empirical mistake.

There is one similarity between argument and the unicorn. We would not want to live in a world where people believed in neither. This is perhaps why Habermas's notion of claims redeemable through discourse was so readily accepted in principle if not in detail. Argument theories are often expressions of our highest hopes, embodiments of our dreams for a better world. The nobility and earnestness of the Athenian model and the committed morality of Habermas's universal pragmatics are core components of our epistemic self-portrait. A community's Weberian ideal types are as important as its practices—sometimes more so, for to describe what people do we often must know what they hope they are doing. Surely we want to be known as much by our dreams as by our practices.

Thus is born, nurtured by our political interests, toughened by our fear that decision making is "play for mortal stakes," a near-aesthetic appreciation of argument as a collaborative achievement to be prized much like fine art, not only for its fineness but for its discipline. Since the decisions that drive our state and shape our society may be unavailable to public scrutiny, the possibility that opposition exists in the private corridors of power becomes our deepest hope—our only reason for confidence in the future.

We needn't be Dewey-eyed pragmatists. Our secular faith may not be wholly naive; the cynic may not be entirely right. The effects of public deliberation may radiate inward to inhibit decision making; even the most cynical public rationales may *bind* their perpetrators to a scrutiny and critique they hope to avoid. Thus we saw a Reagan White House besieged by the entailments of its own rhetoric: "pure hearts but dirty hands," said the *New York Times*. A lofty moral tone in public can tie even the dirtiest hands if conditions are right.

I.2. A Clearer Picture of Argument

We should consider the possibility that argument is a bit too *au courant*, or too chameleonlike. Having something for everyone is more a quality of Rorschach inkblots than of theoretical constructs. There is something suspicious about a construct that keeps company with logicians who disavow psychology, psychologists who denigrate logic, humanists who loathe social science, and antihumanist social scientists. This ubiquity *might* mean that argument is uncontestably important. Or it may mean that argument owes its popularity to its vagueness and ambiguity. Extravagant expectations thrive on ambiguity. Perhaps argument is an icon, rationality's talisman—its vagueness appealing to our impulses toward faith.

Fuller (1983), in critiquing the views of Davidson (1973–74) and Quine (1953), calls attention to the possibility of incommensurability by spurious agreement. Different fields (or "cultures" in Quine's case of the translating anthropologist) use the same word, assuming that it means the same thing, or that they have successfully translated one field's term into another's, thereby authorizing interfield borrowing of ideas. It may take years of compounded misunderstandings before they discover the mistake and expose the illusory progress their interfield discourse had presumably achieved.

The risks of such mistakes are greatest when different fields appropriate the same word to do different work. Informal logicians, for example, organize their work around pedagogical concerns (Tomko and Ennis, 1980); Argumentation scholars focus on formalized rule structures (Ehninger and Brockriede, 1978); social scientists in several disciplines study argument as a symptom of cognitive development (O'Keefe and Benoit, 1982), of conversational structure (Jacobs and Jackson, 1982; Trapp, 1983; van Eemeren and Grootendorst, 1984), of psychological structure (Hample, 1977a, 1977b, 1979b, 1980, 1981), of epistemological practice (Fuller, 1983; Willard, 1982, 1983, 1987a, 1987b), of judicial practice (Rieke, 1982), and of learned discourse. There are enough disciplinary and even cultural differences in this catalog to make critical misunderstanding a likelihood. My aim is not to foreclose or co-opt these approaches but to clarify their fit with the idea of disciplined controversy. The theory defended here may be a platform for clarifying and uniting these divergent traditions.

At first blush, the theory may seem to be little more than Aristotle's dialectic gussied up in modern communication terms. But Aristotle's dialectic uses a serial predicative sense of argument—ordinary arguments being elided syllogisms, things, units of proof, and serial predications. I prefer to avoid a priori requirements for the utterance to be found in arguments except that arguers, like all communicators, employ the full range of available communication modalities, verbal and nonverbal, explicit and implicit. The theory defended here thus defines argument in terms of encounters based on dissensus and regards any communications occurring therein as objects of epistemic and critical interest. It locates argument's epistemic effects in the total package, not simply in implicatures among statements.

I.3. Reformulation of the Argumentation Discipline

My aim is to clarify the breadth, scope, and implications of Argumentation. Having elsewhere announced the intention of rebuilding the discipline from the ground up, and having specified the range of its subject matter (Willard, 1983), I am here concerned with elaborating and refining its architecture. The theory presented here is an overlay to be superimposed on the blueprint sketched in *Argumentation and the Social Grounds of Knowledge*. If successful, it may clarify Argumentation's connections with other disciplines and its prospects for importing and exporting ideas.

The process of defining a live discipline is forever incomplete. The architectural metaphor need not mean that any field is ever finished, standing like a building with hard edges, deep driven anchors, defined through time by its resistance to the elements. Living, breathing communities are not so fixed. Their intercourse with other fields ebbs and flows with intellectual currents within (see Chapter 9). We can freeze-frame them only momentarily. But they are not ephemeral: they thrive on the activities of flesh and blood people; their ideas and practices are real; their contours are not so fleeting as to be beyond description. So I am not asking for help in building an edifice but for help with an inventory of the possibilities in a line of thinking. The litmus test of an argument theory is whether it stimulates and guides useful work. Even if we stumble, the effort will not be wasted. In weighing our theory's possibilities, we may augment the broader argumentation discourse. If this theory is too ambitious or imprecise it may add to the discipline's stock of cautionary tales—the most likely moral being that spacious definitions of argument are too fuzzy.

Lest this sound too Popperian, I do not think that the success and failure of theories is ever so clear-cut that we can expect unambiguous falsifications. Falsified hypotheses do not an abandoned paradigm make. Boredom beggars more theories than refutation. But this theory won't die of blandness.

I.4. A Clarified Relationship between Argumentation and the Public Sphere

This book begins a process that will come to flower in "The Balkanization of Knowledge and the Problem of the Public Sphere"—a movement away from the language of the individualism debate. In advocating a break from this language, I do not mean that every argument theorist explicitly embraces individualism or collectivism, or even that most argument theories start from the question of the individual's relation to society. Individualism has obvious manifestations—witness the discourses surrounding rationality and freedom (Chapters 7 and 8). But its crucial effect stems from its implicitness: the language of the debate is the environment in which argument theories are debated. Its effect is deeply divisive. The Argumentation literature is sharply divided into cognitive, logical, and sociological camps, each nurturing a literature aloof from the others.

My claim, defended here and in "The Balkanization," is that a preoccupation with individuals or with impersonal structure is made easiest by ignoring the facts of communication. If communication is constitutive of person and society, the individualism debate is irrelevant. If cognitive development proceeds by social comparison, then social life consists of communication practices. This subverts the assumption that matters of epistemics, politics, rationality, and the like are best understood within the framework of the discourse on individualism.

If argument is the public sphere's veridical/judgmental method, a theory of argument can be the empirical basis of a philosophy of the public sphere. In describing actual practices, it will explain the effects of pluralism among expert discourse domains, the political implications of incommensurable epistemic claims, and thus the role of argument in public decision making. Ultimately, a philosophy of the public sphere will be a theory of criticism doubly grounded in an appreciation of the epistemic accomplishments of people and the discourse domains in which they move as well as a respect for the relativity that often divides them.

A Modest Proposal

It may seem paradoxical to say that this exposition aims to stimulate further debate. Systematic treatises often have the opposite effect. There is something, well, Catholic—or at least medieval—about laying out a position. It looks like doctrine building. Few spectacles are as discouraging as doctrinal warfare. Great Works, better chanted than read, are carried like icons by acolytes through dirt street villages or wielded like dreadnoughts deployed for battle. Such shenanigans make us occasionally bow to the cynic. We dream of Dewey but get Cardinal Ratzinger.

But competition breathes life into disciplines. They should ring with the jangle of competing theories—some of them seeking to define the whole discipline, if not the whole world. As Boulding says, "Getting there is *all* the fun." The rationale for a systematic start is only that (though vagueness and ambiguity have their uses) clear positions make for good disputes. The theory to follow is a design proposal radically open to amendment. It is trivial if it does not spark critique. The commitment I ask from the reader is to help me make my case as strong as it can be, to plug in better claims than mine if you think of them, to repair connections that I fumble, to engage sympathetically with the construction of the position. Then have at it.

Part I

Argument as a Form of Communication

Introduction

The task of Argumentation is to identify and reconstruct the conditions of dissensual discourse. Its *epistemic interests* inhere in a concern for the social constitution of knowledge, the judgmental, veridical, and rhetorical methods by which communities achieve confidence in beliefs. The point is to explain how groups sustain intellectual stability yet are able to change. One assumption behind this point is that a community's stability and openness to change result from its tolerance of disagreements and methods of argument. Another assumption is that the "force of the better argument," as Habermas says, inheres in a complex package of interaction, inference, and organizational (or more loosely, social) environment.

Argumentation's *analytical interests* reside in a concern for the coherence, structure, processes, and environments of reasoning and utterance. The point is to understand how groups, organizations, and individuals create meaning by conjoining meanings.

Argumentation's *critical interests* reside in a concern for the conditions and possibilities for public discourse within and across communities and with maximizing the possibilities for successful public discourse. The point is to accommodate to the empirical facts of relativity yet to identify the necessary conditions and presuppositions of a public discourse. This interest, like the others, is best served by an empirically accurate explanation of interaction and mutual influence among people and the effects of these on the social domains in which they move. Criticism based on a clear view of the social constitution of knowledge will be less dogmatic and more pragmatically useful.

We need a view of argument that serves these disciplinary interests. This model of argument should be empirically accurate—faithful to the facts of communication—and it should accommodate to the fact that "arguing" is embedded in other practices, institutions, organizations, situations, and concepts. The resulting portrait will be a collage built from a complex package of ideas. Lest this collage be a mishmash of half-baked notions, vaguely threaded together by the theme of opposition, Thomas Kuhn's admonition that ideas take their clarity from their fit with clear theories needs to be kept in mind. Hence my concern with the details of a theory of argumentation.

To "argue" is to communicate. "Arguments" are conversations in which opposition is present. So argument is a form of communication. Assuming that the species has some of the characteristics of the genus, and that it is not exempt from the environmental and internal restrictions of the genus, I prefer to think that a communication theory (and the research tradition it spawns) is the factual ground of an argumentation theory. Argument, that is, becomes a more coherent idea if assimilated into a communication theory.

Chapter 1 establishes the broad tapestry of a communication theory—a merger of constructivism and interactionism under the umbrella of communication concepts and a "profoundly non-constructivist" theory of communication theories (O'Keefe, 1986); Chapter 2 considers the picture of argument ensuing from the theoretical package. The necessary condition of argument is the presence of opposition; its simplest case is a conversation. More complex instances include discussions, debates, the clash of positions in organizational channels, academic disputes, and the battles and skirmishes between competing social and political movements. The fuzziest case of argument may involve a person behaving as if an interlocutor were present, as if opposition is potentially or actually present. Political speakers, for example, attack real or imagined opponents as if their rationales were speeches in a debate. Chapter 3 extends the picture by considering argument as an emergent social reality. Chapter 4 considers the modes of communication we might take to be relevant to argument. Chapter 5 weighs the epistemic effects that may plausibly be attributed to arguments. And Chapter 6 defends the claim that ethos is an inseparable part of the logic of assent.

Constructivism and interactionism, merged as they are here, place a premium on interaction, messages, and the communicative practices underlying both. Differences among people in their beliefs about communication and (thereby) in their creation of messages put a premium on their "positions" (Chapter 12), the analytical moves we have to understand before we can analyze a message as anything but a rationale.

As the interactional theory unfolds, the reader will notice an indifference to another (more common) definition of argument: as a kind of utterance. Chapter 4 makes a case for avoiding disputes about what can or cannot count as argument utterance. If one simply must use the word *argument* to denote utterance, the following usage can coexist with the interactional theory: any claim someone makes when opposition is present or anticipated; or which a speaker, interlocutor, or analyst interprets as an argumentative claim. On this usage, "arguing" refers to participating in an argument and/or making claims construed as arguments. As I work toward the exposition in Chapter 4, it will become apparent why I prefer a broad understanding of the communications that count as "arguments." I am more concerned with what counts *in* than with what counts *as* arguments.

We often speak of "arguments" as contents of larger communications—the particular claims a speaker makes—and of people "arguing thus and so" (Ronald Reagan is arguing that Star Wars research will help the economy). The interactional theory does not prohibit these conventions. It implies a higher unity: when one "makes an argument," and acts as if opposition were manifest or possible; one is *arguing*—meaning that one is entering an institution (Searle, 1969) whose ground rules and etiquette permit, encourage, and even require critique and rejoinder. The scope and ubiquity of this institution is so vast that we find it natural to insist that even persuaders who resist critique are vulnerable. The advertiser may want to avoid criticism, but we can still insist that advertising claims are *treatable* as arguments—that to make any claim at all is to be open to reply.

1

Constructivism and Interactionism

The Case for Assimilating Argument into a Communication Theory

To know is to contextualize. To position an idea in a context is, as Piaget says, to *accommodate* one's preconceived notions to a new idea or to *assimilate* the idea by making it fit one's expectations. In either case, we interpret ideas by placing them in relief against a tapestry of related ideas, changing the figure or the ground as needed.

Argument has historically been grounded in logic. Until the rise of Informal Logic in the 1960s, argument was lodged in remote corners of Logic, Psychology, and Rhetoric as an applied, more indulgent logic, less a "science of pure form" than a purifying therapy for decontaminating ordinary discourse (Begg and Denny, 1969; McGuire, 1960b). The contaminants were feelings, frailties, situations, and institutions which infected logical form.

Argument remains grounded in Logic, despite the revolution fostered by Toulmin (1968). Toulmin wanted to check *Logic's* strain toward autonomy from the empirical world, but his work stimulated a renegade movement (Informal Logic), a new field (Critical Thinking), and the reinvigoration of an old one (Argumentation). This was less a revolution than a legitimation of pedagogical and therapeutic programs of applied logic whose roots reach back to antiquity. Amid much talk of "the demise of formalism," all three fields remain centrally concerned with the formal merits of inference and utterance. What has changed is their focus. The real activities of flesh and blood arguers are now seen as important in themselves and more interesting than empty formalisms.

These fields share the problem of deciding how claims about inferential and argumentative *form* are to mingle with claims about beliefs, practices, situations, organizations, and communities. The facts of human association and interpretation have perhaps seeped more thoroughly into Argumentation than into the other fields (Cox and Willard, 1982), but crowds do not gather to marvel at the clarity of this newly socialized field. Argumentation remains divided between applied formalists, who make the facts of social life fit their analytical preferences, and social scientists, who ignore formalisms and analytical programs. Perhaps this is yet another manifestation of the humanism-scientism schism that splits other fields, but it certainly is not a debate. A de facto incommensurability has crept into Argumentation in which applied formalists and social scientists seem to be going separate ways.

The best critique is a good alternative. This chapter lays out the grounds of an alternative; the second chapter places the figure against the ground. The happiest home for a definition of argument is a theory of communication that conjoins explanations of cognitive processes (interpretation and inference), social processes (interaction and communal practices), and the similarities, differences, and relationships among communication practices (message production and audience adaptation). Communication scholars have labeled this theory "constructivism." At its epistemic base are *Weltanschauungen* assumptions (Kuhn, 1970; Toulmin, 1972; Hanson, 1958). Its substantive content represents a merger of (and expansion upon) personal construct theory (PCT) and Chicago school symbolic interactionism (CSI). The binding agent is a picture of communication.

Positioned in this theoretical context, *argument* refers to a package of empirical phenomena which differs in kind from serial predication. Arguments are happenings whose nature is altered by abstraction from context. They occur in, are affected by, and are intended to affect situations. They are typified by communication which is intended-toward: Arguers mean to say, and are taken by others to say, *particular* things, not just anything their utterances might mean.

The reader who has qualms about overpsychologized or oversocialized views of argument need fear no evil. The theory to follow sees argument as a process whose causes and effects are both private and public. This does not make argument *equivalent* to psychological or sociological processes. Both Socratic dialectic and Aristotle's enthymeme, which I take to be paradigmatic of argument utterances (Willard, 1983), require an interlocutor to grant or attack premises and to complete elided reasoning. Moreover, people do not behave in vacuums. Their intentions and activities are adapted to contexts (competently or not) and channelized by the cultural forms, etiquettes, organizations, and beliefs of their groups. When *A* and *B* argue, they may appeal to impersonal principles that transcend their particular situation and points of view—the authority of discourse domains. Argument is thus a *social* process. The facts of sociality are integral to explanations of the meanings of claims and of the judgmental/veridical practices that authorize them.

Arguments are no more equivalent to social *structure* than they are to psychological processes. They are *processes* bound by *action* (Burke, 1950). They entail utilitarian strategy and tactics, persuasion, message creation, and adaptation to the interlocutor's perspective. They are engagements between people pursuing motives. Whether these motives are a blunt quest of advantage (Burke, 1950), dispassionate critique, or epistemic betterment, the arguer in their thrall is trading in symbols with another person.

The Theoretical Position

The place to begin is not with a full-dress attack on formalism. The demise of formalism is a familiar story, and the complaints that caused it are not the rationale for the decision to see argument as a species of communication. The rationale, rather, lies in the coherence of the communication theory, its research base, the degree to which it squares with Argumentation's disciplinary aims, and the degree to which it requires us to keep our claims about argument consistent with the empirical facts of communication.

1.1. Chicago School Interactionism (CSI)

CSI is a familiar paradigm in the humanities and social sciences, so a brief exposition will do to say how it figures in the theory. But to begin with CSI is to risk a labeling effect, for the social sciences are balkanized as much by metaphors as by disciplinary boundaries. We have (at least) game, dramaturgical, and text analogies (Geertz, 1980), so starting with CSI is like donning a street gang's color: wearing the headband, we are instantly known by all as a proponent of this or that metaphor. As this is to be a theory of argument, one can just imagine the Goffmanesque metaphors (masks, cons, strategies, and ploys) to come.

But CSI does not stand alone in what follows. It is one element of a theory that favors no single metaphor. The language of games is appropriate to some cases; theatrical or ritual metaphors are appropriate to others; and text analogies are appropriate to still others.

CSI grounds the study of action on the fact of human association. People and the collectivities in which they organize their activities are inseparable, for communities exist in and through the communication practices of their members. Social situations are seen as emergent creations derived from the perceptions of the interactants rather than as impersonal roles or structures. In this, CSI shares with constructivism the idea that people interpret events in terms of their private constructions of reality (assimilation) and engage with events by coordinating their lines of action with those of others (accommodation).

Interaction is neither a forum in which preconditioned forces are released or an arena in which psychological predispositions are conditioned into people. The vision is of a person reaching out into the world, affecting events, as well as being acted upon. Social situations are contexts in which people contrive coordinated action by achieving working balances between accommodating their private interests to the perspectives of others and assimilating events to their own perspectives. The root metaphor is the social self, the "inner parliament," which stages the interplay between one's motives and intentions and one's assessment of the perspectives of others. Mead refers to the "I" as a person's goals, the "Me" as the person's importation of the perspectives of others, and the "generalized other" as a person's importation of social norms.

Thus arises a powerful and interesting view of groups and organizations: they are processes, not static entities, they exist in and through the activities of their members—especially their communication practices (Blumer, 1969:6). Arguments are among the most ubiquitous of these practices because disagreement is an important regulative function in collective life.

The ubiquity of dissensus and argument may dilute the cynicism human practices sometimes seem to justify. We need not *assume* that argument is not a myth. We can prove it. As we saw, for instance, the Power Elite model has its uses (indeed argument theories may be seen as elite language games), but it is mistaken to speak of elites (Bachrach, 1967; Rose, 1967) as a unified, undifferentiated, thoroughly integrated and harmoniously fixed entity (Dahl, 1958, 1961, 1967). Many elite theorists hold that "elites share in a consensus about the fundamental norms [property rights, economic individualism, capitalism] underlying the social system" (Dye and Zeigler, 1975:4). But this claim does not mean that elites agree about issues. Elites argue among themselves, like everybody else. The theory of argument fields (Willard, 1982, 1983, 1988) predicts that elites are as balkanized into discourse domains as everyone else—perhaps more so since they are more closely tied to existing structures and have greater stakes than nonelites in preserving them. As a unit of analysis, the homogeneous rubric *elites* has fewer epistemic consequences than community-specific descriptions.

If one acknowledges that organizations are animated by human activities, including conflict, one is less prone to see them as grinding monoliths (Abrahamsson, 1977; Bennis, 1966; Biddle, 1979; Dahl, 1961; Ermann and Lundman, 1976; Frost et al., 1985). One can entertain the prospect that human control is not a foregone option, though it may not fit the dramatic model of leadership one finds in textbooks.

1.2. Personal Construct Theory (PCT)

PCT's root metaphor is the *human as scientist* (Kelly, 1955; Nisbett and Ross, 1980). Humans are forward-looking, calculative beings who explicate events in hopes of predicting and controlling them. People frame actions by construing the available alternatives; they test their predictions against events (Wyer, 1974a; Schutz, 1951). Social scientists must accept "that subjects like experimenters can and do continuously think, theorize, anticipate, experiment, react, create, rebel, and comply, just like everyone else—and what is more they can and do all of these things in any experiment" (Mair 1970:158–59). Behavior is experimental and thus cannot be understood unless one knows the hypotheses being tested by it.

PCT shares with CSI the assumption that private interpretations are not *causally* linked to external events.[1] Both theories assume an external reality whose existence and nature might or might not depend upon someone's thoughts (light exists despite us, but we have a voice in whether it is a wave or a particle); both stress a social reality jointly produced by communicators. Actions have real consequences but are cognitively contrived, not reflections in a mirror of nature (Rorty, 1979). Hence the expression "situations defined as real are real in their consequences" (Thomas and Thomas, 1928).

PCT postulates that "a person's processes are psychologically channelized by the ways he anticipates events" (Kelly, 1955). Continual processes do not start or stop, so PCT does not need such notions as mental energy, drives, conditionings, or stimulus and response. Kelly elaborates his postulate with a series of corollary claims.

The construction corollary holds that a person anticipates events by construing their replications. We look at the world through "transparent patterns or templates" which we create to interpret events. The fit is not always good, but "without such patterns the world appears to be such an undifferentiated homogeneity that man is unable to make any sense of it" (Kelly, 1955:8–9). To construe is to interpret: we note features in a series of elements which characterize some of the elements but not others. A construct is thus a structure of similarities and contrasts, a bipolar dimension on which at least three elements are brought into relation, two being alike and different from a third. To say, "John is Tall," is to say that he is not short.[2]

The *organization corollary* says that we bind our interpretations into progressively elaborated, hierarchically arranged systems. Cognitive systems are (1) *flexible*: open to modification, adjustable as a person accommodates to events; (2) *structured*: their channels circumscribe our navigation; prior assumptions constrict and channelize our thinking as we assimilate events into prearranged structures; (3) *focused*: they exist for a reason, their channels have destinations, they foster appropriate sorts of thinking while inhibiting others; (4) *future oriented*: directed toward prediction and control; and (5) *constructive*: meaning *accommodative*; in using systems we sometimes change them, as in cognitive development. One way to see the relevance of cognitive systems to arguments is to see them as *positions* (Chapter 12).

The *choice corollary or principle of elaborative choice* says that we select interpretations of events that have the best prospects for improving our cognitive systems. Expanding the usefulness of a system entails one of two opposite movements: we either more precisely define a system or we extend its range. Kelly most often has assimilation in mind. When a person must move, "he is confronted with a series of dichotomous choices. Each choice is channelized by a construct. As he reconstrues himself he may either rattle around in his old slots or he may construct new pathways across areas that were not previously accessible" (1955:128). The relations among constructs in a system create pathways or channels. Construing consists of fitting events onto constructs, choosing one dichotomous pole over another, thus building the channels through which we navigate in thought, "the two-way streets along which one may travel to reach conclusions" (1955:126). Inference is navigation along pathways among constructs. Just as navigation requires monitoring and course corrections, thinking moves from point to point in a system. Presumably—Kelly is not clear on the matter—thought is as linear and sequential as a person wants it to be. People, as opposed to computers, do not *have* to suffer von Neumann bottlenecks; they benefit from "massively parallel processing" (to adopt an AI locution).

The *range corollary* says that any construct is convenient for the anticipation of a finite range of events. A construct's "range of convenience" consists of the events for which a person would find the construct useful; its "focus of convenience" consists of the events for which the construct works best.

The *experience corollary* means that "learning" is a process of successively construing events. Werner's (1948) *orthogenetic principle* sees cognitive development as a system's (analogically if not literally Darwinian) evolution from global, undifferentiated simplicity toward increasing complexity, specificity, and differentiation. The succession of events over time "subjects a person's construction to a validation process. The constructions one places upon events are hypotheses . . . to be put to the test of experience. As one's anticipations or hypotheses are successively revised in light of the unfolding sequence of events, the construction system undergoes a progressive evolution. The person reconstrues. This is experience" (1955:72).

The *fragmentation corollary* says that a construct system, if it is big enough, may contain elements that are inferentially incompatible. The greater the complexity of the person's system, the greater the person's tolerance of inconsistencies (see 2.15, Chapter 2).

The *individuality corollary* holds that we differ in our constructions of events. How else would conflict and (thus) arguments arise? But the empirical fact of subjectivity does not impel us to adopt a subjectivist doctrine. Subjecti*vism* is checked by the obvious social fact that group associations authorize claims. Group life is humanity's recurring solution to subjectivism. Thus the *sociality corollary* says that to the extent that one takes the role of another person, construes that other's perspective, one may play a role in a social process with that other. Hence the importance of group life for the suppression of subjectivism—which is what Piaget means in tying the objectivity of thought to its communicability.

The *commonality corollary* says that to the extent that two people construe experience similarly, their cognitive processes are similar. Hence the cohesion of group life and our openness, in varying degrees, to social influence. This corollary thus checks a common mistake: exaggerating assimilation at the expense of accommodation. In focusing on inference, we sometimes describe a privateness and aloneness that contradict the facts of social life. We make it difficult to explain social action, why we find clusters of like-minded people, how community is possible, and how or why socialization and cognitive change occur. To stress uniqueness is to exaggerate autonomy so as to preclude the possibility of communication. But PCT need not be construed so rigidly: the private world it describes is intersubjectively bound.

1.3. Constructivism

This label, first applied to Piaget's genetic epistemology, has been adopted by Communication scholars (Delia, O'Keefe, and O'Keefe, 1982) to label a communication theory (Delia, 1972, 1976a, 1976b, 1977, 1980; Applegate, 1980; Applegate and Delia, 1980; O'Keefe and Delia, 1978; O'Keefe, Delia, and O'Keefe, 1980). Constructivism may be thought of as a broader, more complex, and more social version of PCT, based on PCT but reaching far beyond it because it is not a psychological theory. A psychologist might see perspective taking as the most basic cognitive process; constructivists hold that communication processes are central to our forming of interpersonal impressions. We use constructs to interpret the actions of others, to attribute motives to them. These interpretations are closely allied to our message strategies (Clark and Delia, 1979; O'Keefe and Delia, 1979; Delia and O'Keefe, 1979). Our knowledge of the listener is our basis for choosing strategic alternatives for adapting influence attempts to another's perspective. Construals of listener characteristics are thus a necessary but not sufficient condition for the production of listener-adapted messages. Perspective taking must be supplemented by a "strategic repertoire that must be developed for translating perceptions and intentions into adapted communications" (O'Keefe and Delia, 1982:35).

CONSTRUCTS AND INTERPRETIVE SCHEMES PCT's view of constructs is basically correct, but constructivists refer to "interpretive schemes" to denote any classification device a person uses, even if the device does not fit the bipolar construct mold, for example, general interpretive schemes for conversation (Cicourel, 1974; Grice, 1975). Every interpretive scheme "simultaneously serves the functions of identification and placement. To take an object to be something is to simultaneously place it in regard to its routine functions, its routine occurrence, its expected operation or behavior, and its routine surroundings" (Delia, O'Keefe, and O'Keefe, 1982:152).
Constructs are structures of beliefs and discriminations; schemas are structures for organizing constructs into coherent systems: "Once a schema is invoked to account for the behavior of a person, or for the relations between the person and others, it promotes the

attribution to that person of a variety of related sentiments, abilities, motives, aspirations, character traits, and other qualities" (Crockett, 1977:11). Guided by schemata, impression formation involves interpretation and inference plus the progressive elaboration of one's belief system to accommodate new information. Hence a circular relation exists between assimilation and accommodation: schemata organize our expectations—we interpret and organize new information to fit the schemata we have chosen (Crockett, 1977; O'Keefe and Delia, 1982:42).

Assimilation accounts are too crude to stand alone. One gets an exaggerated individualism, an overpsychologized, too-autonomous person. Two cases in point are the familiar "implicit theory" view (Kelley, 1967, 1971, 1972; Ajzen, 1977; Asch, 1946; Ashworth, 1979; Bem, 1972; Bruner and Tagiuri, 1954; Jones et al., 1971; Ross, 1977; Wegner and Giuliano, 1982) and Heider's (1958) theory of interpersonal relations. The former says that people, as naive psychologists, create explanations of social reality that have "all the features of the formal theories constructed by the scientist. They employ concepts and relationships derived from observation; they provide a structure through which social reality is observed; they enable the individual to make predictions" (Wegner and Vallacher, 1977:21).[3]

Perhaps the most radical statement of this holism (which may have indirectly influenced the others) is that of Quine (1953:40–41), who proposed that scientific beliefs form a web, touched by experience only at some points, but nonetheless so tightly woven that every part of the web may feel the effects of every experience. "Our statements about the external world face the tribunal of sense experience not individually but only as a corporate body." The constructivist's emphasis on situated social interaction suggests that this is an exaggeration. (We will see in Chapter 9 that this holism has more serious defects.) If one sees schemata only as regnant constructs that provide cognitive links among bundles of constructs, one is tempted by the implicit theory model to assume that perceivers are generally or usually concerned with forming organized, optimum impressions of others. It is better to assume that "interpersonal schemata are mobilized by contexts and interactional goals. Such a working hypothesis suggests that the organization of impressions often may not involve an extended understanding of the other's psychodynamic characteristics; indeed we would argue that many impressions, although highly organized and providing useful guides to action, involve only limited attributions concerning the other's personality" (O'Keefe and Delia, 1982:43).

I deal with *you, here* and *now*. This immediate project, not the creation of a comprehensive personality theory, engages my interest.

I do not need to schematize my impressions of you vis-à-vis every possible situation. My rationality is bounded (March and Simon, 1958; Douglas, 1986). Events are punctuated, not a continuous stream, so I deal with them piecemeal; I use my repertoire of interpretations to assimilate events as well as I can. With the press of time, resource shortages, and inadequate information, "optimizing is replaced by satisficing." I do not seek a general impression of a person so much as an impression that will allow satisfactory performance in a particular situation. This squares with PCT's account of assimilation and accommodation. It also limits the applicability of Quine's doctrine of corporate wholeness. Bounded rationality, to be sure, is an assimilation theory: we stop with the first explanation that satisfies us rather than seeking the optimal explanation. But it applies as well to accommodation. We do not revise long-held schemes and constructs for no reason.

Units of Analysis

Social entities of all kinds can be carved up differently depending upon one's interests. Race and national character were interesting units of analysis in Ruth Benedict's day and for a time thereafter, owing to scholars' interests in explaining tribal cultures in contrast to our own, Nazism as an outgrowth of "Germanic traits," and personality types or traits. Even now, references to the American character reminiscent of de Tocqueville occasionally arise (Bellah et al., 1985).

Our characterizations of argument and of the constructs relevant to it are likewise as diverse as our aims and interests. We sometimes focus on the unit of meaningful utterance (Wallace, 1963, 1970), the syllogism, the sentence, the word-object dyad, the text, the text milieu or corpus of a field, the encounter or relationship among arguers, the relations of individuals to groups, organizational structure, political movements and political structure, and at a high level of abstraction, the culture.

Though a single unit of analysis may suffice for a particular interest, it cannot encompass the range of epistemic, analytical, and critical interests we have imputed to Argumentation. The scope of these interests can be suggested by imagining a series of concentric circles surrounding an interaction. At the circle's center, the unit of analysis is *that* situation, its particular details, contours, and points of reference. If A claims X, and X is particular to the occasion, then X has local truth conditions; its merits are fastened to situational particulars. Since A's goals, plans, scripts, recipes, and intentions toward action and utterance are part of the constitution of the context, they are appropriate units of analysis when we seek to understand how A creates a position (Chapter 12), what A intends particular claims to mean, or what A's motives are. How else could we know whether a strategy succeeded or was an optimal path for realizing A's goals? How else can we assess the epistemic effects of argument? To answer such questions, we need to know how (and what) A thinks about communication. Knowing A's views of the possibilities for communicative action gives us a fix on how A translates particular situational features into "exigencies."

In claiming X, A engages B in a public process involving relationships among terms, statements, and ideas. A's success with a logical or procedural etiquette thus becomes relevant as we move further outward on the concentric lines. By going public, A has agreed to play by particular rules and conventions whose systemic structure thereby becomes relevant to analytic and critical analyses.

In engaging B, A may find it necessary to appeal to authority, to the veridical/judgmental standards of a particular *argument field*—thus calling our attention to an even broader unit of analysis, one designed to answer broader questions. X's truth conditions inhere in its fit with a community's substantive beliefs and with A's comportment vis-à-vis that community's procedures.

1.4. Culture and Accommodation

At the circle's outer reaches are slippery abstractions: "society" and "culture"—constructs open to variations in interpretation depending on one's aims (Shweder and LeVine, 1984) and rhetorical methods (Geertz, 1987). Perhaps the most enduring meaning of culture is as a society's substantive content (Linton, 1945), way of life (Benedict, 1934; Williams, 1981), and patterns of behavior which generations pass to their successors (Kluckhohn, 1962). Such equations of culture with substantive beliefs come into play when communication theorists explain the sources of persuasive premises. Call it "Tocqueville's project": public discourse is the *expression* of an underlying corporate structure of conventions, ideas, expectancies, appetites, and values (Wallace, 1970). Public utterance thus succeeds or fails at expressing or matching public opinion. This is a flawed picture, for as we shall see below, communication is not simply expressive. Yet even if it were, public discourse is more apt to "reflect" the tactical positions of leaders than public opinion (Ginsberg, 1986).

Also, culture is a generalization that may obscure differences within a society. Advocates of omnibus definitions of culture sometimes take care to avoid exaggerated homogeneity, but there is still a tension between singularizing culture and taking account of differences between communities. The more one generalizes about "what [or how] Americans think," the more one blurs these differences. Argumentation's epistemic, analytical, and critical purposes enforce the need to account for the heterogeneity we find in societies. Field studies (Willard, 1982, 1983, 1988) give empirical weight to this need.

Perhaps a substantive definition of culture can survive this objection. Tocqueville's project might still be viable if one can describe "the Americans" without succumbing to expansive rhetoric or obscuring differences. Such an exercise might be valuable for certain purposes. We might trace the importance of individualism to other distinctively American ideas (Bellah et al., 1985) or ask whether cowboy capitalism is at the root of American nuclear policy. It may also be that a useful substantive sense of culture is localized to particular fields—that we might speak of a field's culture. These questions are taken up in "The Balkanization" (Willard, 1988). The sole issue here is whether substantive definitions explain the sources of premises—not whether they might serve anthropological purposes (Geertz, 1987; Marcus and Fischer, 1986). For Argumentation's purposes, to explain the genesis of claims, field theory's focus on local intellectual ecologies is more precise and empirically accurate.

There remains a sense of culture that can serve as a unit of analysis for Argumentation under the guidance of the interactional theory. Let's say that a "culture" consists of the things a person has to know and believe in order to proceed normally with fellow members (Goodenough, 1964). "Culture" does not tell us why A (or A's group) believes or does X in particular cases; it describes formal procedures such as the structure of speech acts. The *form versus substance* construct is among Argumentation's oldest—dating at least to Aristotle's distinction between the arrangement of a syllogism's terms and the truth of its premises. The form guaranteed one's inferences but not the truth of one's premises. We may likewise see the conversational structure, for example, adjacency pairing, the fact that questions court answers, requests court compliance, and so on, as a culture's formal arrangements that constitute a tapestry against which particular fields of discourse function.

One can read this formal sense of culture into Delia, O'Keefe, and O'Keefe's (1982:154–55) claim that one does not become a member of a culture merely by coordinating one's constructs with those of others:

Culture is much more than commonality or sharedness in interpretive processes; it is the whole evolving social organization, and conception of reality, and complex of symbolic forms employed by the human group. Individuals become a part of their culture as they become members of the community, as they occupy the places prepared for them in the ongoing process of group life, as they participate in the most basic forms of social organization, and as they come to have cognitive systems in which their most fundamental forms of cognitive representation and behavioral organization are integrated with the meanings these hold for the social group.

This reasoning is not a return to *Seinsverbundenheit des Wissens*. Nor is it a revival of the deterministic view of roles. Nor still does it insist on culture as substance—as in Justice Holmes's famous claim, "We are all tatooed in our cradles with the beliefs of our tribe." Rather, it is an emphasis on accommodation in socialization. Initiates into all communities inevitably first accommodate more than they assimilate. The consequences of such accommodations are seen most readily in communicative acts—the message being the constructivists' central object of analysis.

Competent organizational actors—as opposed to children and novices—may be passive or active, constrained or free, conventional or rebellious for reasons unrelated to accommodation. Consider Weick's (1969) claim that people in organizations do things, retrospectively create explanations of or justifications for their behavior, and then use these explanations or rationalizations to guide future behavior (Cohen, March, and Olsen, 1972; March, 1970; March and Olsen, 1976). Assimilation and accommodation are thus companion processes: people may force-fit complex and ambiguous situations onto their private interpretations; they confront events with the cognitive tools at hand: their social skills, social comparison practices, and methods of justification and explanation—all of these being products of past accommodations.

The formalistic view of culture explains that communication across community boundaries is possible but does not succumb to an exaggerated homogeneity. Moreover, it does justice to the substantive differences we find in life but does not succumb to the opposite error: exaggerating incomprehension—as Kuhn is sometimes accused of doing (Davidson, 1973–74). People can disagree while correctly understanding each other's positions.

Though incomprehension is often exaggerated, the creature does walk among us. As I contemplate my relations with my Roman Catholic neighbor, I sometimes conclude, not entirely facetiously, that we are not of the same species. Short of simple declaratives, we agree on little else. My neighbor does not believe that all questions require answers or explanations for not answering; he is not committed to conversational repair because he believes that opposition stems from his opponent's personal defects; he does not believe that claims should be redeemable except as arguments from authority; he does not believe in turn-taking or that both parties to a conversation should speak. Collaboration on matters of any complexity between us is for all practical purposes impossible. We are demographically similar—white middle-aged males with similar socioeconomic status and educational levels. But the gulf between us is so wide that argument, as defined below, is impossible. Babel isn't a myth, at least not in my neighborhood.

1.5. Three Senses of Accommodation

One reason not to exaggerate homogeneity or cultural determinism is the need to explain the variety of relationships people have with social entities. Whole theories have been concocted as if the world consisted of a single relationship between an impersonal society and one person. The interactional theory avoids this individualism. It locates the epistemic effects of arguments in the "working consensuses" and negotiated settlements achieved by arguers and in the new prospects these exploits make possible. In speaking of accommodations to society, we are not describing a unitary, singular phenomenon but a range of relationships. The language of the individualism debate is thus inappropriate because it disguises differences among people, situations, and communities.

Constructivists hold that a communication theory must be based on a philosophical anthropology if it is to explain accommodation. They are loath to explain cognitive development along universalistic lines (e.g., Piagetian stages) or to equate socialization with assimilation: "In fact, people erect interpretive systems principally through communication with and accommodation to the meaningful, pervasive and enduring social world into which they are born" (Delia, O'Keefe, and O'Keefe, 1982:155). "Because individuals are born into a human community, they enter a world that is already defined, interpreted, organized, and meaningful. The world the individual faces is a world of preconstituted meanings, and it is to this meaningful world that the individual must accommodate" (p. 154). This need not mean that preconstituted meanings are competently or completely presented to initiates, or that these meanings comprise all possible substantive beliefs, or that a society must be seen as harmonious and homogeneous. It means that people's accommodations to social life vary systematically with their communication knowledge and competence.

There are at least three different and progressively complex modes

of accommodation: surrender, socialization, and rhetorical adaptation. These different forms of accommodation correspond roughly
(but are not equivalent) to three different message design logics described below. One can read these distinctions into the CSI literature.

SURRENDER. An extensive post–World War II literature (Fromm's
Escape from Freedom or Adorno et al.'s *The Authoritarian Personality* are typical) sees "accommodation" as a form of surrender, passive acquiescence, or a Marxist existential determination of thought.
We do find true believers, fanatics, martyrs, and sheeplike masses
mindlessly following their leaders, from Masada to Jonestown. Te-
heran's Fountain of Blood is but a common tendency writ large—
that culture's parallel to Arlington Cemetery or Flanders Field.

SOCIALIZATION. The pedagogy of most disciplines focuses on
one's socialization into a community's structure of conventions,
procedures, and beliefs. One learns the "rational" recipes and
acquires status in the group by demonstrating facility with the
community's techniques and methods. Socialization brings commitment, though it is a developmentally more complex accommodation than surrender. Like all successor stages, it feels the
emotional pull of antecedent stages. We do find fanatics and true
believers in disciplines.

RHETORICAL ADAPTATION. Though "rhetorical" connotes "strategy" and "adaptation," many treatments of rhetorical adaptation
have focused on a theatrical metaphor—making "accommodation"
mean dissimulation (pretense, hypocrisy, and deception). Thus Kelman (1961) suggests the importance of compliance in daily life, our
disingenuous behavior in dealing with people who have power to
help or hurt us. And CSI sees accommodation as something actors
do when they submerge themselves in theatrical roles (Goffman,
1959, 1961a, 1961b, 1963, 1964, 1967, 1969, 1971, 1974). Thus we
expect to find individuals adopting public masks of rationality,
friendship, concern, and even citizenship to enable them to enter a
community or to manipulate its folkways for private purposes. Public rationales exemplify this theatricality.

The conventional and rhetorical senses of accommodation square
with the fact that people move from group to group, their allegiance
waxing and waning, their attention ebbing and flowing. We might
call this "multivalence" (Lee, 1966) or "partial inclusion" (Allport,
1933)—meaning that groups get only a psychological slice of the
person.

1.6. Rebellion and Conformity

An *epistemic* reason not to exaggerate the force of culture—either community-specific or omnibus culture—turns on the need to explain how communities both check and encourage dissent and rebellion. Exaggerations of culture make it hard to assess such issues because they overvalue conformity. Too much determinism makes for Whiggish readings of a community's internal debates, thus obscuring the grounds on which communities make dissent "rational" (Chapters 5 and 9).

Toulmin (1972) wants to explain conceptual stability and change in the same terms but resorts to a Darwinian populational language to achieve this aim. The causes of disaffection, dissent, and rebellion may differ in kind from the logics of justification used to defend conventional wisdom (see Chapter 9). A desire for or fascination with new puzzles (Kuhn, 1970) may be tangential to a desire to defeat a prevailing paradigm. Ennui and tedium can seem overwhelming; the puzzles of other fields can seem more attractive; the opinions of renegade colleagues can acquire persuasive power as one's own work seems increasingly Sisyphian. Dissent, in other words, may not be linked to logical anomalies in a prevailing paradigm, though it may eventually attach itself to anomalies. More often, innovators adopt a rhetoric of compatibility stressing continuity with prevailing thought (Gross, 1988). Illusory origins may be flawed history but good politics. Disavowals of revolutionary intent may be disingenuous but rhetorically necessary.

Rationality theorists often put this problem in terms of a person (Toulmin, for example, says that we display our rationality by how we change our minds). But the CSI position attributes the rationality of intellectual change to peoples' mutual accommodations—the social realities they create for dealing with dissent. The choice between stucturalism and individualism is proportionately spurious. We need only an explanation of conformity that does not inevitably make dissent pathological and a way of valuing dissent that does not arbitrarily demean conformity.

Argumentation theorists have mixed feelings about conformity, dissent, innovation, and rebellion. As critics, whose judgments are authorized by particular intellectual fields, we favor continuity with an intellectual status quo. Criticism presupposes a position solid enough to warrant claims, so critics always speak for an existing state of intellectual affairs. But as political animals, especially owing to a century-old concern for debate, Argumentation theorists have a natural affinity for the rebel. They share with journalists an affection for the skeptic, a distrust of received wisdom. They understand that conventions are not unalloyed goods and that pieties and shibboleths often mask harsh motives and corrupt institutions. Call this the liberal presumption (Goodnight, 1980). The conservative presumption resists change in principle; the liberal presumption does the opposite. It emphasizes the power of entrenched interests, human frailties, and the inertial weight of uninspired leadership. A social structure at any particular time is as likely to be an accident of circumstances as an outcome of design. The motives on which institutions are based are as likely to be evil as benign. Since historical forces do not "aim" toward anything (let alone perfection), an institution's current state will reflect the passing fancies, compromises, and expediencies of preceding epochs. On the liberal presumption, then, dissent is in principle rational.

Even the conservative presumption, which puts the burden of proof on the advocate of change, does not make dissent irrational or politically pathological. The advocate of the conservative presumption has two choices to explain intellectual change: to insist that change is a logical progression within an ecology, or failing that, to say that dissensus—a community's encouragement of dispute—yields change. The latter implies that rebels should be tolerated, even nurtured. Not everyone needs be a rebel, but it is valuable to have rebels and skeptics about. Critique is an empty formality in a thoroughly happy community (Willard, 1987a). In a consensualist world, these competing strains create a disquieting ambivalence. We long for the center that will hold, all the while being fascinated by the advocate, the proponent, the rebel. We want the advantages of foundationalism but the prerogatives of the innovator. We want our conformity or dissent to be equally rational even if their rationality differs in kind.

Message Design Logics

Thus far I have considered units of analysis arrayed concentrically around the phenomena relevant to argument. We want to know what is happening when A says X, B disputes X, and so on. Constructivism explains how A intends toward X based on a strategic repertoire. At the center of the concentric circle around A *says* X is the situation: the psychological facts about A and B, the content and contours of the context, the apparent fit of X to the situation, and so on. Moving outward in the circle, X may be indexical to assumptions and beliefs embodied in a local community. Still further outward are the cultural conditions of communication. In deciding to use culture more as a formal than a substantive construct, we have ended up saying that the premises of most reasoning, most of the time, arise from specific communities. Using culture as an outer constraint, not an underlying grammar, we have moved toward saying (Chapter 2) that interpretive procedures are not analogous to Chomskian transformational grammars.

But reasoning—indeed every aspect of arguments—arises also from local *strategic* needs. Though an utterance or speech act might bear multiple, ambiguous, even conflicting meanings, or be taken variously by different interlocutors, or be so lightly held that an interlocutor's reformulation will be accepted by a speaker, we nonetheless find it natural to think of arguers as people pursuing particular purposes.

Seeing message creation as a strategic shaping of means to ends has been a standard part of rhetorical theory since Aristotle. But Argumentation has yet to account for the relationships between message characteristics and the assumptions people use to create them. It may be plausible to think that there are knowable links between one's interpersonal impressions and the messages one produces, but we might be hard put to describe that link. The argument analyst, like the arguers he or she studies, needs a communication theory that specifies how ends get translated into means—the premises one uses to speak meaningfully in a context, to decide upon the effects one can achieve with communication, and to select the best means of achieving those effects (O'Keefe, 1986). Seeing arguments as strategic adaptations is consistent with constructivist thinking, but constructivism lacks a coordination mechanism to explain how one's cognitive repertoire gets translated into adapted communication. Taken alone, constructivism implies that interpersonal communication seeks and achieves *shared meaning*. But communication does not require shared meaning: it needs only a sufficient *illusion* of shared meaning, or a working consensus, to make coordinated action possible.

The constructivists have developed message analysis systems for classifying messages (dealing with persuasion, regulation, comforting, conveying bad news, and resisting compliance) according to how they deal differently with situational demands for considerateness, reconciling conflicting desires, and the elaboration of feelings and perspectives. The most decisive dimension along which messages seem to differ is the integration of multiple goals (O'Keefe and Delia, 1982). O'Keefe and Shepherd (1985) developed a system for analyzing the different goals communicators pursue in arguments and the ways they deal with conflicting goals. Their subjects used three different ways of balancing conflicting goals: "Some persuaders simply forged ahead with no effort to deal with more than one goal; some persuaders would pursue the main goal (persuasion) and handle the problem of showing respect and consideration by appending conventionally defined forms such as hedges, compliments, apologies, and accounts to their messages; and some persuaders included explicit contextualizing phrases and statements that redefined the situation as one in which there was no conflict among goals or wants" (O'Keefe, 1985:2). Do these different approaches signal the existence of three different ethnotheories of communication?

O'Keefe (1985, 1986) proposes that there are systematic individual differences in "the kinds of premises used to generate messages," that people use systematically different communication-constituting concepts (different implicit theories, if you will) that yield different patterns of message organization and interpretation, and thus that it is possible for the facts about communication to be "systematically different for different people." She identifies three views of communication, each "associated with a constellation of related beliefs: a communication-constituting concept, a conception of the functional possibilities of communication, unit formation procedures, and principles of coherence" (O'Keefe, 1986:6). She terms these message design logics (MDLs) "Expressive," "Conventional," and "Rhetorical"—labels that represent not merely a classificatory device for deriving coding schemes but a grammar that explains the production of particular message characteristics. Like interpersonal complexity, the three MDLs consist of developmentally progressive stages (the more complex subsuming their simpler precursors) corresponding to constructivism's orthogenetic view of development. Unlike interpersonal complexity, the MDLs represent a person's knowledge about communication per se.

The root assumption of the *Expressive MDL* is that "language is a medium for expressing thoughts and feelings." Communication is a process in which one expresses what one thinks or feels so that others can know what one thinks or feels. Successful communication is clear expression—messages being repositories for meaning pretty much independent of context. Expressives thus impress us as being rather literal in their creation and understanding of messages: they do not see that expression can be made to serve multiple goals, and "they interpret messages as independent units rather than as threads in an interactional fabric, and so seem to disregard context" (p. 6).

What can communication accomplish? The Expressive thinks that "the only job a message can perform is expression" (p. 7). The idea that messages can be strategically (rhetorically) designed "is foreign and mysterious to the Expressive communicator—messages are understood as simple expressions of beliefs" (p. 7). How can intentions relate to messages? Either the message "fully and honestly" expresses the speaker's private views or it conveys some distortion— a lie or a tactfully edited version of the truth. "A desire to conduct communication as full and open disclosure of current thoughts and feelings, concern for the fidelity of messages, and a deep concern with deceptive communication are thus characteristic of an Expressive view of message function" (p. 7).

The symptomatology diagnostic of expressiveness is proportionately straightforward. First we expect to find expressive messages with pragmatically pointless content. By this O'Keefe means a lack of editing, lengthy expressions of the speaker's wants, even if the listener has already heard them or can do nothing about them, marked redundancies (not mere wordiness but repeating the same thing noncontiguously), complaints the listener can do nothing about, noncontingent threats, and insults. Second, Expressives somehow ignore the task at hand: "Semantic and pragmatic connections between Expressively generated messages and their contexts and among elements within Expressive messages tend to be idiosyncratic and subjective rather than conventional and intersubjective. When one asks of an Expressive message, why did the speaker say this now, the obvious answer is generally: because the immediately prior event caused the speaker to have such-and-so reaction or to make such-and-so mental association, and the speaker then said what he or she was thinking" (p. 8).

The root assumption of the *Conventional MDL* is that "communication is a game played cooperatively, according to socially conventional rules and procedures." The Conventional view thus subsumes the Expressive: "Language is a means of expressing propositions, but the propositions one expresses are specified by the social effect one wants to achieve"—one accommodates to conventional methods, as, for example, speech act theory suggests (Searle, 1969; Grice, 1975; Brown and Levinson, 1978).

The Conventional's basic view of communication is that it is constituted by cooperation. One plays the game, follows the recipes, and obeys the rules. Competence is a matter of appropriate performance: one succeeds insofar as one occupies the correct position in a situation, uses one's conventional resources for obligating the interlocutor, behaves competently as a communicator, and is dealing with an equally competent and cooperative interlocutor. We thus expect to find in conventional messages a "clearly identifiable core action being performed"—one easily characterizable as a speech act. We expect speakers to mention the felicity conditions of the core act, the structure of rights and obligations that empower the act, and (possibly) mitigating circumstances, for example, excuses. Messages will thus be related to contexts in predictable ways:

Just as the connections among message elements involve classic pragmatic coherence relations, the connections between messages and their contexts display a conventional basis for coherence. In contrast to Expressive messages, which are characteristically psychological and reactive in their relation to context, conventional messages bear a conventionalized and rule-following relation to context. If one asks . . . why did the speaker say this now, the answer is generally that this is the normal and appropriate thing to say under the circumstances. (Pp. 10–11)

The basic assumption of the *Rhetorical MDL* is that "communication is the creation and negotiation of social selves and situations." In this MDL, one's conventional knowledge is subsumed within a view of selves and situations as mutable rather than fixed (a view I shall later resurrect as seeing oneself as a belief-forming process). The key to the Rhetorical MDL is seeing meaning in terms of "dramaturgical enactment and social negotiation. The argument criticism makes information about the subtleties of verbal behavior constantly relevant to the process of message planning and interpretation: knowledge of the ways in which communicative choice and language style convey character, attitude, and definitions of the situation is systematically exploited to (on the one hand) enact a particular social reality and (on the other hand) provide 'depth interpretation' of received messages" (p. 11).

In the Rhetorical MDL, the function of messages is negotiation. Different speakers can adopt different voices and thereby talk different realities: "The one thing Rhetorical message producers must accomplish in a social situation is the achievement of a consensus regarding the reality in which they are engaged, coming to employ a common descriptive vocabulary and finding a common drama in which to play" (p. 12). Thus the Rhetorical MDL puts a premium on harmony and consensus:

They tend to ignore power and resource control as a means of conflict resolution; they persistently underestimate the force of social convention and routine and overestimate the individuality and creativity of themselves and others. They value psychological analysis and careful listening, for these form the basis for deep and individualized interpretations against which to test an emerging sense of intersubjective understanding. Their messages are characteristically proactive rather than reactive; their use of communication is dominated by the goals they want to achieve or facilitate and so messages are designed toward effects rather than in response to the actions of others. (Pp. 12–13)

The Rhetorical MDL also displays a characteristic pattern of content and structure: we expect to find "elaborating and contextualizing clauses and phrases that provide explicit definitions of the context," a definite sense of role and character "through manipulation of stylistic elements in a marked and coherent way," and "classically 'rational' arguments and appeals designed to persuade the hearer that the speaker's symbolic reality is true or correct (but not legitimate or powerful or conventional)" (p. 13).

The Rhetorical MDL yields messages with characteristic connections to context. They are neither reactions nor conventional responses but forward-looking and goal-connected. "If one asks of a Rhetorical message, why did the speaker say this now, the answer is generally: because they wanted to pursue such-and-such a goal. Similarly, if one asks of a rhetorical message, what connects all these elements as a common theme, the answer is generally: These elements can be interpreted as steps in a plan or as moments in a coherent narrative or as displays in a consistent character (and usually all of these). In short, the internal coherence of rhetorical messages derives from the elements being related by intersubjectively available, goal-oriented schemes" (pp. 13–14).

Each of the MDLs contains a logic for dealing with multiple and conflicting goals. If I argue with you to pursue personal goals or to correct your behavior or impede your goals, but I also want to remain polite and considerate, my assumptions about communication will make up my MDL. An Expressive believes that the purpose of communication is the clear expression of thoughts. Thus, I will be tactful. I can edit the message, distort it, or be less than frank. A Conventional will be polite by using off-the-record communications and conventional politeness forms such as apologies, hedges, excuses, and compliments (Brown and Levinson, 1978). A Rhetorical assumes that communication creates situations and selves; the solution: be someone else by transforming one's identity. "If one assumes that selves are socially constituted then they are changeable through taking on a different character in social interaction. This is the rhetorical solution—to cast oneself or one's partner into a role in a new drama in which there is no conflict of interest or implication of shame" (p. 17).

1.7. Intentions Translated to Performance

Constructivism is a strategic repertoire theory: it explains the acquisition and nature of the cognitive contents that affect one's attributions of internal states to others; it puts a premium on the idea of interpersonal cognitive complexity and thus to the development of communication skills such as perspective taking and adapting messages to another's perspective (Applegate, 1978; Applegate and Delia, 1980; Clark and Delia, 1976, 1977, 1979; Crockett, 1965; Delia, 1972, 1974, 1976c, 1980, 1983; Delia and Clark, 1977; Delia, Clark, and Switzer, 1974, 1979; Delia and Crockett, 1973).

But interpersonal complexity is not a person's only resource. Nor are accurate interpersonal impressions the only prerequisite to, or even a necessary condition of, successful communication. One needs knowledge about communication, what it is, what it can do, and how it works. A's success in arguing with B may symptomize not A's accuracy in assessing B's perspective but A's knowledge of and assumptions about communication. A and B might share spurious agreements, illusions of shared meaning, but nonetheless succeed in accomplishing coordinated tasks.

The focus on MDLs thus steps beyond constructivism's focus on interpersonal complexity to explain the translation of intentions into communication performances. Expressiveness is a performance ceiling, an inability to translate intentions into actions. But to label someone an "Expressive" is not to impute a *personality type*. The claim is that an Expressive cannot proceed rhetorically without changing his or her picture of the functions and possibilities of communication in the situation. Whether one is *able* to change depends, among other things, on one's knowledge of communication. A problem for argument critics and analysts may arise in cases in which obviously Expressive communications lend no clue to the communication strategies of the speaker. Since Rhetoricals can introduce Expressive tactics into conversations, one would need a description of the situation dense enough to reveal the difference between expression for a rhetorical purpose and expression by an Expressive.

The issue of how one's cognitive development—especially one's interpersonal complexity—limits one's ability to *use* (say) the Rhetorical MDL is a separate one. In the absence of evidence, whether one might find a preponderance of people at certain levels of interpersonal complexity using this or that design logic is an interesting but open question.

What assumptions about argument can one draw from this? Rational goals analysis says that messages are means for achieving situationally defined ends. The MDL model implies that messages within—and the epistemic possibilities of—arguments differ systematically according the MDLs in use by arguers. We further expect to find that arguers are at least sometimes not just arguing. In balancing conflicting or merely different goals, they may also be doing other things: being tactful, conventionally polite, or rhetorically adjusted to a situation. For critics, this puts a premium on dense situational descriptions as paths for getting at both the meanings of texts and the nature of the interactions they study.

The MDL notion also exposes the degree to which argument theories have taken one or another MDL as paradigmatic of all communication. The Expressive MDL, for example, predominates in pedagogical works (Chapter 11). An argument is a "position which is reasoned out" (Wilson, 1980:3) in which one expresses one's position publicly (Barry, 1976; Brody, 1973), with the choice of being tactful or dishonest ("When arguing, it is human nature to present every reason you can think of that is favorable to your position, while omitting those that are unfavorable" [Kahane, 1971:4]). The pedagogical origins of Informal Logic come into play: one wants a correctly reasoned position correctly expressed.

The Conventional MDL arises in normative theories. Some theorists explicitly embrace or at least acknowledge speech act theory (Johnson and Blair, 1980; van Eemeren and Grootendorst, 1984; van Eemeren, Grootendorst, and Kruiger, 1983, 1987) and constructs such as intersubjective validity (Barth, 1972). The Erlangen School's stress on the regimentation of discourse within a clear-cut rule structure (for ensuring semantic correspondences among interlocutors' uses of terms in elementary sentences, for example), the Amsterdam School's emphasis on rule-driven dialectic (van Eemeren and Grootendorst, 1984), several of the normative rule-based theories of argument fields (Naess, 1966; Crawshay-Williams, 1957), and the anthropological field theories (Toulmin, 1972) all share the assumption that discourse can proceed in contrived as well as naturally occurring circumstances.

The Rhetorical MDL is most often discussed with an eye to symbolic transformations—as Burke, for example, focuses on the dictatorship of form and its transformational possibilities. In Argumentation, the rhetoric-as-epistemic model has been given a systematic bent and treated mostly within the Expressive and Conventional rubrics. From the peripheries of other disciplines have come suggestions that form and style are integral to substance: "The question of style arises not in trying to package a finished product of thought, but, rather, in actually producing the thought" (Fuller, 1982:3; see Gross, 1988; Geertz, 1988).

Across this breadth of concerns—from the Expressive to the Rhetorical—is an overlaid unifying concern with adaptation and accommodation, processes I take to be definitive of Argumentation's subject matter. I have elsewhere (Willard, 1987c, 1988) argued that this organizing concern applies to the variations among human practices that affect the creation, acquisition, curatorship, and revision of knowledge, and thus comprises a new discipline, Epistemics.

1.8. Individuals and Collectivities

I claimed in the Introduction that a communication theory would expose the effects of the language of individualism and help us avoid the framework of the individualism debate. There are three signs that it has.

First, the decision to see argument as a form of communication suspends the *opposition* between individualism and holism. The point is not that Hayek, Watkins, Popper, et al. have won the day over Mandelbaum, Broadbeck, Gellner, et al., but that a focus on communication as the constituting agent of communities bypasses the opposition. The interactional theory diverts attention from questions about the individual's relation to society, or the differences between public and private meanings, toward an interest in the working agreements speakers achieve. The theory predicts differences among people, situations, and organizations based on (and in turn affecting) differences in local communication practices. Questions about meaning and influence, and more general questions about how communities create, defend, use, and change knowledge, thus turn on these practices. Questions of freedom and determinism turn on individual differences in cognitive attainment, reflectiveness, and ways of thinking about communication.

This emphasis on communication yields a useful way to read the organizational literature. Students of argument and epistemics need evidence about practices, but the evidence is embedded in a variety of theories. These theories emphasize that (1) individuals may have dramatic effects on organizations; (2) individuals may be confined and bound by roles; (3) organizational structure (or purposes) can shape individual action (and motives); (4) meanings are in people and (thus) communities are individuals writ large, and (5) individuals are communities writ small. The individualist sees these theories as competing answers to the organizing question of the individual's relation to society. But the striking thing about these theories is that each has merit: some people do exert dramatic influence while others passively acquiesce to organizations; meanings are in people, yet communities constrain idiosyncracies. So how can leadership be sometimes a myth and other times a dramatic reality? How can passive followership—and the obvious fact that organizations color our thinking and narrow and constrain our options—be suspended to allow for organizational growth and innovation? The interactional theory points to differences in (and a synergism among) people, situations, organizations, and communication practices (see Giddens, 1974, 1977, 1979).

Second, there are striking parallels between PCT's account of individual minds and *Weltanschauungen* accounts of social ecologies. The idea that cognitive systems are ruled by organizing constructs is analogous to Kuhn's (1970) belief that scientific communities are guided by paradigms. That a person's thinking is channelized by a priori assumptions squares with Toulmin's (1972) populational explanation of intellectual ecologies. That collectivities display a timidity or openness to change parallel to the cognitive preferences and styles of their members squares with PCT's Principle of Elaborative Choice. These parallels impute conservatism to cognitive and collective perspectives, a tendency toward self-preservation (and proportional inhibition of and resistance to innovation).

We thus bypass an array of questions that anyone enmeshed in the framework of individualism might be prone to ask. We have, for instance, a sharp contrast between our theory and the classical sociology of knowledge. Are we resurrecting the Marx/Durkheim/Mannheim vision of *Seinverbundenheit des Wissens*? No. Are we making deterministic claims about psychological processes à la Pareto, De Gre, or Scheler? No. Are we saying that social life is epiphenomenal to individual minds? Emphatically not. *Wissensoziologie* got its psychological determinism from assumptions about the relation of individuals to society. It is no accident that its proponents produced no communication theories or that its opponents such as Sorokin insisted that minds and society were independent variables.

I underscore the similarity between *Weltanschauungen* and constructivist accounts to stress the functional fit between people and their communities. The CSI claim that collectivities exist in and through the activities of their members implies the centrality of communication practices to social life. Yet these practices are equally central to cognitive life. Since these practices arise from the interpretations actors impose on events, explanations of the relation of individuals to society will be circular and functional (Douglas, 1986; Giddens, 1974, 1977, 1979; Ranson, Hinings, and Greenwood, 1980).

In claiming to bypass the opposition of individual and society, I must disavow one interpretation that might be given to this reasoning, namely that it is a resurrection of a physicalist doctrine. To claim that psychological and collective ecologies are similar and functionally related is not to assert *self-similarity*. Once a discredited doctrine, the idea that very small entities are isomorphic to very big ones (and hence that there is a unity between the quantum and cosmological domains) is enjoying a renaissance. But the present proposal only seems similar. Whether or not one can find "the universe in a grain of sand," it is mistaken as Mannheim discovered, to think that any individual could be a perfect replica of a collectivity (Argyris, 1957, 1964; Dahl, 1967; Ermann and Lundman, 1976; Farr, 1981; Grunig, 1975, 1978; Jehenson, 1973). If one takes account of multivalence (Lee, 1966), incompetence, specialization, and other human limits, one would not suppose that an analysis of the logical workings of a text milieu reveals the cognitive workings of the readers of those texts. Nor is it plausible to assume that microanalytic studies of a single person's inferences would *necessarily* yield predictions about the outcomes of collective deliberations (March, 1962; March and Olsen, 1976).

In sum, the language of the individualism debate is inappropriate to the phenomena surrounding argument. Explanations of argument require a benign circle: empirical accounts of inferences, messages, and social environments. Arguments affect people, who in turn affect and are affected by their fields of discourse. These mutual influences vary with differences among people, situations, organizations, and communication practices. It is thus inappropriate to seek a single theory explaining *the* individual's relation to *the* community.

Summary

So argument can be seen as a species of communication, not logic. We have started to define this ground by specifying some units of analysis pertinent to interaction. In avoiding the caricatured relation of individual to society fostered by the individualism debate, we have opted for CSI because it sees social entities (groups, communities, etc.) as existing in and through the communication activities of their members, and for constructivism because it defines the individual-society relationship in terms of communication practices. The merger of these positions dissolves the contrast between structuralism and individualism.

The species bears the stamp of the genus. Argument is thus a *cooperative* activity involving joint action, intersubjective meanings, and accommodations to people and institutions; an *intentional* activity involving speakers who mean to say particular things; and a *creative* and *strategic* activity involving not only listener adaptedness and strategic repertoires but also a *translation* of one's perceptions and intentions into particular communication strategies. To *adapt* to persons and situations is to attribute characteristics to them and to assess the fit between these attributions and one's intentions. To *translate* these cognitive achievements into strategies is to use one's communication knowledge to capture a functional fit between one's goals and messages.

To avoid overpsychologized and oversocialized views of arguers, we have decided that arguers are people seeking balances between their needs to assimilate events to their preferred cognitive tools and to accommodate to public codes, etiquettes, and standards. We expect to find variety in their solutions to this problem and, as well, to find that arguments play a role in such juggling. We should expect to find systematic differences in people's assumptions about communication and (thus) about the nature, purposes, and effects of the messages they create. An argument theory, therefore, will not be a monolithic description of a single discourse derived from a unitary human nature but a picture of a pluralism of discourse animated by many voices.

Notes

1. Historically, proponents of PCT and CSI were (circa 1955) refuting versions of Analytic Philosophy and Psychology which held "concepts" to be features of, or naturally related to, their referents. Against these views, the relation between thought and its objects was held to be arbitrary and not a matter of natural categories (cf. Jabobs and Jackson, 1981). Kelly insisted that constructs are features of our thinking—different in kind from concepts. Thus both PCT and CSI adopted a one-way causality (humans cause actions in the external world) but resisted returning the favor (both theories are unclear about how externalities relate to thinking). Both theories thus undervalue communication. They do so unnecessarily: if situations are comprised of human interpretations, such influence surely works both ways. Thus both PCT and CSI can be modified to account for the degree to which contexts call forth behavior or to which people accommodate to externalities.

2. I doubt that Kelly read Burke or Saussure, yet there are parallels between his view of dichotomization and Burke's "universal negative" and with Saussure's proclamation, "In language there are only differences."

3. Wegner and Vallacher say that, if there is a difference between formal and naive theories, it lies in the tendency of ordinary reasoners to *assume* that their beliefs are correct. Perhaps a more basic difference lies in the professional's belief in intersubjectivity, publicness, and replicability of results. But this does not deny that people fit their actions to their theories (Abelson, 1976; Ajzen, 1977; Barker, 1981; Berger and Calabrese, 1975; Bromley, 1977).

2

Argument as Interaction

The preceding view of communication entails a particular picture of argument: *argument is a kind of interaction in which two or more people maintain what they construe to be incompatible positions*. This definition needs to be fleshed out—first by differentiating the complexity of arguments, and second by unpacking the definition's key terms and phrases.

Three Levels of Argument

This definition encompasses at least three levels of activity distinguished by the substance, sources, complexity, and refinement of the assumptions and rules the arguers follow.

2.1. Naturally Occurring Argument

"Naturally occurring" is used variously. Here it denotes arguers in the natural attitude, untutored in argument techniques but sufficiently competent to engage in interaction. Arguers in naturally occurring arguments might display any of the three levels of accommodation and three MDLs, but the shape, scope, and outcomes of their arguments will be powerfully influenced by conversational rules. The conversational system structurally prefers agreement. Disagreement is a "trouble," argument a troubleshooting mechanism (Jacobs, 1987); the point is to repair the conversation and get on with other business. This purpose is *pragmatic*, not epistemic, justificatory, or deliberative (Jacobs, 1987). Argument at this level "is about speech acts rather than about propositions in the logician's sense, and . . . the issues which structure ordinary argumentation are felicity conditions for the performance of the speech act provoking the argument" (Jackson, 1987:217).

2.2. Epistemic/justificatory/deliberative argument

Not all arguments start from illocutions gone awry. In addition to repair, ordinary arguments may also (or instead) display the epistemic, justificatory, and deliberative motives naturally occurring arguments lack. Untutored and educated folk alike do argue about ideas; and they do so in decision-making contexts institutionalized in a variety of forms. Substantive disputes turn on formal or substantive rules which do more than regulate speech acts. Ordinary arguers appeal to proverbs and folk bromides, as well as to intellectual principles that have filtered out of academe. These can be divided roughly into two categories: deliberative rules (folk argumentation theory, including principles of debate, negotiation, logic, evidence, and presumption) and interpersonal rules (including principles for maintaining relationships, face, and social dominance).

Conversational rules are not irrelevant, but they may be superseded, subordinated, or submerged beneath other goals and rules. When the *point* is to argue, conversational maintenance may be equivalent to letting disagreement flourish. The preference for agreement may be (1) subordinated to one's need to explore an issue, deliberate about a policy, maintain face, or to sustain social dominance; or (2) contradicted and replaced by the conservative presumption in a debate: the former in principle favors a speech act, the latter in principle opposes every proposal before a prima facie case has been made (Jacobs, 1987; Goodnight, 1980). Moreover, debates use constitutive rules that supplant conversational rules (turn-taking specified a priori—the affirmative speaks first and last, the negative speaks every other time; utterance length is controlled; admissible evidence is predefined by rules known in advance) and by regulative rules which superficially resemble the constitutive rules of conversation (e.g., "be relevant" or responsive to the opponent's claims, observe the burden of rejoinder).

2.3. Disciplined Discourse

Disciplined discourse presupposes that rules are in principle open to scrutiny and objection concerning their substance and application. Disciplined arguers work in the natural attitude but with substantively different background awarenesses. They assume that their epistemic and decision-making practices are (1) protected by institutions which are founded upon reflectively adopted and in principle defensible ideals; (2) guided by reflectively adopted procedural rules; (3) indexical to specific authoritative (disciplined) bodies of knowledge; and (4) in principle open to critique. Scientific discourse can be seen as a formalized valuative and judgmental system (Rescher, 1970, 1977a, 1977b); as a general method of intellectual life (Ehninger, 1970; Wenzel, 1979, 1980); or as discourse guided by negotiable (but once negotiated, fixed) rules, as in jurisprudence.

"Having an argument" is thus one of the cooperative enterprises conversation makes possible. The point is not to stifle disagreement but to let it flourish. The purpose of debating, of decision making, or of arguing the morality of abortion with our neighbor is not to grant requests or get on with a nonargumentative conversational project. The substantive disagreement is the point. Political and legal debates, for instance, assume that disagreement may be permanent. Decision making, quality circles, unanimous consent agreements, and agency rule-making promote cooperation without requiring agreement.

The distinction between 2.2 and 2.3 is not a matter of *informal versus formal* argument. Ordinary and disciplined discourse can be equally formal or informal. Debate is as institutionalized in the public sphere as in the academic, and most proposals for formalizing disputes (e.g., van Eemeren and Grootendorst, 1984) apply to both. The distinction, rather, lies in the relationship between the arguers and disciplinary knowledge and rules. Ordinary arguers often make statements that are indexical to authoritative domains. But they are *users* rather than curators or creators of disciplined knowledge.

Expressive, Conventional, and Rhetorical MDLs will be found at all three levels, as will the three modes of accommodation. All three levels of argument can occur in the natural attitude or be subjected to reflection and thus adjusted. The extent to which the three levels of argument can be treated as a value hierarchy depends upon the purposes and values we want to defend. If we prize social tranquility, 2.1 may be incomparably superior; if we value epistemic progress and critique, 2.3 has the edge.

Given that constructivism is a developmental model, and that we have viewed accommodation and the three MDLs in developmental terms, it might seem that the three modes of argument are like Piagetian stages, the simple ones being developmental precursors of increasingly complex successor stages. But successor stages subsume rather than contradict their predecessors; yet the more complex arguments cut against the conversational system's preference for agreement. Moreover, as a matter of evolution, it is mistaken to think that the facts of naturally occurring argument are the raw material out of which our civilization has contrived refined methods of conventional argument by creating situations and institutions based on reflectively adopted procedural rules. Historically, the contrary has been true: ideal theories (e.g., formal logic) were lenses through which scholars viewed ordinary argument. Prior to Argumentation's turn to conversational and interpersonal studies, naturally occurring argument was considered either too unimportant to merit sustained study or as the poor cousin of more refined modes. Perhaps one reason for formalism's conspicuous failure in Argumentation has been that its veridical purposes do not square with the maintenance functions of naturally occurring argument.

Unpacking the Definition

With these distinctions in mind, we can consider each of the main terms or phrases in the definition. The first important phrase is *Kind of Interaction*.

Two necessary but not sufficient conditions of "having an argument" are that the arguers (1) possess adequate communication competence to form and intersubjectively employ comprehensible utterances and (2) know the rules of the conversational system. When these conditions are met, the sufficient condition for having an argument is that trouble crops up. The simplest trouble may be an interruption in an ongoing coordinated project. More complex troubles may stem from substantive disagreements. Seeing argument as interaction thus requires that we see it as a matter of conversational rules and structure, as a matter of substantive disagreements, as a matter of goal-directed behavior, and as an intersubjective accomplishment.

This explains why arguments occur in going social orders, not why people select argument over (say) violence. Since even children argue (O'Keefe and Benoit, 1982), it is plausible to think that the suppression of violence inheres in a pattern of social suppression that begins early in cognitive development. An argument theory need not explain this suppression, as long as some other theory does, but the theory should account for the fact that argument skills develop coincidentally with other cooperative skills. Argument is thus not an aberration but of a piece with other communication skills.

2.4. Conversational Structure

Naturally occurring arguments are organized events. In most cases it is clear when they start and stop. Arguers' actions seem relevant "given that we know an argument is occurring. In short, arguments are distinctive and coherent interactional events" (O'Keefe and Benoit, 1982:162).

Why is this so? The simplest answer arises from the simplest case. Naturally occurring arguments are organized events because conversation is organized and coherent (Craig and Tracy, 1983). Arguments are mundane yet indispensable elements of everyday life: "Their possibility and use provide a basic condition of all conversational exchanges. . . . Argument regulates in important ways the shape and occurrence of other conversational events." Argument, "whether manifest as an event or latent as an unexercised possibility, leaves its mark on whatever goes on in conversation" (Jacobs and Jackson, 1982:205–6).

Naturally occurring arguments are rule governed because they are collaborative productions in which actors jointly produce a conventional relational structure. They occur because actors need to manage a conversational event—disagreement. Their importance lies in their clear-cut display of what might be called the "trivial minimum" conditions of "having an argument" (Rommetveit, 1980).

At the simplest level, conversational analysts use a "sequencing rules model," which seeks to build "a kind of grammar of argument by locating irreducible conventions that operate directly on the surface level of conversation" (Jacobs and Jackson, in press). On this account, the basic units of talk, adjacency pairs, are coupled speech acts (question-answer, request-grant, request-refusal, and the like), which produce sequentially implicated turns and provide for structural expansion into "broader patterns of turns." The first pair part (FPP) of an adjacency pair establishes a "next turn position," which is expected to be filled by a second pair part (SPP). "The interpretive frame established by issuance of an FPP makes the SPP conditionally relevant on the occurrence of that FPP. While other acts may be done in the next turn position, the SPP is conditionally relevant in that what these other acts are doing will be interpreted with reference to the nonoccurrence of the expected SPP" (Jackson and Jacobs, 1980:251). Of the possible responses we might imagine to an FPP, we can usually distinguish the one a particular FPP is designed to get, the structurally preferred SPP. Requests court acquiescence, questions court answers: "The preference for agreement operates on SPPs by creating a general presumption for agreement in the absence of a good reason to do otherwise; it operates on FPPs by promoting the production of turns that will get agreement and by suppressing turns that will not" (Jackson and Jacobs, 1980:253).

Perhaps the sequencing rules model is sufficient for describing the simplest, most automatic conversational adjustments to disagreement. By itself, however, the model ignores the functions communicative acts may serve (Jacobs and Jackson, in press). It cannot explain the variety of coherent replies to an FPP that do not fit the SPP mold or that a range of strategic replies may be germane to an act (Levinson, 1983). Speech act theory (Searle, 1969, 1975) can serve as a higher level functionalist explanation of phenomena inexplicable in adjacency-pair terms alone. But speech act theory has its limits: the idea that illocutionary force resides in the deep structure of an act rather than in the thinking and negotiations of speakers presupposes a dubious view of communication (3.1, Chapter 3).

Of central concern to conversation analysts are empirical anomalies that "arise from the fact that people do not generally interpret and respond to others in terms of the *types of acts* being performed, but in terms of the perceived goals and plans of the communicator" (Jacobs and Jackson, in press, 21). Conversational analysis has thus evolved into a focus on the "goal structure of speech acts" (Jacobs and Jackson, in press, 23). Arguments are coherent not by virtue of universal, context-independent structure and form but by virtue of the relationships between a speaker's goals and the argumentative moves she or he makes.

This brings argument more properly into the domain of intersubjective perceptions. We may thus speak of arguments as "encounters," which are shaped by "relationships" and by taken-for-granted realities, "what everybody knows" (Cicourel, 1974). This vocabulary differs from the structure-based terms of speech act theory (Streeck, 1980; Scheflen, 1974). An example may clarify this difference. If *A* argues that economic prosperity trickles down, *B* may take up the challenge not because *A* is arguing but because *B* is enraged by the substance of the claim. *A* might have argued many opening gambits that *B* would have declined, but this one rouses *B* to respond. In this case, the *illocutionary* and *perlocutionary* forces of arguing that prosperity trickles down are inseparable; the illocutionary force does not reside in the deep structure of *A*'s claim but in *B*'s reaction to it. And *B*'s reason for objecting to the claim may be idiosyncratic to a relationship with *A*. *A* is wealthy and smug: the dispute is about *A*'s self-serving attitudes. In this case, the relationship between *A* and B, its historically developed content undergirding all talk between A and B, overarches the systemic requirements of conversation.

2.5. Social Relationships and Encounters

There must be a relationship before an argument of any complexity can occur (Forgas, 1979; From, 1971). Even first encounters between strangers ("How about them Mets?"), operating on a level of superficial appearances (Cicourel, 1974; Goffman, 1959, 1963, 1967, 1971), require the speakers to assume enough taken-for-granted background to permit coherent statements. To *strike up* or to *take up* a conversation with a stranger may require more complex motives and assumptions than conversational maintenance.

The relationship construct describes the preconditions of intersubjectivity. Conversations are not just scenes in which autonomous bundles of strategic repertoires butt heads; they are outcomes (and symptoms) of broader commonalities. These commonalities may but need not be "shared meanings," for relationships may be founded on mistakes, partial understandings, or public agreements unrelated to private beliefs. Unfortunately, relationships have often been defined without regard to differences in simplicity and complexity among participants. Standard definitions have held that relationships are (1) the "mutual subjective orientation of the participants" (Scheff, 1970:194); (2) "the behavior of a plurality of actors in so far as in its meaningful content the action of each takes account of that of the others and is oriented in these terms" (Weber, 1947:118); (3) "a symbolically recognized probability of recurring interaction between two persons as distinctive individuals based on some functional fit between their respective roles and/or selves" (McCall et al., 1970:172); and (4) communication vitalized by an interpenetration of perspectives (Dewey, 1929) or reciprocal perspective taking (Mead, 1954). The Dewey-Mead view stresses "co-orientation" as the defining characteristic of social relationships. Phenomenologists such as Schutz (1945a, 1945b, 1951, 1953, 1962) use the term *intersubjectivity* to describe "joint awareness" or the "reciprocity of perspectives" (Cicourel, 1970; Goffman, 1959).

Schutz emphasized the hierarchical or multilevel nature of a reciprocity of perspectives. Marcoups and Bassoul (1962) term it a "mirror game." Think of the endless chain of reflections we get if we place two mirrors facing each other. We can distinguish only a few individual steps or successive reflections; they blur together. But we can sense the impact of the collective importance of successive reflections for our relationships with each other. We have a "spiral of reciprocal perspectives" (Laing, Phillipson, and Lee, 1972). This is analogous to Garfinkel's view that "the person assumes, assumes that the other person assumes as well and assumes that as he assumes it of the other person the other person assumes the same for him" (1964:237). Thus Schelling (1948:40–41) in discussing the Korean peace talks notes that recognitions of war limitations could never be unilateral because only mutual recognition would give them force: "It was not just that we recognized and they recognized it but that we recognized that they recognized it and they recognized that we recognized it and so on. It was a shared expectation. To that extent it was a somewhat undeniable expectation."

There is a circular relation between encounters and relationships. Relationships begin with encounters and, over time, undergo successive evolution toward refinement and greater complexity as they guide more encounters (Altman and Taylor, 1973; Berger and Calabrese, 1975; Forgas, 1979; Duck, 1973, 1982; McCall, 1970). Encounters are thus doubly important: they are symptoms and contributory causes of relationships. An encounter may change a relationship, but the relationship makes the encounter possible and gives it at least some of its content (Berger, 1979; Berger and Calabrese, 1975; Berger and Douglas, 1981). Encounters deal with particular matters; relationships deal with the members' identities.

There are in this scheme three levels of coorientation: agreement, understanding, and realization. If *A* and *B* express agreement on *X*, they "agree." If *A* believes (correctly or not) that *B* agrees, there is "understanding." If *A* believes (correctly or not) that *B* believes that *A* agrees with *X*, "realization" has occurred (Laing, Phillipson, and Lee, 1972:64–92). A coorientation, therefore, is a broader intersubjective achievement than (say) illocutionary force—which is not supposed to be an intersubjective achievement so much as a fait accompli wired into the deep structure of an act. For reasons that will soon be clear (Chapter 3), a dense description of a coorientation better fits the idea that arguments take their coherence from speakers' plans and goals.

This definition of argument as a coorientation within an encounter rules out (perhaps too arbitrarily) engagements in which one actor is arguing but the other is not. If our hierarchy of arguments is authentic, we should expect to find people who want to treat *any* opposition as a simple conversational hitch *and* people who turn simple hitches into pitched battles. Expressives may press their points despite their interlocutors' attempts to disengage. Indeed, we often see cases in which one speaker wants to persuade, not argue. If I want to argue and you don't, we have failed to arrive at an agreed-upon definition of situation. Our perception that we are working at cross purposes *is* a coorientation but one that augers ill for collaborative success.

2.6. Parity Is Not Needed To Have an Argument

Some parity is required for an encounter to occur. Speakers must be sufficiently competent to realize that they are interacting. Even the Expressive has to have cracked the code (O'Keefe, 1986). Moreover, parity has its uses: think of any face-saving context—diplomacy or a cocktail party: I'm lying; you know I'm lying; I know that you know; you know I know that you know; and so on. The lie succeeds as a social artifice by virtue of a complex intersubjective achievement. But this does not mean that arguments require parity or participants of equal perspicaciousness and position.

We know by experience that we are not equally matched in all our encounters. Confidence tricks would be impossible if everyone conversed at parity. Think of a parent arguing with a child (not always a conflict of two different MDLs). Experience usually gets the better of innocence. The adult sees deeper than the child. And the child sometimes wins without knowing why. The charm of innocence is a feature of the adult's thinking, not the child's. Or consider two chess masters making moves and countermoves. Imagine the moves they don't make and the experience and insight that help them avoid inferior moves. Now imagine a master playing a novice. Think of the shortcuts the master would not contemplate with a peer but which are serviceable against the novice. The master is thinking rings around the novice. But occasionally the novice may catch the master at one of these shortcuts, just as children sometimes catch adults, striking home with more power than they put into the pitch.

Imagine an argument between an Expressive and a Rhetorical. The Rhetorical might make tactical concessions for reasons too complex for the Expressive to understand, yet the Expressive might then hold the Rhetorical accountable for the exact wording of his or her concessions, thus getting the Rhetorical into unanticipated trouble. Or the Expressive might wear the Rhetorical down by reiterating a litany of complaints or expressions of principle. Exhaustion doubtless decides more arguments than we would like to admit.

Communicative competence aside, parity is also tied to the possession of information and to mistakes people make in assuming that others have the same information or share their organizing concerns (Rommetveit, 1974, 1978). Rommetveit (1980) refers to a speaker's proceeding on the assumption (or as if) a hearer knows what the speaker knows as *prolepsis*. In discussing the psychological effects of "evoked sets" (that we interpret events in terms of whatever is occupying our attention and thus overestimate the degree to which we and others understand messages), Jervis (1976) offers examples (military blunders, airliners being shot down) involving speakers incorrectly assuming that others know what they mean. A general on a hill sees things a commander down on the plain can't see; failing to realize this, the general gives fatally ambiguous orders. Exchanges of all kinds—and especially arguments—between people possessing disparate information or people with different concerns on their minds may be irremediably unequal. The intersubjectivity made possible by reciprocal role-taking does not depend on equality, parity, or symmetry of power positions.

The fact that arguments neither need nor presuppose parity is another case in point against equating any but the simplest arguments with the structure of speech acts. If we think of such disparities as *substantive* inequalities, it is easy to see that they work against *formal* distributions of power such as a speaker's control over his or her own meaning. Consider the Expressive:

The circularity inherent in actions of communication does *not* imply that the two participants assume joint or equal responsibility for what is being meant by what is said. The speaker monitors what he says in accordance with what he assumes to be the listener's position, yet in order to make *his own private world* comprehensible to the other. What he says may still turn out to be an incomplete and very poor expression of what he means. But he cannot possibly misunderstand *what he himself intends to make known*. Only he, *not* the listener, can decide *what is being meant* and *whether it is being misunderstood*. Thus, control of the temporarily shared reality at any given stage of a dialogue is, under conditions of perfect equality or symmetry between partners, in principle, unequivocally determined by *direction of communication*. (Rommetveit, 1980:133)

The direction of communication is decisive, then, in "conditions of perfect equality or symmetry." Substantive disparities of the sort we have been considering would thus cut against the speaker's control, as in the case of a parent (or teacher) who not only adjusts the child's (or student's) expressions but critiques and attempts to change the child's (or student's) intentions. An interlocutor might well understand an arguer's intentions but refuse to honor them.

So claims about the effects of arguments cannot bracket the issue of parity. The claim that the possibility of opposition (the *tu quoque* possibility) is a constraint on actors and the stronger claim that arguments have epistemic importance (Chapter 5) must be adjusted to square with the ubiquity of inequality. As in Jurisprudence mismatched interlocutors make for a vacuous clash.

2.7. Background Awarenesses

It is a serious but nonfatal flaw in theories of relationships that they make no distinctions between simple and complex perceivers and (thus) between simple and complex relations. These theories can be stretched to accommodate to differences in the ways people assimilate, accommodate, and design messages.

We can appropriate the ethnomethodologist's term *background awarenesses* to describe the assumptions behind our mutual perceptions (Hymes, 1972; Garfinkel, 1967; Gumperz, 1972; Kreckel, 1981; Rommetveit, 1974). The assumption is that every conversation takes place against the background of a "world silently taken for granted" (Berger and Luckmann, 1966:172), the tacit, taken-for-granted assumptions that lie behind our speech and action (Schutz, 1945a, 1945b, 1962).

At the simplest (2.1) level are formal cultural principles. Searle's (1969) famous example asks us to think of the knowledge we need to understand that "is there any salt?" means "please pass the salt." Conversational structure (adjacency pairs, turn-taking and the like) may explain the coherence of the simplest arguments, though a more complex view of intersubjectivity is needed for more intricate cases (McLaughlin, 1984; Craig and Tracy, 1983; Brown and Levinson, 1978; Daly et al., 1985; Hancher, 1979). Speech act theory has been critiqued (Rommetveit, 1980; Streeck, 1980) for its tendency to study trivial acts such as requests to pass the salt and to take out the garbage: "Whereas speech acts in which speakers send other people to prison or fine them money, offer or decline marriage, make important contracts, and generally engage in socially significant acts are ignored" (Stubbs, 1983: 490). This is not a devastating criticism *if* the structure of speech acts is not taken to be the controlling intelligence behind the emergence of argument strategies (3.1, Chapter 3). The case for convention need not be made at the expense of intention. Complex arguments obviously have conventional structure. But they also benefit from the facts of relationships (Duck, 1973, 1982), etiquettes (Emerson, 1970a, 1970b), coorientations, epistemic assumptions (Garfinkel, 1962, 1967), and field-based procedural rules (Darden and Maull, 1977).

2.8. Dissensus Refined

It may seem trivial to say that arguments require dissensus, but this claim is one of the few points of agreement among Argumentation theorists. Arguments are coherent as interactional structures at least partially because they stem from relationships containing or permitting opposition (O'Keefe and Benoit, 1982; Benoit, 1981). If consensus consists of an "infinite series of reciprocating understandings among the members of a group" (Scheff, 1967b:32–46) and dissensus consists of perceptions of a lack of agreement at one or more levels of coorientation (Duck, 1982), "argument" must be an encounter based on dissensus.

Argument and *dissensus* are not interchangeable synonyms. Not all dissensus issues in arguments. You and I may ignore our differences vis-à-vis X because our agreements on Y and Z are more important or because overt disagreement might jeopardize our relationship. Diplomacy and negotiations often require that disagreements be submerged beneath the needs of the moment, even beneath illusory agreements. Dissensus, then, is a necessary but not sufficient condition of argument.

An argument is a social encounter built upon the following minima: I assume that we disagree; I assume that you assume we disagree; I assume that I am arguing and that you agree that I am arguing; you assume that you are arguing and that I would agree that you are arguing. These are metacommunicative assumptions which are independent of the subject matter at hand. All four assumptions are "episodic" attributions (situation-specific attributions to a person, for example, that he is lying) rather than "dispositional" attributions (imputing enduring character traits, for example, that she is a liar (Warr and Knapper, 1968). Dispositional constructs ("schemas" in Chapter 1), because they are embedded in larger interpretive systems, are the bases of our episodic interpretations. But arguments, as opposed to other interactions, lead us to employ cognitive schemes appropriate to dissensual interaction. Excepting Expressive MDLs in naturally occurring (2.1) arguments, for example, witnessing behavior (Jacobs, 1982, 1983), in which one's concern is expression regardless of its fit with context or effect on others, most arguing (2.2 and 2.3) shares the hypothesis-testing nature of interaction in general.

It is plausible to think that methods of hypothesis testing differ systematically and even covary with differences in MDLs. The Expressive (in 2.2 and 2.3) will have some simple truth tests. The Conventional will assess a claim's fit with an ecology. And the Rhetorical will aim at strengthening his or her thinking, not the other person's—aiming not to arrive at a deep understanding of the other person (building a theory that perfectly explains the other's perspective) but to derive cognitive representations that enhance his or her own thinking and facilitate successful moves in a situation.

Coorientation is not synonymous with consensus, but it is a pre-condition of recognizing a disagreement. How else could I know that you believe X while I believe not-X? Why would I bother to engage you in argument about X if it were not important? And what would make it important except the terms of our relationship? Arguments are thus intrinsically cooperative achievements: we need at least some negotiated or assumed ground and at least some cooperation to agree that we disagree. Goffmanesque strangers could not begin an argument without first creating a sufficiently detailed relation-ship to make it possible to discover a disagreement. And most of our important interactions are not with Goffmanesque strangers.

The definition of situation "we are having an argument" reflects at least a third-order coorientation: you and I disagree, we both see that we disagree, and we both see that our disagreement stems from some incompatibility between our beliefs. We perceive dissensus:

Consensus exists between two persons, with respect to issue X if there is an infinite series of correct, mutually reciprocating attributions. In actual research, it would not be necessary to measure the entire series. We could assume as the actors probably usually assume, that if we find accord at the first three levels, that consensus exists. The operational measures of con-sensus, then, are three questions to each of the two persons in the trans-action: Do you agree with statement X? How will the other person answer? How will he think you have answered? If accord exists at all three levels, we will take the answers to be evidence of consensus. If there is lack of accord at one or more levels, we will define the situation to be one of dissensus. (Scheff, 1967a:225)

Our relationship coorients us so that we can know whether we agree or disagree and know whether our disagreement is important. Some people "may be able to disagree, to see that they disagree, to un-derstand the other's position even in disagreement and through a combination of understanding . . . with disagreement . . . maintain a reciprocally satisfying relationship" (Laing, Phillipson, and Lee, 1972:102–3).

2.9. Relational Rules for Interaction

Naturally occurring argument (2.1) differs from its more complex cousins in that its object is the repair of an ongoing cooperative project that has developed a hitch. Arguers at levels 2.2 and 2.3 may seek to repair ideas, relationships, and institutions and to balance multiple goals simultaneously, for example, idea or hypothesis testing, face-saving, domination, or even amusement. At least some of these goals come from the personal relationship between the speakers. A relationship between *A* and *B* might be nearly as idiosyncratic as (say) *A*'s private inferences—perhaps a unique social world (Shibutani, 1962). In dealing with each other, *A* and *B* have "gone public"—meaning they have transcended the idiosyncracies of their private psychologies. But they have "gone public" in a restricted sense: their relationship can have private languages or intimate meanings unavailable to outsiders. Contained within it are "special views of self, unique vocabularies of meaning and motive, and most important, symbol systems that have consensual meaning only to the participants involved." Over time, relationships develop rules "specifying acts of deference and demeanor . . . mechanisms for regulating knowledge, secrecy, and personal problems endemic to the relationship . . . [and] task structures to specify who does what, when, where, and with whom" (Denzin, 1970:71). These rules endow the relationship with order and predictability by affording each actor expectancies about the other's behavior. Some rules will be idiosyncratic and context-specific—the appropriateness of a rule being an outcome of a definition of situation; others will reflect the broader social milieus in which the actors move.

Some arguments may be encapsulated in a relationship virtually as private and idiosyncratic as someone's cognitive system; others are indexical to external assumptions and conditions. The arguers, that is, call outside assumptions, principles, and rules into play as needed. To coin a contradiction in terms, rules are ad hoc a prioris: we select the rules that help us make our cases, ignore the ones that don't, attack the rules that impede us, and then act as if our preferred rules are Platonic universals (see Davidson, 1968; Austin, 1975; cf. Anscomb, 1959; Kovesi, 1967). "Relationships may validate, redefine, or make relevant rules from another moral order, be they civil-legal, polite propriety, or another relationship of the same class. Therein lies their signal importance for the student of deviance, for they represent the ways members of any society make that society's rules" (Denzin, 1970:71).

If I accuse you of being unfair, you might demand to know what I mean by fair. If you accuse me of inconsistency, I might refuse to admit that consistency is important or germane. Both cases appeal to, use, and perhaps dispute the applicability of rules. It thus seems plausible to say that arguments differ from other interactions in that they require more elaborate and defined rule structures and these rules are themselves more apt to come under scrutiny. Points of procedural dispute may become stases beyond which the encounter cannot move until a settlement is reached.

This view of relationships and rules puts a methodological premium on understanding how arguers organize phenomena, interpret situations, and adapt their actions. The study of argument thus requires an ethnoscientific move—an attempt to understand arguments from the arguers' points of view. Ethnoscience and ethnographic work are well established in several disciplines—most prominently Anthropology and Sociology. But it may clarify our argumentation theory to specify the ethnomethodological assumptions appropriate to it.

2.10. The Ethnomethodological View: Culture Revisited

O'Keefe (1979) argues that there are two distinct versions of ethnomethodology. Following his reasoning, the ethnomethodological view most appropriate to the interactional theory is that developed by Cicourel (1970, 1974); the less appropriate view is that of Garfinkel. Garfinkel (1964) emphasizes overt behavior. Meaningful events are "entirely and exclusively" behavioral events in a person's environment. Cicourel uses mentalistic notions, cognitive procedures and schemes, to explain how actors interpret other people and events. Garfinkel sees sense of "rules," not as generating mechanisms of action but as post facto conversational practices that create and sustain the appearance of orderliness in social events. Cicourel views rules as the tacit or explicit guidelines or recipes for social practices. Garfinkel believes that we make sense of others' actions as an overt feature of talk, a characteristic of speech acts, whereas Cicourel sees sense-making as a cognitive process that affects talk and is itself affected by talk. Garfinkel locates the artful practices of ordinary actors as identifiable features of talk, not as characteristics of a person's cognitive system; Cicourel locates artful practices in cognitive systems and intersubjective agreements. Garfinkel follows a tradition allied with the thinking of Ryle and Malcom; Cicourel is heavily influenced by Schutz.

These differences yield different research programs. Garfinkel would have us locate the artful practices of argument as things in the talk—observable characteristics captured in texts. Following Cicourel, we would rely less on texts, though we would not ignore them, preferring participant observation and free response research techniques to discern the interpretive rules arguers use. Nonetheless, Cicourel acknowledges a debt to Garfinkel—for, among other things, his view of interpretive schemes.

How do people select rules? On what bases do they define their situations, interpret the motives and intentions of others, and frame their own courses of action? The constructivist's answer is to point to the cognitive schemes people use to organize their impressions: "We see interaction as a process in which persons coordinate their respective lines of action through the application of shared schemes for the organization and interpretation of action. Persons' actions are channelized by interpretive schemes: Individuals act on the basis of their conception of what a situation is, contains, and demands; that conception is created through the application of interpretive schemes; and as a result, the interpretive scheme outlines a set of alternative courses of action an individual may follow" (Delia, O'Keefe, and O'Keefe, 1982:156).

For our formalistic view of culture the organizing question is, at the most general and abstract level, what must we know and believe to operate successfully in a society? What are the rules or recipes we must follow to function normally? Cicourel (1974) proposes a six-part answer. These abstract interpretive procedures are a "collection of instructions" describing appropriate behavior expected of members, a "sort of continual (reflexive) feedback whereby members assign meaning to their environment." Such instructions cannot be equated either with deep structure syntactic rules (in Chomsky's sense of context-free rewriting rules that allow transformations), with surface rules, or with particular substantive beliefs speakers might have or intersubjectively create:

If syntactic rules govern the lexicon and the context-free rewriting rules for defining the grammatical relations determining semantic interpretations, then the structure of social interaction (or the scenic features of social settings) would not possess independent status, but always be "known" to members of a society vis-à-vis grammatical rules. Hence social reality would be generated by universal features of language. . . . Cultural differences would presumably stem from some as yet unknown higher order grammatical rules that would permit variations in expression, but would remain consistent with universal features of a grammar's three components. (Cicourel, 1974:48)

Cicourel thus proposes to ignore Chomsky's transformational model and to assume instead that, though the interpretive procedures *constrain* action, they have no grammatical-creative link to particular substantive outcomes.

The six interpretative procedures as Cicourel presents them are as follows. First comes the *reciprocity of perspectives*, which I have already discussed. It functions as the precondition of behavior in the natural attitude. In entering an encounter, you and I both assume that, if we changed places, we would see the encounter similarly and that as a working assumption, we can disregard our idiosyncracies.

The *et cetera assumption* is Garfinkel's (1964). Our utterances are elided, enthymematic, presupposing shared background knowledge. We have to fill in the blanks of other people's statements, or at least proceed as if we can, even when their statements are ambiguous. The et cetera assumption serves the function of "allowing things to pass despite their ambiguity or vagueness, or allowing the treatment of particular instances as sufficiently relevant or understandable to permit viewing descriptive elements as 'appropriate.' What is critical about the et cetera assumption is its reliance upon particular elements of language itself (lexical terms, phrases, idiomatic expressions, or double entendres, for example), and paralinguistic features of exchanges for 'indexing' (Garfinkel, 1967) the course and meaning of the conversation" (Cicourel, 1974:53).

Normal forms refer to the appearances of normalcy, of what constitutes acceptable talk and demeanor. Communication competence consists of one's mastery of acceptable, normal procedures in a group. We know the natives by observing the ease and facility with which they unreflectively appear normal. In PCT terms, we assimilate the alien to the known to make it predictable. In dealing with aliens, with whom the reciprocity of perspectives is in doubt, we "normalize" them by interpreting their ambiguous communications charitably in *our* terms. Hence our tendency to understand foreign cultures in terms of our own and to translate the motives we impute to aliens into a language of motives common to our own milieu. This confirms Fuller's (1982) intuitions about incommensurability by spurious agreement. In doubtful cases, we assume similarity and agreement.

The retrospective-prospective sense of occurrence is our ability in conversations to wait and see. When someone's utterance seems incomprehensible, we assume that some later statement may clarify it, thus sustaining the social structure despite vagueness: "Waiting for later utterances (that may never come) to clarify present descriptive accounts, or 'discovering' that earlier remarks or incidents now clarify a present utterance, provide continuity to everyday communication" (Cicourel, 1974:54).

Talk itself as reflexive. We expect normal scenes to contain talk, to be built upon it in fact, and we fully expect that talk will reveal to us the nature of a scene as we deal with it and that it will keep us informed of how things are going. As Garfinkel says, talk is what tells us all is well and allows us to explain such normalcy to initiates.

Descriptive vocabularies as indexical expressions. Expressions do not come from thin air. They are indexical to something. Characteristically, we think that expressions refer to bodies of knowledge, practical traditions, discourse domains, or fields. We assume that a speaker takes it for granted that we can draw the links between his or her expressions and the bodies of knowledge or practices to which the expressions refer. It would not be surprising to learn that indexicality covaries with the simplicity or complexity of an arguer's MDLs. The Expressive's statements may refer to beliefs; the Conventional's statements are indexical to particular intellectual ecologies; and the Rhetorical may feel free to jump about from one domain to another depending on the needs of the moment. The Expressive will feel bound by the truth; the Conventional will feel bound by the community; and the Rhetorical will feel bound by the project at hand.

Hence our formalistic sense of culture: the recipes and rules of conversational structure and repair and interpretive procedures that explain how social order is possible and sustained over time. These principles gain importance in complex arguments (2.2 and 2.3), where deeper matters than conversational repair are at stake such as additional, different, and occasionally competing surface rules and substantive beliefs. For instance, in naturally occurring arguments (2.1), the conversational system's preference for agreement "amounts to a presumption in favor of any speech act, so that it is rejection of the speech act (not as in debate or other forums for critical inquiry [senses 2.2 and 2.3], acceptance of a proposition) which must be accounted for" (Jacobs, 1987:234; Jackson and Jacobs, 1981a). The conservative presumption contradicts the preference for agreement. So argument 2.1 differs from 2.2 and 2.3. In the former, arguers "are able to treat disagreement as a local problem, not as a general skeptical framework for organizing their alignment with one another" (Jacobs, 1987:234); in the latter cases, skepticism is part of the etiquette.

2.11. Organizing Schemes

In contrast to Cicourel's interpretive procedures, which apply universally, we might speak of more specific yet still abstract recipes and rules. Delia, O'Keefe, and O'Keefe (1982) use the construct "organizing schemes" to describe particular definitions of situation or typifications (such as normal ways to run a meeting or discussion, or recipes for behavior in public places) and habitual routines for accomplishing regular tasks.

Arguments are built upon organizing schemes. Though interpretive schemes can be idiosyncratic because they are constructed from a person's cognitive stock, "organizing schemes are necessarily social. [They] exist to classify acts in relation to other acts, to fit together the lines of action of independent persons. Organization schemes are essentially coordination devices that allow one person to produce acts with recognizable implications for another person's behavior and permit persons to respond coherently and appropriately to acts that have been produced" (Delia, O'Keefe, and O'Keefe, 1982: 157). Dissensus is the organizing scheme on which we are focused: it normalizes opposition by calling up recipes for appropriate behavior.

Emerson's (1970a, 1970b) studies of gynecological examinations are interesting cases in point. They underscore the importance of sustaining a nonthreatening definition of situation. Gynecological examinations cannot proceed solely by medical definitions; they are a "dissonance of themes and counterthemes." They display multiple contradictory realities which must be balanced if the situation is to succeed. The medical definition runs like this: "This is a medical matter, not a sexual assault; this is how we do things; nothing unusual is happening here; this is a routine technical procedure." The patient and the staff need this definition of situation—the patient to protect her dignity and the staff to keep things professional and to cajole the patient into cooperation. Weighing against this medical definition, however, is the incompatible theme that the patient is a person who cannot be treated impersonally as a mere technical object. Rituals of respect, Emerson says, are rigidly maintained to counterbalance the medical definition. Although the examination is "just an ordinary procedure," allowances are made for the patient's privacy, embarrassment, and "the presence of a nurse acting as 'chaperone' cancels any residual suggestiveness of male and female alone in the room" (1970a:81). So goes the balancing act between two incompatible definitions of situation: "Sustaining a sense of the solidness of a reality composed of multiple contradictory definitions takes unremitting effort. The required balance among the various definitions fluctuates from moment to moment." The appropriate balance depends on the immediate task. "Once one matter is dealt with, something else comes into focus, calling for a different balance" (1970a:92). Contradictions between the competing definitions must not become explicit. The actors hedge as much as they can to allow ambiguity to absorb the tensions that arise. Thus we see people engaged in an emergent adaptation to a situation's demands, balancing the need to treat the patient like a valuable human being with the need to maintain sufficient professional distance. A similar account appears in Ball's (1967) study of an abortion clinic. The professional medical definition of situation weighs against the assumptions of illegality that some patients have. Presumably, these competing definitions might weigh against some of the counterthemes suggested by Emerson.

So arguments may arise from and turn upon incompatibilities among situational definitions. Perhaps ambiguity has failed, leaving the actors unable to avoid explicit confrontations. But "we are having an argument" is a mutually arrived-at definition of a situation to be weighed against other definitions. If there are too many disputes about definitions, and if they become too explicit, they may end the argument and foreclose the possibility of future argument by muddying the relationship with uncertainty (Planalp and Honeycutt, 1985).

Arguments do not suspend etiquette. They are at least as rulebound as other forms of interaction, but they substitute one etiquette for another. In complex arguments the presence of conflict introduces expectations that differ from those of usual conversation. Challenges, demands, and attacks that would be out of bounds in ordinary discourse are proper in arguments as long as they stay within conventional bounds of civility. These boundaries are defined by reference to (say) one's view of honesty and morality, one's Christian duty, or the standards of professionalism in a discipline. Arguments cannot succeed without strong underlying cooperative bonds that keep the dissensus psychologically and sociologically manageable.

2.12. Two or More People

Arguments involve people (not impersonal symbolic or propositional serial predications) using symbols for some purpose (see Barker, 1981; Brockriede, 1975, 1977). And it takes at least two to tango. Even if by *argument* we mean utterances, illocutionary acts, or serial predications—which the interactional theory does not—we still need at least two people. "Arguing that" or "making an argument" presupposes an act with illocutionary and perlocutionary effects. Hancher (1979) has called attention to speech acts that require joint action such as making a bet or "promising that" (O'Keefe, 1982). "Arguing that" analogously presupposes the presence of a listener because it may involve stages of reasoning which a listener must accept before the arguer can move on. In this sense, "arguing that" seems to be a paradigm case of what Mead calls the "conversation of gestures." As in all interaction, meanings, agreements, and disagreements emerge from the give and take. Strategies are accommodated in a process of mutual adjustment. The statements and conversational moves we make in arguments are thus what Mead calls "significant gestures"—moves embedded in a social act whose final cause is an effect on someone else.

This focus on people revives the concern revised in Chapter 1 with competence. Constructivists reject the generativist view of competence and its idealization of a homogeneous speech community (Delia, 1983) in favor of an emphasis on multiple competencies (Filmore, Kempler, and Wang, 1979), individual differences, and viewing language as a mode of action fitted to local goals. On this account, it is plausible to say that argument competencies are of a piece with a person's abilities to adapt linguistic and social knowledge to particular situations to produce effective communication. Obviously, argument requires a cognitive skill for organizing and marshaling one's beliefs and interpretations (Applegate, 1978, 1980; Applegate and Delia, 1980; Benoit, 1981; Clark and Delia, 1976, 1977, 1979; Delia and Clark, 1977; Delia, Kline, and Burleson, 1979). Obviously, too, argument implies the existence of a grammar for translating one's intentions and strategic repertoire into effective messages in a public code (O'Keefe, 1986). Whether these skills are related to or complementary with subject matter competence has not, as far as I know, been studied.

Perspective taking is among the most important—and developmentally clear-cut—competencies. Bronson (1975) analyzes interactions between young children and concludes that 40 to 50 percent of the sequences involved overt disagreements. O'Keefe and Benoit (1982) similarly report that opposition is common among two- to five-year-old children. The chief difference between O'Keefe and Benoit's older sample and Bronson's younger one inheres in the developmentally more sophisticated perspective-taking abilities—and greater flexibility in conversational strategy (see Ervin-Tripp, 1987)—of the older children. The older children are better able to center their attention on other people as obstacles as well as instrumentalities. This more sophisticated and enlarged competence for interaction seems to be acquired as a part of language acquisition:

This hypothesis is supported by evidence of very early emergence of sophisticated argumentative skills like reason-giving. . . . Children's arguments occur within children's conversations; in producing arguments children call on their general conversational skills. Given that children begin producing arguments as they master language and discourse structures, it is reasonable to suppose that learning to argue is a component or product of learning to speak. . . . The ability to have a conversation depends on four related kinds of knowledge: knowledge of the turn system, of language (including knowledge of speech act organization), of principles involved in coherence production, and of the repair system. (O'Keefe and Benoit, 1982: 172–73)

So an "impressive battery of conversational tactics" is mastered early, permitting the inference that the development of certain forms of reasoning (e.g., moral reasoning) is an integral part of cognitive development, which in turn undergirds development in one's ability to argue (Burleson, 1981, 1982; Yingling and Trapp, 1985).

2.13. Saying and Maintaining

The term *maintains* is deliberately ambiguous between two consistent but different meanings. It might be synonymous with *says, states, avers,* or *supports.* Or it might refer to maintenance. One does maintenance on an objectified position, rationale, brief, or perspective (as one fine-tunes the National party platform or puts loopholes and waffle words in a legal brief, or excises or enhances a position statement's ambiguity). One's position is thus more than a belief. It is a constellation of claims organized into a rationale. This sense of position-as-rationale is augmented in Chapter 12 by a sense of position referring to the analysis of the coherences between one's statements and beliefs. Such analysis is analogous to maintenance. Arguers often serve maintenance functions for public positions, just as a maintenance crew keeps a building clean and structurally safe.

Maintenance would not function in naturally occurring arguments in which conversational repair is at issue. It perhaps exemplifies the tendency of more complex motives and goals to differ from the mandates of conversational structure. Maintaining a position, in the sense of keeping it healthy—resistant to outside infections—might entail maximizing its exposure to criticism, a process on a par with inoculation.

2.14. The Sociologic of Incompatibility

The next key phrase in the definition is "incompatible positions." An early version of this definition of argument used the phrase "mutually exclusive propositions" (Willard, 1978a), but the present wording is better. "Incompatible" is looser than "mutually exclusive." You and I might disagree though others think we are mistaken, or disagree not about decisive incompatibilities but about whether one view is marginally better than another, or about narrow matters inside a large frame of agreement. "Mutually exclusive" smacks too much of formal logic. "Incompatible" might include "mutually exclusive," but allows for less dramatic differences.

Incompatibility might refer to either of the two senses of "position." Usually, though, opposition manifests itself in arguments through interpretations of public rationales intermingled with attributions of intentions to people associated as authors or advocates with public positions. This deliberately ambiguous sense of "position" refers both to claims and intentions and is thus shorthand for "standpoint," "perspective," "point of view," or even "worldview." It thus includes simple expressions as well as carefully crafted positions.

I prefer "position" to "proposition" both because positions are not entirely propositional and because their pragmatic effects do not depend on features structurally belonging to a discrete act. As Goffman (1959) says, actors present themselves to one another by actions that have multiple meanings; they are able to select appropriate meanings by virtue of nonverbal cues, past actions, and prosody (Kreckel, 1981:118). Contrary to the predictions of speech act theory, the illocutionary force of a proposition may be less a structural property of the proposition, or the act that carries it, than it is a feature of an interlocutor's imputations of motives to a speaker based on evidence outside the act.

In speaking of positions as rationales as well as the creative and analytic processes by which people orient themselves to public claims, we run the risk of making disagreements seem to be straightforward matters of logical incompatibility. We might conclude that spotting disagreements is a matter of sifting through texts for incompatible claims. Disagreements *might* be so straightforward, but they might also stem from differences (e.g., in evoked sets) that are not in the talk. "Perceptions are influenced by immediate concerns ('evoked sets') as well as by more deeply rooted expectations. We perceive and interpret stimuli in terms of what is at the front of our minds—the information we've received recently" (Jervis, 1976:203). Our interpretations of claims as well as our analysis of our own statements will reflect our immediately organizing concerns. It should come as no surprise that we often err in assuming that others share our organizing concerns and thus that we need not fully explain ourselves. And "when actors send complex and subtle messages, these problems are compounded. And matters are not helped when receivers are attuned to subtleties, because in searching for subtleties the impact of the receiver's expectations is increased" (p. 205).

So the genesis of disagreement is tangentially related, if at all, to logic. Dissensus may be tacit even though it yields propositional utterances. Thus it is not uncommon to find people hotly disputing claims that seem compatible to us. We either do not see the assumptions that make them incompatible or we cannot see the evoked sets that make spurious agreements or genuine disagreements inevitable.

2.15. Cognitive Dissonance and Complexity

Arguers often appeal to consistency, but it is a mistake to equate dissensus with cognitive dissonance, imbalance, incongruity, or asymmetry. The assumption is perhaps older than Aristotle that people by nature seek balance in their cognitions. The early cognitive dissonance theorists went so far as to equate dissonance with Freudian drives. Perceptions of inconsistency thus generated something analogous to a muscle cramp, or a severe headache, or in the case of Newcomb's "strain toward symmetry," a hernia. The research guided by these theories proves only that people strive for consistency in some contexts and not others. It very much matters what they think they are doing. Delia (1976a, 1976b) thus ties subjects' definitions of situation, as emergent interpretations of encounters, to the choices people make among cognitive rules (see Cronen and Mihevc, 1972; Rubin, 1977, 1979). There can be "authority" orientations, "problem-solving" orientations, "identity" orientations, and "consistency" orientations. So consistency is a construct, not a fact of nature (Kelly, 1955)—a rigor people can choose to impose on their thinking when they believe that consistency is important, a rule they can refer to, a standard they may appeal to.

Moreover, cognitively complex people can tolerate more inferentially incompatible information than low complexity people (Crockett, 1965; Press and Rosencrantz, 1969; Nidorf and Crockett, 1965; Press, Crockett, and Delia, 1975; O'Keefe, 1980; O'Keefe and Sypher, 1981). In Kelly's terms, a person with a differentiated, complex cognitive system might choose to tolerate or bracket inferential incompatibilities because the system of constructs in which the incompatibilities lie suggests either higher syntheses or reasons for suspending judgment. More complex persons are better able to reconcile or tolerate incompatibilities. They are able to place competing ideas in a larger context, which can overarch the incompatibilities—why else the hobgoblin of *little* minds?

An argument creates an interlocked web of shared assumptions, stipulations, rules, and meanings that is analogous to the relative cognitive complexity of the arguers. Thus we plausibly expect some arguments to be more complex than others. The interesting empirical question is whether, like their cognitive counterpart, complex arguments are as tolerant of inconsistency as people are.

Summary

The claim that argument is a species of communication is now perhaps clearer. Argument is a variously complex activity because opposition can be greeted by various human intentions, ranging from repair to curiosity and playfulness to epistemic, deliberative, and scholarly motives. I have defined argument as an interaction—meaning that it benefits from conversational structure as well as relationships and coorientations. The focus on relationships and coorientations leads to an ethnomethodological stance toward the creation of intersubjective realities and, as will become explicit in the next chapter, a developing suspicion that arguments do not get their coherence solely or centrally from the illocutionary force of speech acts.

Arguers are doing something in particular: they "maintain positions" that seem (to them at least) incompatible. They are engaged in a public process in which opposition is manifest between claims and positions. They are engaged in an enthymematic process in which meanings and claims may remain implicit. Chapter 3 builds upon this idea to explain *emergence*, the idea that conversations develop and change over time. Chapter 4 expands upon this emphasis on *enthymematic* utterance by maintaining that every communicative vehicle arguers actually use is relevant to any claim about the effects of arguments.

3

Argument as Emergent Action

The argument-as-interaction view implies that arguments are scenes unfolding over time. Conversations are not fixed tableaux, arrested in time, patiently awaiting the analyst's convenience. Arguers are not mannequins, frozen in position. Nor, to shift metaphors, are they stage actors, stuck with the playwright's lines, doomed to the author's plot. All of these metaphors are at odds with our theory, which sees arguers as creative participants acting in concert, collaboratively creating, shaping, and changing events by interpreting their options and strategically adapting to the expectations and actions of others. "Actors are capable of creative originative action, and consequently, communication is not completely bound by its past, but involves an emergent process in which social, that is to say intersubjective, reality is constituted" (Delia and Grossberg, 1977:36). Arguers do not just benefit from social organization, they create, alter, and renew it.

Emergence

Arguments, then, are "emergent." We make them up as we go along. We improvise, change course, and adapt to developments. Our positions flex and strain as we modify claims, concede points, and attack the claims of others. As the issues and argumentative conditions undergo permutation, we may adjust our goals, calibrate our stances, and fine-tune our claims. If we have the requisite cognitive schemes and communication knowledge, we rise to the demands and seize the opportunities offered by the dialectical give and take. Arguments, we might say with Henry James, present "fine chances for active minds." If we are unimaginative and literal in our understandings of communication, our arguments may be tedious and circular—emergent, perhaps, only in getting louder.

Seeing argument as emergent cuts against three reified images— the *speech act*, if seen as the basic communicative process; the *situation*, if seen as a concrete, impersonal structure of exigencies, constraints, and possibilities; and the *argument utterance*, if understood (solely or paradigmatically) as a claim connected to a reason. These images—act, situation, and utterance—are indispensable to our picture of argument. But they are sources of confusion if understood in an overly determined and abstract way. Just as layers of rust blur and exaggerate the original shape of an object, a fascination with structure and determination can obscure the empirical phenomena surrounding opposition. That speech act theory is overly determined, abstract, and structured is the first claim to be considered. That explanations of situation and utterance run the risk of exaggerating impersonal logic and structure at the expense of people will occupy the remainder of the discussion. The assumption behind all three claims is that reifications of structure obscure emergence. Put differently, the facts of emergence work against a preoccupation with abstract, reified systems rather than flesh-and-blood arguments.

3.1. Speech Acts

Speech act theory (SAT) (Searle, 1969, 1975) plausibly explains aspects of emergence. A new speech act introduced into a conversation may change the conversation's course. The act's illocutionary force may influence subsequent events by leading speakers into institutions that have conventional architectures of obligations. "Proposing," for example, summons conventions associated with *presumption* (Goodnight, 1980) or *burden of proof* (Kauffeld, 1987). Conversations may change course and arguments may take new twists when an arguer is seen as "conceding that" or "challenging that."

This concession to SAT is an ethnomethodological, not a philosophical, move. If "convention" is taken in a loose nonphilosophical way to mean common knowledge of etiquette, protocols, proprieties, customs, and rules, then most acts can be seen as implying conventions. Conventions are "what everybody knows," basic and normative rules for the negotiation of status and role (Cicourel, 1974, 1970), public rituals like weddings and funerals, or arbitrary architectures such as game rules.[1] Conventions, so viewed, are taken-for-granted expectancies—part of the predictability built into social life—ranging from cultural forms (conversational structure) to local community beliefs. "Arguing that" or "making an argument" may summon one architecture of obligations among people accustomed to dialectic, such as academics, and quite another to the untutored. Even those who share the institutions of presumption or burden of proof may differ about how one meets the obligations these constructs imply.

SAT uses a technical sense of "convention" (Lewis, 1969). Austin (1971) holds that some conventional acts (such as marrying and game moves) share a family resemblance with some speech acts (such as promising). To assert that "language is conventional" is presumably to say that speech acts carry sedimented traditions, the traces of what may once have been explicit agreements but are now impersonal elements of language. This use of "convention" connotes a different issue agenda than the ethnomethodological view. Under the latter's regime, we need not see conventions, as Hume did, as agreements (e.g., Quine, 1960), or worry about defining conventions "independent of the fact or fiction of convening" (Quine, in Lewis, 1969:xii), or concern ourselves with the cogency of the conventionalist's position vis-à-vis the analytic-synthetic distinction, or debate whether conventions are agreements or empirical regularities. Under the ethnomethodological regime, they might be both. They will vary in force and explicitness and be variously open to interpretation, permutation, and adaptation. A debate about *convention versus intention* would thus be another tedious offshoot of the individualism debate.

Conceding that SAT, *mutatis mutandis,* explains aspects of emergence, I still think that "illocutionary force" is inferior to the constructs "relationship" and "coorientation." The latter terms conjoin intentional and conventional acts and lend importance to interpretive and creative processes. "Illocutionary force" exaggerates even this relaxed sense of "convention" at the expense of these processes and thus does not easily comport with our communication theory.

The reasoning that follows differs from some recent critiques of the Searle/Austin view. There has emerged a "second generation" of SAT (Kauffeld, 1987), which holds that illocutionary acts are not strictly speaking conventional but are based on practical necessity (Holdcroft, 1978; Richards, 1971; O'Neill, 1972). The impetus for this movement, however, is a desire "to reconcile our understanding of the ways ordinary language is used with the discoveries in logic that promoted the notion that an ideal language is needed for cognitively adequate representation" (Kauffeld, 1987:3). While agreeing that illocutionary acts cannot be strictly speaking conventional or entirely conventional in the ethnomethodological sense, my objection is that SAT's view of illocutionary force requires a dubious view of communication.

To start, it is not plausible to think that the speech act, as SAT defines it, is the "basic unit of communication" (Searle, 1969: 21). Our whole theoretical apparatus cuts against this belief. We have posited a distinctively social framework overarching individual intentions (Scheflen, 1973, 1974), a vision of *collaborative* reality creation, a sense of *organizational context*, which describes rules and expectancies that may shape an act's illocutionary force, and a vision of *interpretive* processes that implies that arguers' mutual responses are not limited to or determined by the acts being performed. The interactional theory puts a premium on the *goals* arguers are pursuing and on their abilities to translate motives and strategic repertoires into action. Chapter 4 presents a view of nondiscursive elements which implies that "human communication takes place in a pluralistic, only partially shared, and only fragmentarily known social world" (Rommetveit, 1980).

So it takes an implausible view of communication to see the speech act as the basic unit of communication. Rommetveit (1974, 1978) believes that SAT is a Trojan horse filled with tacitly monistic assumptions about a homogeneous speech community sharing common rules and meanings. Witness SAT's focus on *literal* expressions in unambiguous contexts: the things fiated out of the speech act—nonliteralness, ambiguity, and the like—arguably compose *"the basic existential conditions of human interaction and discourse"* (Rommetveit, 1980:113). The interactional theory sees talk as enthymematic—nonliteral, ambiguous, and elided. The intersubjective reality necessary for enthymematic speech is achieved by reciprocal role-taking, not speech acts that have their illocutionary force engraved on their backs. Searle acknowledges that a speech act is not complete without a hearer's interpretation: the hearer must agree with the illocutionary force of the act. But he holds that the listener's agreement is prefigured in the architecture of the act. Because speaker and hearer have a "shared mastery of the rules" (1975:313), both are able to see the illocutionary force of an act beneath the surface. Since the rule system is shared, one can find the whole communicative act built into the speaker's statements.

Communication is thus reduced to a speaker's intentional literal utterances plus a hearer's reactions in unambiguous contexts. The coorientation notion does not require these restrictions. Streeck (1980:145) argues that illocutionary force is not inherent to acts but to their pragmatic connections with contexts. Searle's claim that illocutionary force resides *in* the act "amounts to a reduction of what goes on *between* people to the actions which *individual participants* perform (or intend to perform). As a result his theory misses the *intersubjective* quality of communication and is unable to explain how intersubjectivity is achieved." What counts, Streeck says, is an interlocutor's response, the agreed-upon interpretations that make the response comprehensible, and provisional settlements that permit the conversation to take new paths. Every speech act "is directed to and must be ratified by an audience" (Duranti, 1986:243, 1987; Brenneis, 1987). So SAT's treatment of any unit of utterance "may be quite different from the way in which it was heard and dealt with as it was spoken" (Goodwin and Goodwin, 1987:4).

Searle's claim that a shared mastery of rules makes understanding possible is thus "incomplete and overdetermined"—incomplete in that it disregards implicit understandings, ambiguities, task-specific purposes, negotiated compromises, organizational contexts, topical effects, and definitions of situation; overdetermined in that it requires speaker and hearer to assign the same meaning to an act.

Given the enthymematic nature of speech, it is not surprising that illocutionary markers are seldom explicit. But why—apart from an arbitrarily assumed "shared mastery of rules"—is it possible for illocutionary markers to remain submerged or hidden (Kreckel, 1981)? A single speaker can only partially control an argument's emergence. The twists and turns of arguments are to some extent unforeseeable. Since arguers often insist upon their interpretive prerogatives, one might be unable to predict even his or her own strategic moves. This variability requires arguers to "constantly adapt previously reached agreements to new circumstances without making these readaptations explicit and 'sound.' Tacit reinterpretations of prior understandings in the light of upcoming contingencies must be possible" (Streeck, 1980:146).

Since illocutionary markers are not all that remains hidden, perhaps the mechanisms that permit economies in general are causally related to hidden illocutionary markers. Surely relationships, perceptions of intentions, and immediate task concerns determine how the illocutionary force of "arguing that" or "conceding that" are taken. Such attributions may be nonverbal, or partially unexpressed, or so deeply embedded in the background of a conversation that they cannot be said to be components of the deep structure of an act. "Actions that, on the surface, have narrowly utilitarian motives and consequences are read, in context, as conveying information about their authors and their author's perspectives. Verbal utterances . . . also convey, in a nonliteral mode and in light of the context of utterance, quite different information about speaker and situation" (Athay and Darley, 1981:286; Goffman, 1959, 1974; Labov and Fanshel, 1977).

I thus read Jacobs and Jackson's (in press) "rational" model of the goal structure of speech acts as a move away from seeing illocutionary force as residing in the deep structure of acts. Speech acts become ethnoconventional means for achieving goals—"elements of plans for getting things done" (p. 23). Arguments are coherent because utterances in them are contributory to goals: "Within this rational model, speech act rules are seen as definitions of belief/ want contexts—bundles of intentions, beliefs, and presumptions— associated with the use of certain means to pursue certain goals. Felicity conditions, within such a model, are not merely conventional requirements for appropriate action; they are rational preconditions for achieving some goal" (p. 24). This focus on conversational goals explains enthymematic utterance without appeal to a mystical belief in shared rule mastery: "Understanding in natural discourse is understanding for practical purposes" (Streeck, 1980:146).

Since arguers *disagree*, it is hard to see how SAT can explain an interactant's decision *not* to argue, or to modify the topic, or to take position Y and not X, or cases when illocutionary force is understood but disregarded, submerged, or modified. As we shall see, one's decision to disengage from argument—to save face or salvage a relationship—may spring from attributions to others which differ from the illocutionary bonds that have been operating in the interaction. One needs enough flexibility to explain how an invitation at the outset of a conversation can transform into a command (Streeck, 1980) or how comfort-intending communications might be construed as invitations to argument.

Perhaps these objections move us so far from SAT that we should not use the term *speech act* at all. In arguing that Searle's emphasis on shared mastery of rules uses a flawed picture of communication, we have certainly opted out of the details of the theory. In seeing convention as an ethnomethodological construct, in subordinating illocutionary force to relationships and coorientations, in placing illocutionary force within the perspectives of speakers rather than in the deep structure of utterances, and in seeing conventions as *local* phenomena, we may have jettisoned the heart of the theory.

But an argument theory needs some account of acts by which speakers enter institutions. "Promising" does bear an impersonal architecture of obligations. It is implausible to speak of promising (and of calling someone to account for breaking a promise or of holding someone to a promise) without focusing on conventional obligations that transcend an individual's idiosyncracies and preferences. Moreover, factual claims imply institutionalized credibility: they cannot be made unless the speaker is seen as in some sense speaking for an expert domain (Chapter 6). One might claim, while chatting about recent headlines: "Journalists are too tough on airline pilots; it's easier than you think to land at the wrong airport." Two expert domains are called into play. Whether landing at the wrong airport is an egregious or pardonable error, and whether in any case journalists are too tough, are questions that place the speaker in a conventionally understood position of "speaking for" as well as about a field. Whether or not credibility arises as an issue, the substance of the factual claims designates some of the grounds for an ensuing argument and carries conventional implications for expert and untutored arguers alike. There is a difference between "arguing *as* a physicist" and "making a claim based on Physics." The former implies tougher (or perhaps more bureaucratic) credibility standards than the latter. Both, however, put a speaker on *particular* substantive grounds.

So even though we seem to have left SAT, we have not jettisoned the idea that substantive claims may be taken as carrying conventional obligations. Argumentation theories have to explain how claims can move arguers onto particular grounds. Since claims may be seen as acts, they may be seen as invitations to enter particular institutions.

3.2. Situations and Contexts

My concern with reified views of situation does not stem from a preoccupation with extremely impersonal or deterministic views of situations. My claims do apply to theorists such as Bitzer (1968), who imputes to the "Rhetorical Situation" structural characteristics independent of the personal perspectives of the actors in it. But such formulations have been criticized (Vatz, 1973) severely enough that it is doubtful that many Argumentation theorists still see the situation as an utterly impersonal structure. My concern is with a subtler temptation to acknowledge the importance of interpretations and strategies, yet to devalue them in one's explanation of how arguments yield critical decisions—to credit good outcomes to impersonal rules and constraints. The following reasoning thus bears a resemblance to the objections just raised against the overconventionalized view of illocutionary force. Because we want to say clear and determinant things about situations, we run the risk of exaggerating their conventional structure and force.

The risks of such exaggerations arise in discussions of contrived, normatively driven argument settings as the law, academe, and science. Some questions (e.g., "Why is science the most consistently successful epistemic enterprise?" [Toulmin, 1972; Popper, 1963, 1982]) provoke conventionalist replies in hopes of avoiding psychological or sociological explanations. Argumentation's pedagogical thrust similarly courts conventionalist, rule-based replies to questions of critical decision making and rational conduct (Barker, 1981; Barth and Krabbe, 1982; Copi, 1978; Freeley, 1981; Kahane, 1971; Rieke and Sillars, 1984). This puts a premium on conventions and the critical effects of rules.

At the risk of underestimating these effects, I want to emphasize the nature of situations as constructive accomplishments. This emphasis does not contradict particular normative claims: it implies only that normative preferences should not be mistaken for empirical claims. CSI sees situations as composed of actors' interpretations, definitions of situation, and strategies. Constructivism assumes a coherence between actors' actions and their strategic repertoires for achieving an intersubjective working consensus with others. But the view of messages developed in Chapter 1 says that actors need not share meanings so much as sustain sufficient agreements or illusions of shared meaning to permit coordinated action.

This picture cuts against the practice of adopting a normative model as a basis for empirical claims. Not all situations share the explicit rule structure of (say) legal proceedings. Ordinary situations do not always come with their entailments and requirements plainly stamped on their faces; nor do they usually restrict actors to only one or a few options. Organizing procedures do not follow automatically from context but must be created, culled from one's cognitive repertoire, and more or less clearly announced to others. Since these procedures may evoke disagreement, they may require negotiation and adjustment. Since the procedures are deployed in a context whose meaning is emergent, they may undergo change as actors accommodate to one another: "Interactional structure and coordination are not achieved through the simple application of rules but are created as participants implicitly negotiate an orderly scheme for their interaction and attempt to display their adherence to that orderly scheme" (Delia, O'Keefe, and O'Keefe, 1982:158). For this reason, the constraints of a situation are features of an intersubjective cognitive map as well as emergent strategies for accomplishing (and negotiating) ends, not an impersonal situation.

So the problem is not that Argumentation scholars confuse normative and empirical models, though some once did, but that their normative preferences lead them to inflate the effects of social structure. Actors' interpretive prerogatives become distortions or pathologies of norms. Translated into a pedagogical focus, this preference for convention slickens an already slippery slope.

3.3. Structure as Form and Procedure

"Structure" brings two allied metaphors into play: Aristotle's view of form and substance and the idea of rational procedure constraining or shaping the raw materials of nature. Both metaphors are easily exaggerated—not just to the point of caricature but to a point that they become empirically wrong. Historically, form and procedure are among Argumentation's most enduring themes. Many theorists speak of "structure" as predication, for example, a syllogism's arrangement of terms. Aristotle's practical, dialectical, and rhetorical syllogisms were impositions of form on beliefs. And normative rules have been seen since antiquity as constraints upon the otherwise explosive raw material of human nature. Even in speaking of conversation rather than utterance, we feel the pull of these metaphors. There must be a raw material—the conversation of savages—upon which we want to impose constraints.

The idea of civilized constraints is among the most persistent themes in Western thought. The contrasting picture is of primitive man—a narcissistic, morally blind brute possessed by powerful instincts for aggression, herd followership, and (in Aristotle's terms) a subordination of the rational to the animal. The Romantics' noble savage was a momentary aberration: the more enduring portrait is of a slothful lout, generally thoughtless, sometimes dangerous, always less than he or she might be. Hence civilization's shackles: its rules and etiquettes repress our instincts and make us toe the line. The brute is stilled, not killed; it remains an ominous possibility lurking beneath the civilized veneer. But its power wanes as civilization waxes.

There is a palpable animus for the individual in this portrait. It resembles the nineteenth-century diagnosis (by Burke and the French theocrats) that individualism could only be a social and political pathology. Human frailty explains the genesis of error; conformity to conventions explains rational action. The individual is raw material to be shaped and molded by society. Thus the shackled brute's raw power is harnessed to do socially acceptable work.

To emphasize the exaggeration in this picture is not to advocate the opposite extreme. Lukács's (or Twain's) dichotomy of an autonomous, free-willed individual at constant odds with the "deadening conformities" of society is too romantic and strays too far from the facts of socialization and cognitive development. The advantage of the CSI view is that it dissolves the contrast. If social organizations exist in and through the interactions of their members, they cannot be contrasted with those activities.

Similarly, one can so exaggerate the importance of form as to conclude that arguments, once started, have determinant outcomes. If we could know the starting points, rules, and permutations the claims are likely to take, we could predict the final result. This hope for a transformational calculus to determine the outcomes of lines of thought has been fashionable at least since Leibniz, and has lately been transformed into a software problem. Computerized decision making is thriving in many fields. Information recognition schemes channel data through optimum decision scenarios which translate their results into recommendations or technical guidance. Thus current generation airliners are capable of completing flights by themselves—their flight crews confined to a new euphemism, "flight management." Can we likewise think of "dissent management" and "emergence control?" Can organizations rely on computerized controversy? Can we specify conversational and propositional calculi with enough precision to compel optimum outcomes? Sweeping questions, these, but it may pay to resist sweeping answers.

In working with software, we are drawn by the software's logic to seek as much rigor as possible in specifying a routine's use conditions. Once one sets up a data base, creates calculation rules, and has successful results, one wants to apply the system to as many phenomena as possible. If something does not fit the program's range or focus of convenience, one is tempted to increase the specificity of the program's starting conditions, hoping to beat the problem to death. For cost-benefit scenarios the solution to problems of reduction is more reduction.

It is sometimes valuable to bludgeon problems by hitting them with ever bigger trees, but looseness has advantages as well. Turbo Pascal is not the only answer to ambiguity. Just as artificial intelligence programs have proved less flexible and imaginative than human inference because they lack "massively parallel processing," decision-making programs may prove less innovative and adaptable because they lack context. An analogy may prove this point. Chaos physicists speak of extreme sensitivity to starting conditions to explain the unpredictability inherent to some phenomena. Weather follows roughly analogous paths, but only incidentally the same path, because it makes all the difference in the world when and where a weather system starts. Once started, a storm follows broad patterns common to storms: it is better than a guess that it will weaken and die but anyone's guess where or how fast it might move. Part of this unpredictability exists because, though we use a language of starts and stops to describe apparently discrete events, storms have their genesis in *continuing* conditions.

The idea of continuing conditions brings us back to emergence. "Extreme sensitivity to starting conditions" means that even if we could know where a process starts, freeze it for a moment of measurement, dump our measurements in a Cray and calculate all imaginable parameters, we could not confidently predict its course. In their course of life, storms produce turbulence, changes in power, and directional zigs and zags. Yet storms may be more predictable than arguments. We do not think of storms strategically adjusting their activities in order to intensify, survive, save face, adapt to others, or achieve dominance, but we do think of arguers this way. Human affairs are at least as variable as the weather and arguments are perhaps more variable affairs than most. So we speak of strategy and tactics as emergent over the span of single or multiple encounters. Arguments thus exhibit extreme sensitivity to continuing as well as starting conditions.

3.4. Claim-Reason Complexes as Arguments

A widely used definition of *argument* is as a claim connected with an explicit or implicit reason. Let's call this the *claim-reason complex* (CRC) view. The CRC view might take any of three forms: (1) a *stipulative definition*, holding utterance to be argument only if it consists of a claim straightforwardly connected to a supporting reason; (2) a *loose definition* that attempts to accommodate to the facts of emergence; and (3) an *analytic abstraction from talk*, a CRC that the analyst can pull out of the talk. It is no mean feat for a construct to be vacuous in any of three guises, but the CRC view is a triple threat.

In the sense that no stipulative definition can be wrong, the definition of argument as a straightforward CRC always succeeds on its own turf. One unquestionably can find empirical instances of one's definition ("Reaganomics is sound economics, *since* the trickle-down theory is true, *since,* and so on"). Undoubtedly dual-clause claims connected by *since, because,* or *for* (or adjacent utterances presumably enthymematically connected) differ from other utterances. I further concede that the CRC view (if one insists upon it) can cohere with the interactional view. My point is not that CRCs cannot be seen as argument utterances or that they never occur in talk, but that they are not typical of the utterance one finds in arguments.

The minimum requirement of a paradigm case of the talk in arguments is that it be enthymematic.[2] Implicitness, economy, and ambiguity (and the ability of speakers to trade on implicitness, benefit from economy, and disambiguate utterances) are the most striking features of speech. Speakers *can* observe Grice's quantity maxim because normal talk presupposes interpretive procedures—the reciprocity of perspectives, the et cetera assumption, normal forms, the retrospective-prospective sense of occurrence, reflexivity, and indexicality (Chapter 2). So we do not expect people to speak in tightly bundled CRCs. We expect CRCs to *emerge* in the give and take and that each CRC owes its *structure* (its existence as a *complex* or unit of meaningful utterance) to the collaborative and cognitive achievements of the speakers. Consider a made-up case:

(1) *A*: Reaganomics is sound economics.
(2) *B*: What do you mean by "sound"?
(3) *A*: It explains how the world works.
(4) *B*: I'll bet most economists don't buy that.
(5) *A*: I'll bet they do.
(6) *B*: Prove it.
(7) *A*: You prove it.
(8) *B*: I think it's a way of ignoring the poor.
(9) *A*: The poor are better off now.
(10) *B*: You believe in "trickle-down"?
(11) *A*: Trickle-down is true.

And so on. This process of emergence might continue indefinitely. Line (3) is not a reason for (1). A side issue (an authority appeal) is briefly explored (lines 4 through 7) yielding no reason for (1). The challenge at (8) yields (9), which *might* be a reason for (1) but lacks a clear link to (1). This unclarity leads to a pinning move at (10), yielding (11). If this concededly oversimple example comports with our intuitions as language users about how arguments go, it is plausible to think that real conversations may embed claims and reasons even deeper in distractions, side issues, and politesse. Tightly bundled CRCs may thus be exceptions, not the rule.

There is a parallel between the CRC focus and the reasons one might have for preferring SAT. On one hand, one might favor the CRC focus because it takes the ambiguity out of identifying speech acts. If we find a tightly bundled CRC in the talk, we have found a clear-cut speech act. Conversely, it might be thought that SAT takes the ambiguity out of identifying CRCs. But neither case is convincing. To concede that the connections among conversational moves are stretched out, implicit, and negotiated is to cast doubt on whether it is useful to think of "arguing" as a speech act at all. It is plausible that conversations verge on becoming arguments when the illocutionary force of a claim is seen as "arguing that," but it is not clear that any claim carries with it a conventional deep structure invariably to summon up in the hearer the right shared rules. If it takes two or twenty moves to get a CRC into the open, then what happens until the illocutionary force kicks in? What conventional structure is ruling the conversation? Not the illocutionary force of (1), if it is ambiguous whether A is "arguing," "proposing," "claiming," or "whining." Apart from B's cognitive stance and attributions to A, claim (1) might have any number of meanings. I think that the coorientation "we are arguing" is ruling the interaction without a clear-cut CRC. Opposition is manifest: B demands clarification, then presents a counterclaim even though A's whole CRC is not out on the table. Since the opening gambit does not fit the CRC criterion, and there is no reason to think that the illocutionary force is in the deep structure of a particular claim, then the conventions of "arguing" are features of the arguers' interpretations and negotiated agreements.

So the *stipulative definition* is hopeless. It restricts "argument" to atypical utterances. It brackets the facts of interaction as if they were inessential scenery. Ultimately it has no point. To advocate speaking in tightly bundled CRCs would entail making a case against the ways conversational arguments normally move. This, as far as I know, has not been done. Indeed, no advocate of the CRC view explicitly rejects the idea of emergence, perhaps because most CRC advocates discuss interaction and utterance separately, or discuss utterance alone, leaving interaction for others to study. Whatever the reason, the CRC literature does not prohibit interactionists from speaking of emergence. Recognizing that stipulative definitions are hyperbolic and arbitrary enough to do violence to the talk one ordinarily finds in conversations, follows these CRC advocates have tended rather more toward the *loose definition*. Utterances need not be tightly bundled; they need only be perceivable as CRCs. The claim and reason (or evidence) need not appear in tandem; they can be separated by any number of conversational moves.

But advocates of the loose definition nonetheless insist that a CRC be present in a conversation. Brockriede (1977) holds that conversations cannot be *genuine* arguments unless they contain CRCs.[3] He presumably means to distinguish genuine arguments from quarrels, spats, tiffs, and rows (and thus "arguing" from wrangling, bickering, squabbling, and the like). With O'Keefe (1982:11) I wonder whether these things "are all that carefully distinguished from one another in everyday talk." Moreover, a *pedagogical rationale* has crept into an empirical argument. Perhaps one can make a case for emphasizing normative ideals and thus of speaking about "genuine versus spurious" arguments or of aesthetic or literary merit. But a pedagogical rationale should not masquerade as an empirical *definiens* if it arbitrarily narrows the *definiendum*.

As a matter of *defining argument*, the *analytic abstraction* view is empty. Perhaps one can cull CRCs from the messiest squabbles. But in sifting through a conversation to glean *units* of meaningful utterance, one may be doing something different in kind from what the arguers are doing; and one is not studying the argument as it happened. What one *is* doing may be valuable: in finding units in conversations, even if the analyst utilizes them differently than the arguers did, new argumentative possibilities may be seen. The point is to study how things might have gone, or how they might better have gone given the arguers' goals, or how public issues are translated into particular issues in arguments. My only point is that these values have nothing to do with defining CRCs.

3.5. SAT: Threat or Menace?

I argued (3.1) that illocutionary force should be seen in terms of an ethnomethodological view of convention and that Searle's version of SAT trades upon an eccentric view of communication. Problems with the CRC focus accentuate this muddle: the features of conversations that make arguments possible reside at least as much in relationships and coorientations as they do in the talk. Yet, argument theories must explain the conventional force of *acts*—how the introduction of an act creates felicity conditions for subsequent acts (Jackson and Jacobs, 1980, 1981a; Jacobs, 1986; Jacobs and Jackson, 1981). The ethnomethodological solution to this tension succeeds at the price of stretching SAT's constructs so far that they may be unrecognizable—so far that it is perhaps more trouble than it is worth even to speak of speech acts.[4] What do we stand to lose by this?

It might be thought that we lose a precise way of naming utterances, though (as we saw) SAT does not make it easier to spot CRCs. Perhaps the best way to assess this apparent loss of precision is to consider distinctions argument scholars have in fact made.

O'Keefe prefers "making an argument" to "arguing that" because "arguing that" is at least sometimes "not very different from 'claiming that' or 'suggesting that' " (1982:12). Indeed. It is hard to imagine an argument in which arguers are not "claiming that," "stating that," "suggesting that," "challenging that," or "conceding that"— and in doing all these being seen as "arguing." Consider Austin's example, "proposing that." Proposing is a routine invitation to argument because it naturally gives rise to certain argumentative conventions such as presumption and burden of proof. But so do "claiming that" and "maintaining that." At minimum, then, there are multiple names for the same act. One *might or might not* find important differences (or *any* differences) between "saying that," "claiming that," and/or "arguing that."

It might be thought that avoiding SAT deprives us of the game metaphor. SAT and conversation analysis certainly trade on a metaphor with game rules—often to advantage. This is owed to Wittgenstein, who spoke of "forms of life" and "rules of the game." But the game metaphor, taken loosely enough to be plausible, does not require SAT. I interpret Wittgenstein's reference to the rules of the game as a loose expression, on a par with saying of a biotechnologist who surmounts the political hurdles involved with grantsmanship, "she or he knows the rules of the game." Or in the words of one academic (reconstructed from memory): "No curriculum committee's gonna let that get explicit. Sociologists don't dump on psychologists for teaching sociology cause they know they're vulnerable for teaching psych [in their courses]. And everybody teaches psycholinguistics. Everybody knows course proposals are lies. They know the rules." So rules can be explicit or implicit—at the foreground of controversy or so embedded in the background as to be taken for granted.

Avoiding SAT, we lose a literal game metaphor. But surely no one believes that arguments or any conversations proceed literally like games, or even that the game metaphor should be the organizing metaphor to describe argument. The metaphor works best to describe entering *particular* institutions—as one among many moves arguers might make.

Let's take a case that seems to exemplify the conventional importance we have imputed to acts—an act that, once introduced, can change the course of subsequent events. It seems to me that "conceding that" is a paradigm case. But "conceding that" presents two difficulties for the game metaphor. First, one can "concede" piecemeal (I can concede two of your points but reject two others). Or if you defend trickle-down theory, I might concede that your theory is *half right*. But one cannot acquiesce to game rules piecemeal. I cannot halfheartedly concede that "knight takes pawn" in a certain position is an illegal move; nor can I halfheartedly make the move (however ambivalent and irresolute my feelings and beliefs about the move may be).

Second, we have decided that arguers are "maintaining positions" (Chapter 12). The emergence notion implies that positions defended by agile arguers can flex, strain, and change as an argument proceeds. This is just the opposite of how one's chess position is said to change. It is unnatural to speak of a chess player's "position" before the game starts. "Chess positions" are what we have on the board after each move—the realities one must work with. "Position" in argument, I should think, refers to a person's interpretations, which, in changing, may also change the meanings of previous moves as well as the possibilities for future moves. An arguer's position is thus as inflexible as she or he makes it. Put another way, "conceding that" is an act with conventional implications, but it very much matters what is conceded and how the concession is interpreted.

So I do not see that much is at stake in avoiding SAT. It proposes an implausible picture of communication; it does not satisfactorily explain the meanings of acts; and it exaggerates the sharedness of meaning needed for concerted action. We stand to lose only caricatures. On the theoretical grounds established here, "we are having an argument" is a definition inferred from and yielding the expectation of opposition. This coorientation may be a dimly perceived background awareness or an explicit claim; it may arise from something in the talk or from nothing in the talk. "Having an argument" does not dictate what forms opposition might take, what the arguers might say, and what twists and turns the argument may undergo. "Arguing" implies no particular rules, except that the interlocutors have not drawn knives. "Arguing as a physicist" does imply particular rules because "speaking *as*" anything involves entering a domain of discourse. Argument rules may be variable, but they are pragmatically tied to local conventions.

The Better Part of Valor:
How Arguments Flare Up and Simmer Down

Despite the differences between views of speech acts, situations, and CRCs, there are similarities in the objections appropriate to them. All three undervalue speakers' interpretive procedures and exaggerate the conventional force of impersonal entities—the act, the situation, and the CRC. The facts of relationships and coorientations are damaging exceptions to these conventions. The evidence to which I now turn further emphasizes this common weakness.[5] All three models fail to explain how and why arguments simmer down.

The speech act "promising" holds until one fulfills or breaks the promise; but "arguing that" has no shut-down principle wired into its deep structure. "Making an argument" has an end point: one gets the last premise out. But this says nothing about how conversations proceed. Presumably even the staunchest CRC advocates do not see conversations as loose contexts for isolated performance—making "arguing" analogous to a cadenza in a concerto: a sudden break in the action for solo performance. This would make "thesis-antithesis-synthesis" an isolated set piece like the *Lazzi* of the *Commedia de'l Arte*.

The reasoning behind seeing "making an argument" as a speech act does not (again apart from the "shared mastery of the rules") explain what happens next. An interlocutor's reply is irrelevant to the definition of "making an argument." If we take the formal principles of "culture" as the whole story, they would yield an implausible picture of simmering down. Arguments would be said to end because requests are granted, explanations are found satisfactory, or agreement is reached. As we will see, complex arguments (2.2 and 2.3) often simmer down without resolutions being reached: someone becomes too emotional, a relationship is endangered, or the argument starts to seem pointless.

The situational view speaks of "exigencies" but less clearly of solutions or end points. One could doubtless point to impersonal situational variables that work against sustained argument; but surely one's explanation would become increasingly psychological (and dependent on the idea of intersubjective understandings) to explain how and why arguers decided to shut argument down. The CRC view explains neither an argument's flare-up or simmering down. The concern of that model is with defining a kind of utterance as argument.

Seeing arguments as conversations does not preclude the claim that disputes might be sustained over many encounters, that they are developmental aspects of relationships as well as circumstantial features of encounters. Spouses, for instance, may sustain disputes about child rearing, sex, or finances over years, their differences flaring up and simmering down across numberless encounters. They might well call it the "same old argument," but just as their relationship undergoes developmental change, as the shared histories presupposed in their talk expand, the "old argument" becomes more enthymematic, refined, and complex.

In interviews, I have obtained descriptions of this pattern. Spouses, close friends, business associates, and siblings point to a recurring dispute, often a serious one, that is the "same old argument." This permits the inference that social relationships are built upon regulative assumptions that allow ongoing disputes to flare up occasionally and ensure that they will simmer down before permanent damage is done to the relationship. Whether these regulators are automatic, on a par with a thermostat, or emergent in particular encounters need not concern us. They are likely a little of both.

Disagreements can flare up and simmer down even in a single conversation. It appears that arguers employ a cooling-off period, intending to return to the dispute later. Hence:

P: I dunno. He seemed; I felt uncomfortable, I guess. It seemed like a good plan to talk about something else.

Q: Things were getting hot; he's gonna punch me out. I didn't think about it. . . . X came in and I just wanted to talk about that [a new subject].

Ambiguity, for instance, may be a relationship's most important protection, both as an automatic social practice and as an emergent practice in a situation.

3.6. Ties That Bind

Withdrawal from arguments has not been studied, though some research bears on it tangentially. Interactants, for example, avoid expressing very negative evaluations of others, across a continuum of social distance, and restrain themselves from communicating their private negative evaluations of others as strongly as they might believe them. Mayer (1957) asked college women to imagine that they had a very low opinion of a friend's romantic entanglement and to specify the conditions in which they would communicate this low opinion to the friend. Mayer reported a "marked tendency" in his subjects to withhold negative comment, both from close friends and from more distant acquaintances. They would give mild versions of their private views "only if asked." The conclusion was that the "self-restraint of friends" is a powerful force in social relationships.

Another relevant finding is that people have a better idea of who likes them than of who dislikes them—perhaps because people communicate liking more readily or accurately than they do dislike (Tagiuri, Blake, and Bruner, 1953). There is also evidence that people distort negative evaluations of themselves (Buss, 1961; Harvey, 1962; Harvey and Clapp, 1965; Harvey, Kelley, and Shapiro, 1957).

People are hesitant to take up interactions with people believed to be hostile or cold to them (Newcomb, 1947; Kelley, 1950).

3.7. Simmering Down

Let's say that you and I are arguing, as we often have, about a recurring dispute. We may think that it is a routine argument; nothing unusual is happening. If one of us becomes upset, the argument may become too heated, too emotionally involved. We may mutually or individually decide to end the argument to avoid undesirable consequences. "The friendship is in danger" would be a red flag of warning to shut things down. Somewhat differently, we might decide to disengage to avoid a public scene, promising ourselves to resume combat as soon as it is convenient and safe.

Observations and interviews consistently reveal arguers who end arguments because they have become repetitive or because the discussion has reached a stasis beyond which the participants cannot progress. This permits the inference that untrained arguers believe that arguments should accomplish something. The following hand-recorded exchanges are characteristic:

W: We're not getting anywhere with this. I don't see what good it is to just keep going round and round. . . .
B: You want something I can't or won't [gesture = I grant the point] give and I think you're unreasonable. . . . We've done this fifty times and it's never getting us anywhere.

Interviewed subsequently, W displays the elements of a folk theory of argument. Asked what he expected to get out of an argument, he replied, "Some decision, change; don't debaters talk about problem solution? If we argue, we ought to solve problems." Good arguments solve problems; bad ones do not.

Twenty-five undergraduates at Dartmouth College were interviewed to discover what, if any, assumptions about argument they used. The pretext was that of a study of recall ability: "I am studying people's ability to remember conversations. I am going to ask you to recall a conversation you have had with someone recently. I will ask you for as many details of the conversation as you can provide. For instance, have you had any arguments lately?" Invention is as revealing as a good memory. For the purpose of understanding how ordinary arguers construe argument, it seems plausible to think that even the most fanciful reconstructions would yield information about how the person understands argument. Whatever the merits of this assumption, no interviewee asked, "What do you mean by argument?" Instead, each one produced an example of interpersonal conflict.

Untrained arguers distinguish fights from arguments. Fights consist of expressive communication; arguers state their positions, caring little or nothing about contextual particulars, persuading the opponent, strengthening their own thinking, or learning more about the other's views. Consider this description of a lover's quarrel: "When you sometimes get mad and blow up; that's all you can do. That's fighting. When you argue, you can get mad, but you're also arguing, figuring out some problems. That's why we have arguers. There's problems; there's arguers." So the language of problem-solving has found its way to an educated but untrained person. Arguments are supposed to accomplish something. Some resolution is expected.

A PROBLEM-SOLVING ORIENTATION IS COMMON. A consistent theme in the interviews was that arguments do not just spring up; they are caused. People argue because problems divide them; and it is permissible as well as common for people to argue to find solutions to problems. Thus arguments are supposed to get somewhere, either solving or suppressing a disagreement. Arguments that are "going nowhere" are not worth continuing. Although it might be thought that this result is an artifact of a university education, a comparison of the following explanations is instructive. The first speaker is a Dartmouth undergraduate, the second a high school graduate:

A: People wanna do different things. This is why arguments happen. The thing arguments do is allow people to get together on doing things. That's what a social system is. Negotiation is a good word. Maybe compromise.

B: You wanna do one thing, me something else, but we gotta do it together, like the army or Congress. People have to live together. So I want to do something and you wanna do something. We argue.

Both speakers express apparently similar sentiments; both presuppose some ulterior purpose for arguments; both presuppose a pragmatic, utilitarian expectation that arguments will accomplish something.

ARGUMENTS GOING NOWHERE ARE UNPLEASANT EXPERIENCES. They are apparently both frustrating and "dangerous"—meaning potential causes of emotional outbursts and even violence. A typical view: "wasted effort; lots of work but nothing done." Even the interviewees who said they enjoyed arguing for its own sake added the caveat that arguments become unpleasant and sometimes threatening when they go nowhere. This squares with reports that disagreement can harm group morale when criticism is directed at persons rather than ideas or when arguments become quarrelsome (Schultz, 1983; Torrence, 1957; Ziller, 1955).

O'Keefe's description of Expressive MDLs leads us to expect to find emotional outbursts in which Expressives rehash old disputes without making any special attempts at persuading. An example (reconstructed from memory) comes from a planning committee at a metropolitan university:

RAY: [red faced; upset] Dammit! I've told you people. [Pause] I've told you hundreds of times. [Lecturing] You don't start with money and work backwards to programs. You decide what the programmatic needs are, then make a recommendation. Money should come after all that. [The others have obviously heard this before. There is a professional, not an embarrassed silence.]

BOB: Well, I don't think the program's hurting here.

Bob has neither agreed nor disagreed. But Ray's outburst has been effectively set aside as irrelevant to matters at hand (which are to start with available money and decide on programmatic options).

CONVERSATIONAL STRUCTURE IS NOT THE ONLY THING THAT PREFERS AGREEMENT. The reader who is unconvinced by my objections to SAT may feel that the simmer-down effect is being overpsychologized here. However an antipathy for disagreement is the most uniform and universal finding in the interviews: arguments should be avoided whenever possible; disagreements are impediments to getting things done; they become unpleasant; only quarrelsome people really like them; disagreement is inevitable, but best kept submerged. Argumentativeness is impolite, a personal flaw for which there are no commendatory adjectives. Argument-prone people are truculent, bellicose, belligerent, or, in the technical parlance of the silver-tongued devils in my sample, *chickenshits*, *horses' asses*, and *assholes*. This desire to minimize conflict seems to be a general rule. Exceptions are permitted only in situations that promote disagreement (e.g., debates, seminars, and decision-making processes). So the simmer-down effect is of a piece with the methods people use to control the emergence of disagreement. It is thus no accident that conversation prefers cooperation and agreement. On the evidence of the interviews, the people who follow the rules for maximizing cooperation and agreement do so because they agree with them.

This desire to keep the peace should be especially obvious on occasions most dependent on etiquette. In dealing with strangers, one has no enduring relationship to smooth over difficulties or to keep disagreement manageable. Discovering disagreements with strangers is analogous to lifting a rock, exposing myriad squirming, crawling, and loathsome creatures to light. If we *must* lift the rock we lift slowly, letting the creatures scuttle out of sight so we do not have to see them. The conversational analog to lifting rocks slowly is account sequencing (McLaughlin, Cody, and Rosenstein, 1983)— a way of managing "the discovery of difference" and of negotiating the disposition of conflicts. At the first sign of disagreement, *A* reproaches *B*, alerting *B* to the fact that *B*'s beliefs, aims, or actions do not square with *A*'s and that *A* sees this discrepency as important. *A* presumably has not reproached *B* on grounds of doctrinal purity but in order to maintain the peace. With the ball in *B*'s court, *B* can account, justify, wheedle, disengage, or back off the disputed ground. If *B* backs off, the disagreement has been isolated and quarantined. But *B* might not back off if the disputed matter seems more important than a relationship with *A*. Acquaintances, of course, have more to lose than strangers, and may keep their relationship, if they value it, out of harm's way by honoring reproaches (Adams, 1983, 1985; Newell and Adams, 1985; Newell and Stuttman, 1983; McLaughlin, Cody, and O'Hair, 1983).

I argue (5.5, Chapter 5; see Willard, 1987a) that the preference for agreement may be socially beneficial, yet pathological—especially for decision making in complex organizations. It cuts against what we might call the dialectical motive—which values the disciplined testing of ideas. The point is to lay bare the details of a position, to make sure we see the scuttling creatures. The Socratic chain of questions, leading the asserter backward toward the grounds of a claim, seeks to sharpen disagreement, to leave nothing to piety and privacy. It values everything but keeping the peace. Since antiquity, this intellectual model has been thought to have therapeutic value. Untrained arguers make mistakes; dialectic cuts through the mistakes. I am describing, of course, a fundamental pedagogical value underlying Argumentation and Informal Logic—and arguably a value virtually definitive of academics. A failure to appreciate the degree to which the dialectical motive contradicts the preference for agreement may be a serious flaw, for it yields a pedagogy based upon a mistaken audience analysis.

Summary

Arguments, like all interactions, occur over time; they start and stop, flare up and simmer down. They are sequential: ordered serially according to conventional principles (questions court answers, greetings are paired, movements are based on preceding moves, topic shifts are negotiable, and so on), yet they are also emergent. They are heavily reliant on talk. Their continuity arises from topical coherence, adaptation to situation, and procedural etiquettes for turn-taking, interruptions, etc.

Why is emergence important? First, ambiguities can be transformed, either into agreements governed (say) by topical coherence or into disagreements causing (perhaps) topical shifts. Ambiguities are the inevitable price of economies in speech; the greater the economy the more enthymematic the utterance. Searle (1974:16) says, "We pay a small price for such economies in having ambiguities, but it does not hamper *communication* much to have ambiguous sentences because when people actually talk the context usually sorts out the ambiguities." But perhaps economy is more expensive than Searle thinks. If talk keeps ambiguities submerged beneath a larger interest in cooperation, then it favors the momentum of established projects and works against the dialectical motive (Willard and Hynes, 1988). The emergence of disputes is thus a phenomenon of urgent interest. The question of how disputes are able to flourish in spite of the preference for agreement is central to understanding how (or whether or not) ordinary speakers value argument and how they might be persuaded to value it more.

Second, just as the ambiguities in enthymematic speech are sorted out through talk, we expect that the give and take of arguments will result in at least some claims changing in meaning. If the analyst catches a claim at the wrong point in an exchange, i.e., at a point before it undergoes modification, misunderstanding may result. Third, even at the end of an argument, the revisions in a claim may not be apparent on its face: the retrospective-prospective sense of occurrence facilitates a speaker's ability to take foregoing modifications for granted. The *mutatis mutandis* is taken-for-granted by the arguers but might not be apparent in the text.

Notes

1. We know *roughly* what to expect when we go to a wedding but not whether the woman will promise to obey the man, or whether the spouses will make their pledges to a priest, a justice, or each other. As an abstract, allegorical act, a marriage (Gertrude Stein might say) is a marriage is a marriage. But every wedding is more than that—perhaps embodying a whole list of conventions and idiosyncracies.
2. Even if the inquisitorial nature of arguments can force arguers to be

unusually explicit about the assumptions behind their claims (see Chapter 4), the difference between enthymematic arguers and other speakers is surely one of degree, not kind.

3. Brockriede (1977; see also Burleson, 1979a) couches his insistence that conversations contain CRCs in a different language: O'Keefe's (1978, 1982) distinction between argument₁ and argument₂. I avoid this usage because the interactional model makes it pointless to settle on any one definition of argument utterance.

4. The most prominent advocate of seeing "argument-making" as a speech act is fervently lukewarm: "Although I will use the term 'speech act' in describing argument-making, I place no great stock in that usage" (O'Keefe, 1982:13). This is an odd expression. Imagine a Jesuit saying, "Though I speak as a Catholic priest, I place no great stock in that label." Or, "I'm playing chess, but I place no great stock in the rules of chess." O'Keefe's claim is even odder: absent disclaimers to the contrary (O'Keefe quotes Searle authoritatively, then uses "speech act" without comment), the term *speech act* conjures SAT, which implies that the locutionary/illocutionary force of naming a construct a "speech act" carries with it the public conventions associated with that label. Apart from an allusion to argument as a *collaborative* enterprise, O'Keefe does not take up the question of *where* illocutionary force resides. So it is not clear whether O'Keefe prefers a view of convention and of illocutionary force different from Searle's. I take it, then, that even though examples of "making an argument" can be made to fit Searle's model, O'Keefe is loath to gush over its importance.

5. This section is more a reminiscence than a proper research report. It is based on eighteen years of unsystematic work with university debaters and thus cannot possibly masquerade as rigorous social science. It also represents six years of more systematically organized observations. The evidence consists of hand-recorded or taped arguments—by students, colleagues, and strangers in airports, hotel lobbies, and taverns. These are overheard arguments—the kind one happens to hear in public places, not those people have in more private places. In some cases involving students, the overheard snatches have been fascinating enough to prompt further questioning.

The weaknesses of self-reported data are notorious (see Hample, 1984; Trapp and Benoit, 1985; Trapp and Hoff, 1985). But argument researchers are not hunting subtleties. If spouses report an ongoing dispute and their veracity is confirmed by other observations, it is plausible to believe them.

4

Argument as Utterance

The twenty-year interregnum since the demise of formalism has been marked by debates about the comparative superiority of different definitions of argument (Balthrop, 1980, 1982; Brockriede, 1975, 1977, 1985; Burleson, 1979a, 1980, 1982; Kneupper, 1978, 1979, 1980; McKerrow, 1980; O'Keefe, 1977, 1982; Wenzel, 1980; Willard, 1976, 1978a, 1978b, 1981, 1982; Zarefsky, 1980). The main point of dispute has concerned the characteristics *utterance* must have to be properly called *argument*. Alternative answers to this question have equated *argument* with (1) serial predications, (2) the speech act "making an argument," (3) CRCs with overt or covert claim-reason links, and (4) cognitive processes. These disputes proved inconclusive partly because some of these senses of *argument* are incomparable. They represent different research and analytical programs focusing on different phenomena.[1]

In this context the interactional theory may seem strangely silent and equivocal—like a stranger moving cautiously through a feuding village. The theory does not prefer any one sense of utterance over the others; it does not favor any of them as a paradigm case; it can neither referee nor stand to benefit from these disputes. Such neutrality, of course, raises suspicions on all sides. Neutrality is intolerable if one equates Argumentation's disciplinary health with achieving consensus around a definition of utterance.

Grounds for a Different Question

But it's a strength, not a defect, of the interactional theory that it avoids the utterance debate. It poses a better question. Instead of asking what characteristics utterance must have to be properly called *argument*, our theory asks, "Once we have an argument, what sorts of communications do we find in it?" This question courts two different answers. First, arguers, like all communicators, use any or all of the communication vehicles available to them: serial predication, claiming, and reason-giving, as well as proxemic, paralinguistic, gestural, and facial cues. Once we have an argument, *anything* used to communicate within it is germane to an analysis of how the argument proceeds and how it affects the arguers. The second answer concerns how we should name the communications we find in arguments: if one simply must use the term *argument* to refer to communications within arguments, then *argument* may refer to *whatever* communications one finds in polemic conversations.

With this second answer, I may seem to be entering the utterance debate, not opting out of it. And botching my entrance at that, for it is eccentric inside that discourse to define *argument* as proxemic, paralinguistic, gestural, and facial cues. But inside the interactional theory, the second answer *is not a definition of argument*. It is a definition of a sphere of relevance. The analyst guided by the interactional theory wants to know what affects the progress and outcomes of arguments. My answer is a package deal: any of the symbolic activities going on in an argument may affect its progress and outcomes.

I would be content never to use *argument* to designate utterance— to use the term solely to denote polemical interaction. This is an easy convention to adopt. Instead of using *argument* to define other words (predication, CRCs, and the like), one uses the other words. It is more precise to say that "John is claiming that" or "John is giving reasons" than to say "John is arguing." The latter expression requires a further claim, "by 'arguing' I mean 'giving reasons.' " Under the regime of the interactional theory, little is at stake in disputing whether John's reason-giving is a paradigm or a fringe case of arguing or whether John can be said to be arguing when he is thinking.

This preference cuts no ice with proponents of the various views of utterance; nor can it overcome the inertia of entrenched popular usage. I am resigned to the fact that argument scholars will continue using *argument* to refer to serial predications, psychological processes, communicative acts, claiming, and reason-giving. What follows reflects this resignation plus the belief that the debate about "argument utterance" is radically devalued by the interactional theory.

4.1. A Defense of the Question

Defining argument as interaction obliges us to see arguers as communicators. Communicators, we know, employ the communication modalities at their command: verbal and nonverbal, explicit and implicit. The arguers we study are equally versatile. Though arguments introduce *unique* conventions (overt opposition being acceptable in arguments but not all other interactions), there is no reason to think that the species differs from the genus. It seems prudent to say that any communications in a polemical conversation may be relevant to its outcomes. We should expect that ordinary arguments will not resemble textbook cases of speakers trading serial predications. A case in point follows:

Example 4.1
[Recorded from memory]
Two academics are discussing a proposed newcomer to their department:
c: An FTE is an FTE.
t: [Whines; shakes head; sour facial expression] Noooooooooooo.
c: Look, we ain't gonna get more lines anytime soon; this is yer classic bird in the hand.
t: [Shakes head; whines; repeats facial expression] Noooo.
c: I can't lose sight of, a whole FTE. Man! A whole line.
t: [Whining] An FTE is not an FTE. [Shakes head; holds hands to head as if suffering from a headache]
c: We can get the guy to teach some things for us.
t: What things? What does he do for us?
c: He can teach the baby course.
t: [Whines] Ohhhh. We don't neeeeed it.
c: Look, man, law of the jungle: expand or die.
t: Expand *and* die. Bloated.

Example 4.1 seems intuitively typical of ordinary speech. The striking feature of the text is its embeddedness in a mature relationship between C and T and its dependence on a retrospective/prospective sense of occurrence and indexicality linking this conversation to many past conversations. The whine, for example, is intended by *T* (and taken by *C*) to stand for previous conversations about local bureaucratic limitations, weaknesses of the person being discussed, and their shared estimations of their organization. The whine and the sour, pinched facial expression capture a view *C* and *T* share of some common acquaintances and thus function as full-fledged objections that cause *C* to defend his claim.

The text is too sparse for logical analysis. One cannot formally assess "an FTE is an FTE" without knowing what *C* means. One can say that *C*'s reason is weak, but it is unclear from the text whether the reason is produced to support "an FTE is an FTE" or some other claim that is taken for granted. The latter was the case but is so deeply embedded in the background assumptions of the speakers as to be invisible in the text. Both *C* and *T* know that "an FTE is an FTE" is not the claim at issue. It is an opening move to "this is yer classic bird in the hand."

T gives no explicit reasons, but his whines and grimaces are pivotal to the conversation's progress. He is participating in the argument whether or not his utterances fit anybody's criteria for "making an argument." Like any language user, *T* depends upon *C*'s memory of past conversations to give sense to *T*'s utterances—an assumption typical of enthymematic speech. The substitution of paralinguistic cues for serial predication is an economy measure available to arguers with mature relationships. The relationship's history permits a shorthand that yields the benefits of dissensus without its costs in time.

Another example of deep embeddedness in a relationship involves speakers who are not—and know they are not—speaking literally. Example 4.2 was tape-recorded. The speakers are two students:

Example 4.2

P: Queers are always jumpin you in the john.

T: That's only a tiny percentage; there's more hetero rape by far.

P: That's just cause they haven't studied it enough.

T: There's lots of stuff done on gay lifestyles. Most of them couldn't care less about jumping straights in johns.

Two people are apparently discussing statistical generalizations. Nothing in the talk suggests otherwise. The exchange is unusually propositional; both speakers (perhaps because they are trained debaters) use complete, propositionally formed sentences. The instruments of propositional logic might seem appropriate to this exchange. "Queers are always jumpin you in the john" is a claim for which warrant and backing are gradually secured. But nothing of the sort is happening. *P* and *T* are speaking indirectly about *P*'s roommate who has just "come out of the closet." *P* is expressing fears and is being reassured by *T*. I asked *P* what they were talking about:

P: [Smiles] Well [long pause] we were really talking about *X*.
w: Why did you couch everything in statistical terms?
P: It seemed kinda gross to talk about a good friend that way; 'sides, I'm not sure any of that stuff applies to him.

The news of *X*'s "coming out of the closet" stimulated the exchange between *P* and *T*, who are close, long-term acquaintances. So although the text can be abstracted from context for certain analytical purposes, it cannot be abstracted from *P* and *T*'s relationship for our purposes. If we want to know why *P* is reassured or how his claims were tested against *T*'s views, we must know how *P* and *T* intend toward their utterances.

Speaking indirectly or in codes is an unremarkable, ordinary accomplishment of language users. Ambiguity and evasion are valuable tools for accomplishing complex social tasks such as being polite while insisting on one's point of view. As Goffman says, the public masks people use and the etiquettes they obey often require indirection, vagueness, ambiguity, and ritual untruths. Even the Expressive in being tactful will attempt concealment. The Conventional has an appropriate arsenal of polite maneuvers. And the Rhetorical may adopt whatever measures seem warranted by the situation.

So I prefer to regard any communications occurring in an argument as "argument utterances." Although arguers do many things intentionally, I do not want to restrict argument solely to what Mead called "significant gestures" (see, e.g., Jacobs and Jackson, 1982). Significant gestures are defining characteristics of argument: they represent a person's adjustment of his or her behavior toward others; their purpose is to have effects on others; they are, as Goffman (1959) says, given, not simply given off. But messages are also given off. How else are irony and sarcasm possible?

Silence, for example, is both given and given off. Whether silence means acquiescence, denial, defeat, or tactical adjustment, and whether it bears upon the relationship of the arguers, the substance of their argument, or both, it is a notable occurrence and a continuing problem of management. In ordinary etiquette, silence is an accepted but ambiguous option: if *A* asserts *X* and *B* remains silent, *A* might interpret *B*'s silence as acquiescence, thereby proceeding to additional claims based on *X*, or as disagreement, thereby proceeding with defenses. In either case, silence has called the shots.

Example 4.3
In a baggage claim area at Los Angeles International Airport, a man graps a brown suitcase from the conveyer belt. A woman has also started for the bag but stops as the man grabs it. The man notices her action.
MAN: Eh, I'm pretty sure this's mine. [looks it over]
The woman looks at the bag.
MAN: Better check the tag. Whoops! Maybe this is yours.

The woman, I submit, made a claim on the man's attention and belief. The evidence: (1) the man acts like someone who has been challenged: he gives a reason for his behavior addressed to the woman; as she continues to look at the bag, he feels obliged to check the tag; he believes he is being communicated to, that she is asserting ownership; he obviously does not construe her silence as acquiescence; and (2) after the man, smiling sheepishly, backs away from the bag, the woman immediately steps forward and claims the bag; the man was not wrong: she *was* claiming ownership.

Silence is also a resource, especially in alliance with deliberately vague expressions, for maintaining ambiguity and thereby avoiding overt opposition. Consider a case in which one speaker (C) does not want to give the other (R) what R wants.

Example 4.4
[Reconstructed from memory]
R: [Climbing stairs] Charlie, you know I still need that schedule for the classroom.
C: [to passerby] Hey, George, how're you doing? [C and R climb another full flight of stairs]
R: You know, 309.
C: Yeah, I'll have to write that up. Get it all . . . put together. [trails off]
R: Can you get it to me soon? I mean, it's really important so I can schedule.
C: [Silence—as the speakers climb another flight]
R: Are we together on this?
C: OK, let's look at the printer; I guess this's what everybody's getting.

Clearly C wants ambiguity. He does not want to challenge R openly, but he does not plan to give R the schedule. As the speakers finish their climb and enter an office, C changes the topic. R realizes the C's silence means *something*, so he seems concerned with disambiguating it. Again, silence has called the shots. R's opening move is bypassed, its illocutionary force lost in an intentional muddle of ambiguous expressions and silence.

Now for an extreme case—introduced not to defend silence as a paradigm case of arguing but to prove that dissensus does not depend on words.

Example 4.5
[Observed by the author]
There has been a sudden cold snap: the temperature has dropped radically in two hours. A shabby, scantily dressed man (fitting the usual sense of "bum," "street person," or "wino") approaches the entrance to a luxury hotel in Pittsburgh, Pennsylvania. The bum makes eye contact with a policeman standing beside the entrance. The bum turns his eyes toward the hotel lobby, as if requesting permission to enter. The policeman stares impassively at the bum— a hard stare, no gestures. The bum hugs his arms to his torso, as if cold. The policeman maintains the stare directly at the bum. The bum looks once more at the hotel lobby, shrugs, and moves on.

Concededly an extreme case; certainly not a paradigm case; but nonetheless it is a clear-cut case of interaction based on dissensus. We have an interaction made up of moves intuitively typical of a culture's communication system. A request is made; a reason is given. The request is denied; no reason need be given. The request violates taken-for-granted knowledge (cops do not let bums loiter in luxury hotel lobbies). The request and refusal both depend upon "what everybody knows."

Examples 4.1–4.5 buttress the case made in Chapter 3 against SAT proper and intensify the doubt that illocutionary force, even re-formed to fit the ethnomethodological view, can be made applicable to ordinary speech. All four examples embody emergent strategies. All four display nonverbal elements (and implicit background relationships) inextricably linked to verbal elements. Constructs like "relationship" and "coorientation" are better suited to explanations of such arguments. If you find the case against SAT convincing, all four examples are unremarkable, even though they display people participating in but not "making" arguments.

If you are not convinced by the case against SAT (perhaps you still want to see "arguing" as essentially or paradigmatically a matter of "making arguments"), then all four examples may seem problematic—especially if you concede that they are plausible instances of ordinary speech. Obviously there is a disagreement here, but it will pay to be clear about what the disagreement is. You may concede that silence is important to interaction but resist the claim that silence or other nonverbal cues are cases of "making an argument" (O'Keefe, 1982).[2] But no such claim is being made. The claim, rather, is about the sphere of relevance mandated by the interactional theory. The four examples show people participating in arguments, even though their messages do not meet the SAT criteria for "making an argument." If examples 4.1–4.5 seem paradoxical (by having people "arguing" who are not "making" arguments) they are so only inside the framework of SAT. Inside the interactional theory, it is fruitless to debate whether one or another form of communication fits SAT's formula for "making an argument."

If you *still* prefer to remain within SAT, it may still be possible to avoid the dispute about what counts as "making an argument." Instead of debating whether the term *argument* should be reserved solely for communications that fit the SAT criteria for "making an argument," it might be instructive to ask whether the illocutionary force definitive of "making an argument" is but one element in arguments. One might see illocutionary force by analogy (1) to an automobile's starter: essential for getting the car started but unessential to the functioning of a running engine, and (2) to a gear shift that moves an ongoing force onto a different plane, but having done its work recedes to the background. If one simply must believe in illocutionary force, one need not see it as the necessary and sufficient cause of argument.

Another point of rapprochement bears mention. If you find the examples plausible, share the reservations about SAT, and accept the ethnomethodological view of convention, you are not compelled to equate utterance with serial predication. You are freer than the speech act theorist proper to say that illocutionary force resides in the imputation of intentions to a speaker. "Making an argument" might refer to whatever symbolic exchanges get an arguer's meaning across. Recall T's whines and facial expressions in 4.1. Clearly, T is arguing, and his interlocutor takes him as arguing, long before he gets to his first proposition, "an FTE is not an FTE." Moreover, we can imagine cases of misstated intentions. If I am splitting a baked potato and say, "please pass the salt," you might correctly hand me the butter if you know I hate salt. If I am holding a coffee pot but ask you if you want candy, you might well nod, fully expecting to get coffee. The imputation of intentions in cases of this sort may be irrelevant to a statement's illocutionary force. The coorientation more than a speech act ratifies one's status as a participant in an argument. In example 4.1, the speaker opens an institutional door that gets him into an argument. Groans and shaking heads serve this function as readily as propositions.

4.2. Serial Predication

Having elsewhere discussed the defects of serial predication as a paradigm case of argument utterance (Willard, 1983), I will not belabor the obvious: just as we would not defend silence as a paradigm case of "arguing," we should not defend serial predication as a paradigm case. Neither exemplifies the range of communication modalities available to arguers. Nor is paradigm case reasoning necessarily the best way of assessing the competing senses of argument. A field's paradigm cases may be artifacts of its textbook writing practices, or, differently, products of statistical drifts in a field's state of majority opinion. Whatever the current scholarly consensus may be, serial predication is Argumentation's textbook case nonpareil. Though Argumentation's paradigm cases and textbook cases may be one and the same, this match (I think) is a symptom of developmental immaturity. Suffice it to say that a field's textbook cases are sociologically and (thus) intellectually important—both because they affect the field's socialization processes and because they shape the field's thinking in nontrivial ways. Thus what follows concerns serial predication as a textbook case.

The interactional view does not deny that for some purposes serial predication is preferable to other modes. The theory implies only that serial predication is too narrow a model for defining the utterance that counts in arguments. Seeing serial predication as the main instantiation of argument yields (for our purposes) an implausible view of how arguments work. We doubtless can find meanings in statements that would surprise the speakers (Swanson, 1977a, 1977b). But the interactional theory holds that utterances are intended-toward. Speakers intend their utterances to have specific meanings.

Let's consider a case in which serial predication is the least interesting thing happening and which seems like a confrontation between users of Rhetorical and Expressive MDLs:

Example 4.6
[A Reagan administration spokesman answering a question from the press]
We are not considering a military option [in Nicaragua.] We have never considered a military option.

What might this mean? Is it a message to Managua? "We're poised to strike; we have our options planned; beware!" Is it a message to Moscow? "We can and will execute a military option; we're preparing the public for it." Is it a message to the Contras? "We're laying the public justificational groundwork; hold on; our troops are coming." These possibilities presuppose a Rhetorical MDL creating predesigned symbolic conditions. It is not just that the speaker intends the opposite of what the words say, or even that diplomatic sophisticates did not seem to consider the possibility that the intentions matched the words, but that the intentions might bear no relation to the words. Maybe actions do speak louder than words.

Propositional logic prefers an Expressive MDL. Its questions are as follows: Is the claim true or false? Does it accurately express the administration's intentions? Diplomatic naiveté aside, the limits of the Expressive MDL are apparent if we think that the effect of this communication comes not from the words but from the act of making a public pronouncement.

The locus of meaning is not propositional logic's sole limitation. The argument critic surely wants to know how ideas progress in an argument. Exemplifying (let alone restricting) argument to serial predications would lead one to see opposition as residing in statements, not speakers. This is plausibly why argument scholars have used *issue* as a technical term closely allied with propositional expressions and (thus) why they have so widely accepted a Hegelian (thesis-antithesis-synthesis) picture of opposition. People do adopt middle positions, but not all arguments are so simple. Some disputes (e.g., long-running, recurring conflicts) cannot be pressed instanter. Other disputes do not turn on alternative positions on a single issue (environmental disputes, for example, often involve proponents of economic claims versus proponents of natural value claims—positions that cannot be synthesized because they are not logically comparable, though they are politically competitive). In still other cases, there may be no middle position (as a political matter, for example, there exists no occupiable middle position between the pro- and antiabortion positions; abortion laws are not middle positions). Still other disputes (such as environmental issues respecting which both sides must grapple with apparently endless lists of side effects) may be too big, drawn out, and messy to yield clear syntheses. Quine's (1953) doctrine that thought meets experience as a corporate whole seems inapplicable to big, spread-out conflicts in which many issues are at stake (see Chapter 9).

4.3. Must Reasons Be Overtly Stated?

Humpty Dumpty was right. Words can mean just what we want them to mean. If we are indifferent to getting agreement, we can stipulate anything. We can insist, for example, that utterance counts as argument only if it is in explicit syllogistic form—a stipulation not unlike restricting "rationality" to demonstrative certainty. But disciplines are not stipulatory free-fire zones. Restricting argument to syllogisms would be too narrow: little in daily or disciplinary life would count as argument. The stipulation would thus die of neglect.

Likewise, one can stipulate that only discursive claims linked to overtly stated reasons can count as arguments. Some theorists have inferred from this that actors must be making arguments before they can be said to be having an argument (Brockriede, 1975, 1977; Burleson, 1979a, 1979b; cf., O'Keefe, 1982). On this view, presumably not every conversation based on opposition would count as an argument—only the ones containing claims linked to overtly expressed reasons. This ignores how ordinary talk proceeds and obscures the enthymematic nature of communication. Interactants do many things in conversation: they speak, whine, listen, grimace, nod their heads, and gesture. They respond appropriately. They do not, as Aristotle said, deliver orations when a wave of the hand will do. In speaking of children's arguments, and a particular example of a sustained conflict between two children, O'Keefe and Benoit (1982:156–57) make the same point:

> The use of direct verbal appeals, physical assault and appeals to external authority within this sequence indicates that the conduct of disputes can be pursued through a variety of means, only one of which involves direct verbal appeals. And even when verbal appeals are produced, they may be interspersed with other modes of behavior.
>
> It should not be supposed that this is simply "childish" behavior to be explained away in developmental terms. In some adult communities, physical means are preferred for dispute settlement in some contexts (see, for example, Phillipsen's [1975] analysis of blue collar communication). . . . O'Keefe's [1982] analysis suggests that in ordinary usage "argument" refers to virtually any disputatious interaction. It appears that disputes can be conducted in a variety of modes, that verbal exchanges are one such mode, and that different modes of dispute may be employed concurrently or successively within the same dispute. Thus "argument" in ordinary usage is an intrinsically fuzzy concept that can be appropriately applied to a wide range of activities.

The insistence upon claims being linked to overt reasons does not square with how talk ordinarily proceeds. Some "reasons" are obvious from the context and from the relationship uniting the speakers. A case in point is a conversation involving overt opposition but implicit reasons in which the speakers capitalize upon past conversations:

Example 4.7

c: *Eat!!!*

s: [Laughs] Lunchward Ho!

t: I'm not hungry. Soup Kitchen?

c: Trough. Stick your head in; grunt like a pig. Don't have to use plates.

b: I'll go if it's not the trough.

t: Soup?

c: Soup sucks. How bout Chinese?

b: That's OK. I can get veggies there.

"Soup," "trough," and "Chinese" refer to restaurants ("trough" is short for "pig trough"). "Soup sucks" does not refer to food but to likely company if the group goes there. Such economies are typical of ordinary speech. They carry no CRCs, yet positions are taken, and opposition is manifest.

The stipulation also ignores the elided, implicit, indexical (in a word, enthymematic) character of situated utterance (Bitzer, 1959; Delia, 1970; Jackson and Jacobs, 1980; Cicourel, 1974). *Enthymeme* was Aristotle's term for rhetorical proof jointly created by speaker and listener. We do not waste time saying what is manifest, Aristotle claimed. Instead, as in Examples 4.1 and 4.6, we say just enough to get our hearers to supply premises, which they can do because they share with us a common stock of background assumptions and beliefs. Persuasion is thus a two-way street: the persuadee participates in his or her own persuasion by supplying meaning and premises to a speaker's enthymemes.

In naturally occurring argument conversationalists do just enough to get agreement. Because the aim is conversational repair, the requirements for reason-giving cannot be determined in advance (Jackson and Jacobs, 1980). The prediction is that given limitations of time and resources, speakers will "satisfice"—seeking the most efficient adequate solution rather than an optimal one. This efficiency requires that only the minimum necessary information be given explicitly (Grice, 1975):

Enthymemes can be considered a special case of Grice's quantity maxim: be as informative as necessary for the purposes of agreement, but avoid being more informative than is necessary. The rules of conversational turn-taking allow conversationalists to jointly work out the level of informativeness necessary for their practical and communicative purposes. Because recipients of turns always have the opportunity to ask for clarification, repetition, or elaboration in the next turn, an under-informative turn can always be cycled through the repair organization before getting a response. . . . No

mechanism is available for repairing over-informativeness once it has occurred. (Jackson and Jacobs, 1980:263).

It is better to say too little than too much. The former is easier to
repair than the latter. Efficiency and good taste dictate that we not
propound every premise, that we take "what everybody knows" for
granted.

This economy is nowhere better displayed than in its violation in
bad novels and screenplays. Writers with no ear for ordinary talk
cram plot information into their characters' speech, resulting in dialogue that rings false: John says to his brother, "Lydia, our Mother,
wants us to come and live in Sandhurst, our ancestral home." We
see the artifice, the busy novelist dense-packing speeches in a way
normal people do not.

Trained arguers *can* converse in complete units of reasoning. Debaters sometimes do. In some technical forums, especially in complex decision-making contexts, such explicitness has value. Grice's
quantity maxim thus is not a universal rule. But in speaking of
debate and decision making as technical accomplishments, we have
set them apart from normal speech. Discursive serial predicative
speech is exceptional, a refined accomplishment, not paradigmatic
of ordinary utterance, and not especially desirable in routine social
contexts. Ordinary speech capitalizes on the enthymematic possibilities in situations.

4.4. Covert Reasons

To take account of the enthymematic nature of speech, some argumentation theorists modify the reason-giving criterion to say that
the inferential leap need not be manifest in speech. If we can imagine
that a speaker has a reason for a claim in mind, or if we can imagine
some connection to a reason, then we have an argument. But this
is circular. Connections can be conjured even for grunts and gestures.
The sparsest utterance—"no" is perhaps argument's most definitive
utterance—does not come from a vacuum. So the stipulation that
one must be making arguments before one can be said to be in an
argument—when "making arguments" is understood as involving
implicit reasons—is more of a circle than a definition.

It is not a mistake to think that overt claims are linked to covert
attitudes and beliefs. The flaw is in the assumption that argument
utterance differs in kind from other communications. This belief
has been more a political rationale for Argumentation's focus on

"rational" appeals than a substantively justified move. The only unique thing about argument utterances may be that they occur in contexts of conflict. Witness the evidence that argument competence does not develop separately but is acquired as part of learning language: "Children's arguments occur within children's conversations; in producing arguments children call on their general conversational skills. Given that children begin producing arguments as they master language and discourse structures, it is reasonable to suppose that learning to argue is a component or product of learning to speak" (O'Keefe and Benoit, 1982:173). Our conversational skills are of a piece. One might have to learn or refine particular skills, but the defining characteristic of argument seems to be controversy per se. Obvious empirical hypotheses stemming from this conclusion include (1) the inquisitorial nature of arguments forces interlocutors to be more explicit and thus less enthymematic than other conversationalists, the difference being a matter of quantity; quality would depend on the arguers' skills and motives; (2) the controversial, confrontational nature of arguments forces arguers overtly to present reasons more often than ordinary speakers are forced to do; (3) the quantity maxim is less relevant as arguments become more complex. These hypotheses accommodate to the empirical facts yet attempt to recover the intuitions of those who see argument utterance as unique.

If a premium is put on strict demarcations between argument utterance and other communication modes, these hypotheses may seem unsatisfactory. If confirmed, they are unlikely to underwrite claims that argumentation is a unique discipline. But a preoccupation with desciplinary uniqueness may be pathological if we distort our ideas to fit academic politics. I think (Chapter 9) that Argumentation's boundaries with other research traditions in Communication (and with other disciplines such as Informal Logic) are fuzzy at best and perhaps only bureaucratic.

4.5. Indexicality

Communication is always indexical, but the degree to which arguers explicitly refer to discourse domains that stand behind their claims may vary with the explicitness with which they are challenged.

Sociolinguists use "indexicality" to label one's interpretation of communicative acts on the basis of background knowledge (Gumperz, 1972; Cicourel, 1974). They hold that messages are imperfect replicas of the backgrounds on which they are based. As one's knowledge is translated into context-specific intentions, indexicality means that messages "are always an imperfect realization of what was in the minds of the speakers and hearers. Background assumptions may be signaled as part of the message through choice of words, speech style or stress and intonation; or they may be implicit in the actors' view of the speech event" (Gumperz, 1972:23). A consistent but broader use of indexicality would have it mean that speakers have a discourse community in mind as standing behind their claims, that they intend their utterances as representatives of some particular domain. Thus, in saying that utterance is indexical, I mean that speakers intend toward their utterances by reference to background assumptions, which may be variously packaged: personal experience, public institutions (e.g., promising or jurisprudence), or epistemic domains.

Though Example 4.3 is a trivial-seeming exchange based on matters of the moment, the behavior of both parties is explicable in light of the conventions they are observing. There exists no published etiquette of baggage claim areas unless the signs are counted: "Many bags look alike. Please check the tag." The man clearly assumed the possibility that there might be more than one identical brown suitcase on his flight, that he had no right thoughtlessly to take a bag, and that it was acceptable and routine for others to challenge his doing so.

4.6. Psychological Terms

Inside the interactional theory, there is not much point in using *argument* as a label for cognitive processes when other terms— *thinking, inference, reasoning,* or *rehearsal*—better serve this purpose. What follows may not convince proponents of the psychological view (Hample, 1977a, 1978, 1979b, 1980, 1981) to refrain from using *argument* to designate cognitive processes. Nor does it imply that the cognitivist does not have a valid point to make. But it pays to be clear about what that point is.

Ever since Aristotle made the enthymeme a species of the practical syllogism, argument and inference have been closely associated if not allied constructs. Yet in this century, through the 1980s, the research traditions studying inference have been sociologically distinct, even isolated, from the traditions studying argument. Inside Argumentation, the cognitivist could hardly be said to occupy a "position": nobody in the *argument* camp either challenged or used cognitive evidence.

The reason for this separateness is one of the few points of agreement among Argumentation theorists: arguments are public; inferences are private. Argument is associated with verbs such as *speaking* or *asserting*; inference is associated with verbs such as *thinking* or *believing*. The popularity of this distinction explains the segregation of the research traditions focusing on argument and thought. Cognitivism became a *position* in the utterance disputes as an accidental by-product of another position—as a way of refuting the received view of texts. It became more a theory of interpretation than of psychology.

Consider the claim, "an argument [unit of utterance] has no existence apart from the perspectives of the speakers" (see, e.g., Hample, 1979b, 1980, 1981; Willard, 1976:313). Taken as a claim about texts, this is manifestly defective: texts obviously have existence apart from any particular reader's perspective. As a statement about someone's speech, however, the claim is more plausible. Critics often need to say what utterances mean. If utterance arises from intentional behavior, statements about someone's cognitive processes are part of the evidence concerning meaning. Not all of that evidence can be found in texts. Construing is not synonymous with verbal formulation because one's behavior "may be based upon many interlocking equivalence-difference patterns which are never communicated in symbolic speech" (Kelly, 1955:50). So it is a mistake to abstract the statements occurring in arguments too far from the phenomenal fields of the people who produce them.

My point is not to expel textual studies from Argumentation. Discourse domains exist in activities, among the most important of which are the accretion of a text milieu, reasoning from texts, and arguing from texts. Textual studies are thus integral to field studies (see Willard, 1983).

Texts can be looked at in at least two ways. A text may stand as the record of an occurrence ("this is what John and Mary said," "the text of President Reagan's speech is as follows") or as a conventional contract ("John is making economic claims and is thus obliged to play by the disciplinary rules of Economics"). The two are not utterly different. The text-as-record can be used as a wedge for getting a speaker to acknowledge a conventional contract he or she has blundered into. But the text-as-record has had unique importance, indeed a position of centrality, in argument criticism. The critic claims that in analyzing a text he or she is analyzing how well an utterance realizes someone's intentions, seeing evidence of someone's rationality, or explaining how or why someone is affected by an argument. The psychological view thus entered the utterance disputes as an objection to such practices.

It is perhaps uncontroversial that messages are not equivalent to intentions. A speaker may be incompetent or mistaken. A Rhetorical may produce a message that disguises or submerges her intentions beneath a facade designed to enhance cooperativeness. But it is wrong to say that texts are not equivalent to messages. Texts obviously are messages: they contain or embody as many messages as the hermeneutic critic can wring out of them. The better-stated claim is that texts are not equivalent to a particular speaker's message—meaning that a text of John's speech might miss nonverbal, contextual, and other nondiscursive elements of meaning. At issue is the status of a text as a purported record of an event, its fidelity in reproducing intentions, messages, and events.

Perhaps the cognitivist wants to use *argument* to describe both inner deliberation and public utterance so as to emphasize the importance of the creative process in which intentions are translated into messages. Yet just as terms like *thinking* save the cognitivist's intuitions about intentionality, there are clearer terms to describe message creation. For example, the CSI term *rehearsal* includes the "I-Me" interactions of the self in which an actor takes the perspective of another to predict the effects and implications of statements and strategies. The term thus differs from argument in the way a stage actor's view of rehearsal differs from performance. The rehearsal is a time for experiments; performance is not. An audience witnesses the performance, not the rehearsal. Rehearsals are private, or at least in the family, benefiting only from past experience; performances are public, benefiting from feedback from the audience.

Obviously, we expect rehearsal to covary systematically with the complexity of the arguers: the Expressive would work on getting his or her words right, or at hiding his or her true intentions effectively; the Conventional would check his or her manners, morals, and facts against a field's etiquette; and the Rhetorical would decide what he or she wanted to create. These varied approaches to rehearsal are objects of equal research interest. Just as a person's intentions are relevant to interpretations of his or her statements, we cannot appreciate strategic mistakes unless we see how they come to be made. The rehearsal process is thus the starting point of empirical explanations of argument. But just as the theater critic would not ignore performance in favor of rehearsals, so too the argument critic must attend opening night.

So *argument* is not the optimal term for cognitive processes. The uncontestable importance of inference does not oblige us to take a position in the utterance debate. Judged as a position in this debate, the cognitive view is unsalvageable—as oxymoronic as "creation science." The importance of the cognitive view is its evidence—bearing, for example, on how texts should be regarded. Intentions and at least some meanings are personal; motives and at least some meanings are indexical to social entities. Thus, although texts have conventional lives of their own independent from the intentions of their creators, this is irrelevant to the status of the text-as-record.

4.7. Nondiscursiveness

Most Argumentation scholars concede that nondiscursive elements may affect interactants' interpretations of utterance. They nonetheless hold that argumentative utterance must be propositional or propositionally explicable (Balthrop, 1980; Burleson, 1979a, 1980; O'Keefe, 1982; van Eemeren and Grootendorst, 1984; van Eemeren, Grootendorst, and Kruiger, 1984, 1987; Fisher, 1980; Gottleib, 1968; Wenzel, 1980). This does not mean that they expect arguments always to contain formal propositions but that the expressions of actors must be publicly understandable, or as Habermas (1984) says, capable of being criticized.

Apparently, the "nondiscursiveness thesis" (Willard, 1981) is read as insisting upon private meanings to the exclusion of public meanings—rather as though "private versus public" were a clear-cut distinction. In the context of the interactional theory, allied with the view of multiple publics, fields of discourse, and perspectives, the issue is more complex—and irrelevant. Under the regime of the interactional theory, the term *argument* refers to interaction; a multitude of other names is available to label the communications occurring within arguments. And a phenomenon's unavailability for analysis does not deprive it of importance.

Here we have a clear-cut case for avoiding the utterance dispute. The dispute turns on how narrowly one wants to construe "argument utterance," "claiming," or "argument appeals." We have already seen that the imputation of intentions is more decisive than the illocutionary force of "argument making" in getting arguments started and that some imputations of intent turn on nondiscursive elements or background assumptions not present in the talk. To test your intuitions on this, consider the following reasoning: if we restrict *argument* to the exclusively discursive, we rule out interesting genres of persuasive communication. Television commercials, for example, combine music, dance, cartoons, special effects, visual images, and words to produce—as Toulmin says—claims on our attention and belief. Persuasive appeals can be designed so that words take their meanings from music or from visual effects. Beer commercials, for example, create a general association of consumption with good living, happy times, and the like. Automobile commercials exploit clever camera work, special effects, and music to such a degree that the words are sometimes the least important elements in the message. Richard Nixon's 1968 campaign commercials used taped passages from his nomination acceptance speech superimposed on films of war scenes. The effect was that doves heard the message as dovish, hawks heard it as hawkish.

It might be objected that persuasive appeals are not equivalent to arguments. To accept my examples as cases of argument is tantamount to making argument synonymous with persuasion and (thereby) Argumentation synonymous with Communication. But why is this an important objection? What is at issue here? If the rationale for distinguishing argument from other communication phenomena resides solely in keeping Argumentation distinct as a discipline, doesn't this mean that a bureaucratic rationale is driving the ideas?

Disputes about the relevance of phenomena arise in every field. Though they are sometimes mere terminological squabbles, such disputes may reflect important field-defining questions. Questions like whether detective stories are "literature," whether psychological terms are essential to explanations of scientific reasoning, whether economic laws are central to sociological descriptions, or whether only deductive (certain) serials can count as "rational" claims are—or may be—more than terminological matters. But I cannot see that any of this applies to the issue of whether it is valuable or necessary to distinguish persuasion from argument. The points of demarcation seem arbitrary; persuasive appeals are claims on attention and belief; they are as logical or illogical as other claims. The intentions of arguers are often (if not paradigmatically) persuasive.

Summary

Professions and disciplines[3] can contain different research traditions (Laudan, 1977)—each going its own way, focused upon particular problems, employing favored methods, yielding research that does not clearly fit with the research of other traditions. A de facto incommensurability may obtain between these fields when their scholars ignore each other's work and speak only to like-minded colleagues. These sovereign domains might happily go their own ways were it not for the confrontations inherent to disciplinary life. They are brought into conflict when, for example, someone proposes a specific paradigm as a universal for the field or when one theory is purported to be better than another. The disputes about competing "senses of argument" have been of this sort.

It may now be clear why I am loath to use the term *argument* to describe utterance and want no part of doctrinal disputes about whether (say) serial predication is a better or more paradigmatic sense of *argument* than (say) waving one's arms or raising one's voice. The competing views, which emphasize different kinds or aspects of speech, have equally plausible justifications. The disputes among them seem inconsequential. And even if these disputes are urgent, they cannot be settled if the views are not comparable. None requires—logically, which is not to say politically—that we accept them only by rejecting the others. Cognitivists, for example, are not forced to equate thought and speech. Advocates of "argument-making" can accept the cognitivist's ideas yet not call them *argument*. My intention thus has not been to convince anyone to abandon or subordinate particular views but to prove that the issue of defining argument utterance and marking it off from other modes of speech is less important than is often thought and that it may be futile. The focus on conversation does not logically replace these views of utterance as criteria for defining *argument* so much as it bypasses them.

Given the pluralism we have to live with, it is not too great a stretch to regard any communications occurring in a polemical conversation as relevant to argument analysis. There is no harm in calling such communications *argument* (or the only apparently redundant *argument utterance*) if one simply must do so, as long as one does not play favorites. I believe that there is little at stake in doing so. Even if you reject my claim, *argument utterance* will still mean virtually anything until further terms are added to specify the speaker's meaning. Moreover, accepting my claim does not demand abandonment of any favored view except the overt reasons criterion.

Perhaps, when all is said and done, you are still suspicious of my claim that the competing senses of utterance are incomparable or that their differences are beyond settlement. This suspicion might incline you to reject an expansive sense of *argument utterances*, but it may not require that you do so. Despite your suspicion, you can accept the claim that the interactional model makes for an expansive sense of what counts as argument utterance. If the interactional model genuinely entails an expansive view, one can grant this entailment without surrendering the prerogative of defending one or another of the special views—the overt reason criterion, again, excepted. Nothing in the interactional theory prevents the defense of normative claims. Nothing in the preceding implies that all communication modalities are equally useful, clear, or efficient for all purposes. Given world enough and time, one *might* be able to mime

"Reaganomics is spurious because the trickle-down hypothesis is false." But words do seem more efficient.

Finally, the interactional view does not preclude or denigrate the study of appeals in sustained vehicles such as speeches, advertising, position papers, and the like. Mass communicators may sometimes be exempted from some conversational rules, but so are some conversationalists. Speeches and advertisements, like arguments, contain claims, appeals, adaptations to listeners, and conjoined discursive and nondiscursive communications. I avoid the dated argot "monological versus dialogical," mainly because that vocabulary implies an opposition between two modes of analysis and orders of phenomena. That opposition was an artifact of how proponents of dialogical views made their cases. Defining argument as polemical conversation does not prevent us from saying that speakers, advertisers, and writers also act polemically. And we are not surprised to find polemicists acting as if opposition were a continual possibility—acting just as conversationalists act when dealing with overt opposition.

Notes

1. Logicians, for example, need no sociological or psychological terms. Formalists can use a narrow sense—or no sense at all—of indexicality. But cognitivists might regard logical form as tangential to explanations of influence-taking. The logician might acknowledge this difference but resist the claim that logic should study cognitive processes. Whether a CRC is valid is a different question from whether *John's* CRC is valid—a matter of logical form in the former case and of intentionality in the latter. How John's message matches his intentions is irrelevant to the former but central to the latter. CRCs may be hermeneutically infinite, but John's CRC is not if he refuses to be bound by every meaning we might wring out of it. If we want to know why John or his interlocutor are epistemically affected by argument, we are appealing to an order of evidence alien to Logic. So a Tarskian need not be concerned with the limits of formal analyses in Argumentation just as the argument scholar need not regard the Tarskian's position as authoritative. Distinct questions and proportionately noncompetitive theories are at issue. Conflicts arise only if we claim to improve formal analysis or if the Tarskian claims to be analyzing ordinary discourse.

2. O'Keefe's (1982) view of "making an argument" does not come from SAT but from paradigm case reasoning (cf. Willard, 1983).

3. I am using *profession* as a rough label for broad associations, e.g., the American Psychological Association or American Meteorological Society. I use *discipline* to designate schools of thought, points of view, or paradigms such as Freudianism, Behaviorism, or Constructivism.

5

Argument as Epistemic

This chapter muses skeptically on the claim that argument has epistemic effects. It concludes that a modest version of this claim can survive scrutiny. That is, quite apart from the epistemic effects often claimed for utterance and serial predication, argument interaction per se has epistemic consequences. We can label this claim "A = E."

Social Comparison

The rationale behind A = E is an ancient one. Ideas that weather the dialectical storm emerge the better for it; people willing to put their ideas at risk are the beneficiaries. Both reflectively and in the natural attitude, we test our views against the criticism of others. We represent our positions publicly[1] thereby subjecting them to criticism. The reactions of others may invite revision and further testing. An opponent may isolate defects in one's reasoning, in the logic of one's position, or prompt changes merely by expressing opposition. An arguer may modify a position on the spot or undergo long-term change as the argument is recollected in tranquility. Epistemic effects are thus aspects of conversational emergence. Refinements and adaptations of one's strategies, working agreements, and definitions of situation often require changes in one's goals, beliefs, and positions.

So arguments are social comparison processes (Festinger, 1954, 1964).[2] The social comparison model proposes a functional fit between interaction and cognitive development. Interaction provides the test of experience and yields orthogenetic growth—movement from diffusion and global evaluation toward complexity, differentiation, and specified evaluations (Werner, 1948). Over time, "children develop more differentiated sets of interpersonal constructs, form constructs for representing and explaining a wider range of human conduct and psychological experience, and acquire progressively more complex schemata for organizing and integrating their attributions" (O'Keefe and Delia, 1982:44).

Perhaps the paradigm case of social comparison (if it isn't the child trying ideas out on parents) is the novice entering a rational enterprise. A = E means that argument is a veridical/judgmental method rational enterprises use to evaluate claims and test positions (Toulmin, 1972; Graham, 1981; Gibbs, 1966; Berger and Luckmann, 1967; Rescher, 1973, 1977a, 1977b). Public knowledge (Ziman, 1968) is by definition criticizable (Habermas, 1984; Bitzer, 1978; Brockriede, 1982, 1985; Dixon, 1980; Ehninger, 1970). Socialization into a discipline has (paradoxically) an indoctrinational and a dialogical quality. One memorizes the famous people, their ideas and methods; one learns the standard research routines and modes of "rational" presentation. Yet novices are expected to test their ideas publicly. Seminars, conversations, examinations, and informal arguments among students and professors are the best checks against individual errors. They are the organization's most decisive instruments for self-perpetuation. They are also the novice's means for understanding the organization's epistemic constitution. Reflective acquiescence, it seems, draws upon the same resources as the socializing forces working against it.

Notice the fusion of cognitive effects, disciplinary discourse, and mass communication in this reasoning. The unifying principle is the idea of "discipline." Individuals discipline their thinking to accommodate to the feedback they receive; disciplined discourse succeeds as arguers acquiesce to impersonal, historically countenanced rules; and the self-regulative nature of debate is therapeutic for mass discourse.

5.1. The Claim Inflates

A = E is usually a carefully staged, modestly put proposal—especially in theories of public discourse (Dewey, 1954; Forester, 1986; Lippmann, 1965; Monroe, 1967; Ziman, 1968). Lippmann and

Dewey do not brandish slogans of the "debate is the cornerstone of democracy" sort. Their thinking is more like Tocqueville's: deliberative excellence is democracy's nascent possibility, planted in shallow soil, like a frail seedling needing stakes and wrappings as protection against the elements. Idea-testing is a kind of development or intellectual isometrics which strengthens both the arguers and their ideas (Mills, 1968). Public discourse thereby becomes a Spencerian survival of the fittest. This struggle for survival is not an ecological happenstance but a social-developmental imperative— the alternative being dissolution, decadence, and decay. As Lippmann (1955, 129) says, "In the absence of debate unrestricted utterance leads to the degradation of opinion. By a kind of Gresham's Law the more rational is overcome by the less rational."

Applied to disciplinary discourse, A = E often becomes a less guarded claim, perhaps because it is more an assumption or prejudice than an organizing problematic. Disciplined discourse is seen as a dispassionate, logical marshaling of ideas or impartial criticism (Gellner, 1982; Laudan, 1977, 1984; Mills, 1968; Newton-Smith, 1982) rather as if disciplinary membership confers immunity to human frailties or at least makes one more prone to tolerance and openness to critique (Johnstone, 1959; Weimer, 1979). This reasoning is sometimes transformed into a pedagogical rationale: critical thinking and dialectical methods are somebody's disciplinary property and historical inheritance. One's subject matter thereby becomes democracy's lifeblood—not bad currency in academic politics. The extravagance of this rationale sometimes obscures the genuine merit of the A = E position, for there *are* reasons to think that disciplined discourse makes for better decision making than ordinary public argument. We perhaps need to rekindle some of the skepticism with which this book began—at least enough to see the difference between A = E and bureaucratic rationales or rhetorical flourishes.

5.2. The Honesty Reservation to A = E

The simplest case is the best starting point. The facile Norman Rockwell idealization of "rational argument" one often finds in textbooks and ceremonial oratory courts a proportionately glib and inflated skeptical reply. Both pictures are dependent on an Expressive view of communication. We must dispose of both caricatures before turning to better-put questions.

The Expressive rejoinder to A = E is that arguers do not always behave honestly. "Rationalities" are described in Chapter 7 as, inter alia, public masks Conventional or Rhetorical communicators adopt for particular purposes. Argument strategies may be part of this mask. Thus the opinion change we think we see in arguments may be spurious, as in the case of studies which report that subjects display opinion change as a strategy:

First, subjects expecting to discuss an uninvolving issue with a peer became more moderate on the issue than did subjects who did not expect to discuss it; further the moderation tendency occurred even when the other's position on the issue was unknown, and even (but to a lesser degree) when the other's position was on the same side as the subjects' but was more extreme. Second, when subjects were then told that they would not have to engage in a discussion of the issue after all, the changes they had exhibited while expecting discussion disappeared; they reverted back to their initial positions without any apparent residual effects. (Cialdini and Petty, 1981:230, referring to Cialdini et al., 1973)

The subjects only appeared to moderate their positions, apparently to "seize the middle of the opinion scale and thereby . . . [achieve] a safe, defensible position" (Cialdini and Petty, 1981:230).

This might mean that public discourse—especially mass communication—structurally prefers blandness. The optimal position is the safest, least offensive one. In this spirit, an academic's admonition about creating a curriculum proposal with a strategic eye to its defense is predictable:

Example 5.1
[Recorded from memory]
c: I want this thing [a document] to be aerodynamically perfect.
t: [Smiles] Nothing sticking out to grab hold of, eh?
c: No rough edges; no handholds. Just smooth surface.

Motives aside (perhaps the speakers want to avoid quibbling objections and getting bogged down in minutiae), what is troubling about this exchange is the cynical inference it permits: public agreements are fraudulent—premised on watered-down, strategically safe positions. Since one cannot always infer private beliefs from the positions people take, it is plausible to expect to find communities paying lip service to principles that few members privately believe. The preference for blandness makes for defensive thinking: the middle position between competing extremes is the one most likely to be right or successful—witness Cialdini and Petty's subjects. The conversational system's preference for agreement may have infected public deliberation.

If these are plausible inferences, then arguments are only apparently epistemic. But this objection does not entirely undercut the claim that A = E. First, the studies themselves emphasized low-involvement topics. Although high-involvement topics also pose a problem for the argument theorist, people who are committed to a position and have thought it through do not "snap back" to their original view after a single event. Second, at least some public moderation of private positions is an effect of someone's general social anxiety and discomfort in social situations (Turner, 1977). Third, the anticipatory shifts measured by these studies do not necessarily represent a conscious strategy of distortion. "Subjects may be unaware that they are shifting; or, as Hass, Mann, and Stevens (1977) explain, subjects may merely be emphasizing a different aspect of their attitudes within their latitudes of acceptance" (Cialdini and Petty, 1981:230). This squares with our multitiered view of accommodation (Chapter 1). One can consciously adopt masks or slip in and out of them unawares.

So Rhetorical and Conventional accommodation to public codes is not invariably dishonest. Nor does it substitute "inauthentic" for "authentic" communication. I do not see how one can suppose that public discourse is a *substitute for* or counterfeit of individual perspectives without assuming the individual to be autonomous. It is the language of the individualism debate—pitting the individual against the public—that makes us think so simply of accommodation as the surrender of individualism. Hypocrisy is perhaps a worthy problem for novelists and perhaps even for fallacy theorists, but it is an inadequate way of seeing accommodation. The radical individualist makes private belief and commitment the measure of worthy participation. Yet the fact that arguers accommodate to public codes and conveniences plausibly proves that they regard the public codes as superior to private ones for certain public purposes. To speak of physics, one needs the language of physics; to have a dinner party, one needs etiquette.

So there is less to this objection than it first seems. In its strongest form, it stems from a spurious contrast of individual and society and achieves its greatest effect by assuming an inevitable opposition between individual and public motives: to go public is to lose oneself rather as actors lose themselves in roles. Unexaggerated, however, the idea that strategic calculations can sabotage deliberation and debate by shielding ideas from scrutiny is a check on exaggerations of A = E. But while this idea inhibits exaggerated claims about argument and knowledge, it does not deprive argument pedagogy of the right to consider the tension between strategy and epistemic hopes. This outcome is enough, I think, to make A = E a nontrivial claim. But this hardly puts the issue of bad motives to rest.

5.3. Pollyanna's Revenge: The Burden of Rejoinder

One way to defend the epistemic importance of argument is to make the following claim: the burden of rejoinder—one's obligation to reply to an interlocutor—is a protection against bad motives. This claim may have merit, but there are reasons for thinking otherwise.

We know by experience that people do not always behave well in arguments. Dialectic and dialogue require tentativeness, a willingness to jeopardize construct systems, an openness we cannot supply if we think that too much is at stake. Though some people manage to distinguish between their points of view and the "facts of the world," others do not or cannot. True believers act as if the facts of the world are at stake; they equate their personal interpretations with obvious truths; if others disagree, they are being perverse; tentativeness is a moral weakness. Others see tentativeness as a strategic weakness (or a cynical ploy)—at best an expendable nicety to be jettisoned in order to win. They are after social dominance; they define the encounter so as to license the strategic moves necessary to achieve dominance.

This is not exclusively an individual frailty. Some public modes of thinking avoid the burden of rejoinder, as the Shiite, for example, eschews dialogue with "infidels," Sunni or Christian. By naming their opponents in a particular way, they deny the obligation to argue. One might also proceed from a doctrine with an exceedingly narrow latitude of acceptance and proportionately broad latitude of rejection (isn't that just what defines doctrinaire thinking?). One thereby concludes that claims falling outside the doctrine are by definition not prima facie. They merit no response. The purpose in naming one's interlocutor is to say *en passant* whether his or her claims are prima facie, through abusive ad hominems or by observing that the interlocutor stands too far outside one's field of discourse.

In the face of zealousness, tactical agility, and relativity across closed borders, it might seem credulous to think that A = E. The burden of rejoinder may seem pathetic, reminiscent of the Maginot Line, encouraging rationality only in those already committed to it.

Once again a plausible reservation has gotten out of hand. That the burden of rejoinder cannot forestall obstructionism or cure zealousness does not disprove A = E. The ardor of committed people is not as relevant to the burden of proof as it first appears. To prove that, we need to work through the reasoning behind the burden.

Aristotle claims that rhetoric serves an epistemic function when we do our best to support even a position we do not believe. In developing the strategies necessary for supporting a position, we better understand its entailments. This does not preclude our becoming more entrenched in our beliefs, but it is plausible to think that epistemic change has occurred if one comes to see one's beliefs as social messages, as claims to be interpreted and evaluated by others. To thrive (or survive) in a community, one must accommodate to discourse expectations ("what everybody knows"). It is this buttressing against the expected objections of others that I take to be the signal epistemic effect upon even powerfully committed arguers. Arguments entail the expectation of reply. The burden of rejoinder is a pivotal component of the reciprocal intentions necessary to produce social action—which means that it enjoins us to behave as fully functioning social beings even when we do not want to.

Moreover, arguments introduce constraints even when tentativeness is bracketed. Let's call this the *tu quoque* possibility. Excepting fanatics, arguers expect attack and criticism. The coorientation, "we are having an argument" (or even the illocution "arguing that") introduces this expectation. Since behavior is experimental, we expect arguers to frame their strategies with an expectation of attack and criticism in mind. Their strategic calculations will take the possible attacks from others into account. One takes care with a position not to seek the truth but to win. Thus Lippmann's (1955, 1963, 1965) "indispensable opposition": we learn more from opponents than from allies, for opponents seize upon flaws in our positions and force us to mend our ideas. And this, Lippmann holds, makes freedom a reality, for we voice our opinions in order to defend and improve them.

There remains, of course, the Shiite. The burden of rejoinder may be a Western peculiarity. But has anyone claimed otherwise? An argument theory speaks to people who are to one degree or another committed to discourse. It is extravagant to expect it to solve every problem of relativity. Nonetheless one important idea has emerged: whatever else it is, Argument is a *value* to be weighed against other values.

5.4. Arguers Should Seek Tentativeness

Cederblom (1986; see also Natanson, 1965) proposes that we should think of ourselves as belief-forming processes rather than as fixed selves. This position is an individualized version of Weimer's (1979, 1984) comprehensively critical rationalism (see also Settle, Jarvie, and Agassi, 1974). This theoretical move is important partly because it illuminates the value-ladenness of one's choice of social scientific explanations. Traditional attitude theory, e.g., would have us see ourselves as relatively fixed prepotencies or predispositions for responding to environmental stimuli. We are our histories. Presented as a portrait of the human condition (as opposed to a portrait of how some people order their cognitive affairs), attitude theory (or more generally, behaviorism) underwrites one's conservative preferences for reacting rather than acting, for keeping old beliefs by blotting out new ones. To emphasize a slavery to history is to justify closed-mindedness.

Cederblom says that, in arguments, we naturally want to already be right. If we associate our beliefs with our self-definitions, a critique of our beliefs is an assault upon us. This thinking corresponds to the notion of ego involvement emphasized by the social judgment theorists. If I believe that my beliefs are better than yours, I believe myself better than you; to admit mistakes is to admit faults. The drawback, Cederblom notes, is that this thinking "stands in the way of improving my set of beliefs." Our wanting to be right all along is psychologically preferable to humility. We see mistaken beliefs as defects in ourselves. This inclines us to reject beliefs that conflict with ours. Arguments in which both parties insist that they have been right all along become "a kind of contest." To admit that the other is right is to lose—and lose more than the argument:

There is some degree of humiliation in losing, and I will do my best to avoid defeat. Because of this, it is unlikely that I will seriously consider the reasons you give for your point of view. I won't want your reasons to be compelling because I don't want to lose. And yet it is ironic that we speak of a "loss" in this situation. What has actually taken place when an argument has been "lost"? I have been given reasons that I now see as adequate for adopting a belief which I previously lacked, of which I can now make use in my dealings with the world. And I have weeded out a belief that I now see as inadequate. Considering myself as a belief-forming process, I have functioned well and am now in an improved position. It is only if I identify myself with my past beliefs that I would have grounds for dismay. (Cederblom, 1986:5–6)

Seeing ourselves as fixed sets of beliefs thus stands in the way of self-improvement.

There is empirical support for Cederblom's claims. Jones and Gerard (1967) describe a "basic antinomy" between the need to be open-minded versus the need to act, the former inhibiting the latter while being superior in fostering one's knowledge of the physical and social worlds. Committedness equals closed-mindedness, stability, and self-protection; uncommittedness equals openness and flexibility. Hass (1975) concludes that uncommitted people are more open to examine a position for its merits whereas commitment leads one to examine a position to decide which claims to make. Hass (1981:163) holds that a person's prior commitments cause intolerance, defensiveness, and resistance to persuasion. "In a more argumentative tone, probing for logical flaws will occur, but in addition one strives to call forth arguments supporting one's own position and refuting that of the source. In other words, the purpose of mustering counter-arguments may be to resist persuasion or to examine the message content, or, more often, it may be some combination of the two."

Cederblom holds that a commitment to dialogue, a commitment in principle to submit one's beliefs to critical tests—is the optimal cognitive response to an intellectual world in which knowledge claims are continually submitted to refinement and change. "Considering all there is to be known, and the way in which theories are continually developed, refined, and replaced, it is surely unrealistic for any of us to take pride in having a set of beliefs that needs little improvement. This seems to be a reason in favor of choosing the alternative of cultivating our ability to reform and replace inadequate beliefs, and to identify ourselves in terms of this ability" (Cederblom, 1986:8).

Nonetheless, we respect the rebel. We do not necessarily denigrate the person who stands up for his or her beliefs, who pushes them as far as they can go, and who has "the courage of his or her convictions" (think of the values embedded in that phrase). Tolerance and open-mindedness can be weaknesses, especially when people behave badly. We hardly respect someone who is willing to "see Hitler's side."

Cederblom's reasoning can survive this objection. The justification for our having the courage of our convictions, I think, differs in kind from the justification of open-mindedness. We value argument for its epistemic effects; we value speech for its social effects. The value of having the courage of our convictions does not depend on our being right; it depends on a community's assessment of its effects. Comprehensively critical rationalism thus does not deprive us of having the courage of our convictions in situations in which that courage counts. In epistemic affairs, however, justified true believers are handicapped.

Cederblom raises one objection to his proposal that will strike a familiar chord to Argumentation theorists—that it is to society's benefit when fully committed interlocutors behave as advocates, making the strongest possible cases for their positions. Argument's epistemic effects, by this reasoning, do not depend on the advocates' willingness to change their minds. Conflict per se yields overarching unities, points of reconciliation, and accommodation. Thus in jurisprudence or politics we leave it to an audience, not the advocates, to determine the outcome. Among debate's most important self-regulative functions is the suspension of judgment; and it is to audiences, not debaters, that we look to achieve this suspension. On this view it is unimportant that the disputants be open-minded—only that they be given a fair hearing.

Cederblom's answer to this objection emerges from his opinion that Samuel Johnson was a great advocate in spite of, not because of, his committedness and zeal. The conflict that society needs for epistemic and deliberative health does not need so much zeal. Argument thrives on tolerance—a fragile commodity when people are standing on principles. Zealousness is perhaps argument's most debilitating pathology. The social divisions that torment societies—doctrinal differences deployed as flesh-and-blood troops in Beirut, the abortion controversy in the West—have surely been exacerbated by the committedness of advocates.

People who know the truth usually behave badly. They want to kill or suppress their opponents, launch holy wars, and enforce their doctrinal preferences. In identifying themselves with their beliefs and taking their self-value from their possession of truth, they devalue their opponents. In owning the truth, they disown ways of testing it; in feeling constrained by the facts, they feel free to bypass procedures for testing facts. Truth courts commitment (why else have the idea?). Commitment perfects itself by intensifying (who honors halfheartedness?). And the tumor metastasizes—invading one's tolerance, civility, open-mindedness, and openness to discourse. Truth, in sum, is an evil idea—at least as bad as expediency.

It is hard to live in the latter half of the twentieth century and not believe in evil, but secular intellectuals may feel sheepish using a construct long thought to have horns and a tail. They believe in deeds, not demons, even if human deeds are often repugnant enough to interest an exorcist. I think that whether or not Satan intervenes in human affairs, his efforts are redundant, for humans forge their own evils. Among them, truth gets results Hell can only envy. The world would be a cleaner, happier place if we awoke tomorrow bereft of it.

But this is an unsatisfactory reply to the objection. To rail against truth does not get around the objection that argument is defenseless against it. It is unobjectionable to ask people to be open-minded, polite, and tolerant, but perhaps argument plays a role in achieving these qualities as well as depending upon them. The claim that A = E is interesting *because* it implies that arguments have epistemic effects even on zealous, committed arguers. Truth, let's say, is the disease, argument the antidote. Just as we would not reject a medical regimen because it was an incomplete cure, if nothing else is available, we need not require that argument be completely or always effective. Perhaps only bullets cure fanaticism but less drastic afflictions may yield to milder cures.

Even if we equate our point of view with the facts of the world, however much we resist seeing ourselves as belief-forming processes, and however reluctant we are to entertain threatening notions which might jeopardize our beliefs and methods, the fact that we must defend our position makes us think about its structure and implications. If arguments have no other effect, they force us to see our beliefs as systems and to evaluate them on these terms. McGuire (1960a, 1966, 1981) has reported a "Socratic Effect" stemming from asking people questions about their beliefs. Socrates, remember, got Meno's slave to change a belief by asking him questions about other beliefs which didn't jibe with the contested belief. While we usually think of persuasion as a process in which a persuader hopes that a listener will accept new information, the Socratic Effect involves getting the listener to work with his or her own beliefs. This supports the claim that interactions that force people to examine their positions *as* positions, to see their beliefs as scenarios open to outside attack, lead them to buttress their views by seeking additional support and by a sort of cognitive housecleaning for visitors: we tidy things up for casual guests and do deep cleaning for the pickiest. We spit and polish for company by enhancing the clarity, consistency, and coherence of our ideas (Watts and Holt, 1970; Henninger and Wyer, 1976; Rosen and Wyer, 1972; Wyer, 1974a, 1974b, 1975; Wyer and Carlston, 1979).

Weighing against our conclusion is the empirical evidence that publicly defending one's position strengthens one's commitment to the position (Cialdini, 1971) and that preparing for public utterance has the same effect (Brock and Blackwood, 1962; Greenwald, 1968), sometimes increasing the extremity with which we hold our views (Jellison and Mills, 1969): "A possible explanation for anticipatory opinion shifts of this sort is that the commitment to public advocacy . . . might cause subjects to rehearse, generate, and critically evaluate the arguments they will have to use in the public presentation. . . . If a person generates and rehearses arguments favorable to his or her initial position, the individual may become even more extreme in that view" (Cialdini and Petty, 1981:218). To say the least, this is not quite what most people have in mind in asserting that A = E. This reservation is nonetheless plausible. Its effect should be to check our tendencies to exaggerate the epistemic effects of argument. But a less generous reading might be that it guts the claim.

Perhaps not. First, the studies are of monological not dialogical communications—a speaker delivering messages to an audience. Arguments, as described here, differ in kind. Second, Cialdini and Petty (1981:218) add the caveat that "if arguments opposed to the person's initial position are generated and rehearsed, movement away from the initial position would be expected." Arguments by their very nature promote just such considerations (Petty and Cialdini, 1976). Third, weigh the evidence for the Socratic Effect against the evidence for the reservation. The two do not contradict because they deal with different conditions, namely, argument's unique effects. In addition, recall the evidence (and the reservations I acknowledged) that people who anticipate participating in a debate moderate their positions, putting them in less extreme and thus more defensible terms than they otherwise would (Wells et al., 1977; Snyder and Swann, 1976; Deaux, 1968; Sears, 1967). Finally, we should not forget that "what all these studies have in common is that subjects believed from the outset that their opinions would be monitored" (Cialdini and Petty, 1981:226). This is on a par with one's knowing in advance that one is going to be in an argument.

So we have a reservation to be weighed seriously against the A = E claim, but which should not itself be exaggerated. Unexaggerated, that is, taking the reservation seriously, A = E remains a nontrivial proposition.

It is plausible to think that arguments have epistemic consequences for arguers as well as audiences. Arguments by their nature promote the examination of beliefs as positions or systems. In this respect, arguments are superior to solitary thought: their give and take yields a criticism that in turn results in a more intersubjectively grounded position. In defending a position, whatever our motives or private beliefs, we come to understand it better, not because we want to but because our interlocutors force us to.

5.5. Valuing Dissensus

Another objection to A = E arises from the evidence presented in Chapter 3. The evidence suggests that the preference for agreement is robust and ubiquitous. Ordinary folk argue only if pressed by events and only enough to *satisfice* (March and Simon, 1965; see Benoit, 1981, 1982, 1983a, 1983b, 1985; Benoit and Benoit, 1987; Trapp, 1983). A pervasive distaste for argument, the objection holds, undercuts any but the most bland versions of A = E.

The preference for agreement, remember, is thought to inhere in three phenomena: conversational structure, a psychological preference for niceness and harmony, and organizational momentum. The relationships among these factors are not altogether clear, for they are studied by different research traditions. Conversational structure is often described nonpsychologically and as if it operates in more or less the same ways across organizational contexts:

The enthymematic character of argument in conversation is a reflection of this presumptive framework within which the regulative force of the preference for agreement operates. . . . The preference for agreement . . . operates to limit the incidence and the exposition of argument to what is necessary for the practical purposes of maintaining a conversational alignment (Jackson and Jacobs, 1980). Conversational partners, then, avoid a stance of unmotivated doubt on the assumption that the other will avoid unmotivated action. So, unlike more traditional analyses of the enthymeme (Bitzer, 1959; Delia, 1970), we do not see production of conversational enthymemes as any active effort by hearers to 'supply' premises for the claims of speakers; rather, we find that conversational enthymemes are the result of a general pattern of assuming the validity of the others' acts and the relevance of their proofs. (Jacobs, 1987:234–35)

Hence Cicourel's retrospective-prospective sense of occurrence. If the enthymeme is sufficiently vague or unobjectionable, it is presumptively acceptable. *Organizational* studies see the preference for agreement as inherent to organizational life (Argyris, 1964; Beckhard, 1969; Bennis, 1966; Conrad, 1985; Guest, 1962; Janis, 1982). Systems theorists speak of organizational structure anthropomorphically, biologically, or in machine metaphors, and thus see the preference for agreement as a determinism. Communication theorists soften this determinism and speak instead of social bonds, rhetorical glue, and communication networks. *Psychologized* versions of the preference for agreement make the preference a feature of people's opinions and attitudes. In Chapter 3, the simmer-down effect was at least as psychological as it was a feature of conversational structure—more a matter of maintaining a relationship than of sustaining a conversational project.

These three sources of the preference for agreement are not contradictory. They are not (or need not be seen as) competing explanations of the same phenomenon. As we have seen, all three are described as creating a kind of presumption. They may in fact be synergistic, as it is plausible to think that organizational momentum might be abetted by conversational repair. In other words, put Jacobs's description of the enthymeme into a particular organizational context. And the motives for maintaining relationships obviously arise in organizations and affect conversations occurring within them.

If the three sources of the preference *are* synergistic—let's call them the Triple Alliance—their joint implication is not a happy one for A = E. By psychological preference, conversational requirement, and organizational mandate, dissensus is an unpleasantness to be restricted, suppressed, and ended as quickly as possible. An ungenerous variation of this objection would put it that the preference for agreement makes A = E impossible (see Janis, 1982).

The answer to this objection, as implied in Chapter 3, is the dialectical motive—a value that works against the preference for agreement. A = E depends on the dialectical motive, so it is plausible to think that A = E is (or can be) as strong as the institutions, organizations, and personal beliefs that favor argument. The hierarchy of motives (2.1–2.3, Chapter 2) is not Piagetian—the complex motives are not evolutionary derivatives of conversational repair—but it is a hierarchy nonetheless. To move from repair to more complex motives is to value argument all the more. The dialectical motive, that is, values opposition for disciplinary and epistemic purposes. Weimer's (1979, 1984) comprehensively critical rationalism is one variation on this theme (see also Settle, Jarvie, and Agassi, 1974); Cederblom's individualized position described above is another.

The empirical question of which value is stronger favors the preference for agreement. But organizations do tolerate dissent (Benson, 1973, 1977); decisions do get argued out, however badly (March and Simon, 1965; Simon, 1976); disciplines do progress. The deficiencies of the dialectical motive may reside in its breach. The issue may come down to questions of how the motive can be strengthened.

Some readers may be hesitant to concede that dissensus is intellectually healthier than agreement and cooperation. Proving that the dialectical motive should wax while the preference for agreement wanes will be an extended campaign—example by example—at least a book-length task (Willard and Hynes, 1988). The thrust of that exposition can only be peeked at here.

After extensive study (Commission on the Space Shuttle Challenger Accident, 1986), the origins of the Challenger disaster remain baffling. Despite the clear and vigorous opposition of its experts, NASA pushed inexorably ahead. Some unexplained force subdued the deliberative process, circumvented the opposition, and marched events onward—as if they were out of human control. A prime suspect was the "pressure of the schedule," but investigators found no evidence that dissent had been held hostage to the schedule. Feynman (1987) blames it on a loss of common interest between engineers and scientists on one hand and NASA management on the other. Ice (1987) notices the momentum of institutionalized projects and the degree to which momentum becomes argumentative presumption. Gouran's (1987) diagnosis is similar—a "failure of argument" caused by project momentum and organizational pressure for agreement and project completion. The common denominator is that Challenger was launched by a strong preference for agreement—the Triple Alliance in full bloom.

Momentum as presumption ought to be an intimidating image, for it implies that an organization's veridical and judgmental apparatuses, however cautious they may be in principle, may be bypassed, muzzled, or diluted by inertia. Organizational projects and goals become conversational presumptions favoring particular acts at the expense of others. Dissent is the first casualty, for it must surmount a formidable conservative presumption (Goodnight, 1982).

Studies of decision making often seem like catalogs of catastrophes. From the Charge of the Light Brigade to the Vietnam War to the Iran-Contra scandal, the history of blunders is less a story of single, definitive errors than of complex packages of mistakes. The British campaign against the Zulu and the Challenger disaster are not similar or different plotted along clear-cut dimensions; they are complex recipes sharing common ingredients but with special touches of their own. So my point is not that the Triple Alliance outweighs stupidity, arrogance, groupthink, botched procedures, conceptual blinders, prejudice, and orneriness but that it nourishes these flaws. Decision making unreflectively subordinated to organizational momentum, relationship and status maintenance, and conversational repair works against good decisions. Enthymemes on automatic pilot are deliberatively inferior to more complex interpersonal processes, for instance, supplying premises. The more that is taken for granted, the more that can go wrong. Thus it is plausible to think that a preference for agreement can be pathological.

The point of epistemic arguments is to "keep the conversation going" (Rorty, 1979). Conversational repair may be subordinated to regulative rules for disputation ("be relevant" or responsive to the opponent's claims, observe the burden of rejoinder). Formal debates suspend or subordinate conversational rules by specifying rules for turn-taking, utterance length, testing admissible evidence, and so on. They require enough civility and grace to allow disagreement to thrive. The interlocutor must supply premises, but is also expected to raise objections. The adversarial context yields not a general psychological skepticism but an institutionalized one.

The Challenger case exemplifies the complexity of public discourse—how technical reservations get buried beneath technocratic hedges, qualifiers, and the political urgency of schedules, how deliberative techniques succumb to bureaucratic inertia, and how secrecy and privacy permit the narrowing of options. The preference for agreement is of a piece with these defects—perhaps their cause.

The horror of Challenger lies in the suspicion that Challenger was launched by the decision-making techniques we use for everything else. As a cautionary tale, the episode implies that well-wrought organizations have inefficiency (perpetual dissensus) wired into their structures.

The foregoing is only a sketch, but it captures the thrust of the full-blown case study (Willard and Hynes, 1988). It can stand here as a plausible reply to the objection that the preference for agreement obviates A = E. Keeping things modest, the advocate of A = E can concede the empirical facts but interpret them as meaning that the case for the dialectical motive is an urgent one.

5.6. A = E Is Equivalent to "Rhetoric Is Epistemic"

It is now common to speak of the "rhetoric of science" (Campbell, 1986; McClosky, 1985; Nelson, 1987a; Weimer, 1979), of "rhetoric as epistemic" (Scott, 1967), and of the two phrases as equivalent (Nelson, 1987b). As McGee and Lyne (1987:398) say, "Arguments are in fact but a special case of rhetorical tactics in general." Does our thinking here jibe with this tradition? The fit seems comfortable, though it may displease those who want Argumentation strictly separated from Communication and Rhetoric.

The expression "rhetoric is epistemic" is variously interpreted. It might mean that rhetorical practices serve knowledge by representing and defending it, thus securing belief in and followers for knowledge. Let's call this the *"Rhetoric as Rhetoric View."* It designates the Platonic belief that knowledge is created and tested by nonrhetorical means but that rhetorical processes may be unpleasant necessities for social influence (Ayer, 1956).

Quite differently, in saying that rhetoric is epistemic, one might mean that rhetorical arguments yield knowledge—that arguing is a social comparison process in which ideas are evaluated and through which people are able to assess the force of the better argument (Berger and Douglas, 1981; Kelley, 1971, 1972). Let's call this the *"Social Comparison View,"* letting it stand for the belief that cognitive development proceeds as the individual tests ideas against the views of others.

Allied with the Social Comparison View, but concerned with the person-as-political actor, is a reading of "rhetoric is epistemic," which we might call the *"Argumentation View."* This is Aristotle's idea that debating both sides of a question allows truth to defeat its opposite. The teleology of truth aside, the argument-as-test idea is important in legal and political thought and is the cornerstone of argumentation theory.

Building on the Argumentation View—and the mirror opposite of Rhetoric-as-Rhetoric—the *"Sociology of Science View"* holds that rhetorical processes are foundational to knowledge claims. Style, for example, is not packaging (or mere embellishment) for otherwise created knowledge but is central to the creation of knowledge (Fuller, 1986, 1987); *ethos* (understood as credibility, authority, and even charisma) is not separate from a knowledge claim's legitimacy but is a foundational component of that legitimacy (Weimer, 1979, 1984).

In saying that rhetoric is epistemic one might also mean to make a hermeneutic claim: rhetorical statements make particular contextualized visions, which we might call implicit and explicit knowledge claims. Let's call this the *"Hermeneutic View."* It labels the view that rhetoric is a process of making known one's subjective interpretations of reality (Balthrop, 1982).

Another meaning of "rhetoric is epistemic" is that rhetorical utterances express political consciousnesses or ideologies. Rhetorical expression is thus seen as a symbolic invitation to enter a way of thinking. Let's call this the *"Ideological View,"* to denote the thinking of fantasy theme, genre, and political critics who stress the expressive, unifying functions of rhetoric.

Still another meaning of "rhetoric is epistemic" refers to acts of witnessing and celebration—the stylized rituals by which people proclaim (and thereby reinforce) their consubstantiality (Burke, 1950). Let's call this the *"Ritualistic View,"* to designate the recognition that rhetorical practices enhance people's confidence in and satisfaction with particular points of view.

Finally, in saying that rhetoric is epistemic one might mean that knowledge inheres in the sociological traditions and groupings that consensually validate claims—rhetoric being the glue that binds these aggregations together. Let's call this the *"Sociology of Knowledge View"* to label two claims: that knowledge and justification are embedded in local community practices that are themselves legitimated by local consensual frameworks; and that rhetorical processes are foundational parts of legitimation.

There are doubtless other meanings one might attach to "rhetoric is epistemic." Most theorists use more than one meaning (Berger and Calabrese, 1975; Bryant, 1973; Bitzer, 1978; Farrell, 1976; Scott, 1967, 1976) or hybrids (Fisher, 1984), although a few focus on one meaning (Johnstone, 1978). Obviously, what the epistemic functions of rhetoric are said to be depends on one's theoretical concerns and assumptions, problem focus, scholarly purposes, and subject matter emphasis.

The expression "A = E" might be taken as equivalent to *any* of these meanings of "rhetoric is epistemic." One has only to concede that arguments have epistemic *effects* to believe that argument practices can serve bodies of knowledge, however derived ("Rhetoric as Rhetoric"), check one's private interpretations against the views of others ("Social Comparison"), permit idea-testing in public discourse ("Argumentation"), create knowledge ("Sociology of Science"), express particular views ("Hermeneutic"), create and sustain public faith ("Ritualistic"), and legitimize the methods and beliefs of communities ("Sociology of Knowledge").

In the context of field theory (Willard, 1983), A = E captures all seven senses of "rhetoric is epistemic" except for the belief that rhetorical means play no role in knowledge creation. A = E means that social influence affects belief and action in cognitive development and in daily life; discourse communities are bound together rhetorically—their *social* coherence arises from the commitment of their members; this commitment combined with routine argument practices affects perceptions of each community's *intellectual* coherence; it follows *ex hypothesi* that things taken as true in different communities are so regarded because of their fit with each community's epistemic framework—its rhetorically secured body of beliefs, assumptions, and procedures.

Summary

Plato said that the spoken word is more powerful than the written—and he did not mean it as a compliment. Words rush by unexamined. One cannot backtrack or check claims against one another. Criticism thrives on leisure and tranquility. Arguments race past like clacking trains.

Argumentation theorists have usually conceded Plato's claim yet held it to be beside the point. Aristotle's famous defense of debating all sides of public questions has been thought to be the nub of the matter. To know the details of one position is to better know the ins and outs of an opposing position. Even if the written word is incomparably superior to oral argumentation, the social and organizational worlds run on interaction. Moreover, oral and written argumentation often interact in real controversies. Thus A = E is conceived here as a position within the interactional theory.

One can attribute epistemic effects to argument without appealing to the outcomes of any particular sort of utterance. Interaction per se, the sheer fact of opposition, introduces cognitive and community effects. In ceding one's private prerogatives to the public court, one becomes open to social pressures, the burden of rejoinder and *tu quoque* possibility, which make for critical weighing of one's claims.

I have taken pains to avoid exaggerating these epistemic effects by considering objections that might be raised. The thrust of this skeptical maneuver is to depreciate the objections. Perhaps the most difficult of these—and certainly the one least put to rest here—is the fact that, while argument depends upon a modicum of good will on the part of arguers, it cannot guarantee that good will. However rambunctious arguers may seem, however loud and objectionable arguments may get, argument is nonetheless a delicate and frangible commodity—one all too easily subverted. But this should make us prize argument all the more. Though it can't defeat zealousness and fanaticism, it is an alternative to them. Since perhaps nothing short of therapy or bullets can cure the worst human motives, argument can't be blamed for its weakness in the face of the fanatic.

Notes

1. To speak of representing positions publicly differs from such expressions as "making our private thoughts public." It captures multiple communication possibilities whereas "making our private thoughts public" presupposes one communication possibility—the Expressive. The social comparison model does not distinguish Expressive, Conventional, and Rhetorical MDLs—perhaps because social comparison is a developmental explanation and Festinger is thinking primarily of children.

2. Festinger's view of social comparison is a psychological—and thus strongly individualistic—theory. It portrays a person grappling with the social world, rather as if Mead's "I," feeling lonely, summons the "me" for reassurance. But this individualism is unnecessary. Inside the frame of a communication (as opposed to a psychological) theory, social comparison is not a confrontation of private worlds but an effect of a distinctively public process. Moreover, A = E is simultaneously a statement about cognitive effects and public methods. It refers to social comparison processes and to the uses to which communities put argument. It implies that argument is a method used by individuals yet countenanced and shaped by communities.

6

Argument as Personal Influence

The claims considered here are that (1) ethos is a pivotal component of the logic of assent and (2) ethos is inextricably tied to "rational" argument. By *ethos* I mean the attributions (Jones et al., 1972; Sillars, 1982) of credibility, status, expertise, and attractiveness people make to communicators. Claim (1) thus means that perceptions of communicators figure prominently in decisions to accept social influence. Claim (2) means that ethos is integral to the "force of the better argument"—an inevitable and sometimes proper part of the calculus for deciding when it is "rational" to accept a belief.

A third claim—that we should guard against overvaluing authority—arises from the defense of the two claims. Claim (2), after all, might be seen as playing into social foundationalism and thus underwriting a preference for conformity over critique. This possible interpretation does not arise from a mistaken impression: the *point* of authority is to silence opposition. Since the interactional theory leads us to value dissensus, the importance of ethos to epistemic organizations is a serious reservation.

Ethos and the Logic of Assent

Claim (1) is superficially innocuous. Nobody would deny that ethos is important in persuasion. Nor would many deny that authority plays a role in disciplined discourse. But one might insist that ethos can and should be separated for analytic purposes from the logical structure of utterances, which in turn may seem to imply that authority is extrinsic to disciplinary structure. Some such assumption must underlie views of argument that ignore ethos (Fogelin, 1978; Olshewsky, 1983; Toulmin, Rieke, and Janik, 1979; Wilson, 1980) and approaches that emphasize credibility but see it as one factor "alongside good reasons and values that contributes to a decision to grant or deny adherence" (Rieke and Sillars, 1984:131). Indeed, most argument scholars who deal with ethos treat it as an explanation of *message acceptance* or *persuasive effect*, rather as if persuasive effects were a different order of phenomena, relevant to but not part of arguments (e.g., Barker, 1981; Cook, 1969; Copi, 1978; Jensen, 1981:213–28; Kahane, 1971; Mills, 1968; Sproule, 1980). A vestigial form of the conviction-persuasion duality seems to be operating: one thinks of persuasive effects as frosting on a cake, or as architectural gewgaws embellishing but not buttressing a structure, or as different orders of process, in the sense that the surgeon does the work but the anesthetist makes the operation psychologically possible.

6.1. Authority

This separation of ethos and argument also arises in discussions of authority. Arendt (1958:86), for example, insists that "if authority is to be defined at all it must be in contradistinction to both coercive power and persuasion through arguments." Her reasoning resembles Kelman's (1961) notion of "identification." One feels the pull of authority as one achieves a satisfying self-definition in relation to another person, group, or institution or seeks "to emulate conduct embodied in an exemplary individual or text" (Connolly, 1987:129).

Claim (1) prevents such separation. It implies that the analysis of arguments must include examination of the interpersonal perceptions guiding them, that *any* perceptions (however disreputable) may come into play in arguments and affect their outcomes. It implies further that "the force of the better argument" may sometimes be inextricably tied to a speaker's credibility. If one acquiesces to the counsel of experts, one presumably does so because one lacks the needed expertise. An example may clarify this point:

Example 6.1
[Hand recorded] Two men are standing in a departure lounge at Logan International Airport. They are looking at a stormy sky.

A: Boy that's ugly. If that thing turns around and comes back, we're gonna be stuck here all day.
B: CNs don't behave that way.
A: What's a CN?
B: Cumulonimbus—thunderstorm. They don't turn around. They're pushed by weather systems. Unless there's sump'n else coming along, we'll get off ok.
A: [Grunts—acquiescing; shifts topic]

This example would be incoherent unless we see B entering an institution of discourse. A's apparent acquiescence would make no sense unless seen as an imputation of expertise to B. B is doing what every arguer who appeals to facts does: standing as a ratified or provisional spokesman for a domain of expertise and thereby entering the zone of control of that discipline. In using meteorological terms, B establishes his bona fides to A's satisfaction. The claim "CNs don't behave that way" thus functions as a scientific fact (see McCloskey, 1985:121–23).

Aristotle called ethos the most powerful means of persuasion—a claim still widely accepted and deplored after decades of research. A's acquiescence to B is thus an unremarkable occurrence explicable according to conventional wisdom about persuasion and ethos. A's acquiescence to B's authority is paradigmatic of the provisional trust situated arguers routinely accord their interlocutors (Jones and Gerard, 1967). For some reason (perhaps B's use of jargon, or past discussions of the weather, or A's ignorance of or indifference to meteorology, or a regard for B built into the relationship), A concludes either that B is speaking competently or that, regardless of A's private beliefs, he will let B's claims stand. His conclusion comports with our intuitions and evidence about how people take influence from acquaintances by imputing credibility to them (Aronson, Turner, and Carlsmith, 1963; Baron and Miller, 1969; Chaiken, 1979; Cook, 1969; Gillig and Greenwald, 1974; Greenberg and Tannenbaum, 1961; Greenberg and Miller, 1966; Hass, 1972, 1981; Norman, 1976). Had A challenged B, he might have asserted equal or superior stature for making meteorological claims or attacked A's implicit claim to authority. The truth conditions of B's claim would inhere not in a propositional calculus but in the outcome of a dispute about his authority to "speak meteorologically."

Example 6.1 comports with our intuitions about local—as opposed to mass media—influence. We need not resurrect Cooley's notion of the primary group (because it ignores multivalence [Lee, 1966]) to think that influence concerning public issues arises from multiple sources—especially one's friends and associates—and not solely or exclusively from mass communications. This familiar claim stems from Katz and Lazerfield's (1964) study. Though the idea of local influence is sometimes ignored by mass communication theorists (e.g., Nimmo and Combs, 1983), it is widely thought to bridle exaggerations of mass media effects. Lowery and DeFleur (1988:166) find it amazing that local influence was ignored by early researchers: "The problem was that the theory of mass society led inevitably to assumptions that people in modern social life were isolated and individualistic. But as research on contemporary populations and social systems progressed, it had become increasingly apparent that the theory of mass society was not a very accurate model. Over and over, the important role of close personal ties in modern life was being uncovered in major research studies on social behavior." B is serving an interpretive, fact-organizing function for A. In accepting B's influence, A is doing something paradigmatic of modern life— accepting local influence about nonlocal matters.

A less congenial inheritance from Aristotle is a value-laden dichotomy of ethos and logos. Ethos is a necessary evil in persuasion owing to the depravity of audiences; logos is the stuff of prudential conduct—the appeals appropriate to people of practical wisdom. This legacy has extended into contemporary Argumentation. Argumentation theorists routinely acknowledge the importance of ethos to persuasion but begrudge it only peripheral importance in "rational" discourse. To accept a claim not on its merits but on an arguer's authority is widely thought to be a mistake—a fallacy or at least an inferior intellectual move. One should look at the arguments, not the arguers.

But there are reasons to doubt this denigration of ethos. As we saw in Chapter 2, when conversational repair is at a premium, one believes one's interlocutor if possible. In complex encounters, arguers cannot always verify claims. What is A supposed to do at an airport? Further, it is socially appropriate—given our assumptions about the relationship between them—for A to trust B. And insofar as knowledge is community property, the social fabric is built upon a division of labor and authority structures (Haskell, 1984). Accepting authority can range from a desire for repair to an acquiescence to community authority. The ethos of the disputants is thus in principle relevant to explanations of how arguments do and should work.

We might expect that disciplinary arguers would be less dependent on authority than untrained arguers, but there is little evidence to support this belief. Both extreme cases (what *did* protect Cyril Burt from critique?) and typical ones (has Positivism persisted solely on the strength of its arguments or partly on the prestige of its advocates?) conspire against the conclusion that disciplines are immune to authority (Bernstein, 1982; Freeman, 1983; Gieryn and Figert, 1986; Kenny, 1986; Kohn, 1986; Peters and Ceci, 1982; Redner, 1987; Ravetz, 1971; Taub, 1986; Whitley, 1984). Provisional imputations of authority, status, and veracity are necessary for research traditions to maintain cohesion and to attract followers. Authority may be more likely to be questioned in disciplines, but this does not mean that an arguer's ethos is irrelevant to a community's acceptance or rejection of his ideas. Example 6.2 is a case in point.

Example 6.2
  A faculty committee is discussing curriculum.
  [A is a newcomer to the university, T is an old-timer]
  A: So we need a rhetoric section.
  T: No no no no no no no no. Can't call it "rhetoric."
  A: Huh?
  T: Can't call it "rhetoric."
  A: [Quizzical look]
  T: [Smiling] I'm talking about the political realities of this place. English owns "rhetoric." Can't use the word.
  A: Oh.

Length of tenure equals familiarity with local politics: *A* acquiesces, and does so "rationally." The force of the better argument here resides not in the structure of a claim or unit of reasoning but in the imputed stature of the speaker, *T. T* does not rely solely upon ethos. He does give reasons—which permits the inference that reason giving in addition to expertise is doubly effective (see Norman, 1976).

In Example 6.2, which I take to typify arguments of this sort, ethos is the engine of a logic of assent. The point is not merely that a person's evaluation of a message may be tied to his or her evaluations of a source (Festinger, 1964; Osgood and Tannenbaum, 1955; Jones and Brehm, 1967; Zimbardo et al., 1965) or that listeners sometimes tie assent to a source's power or attractiveness (Kelman, 1961), but also that assent to authority is the "rational" thing to do (Stich and Nisbett, 1984) .

6.2. Ethos as "Rational" Judgment

Claim (2) implies that arguers are not necessarily mistaken in confederating their feelings and beliefs about speakers with their judgments of speakers' utterances—that some interpersonal perceptions should be parts of "rational discourse."

This claim may seem objectionable. Interpersonal judgments are sometimes ignoble. People judge other people by physical appearance, class, race, religion, sex, and so on. Factor analytic ethos studies permit claims such as *"Tall Men* with *Deep Voices* and *Smooth Delivery* who are *Well Dressed* are more persuasive than. . . . "* Other studies add that *loquacious, confident,* and *poised delivery*—as well as *eye contact, composure,* and *good grooming*—influence credibility attributions (Petty and Cacioppo, 1981). Such lists of ethos variables seem to be dismal catalogs of human frailties—inventories of pathologies that epitomize the disease fields such as Argumentation and Informal Logic arose to cure.

Claim (2) seems objectionable if the interpersonal judgments that make up ethos are thought to apply in all cases. Factor analytic studies often ignore definitions of situation (Delia, 1976b)—leaving the impression that judgments of *similarity* (Byrne, 1971) or *physical appearance* (Bersheid and Walster, 1974) apply (equally) in all situations. On these appearances, claim (2) makes us uneasy because it seems to authorize manifestly inappropriate standards for describing or judging people.

But ethos variables are also tied to other perceptions—especially topics (Goethals and Nelson, 1973) and definitions of situation (Delia, 1976b; Delia, Crockett, Press, and O'Keefe, 1975; Duck, 1973; Fiske and Taylor, 1984; Goffman, 1971, 1974; Jones et al., 1972). A physicist might be beyond critique for preferring tall males with deep voices as dinner companions. But a physicist's professional stature may be integral to the judgments physicists and lay folk alike make of his or her statements.

Claim (2) does not authorize any particular interpersonal perceptions. Imputations of credibility, expertise, and the like are made relevant by people in situations and legitimized (or not) by local communities and conventions. Claim (2) does not deprive a discipline of its prerogatives for defining appropriate credibility. Nobody maintains that *tall, male* physicists with *deep voices* and *smooth delivery* should (or ordinarily do) carry the day over short females with squeaky voices and halting delivery.

Claim (2) says that some interpersonal perceptions are relevant to (and thus appropriate to the "rational" evaluation of) argumentative claims. We do not throw logical form out because people commit fallacies. Argumentation scholars and informal logicians feel justified in maintaining that there are knowable, describable differences between good and bad reasoning; this same thinking can be applied to ethos.

6.3. "Rational" Deference to Authority

What does it mean to say that it is "rational" to defer to authority? Beyond obvious cases of compartmentalized expertise (I trust my doctor, lawyer, dentist, and mechanic to do work I cannot do based on knowledge I have no time to acquire), there are purely intellectual cases in which I defer to a community's authorities:

My belief in evolution rests on no firmer basis than expert authority. Certainly I have not inspected the fossil record for myself, or worked my way through the intricate details of Darwin's argument . . . or followed the debates which led to the present version of the theory. . . . We nonfundamentalist laymen believe in evolution not because we have in mind the evidence and experience it would take to envision the process and grasp it in a fully rational way, but because we trust biologists. Our trust is not blind, of course. We willingly defer to the judgment of biologists in large part because we feel sure they have good reasons for their beliefs and could display those reasons to us. . . . But my confidence that good reasons exist does not change the plain fact that my present acceptance of the theory of evolution is based not on those uninspected good reasons but on deference to authority. What shapes my belief is as much psychological and sociological as logical. And although I think the thought process that leads me to my belief is far sounder than the one that leads the creationist to his, the difference is not a matter of his clinging to authority while I rely on reason: we both submit to authority, but to different authorities. (Haskell, 1984:xi)

Deference to authority is thus *competent* behavior in contemporary society. A university education is largely a socialization process teaching the young to defer to proper authorities (Stich and Nisbett, 1984). The justification of deference is based partly upon the limits of an individual's ability to examine evidence personally, as Haskell says, and partly upon the institutionalization of credentialing. "In order for expertise to exist as a stable and reliable activity, it must be institutionalized in some fashion. In any large and complex community there must be some conventional way by which people can identify an expert" (Freidson, 1984:16).

In addition to individual limits and the institutionalization of credentials, the sheer complexity of modern life—the divisions and subdivisions of knowledge—press even the best educated toward deference to the specialist. "In reiterating that scientific culture is specialist culture—who doesn't know this?—one risks riding an advancing swell of cliché" (Ozick, 1987:3). But if fragmentation and splintering are now taken for granted, the idea that deference to authority is often deference to specialism ought to fascinate us.

To assert that something is true because it occupies a particular niche in an expert community's intellectual ecology, because the truth of the claim would garner a majority in a plebiscite among members of that domain, is a proper mode of argument. Authority, therefore, must be part of any calculus for explaining arguments and their outcomes. The speaker's authority may be part of the truth conditions of his or her claim. Taking the speaker's authority may thus be an integral part of "rationally" evaluating it.

That one can point to historical cases of mistaken consensus does not cut against the Stich/Nisbett/Haskell position that deference to authority is "rational" action. Any consensus may be fallible, but it may still be "rational" to acquiesce to it.

6.4. Credibility Is Enthymematic

In raising objections to the insistence on explicit reason-giving (Chapter 5), no mention was made of a peculiar analytical/critical problem, viz., credibility rarely resides in the talk. If a critic wants to know whether an arguer is "rational" or (conventionally) sound in accepting an interlocutor's claim, the interlocutor's credibility may be central to the answer. The men discussing the thunderstorm (Example 6.1) exemplify this characteristic. If it is "rational" for A to accept B's claim by virtue of B's expertise, then expertise is inseparable from substance in A's calculus of assent. But the credibility on which Examples 6.1 and 6.2 turn is not in the talk. We infer its presence rather as astronomers infer the presence of an unseen planet by noticing anomalies in observable bodies that must be effects of an unseen planet. The behavior we do see is comprehensible if we assume the existence of a hidden entity. Thus we make sense of A's acquiescence to B in 6.1 by deciding that A is imputing credibility to B.

Authority and Modernity

A central theme in the authority literature is that modernity undercuts authority—or supplants it with a less authoritative (which is to say "more human") substitute. Originally, authority had its ontological base in foundationalism: epistemological and value claims were ultimately defensible by appeal to some outside authority—God, nature, and so on. As Arendt says, "Legitimacy derives from something outside the range of human deeds" (1958:82). In a world "drained of telos" (Connolly, 1987:130), authority finds its new location in the conventions of human enterprises (Berger,

Berger, and Kellner, 1973; Bierstedt, 1950; Blumenberg, 1983; Flathman, 1980; Foucault, 1977; Hauerwas, 1981; Hick, 1985; Sennett, 1980).

The foundationalist sees this shift to "human deeds" as lamentable. Yeats's center has not held. Relativism and nihilism loom near. Barbarians are at the gates. One might hope to revive teleology or Aristotle's view of *hexis* (MacIntyre, 1959, 1981) because human authority is "authoritarian" or "bureaucratic" (Goodnight, 1982, 1986; Wolff, 1968). One might hope to ground human authority in a rational telos located in the structure of idealized speech acts (Habermas, 1971, 1973, 1975, 1979, 1984). Or despairing of teleology but distrusting human institutions, one might seek a radical critique of human authority (Foucault, 1972, 1977). Building upon a robust skepticism about human disciplines, one might also hope to institutionalize the ambiguity of authority—to make explicit its fundamentally necessary and inevitably dangerous aspects (Connolly, 1987).

Beside these philosophical treatments of authority, the interactional theory may seem compromised. It collapses ethos and authority and emphasizes their centrality to the outcomes of arguments in communal contexts. In emphasizing the *collective* importance of ethos, It may seem to succumb to disciplinary false consciousness (as Habermas might say) or to an eviscerating piety (as Foucault might say). In making ethos inseparable from and foundational to the logic of assent, It may seem to have dispossessed the individual. Doesn't claim (2) equate the "rational actor" with a company man in a company town?

Once again, the language of the individualism debate is doing its work. If one is concerned with rescuing virtue from the clutches of convention or with deriving an optimally "rational" logic of assent, one's attention is channelized by the dichotomy of individual and community. Reflective thinking becomes the individual's weapon against technical and social control. There is a romantic theatricality to this thinking that disguises both the merit in the position (who can object to reflective thinking?) and a mistake. The mistake lies in pitting individuals against communities, then betting stupidly on the outcome.

Moreover, once one casts the issue of critique in terms of a dichotomy of person and community, one sets the individual off on an impossible quest. Witness Habermas's quixotic goal of a society whose "rational" processes are fully transparent to the individual and thereby matters of agreement or reflectively achieved social contracts. This goal puts a hyperbolic demand on an individual: one learns by doing; but public action makes for private commitment

(Festinger and Carlsmith, 1959; Hovland, Campbell, and Brock, 1957; Janis and King, 1954; Kiesler and Kiesler, 1969; King and Janis, 1956; Miller, 1973; Petty, Ostrom, and Brock, 1984; Petty and Cacioppo, 1981, 1984). Moreover, the breadth and complexity of knowledge in modern life put the individual in an impossible position: we prize expertise and competence while demanding an unattainable breadth of vision; one cannot reflectively acquiesce to the whole of one's organizational position (Argyris, 1957, 1964; Bachrach, 1967; Bennis, 1966; Benson, 1973; Blau, 1955; Dahl, 1967; Hogwood and Peters, 1985). This mistake has its parallel among critics who polish their eminence by insisting on standards no one can meet. Some guard-house doggerel comes to mind:

> Give them goals they cannot meet;
> And they will grovel at your feet.

The problem is putting it all on the individual. If we see critique (Foucauldian, Habermasian, or what have you) as a social enterprise, we move onto different grounds—namely, argument as interaction. And this gets us back to valuing dissensus (Willard, 1987a; Willard and Hynes, 1988). Thinking this way, we retain Foucault's insight that existing orders create selves appropriate to their needs and Connolly's preference for institutionalized ambiguity and a "social ontology of discord within concord." We give the individual reachable goals and resources to draw upon. We need only insist that the move from alienation (an individual's prerogative) to critique and even rebellion is a distinctively social enterprise.

6.5. Ethos versus Opposition

The risk of giving ethos a central place in an argument theory is not that analysts will be unable to distinguish good from bad or appropriate from inappropriate attributions. Rather, an appreciation of the centrality of ethos to communal (and especially disciplinary) life may lead Argumentation theorists to overvalue *authority*. Authority, let's say, is a powerful ethos effect in which a person acquires prestige, status, and stature by virtue of his or her community position or reputation and in which institutions or disciplines are legitimized. As Kuhn (1970) says, we effect entry and achieve status in a field by demonstrating our competence with its methods and adroitness with its procedures. Authority thus arises (or masquerades) as disciplinary merit. Inside a discipline, then, it is "rational" at least provisionally to acquiesce to authority; and outside a discipline, one can do little else but accept an arguer's professional stature as being vouched for by the discipline. Authority encourages trust; trust encourages settlement of disputes and the acceptance of claims.

The unfortunate effect of such authority is to undercut opposition. People hypnotized by the death of teleology may be tempted to make sociological foundationalism an effective substitute. They might prefer conformity to rootless freedom. This might lead them to think that the raison d'être and ideal completion of disciplines is the surmounting—or the ending—of disputes. There are two motives for this pressure to authority: a fear of relativity (which should be counted as among the twentieth century's most recurring phobias) and a hunger for progress.

This may be just the sort of ambiguity Connolly (1987) wants us to institutionalize rather than suppress. As people and societies seek to institutionalize knowledge—to buttress it, firm it up, make it dependable—they risk diluting their most powerful medicine. This permanent tension cannot be circumvented by arbitrarily separating ethos from argument or authority from "rationality." If they are empirically inseparable, as I argue here, then only the most piquantly Foucaldian blindness (or cynicism) could justify our insisting upon their separation as ideals or as pedagogical exemplars.

This permanent tension should be one of Argumentation's organizing interests; the authority of disciplines should be regarded with a disciplined ambivalence. I am not reducing disciplined argument solely to authority. Petty and Cacioppo (1979, 1981, 1984; Petty, Cacioppo, and Goldman, 1981) emphasize that ethos effects are most pronounced in cases of low issue involvement. Surely we will find high issue involvement in at least some cases of disciplinary arguments. Thus though disciplines are built upon authority structures—and disciplinary actors cannot be said to be immune to authority—we still expect innovation and change to occur. The ubiquity of conceptual change should allay any fears that the human disciplines will suddenly find themselves frozen in place. Manifestly, the crisis of modernity is due for a gold watch, yet the disciplines plod onward, resisting and embracing change.

Summary

Any account of the public sphere must include assumptions about authority. Since our political and juridical discourses are inextricably linked to a rule by experts, argument studies may illuminate the intersections of expertise and logic as they affect decisions to accept persuasive influence and as they affect public veridical folkways.

The connectedness of public and private affairs is exemplified by their common dependence on authority. Claim (1) thus displays the centrality of ethos to a logic of assent. Claim (2) emphasizes that acquiescence to authority is at least sometimes the "rational" solution. Both claims make the most sense when understood outside the terms of the individualism debate.

To show the importance of removing authority from the individualism debate, I have considered claims (1) and (2) vis-à-vis the ongoing critique of modernity. The concern has been to defend the interactional theory against the charge that it plays into social foundationalism, which claim (2) prima facie appears to do. But this bad appearance is an artifice of the language of individualism. The interactional theory puts the matter in terms of a tension between pressures toward conformity (acquiescence to authority) and rebellion (or intellectual change). Since both forces occasionally triumph, it is a mistake to exaggerate either. Ethos works against opposition, but opposition has resources of its own. The key to respecting the ambiguity of authority is, following Connolly, to exaggerate neither side but to accept their competing claims.

I had nearly finished this book when I encountered Connolly's *Politics and Ambiguity* (1987). Though I think that Connolly does not fully escape individualism, it is notable that he sees the need to do so: "The attraction of the liberal doctrine resided largely in its desire to acknowledge together the claims of public authority and private prerogative. But, as its conceptual resources have lagged behind changes in the structure of modern life, this attraction has faded. The web of social life is now too tightly drawn to sustain this picture of public authority and private refuge" (p. 72). Though Connolly embraces a "social ontology of discord," I think his contribution lies elsewhere. Because he lacks a theory of argument, he has no way of guaranteeing the discord. But his emphasis on institutionalized *ambiguity* seems to me to be a powerful idea (for a striking comparison, see Levine [1985] and March and Olsen [1976]). Connolly reasons that collectivist theories of legitimacy "provide the most refined instruments with which to probe subterranean developments in our civilizations" but that these instruments must be refined or replaced through a critique made possible not by resolving ambiguities or by siding with one or another side in current disputes but by establishing ambiguity at the very center of our understanding of knowledge-producing processes and organizations. That authority is repressive yet necessary is not a *debate* but a starting point.

Part II

Argument's Family of Terms
Introduction

One implication of the interactional theory is that argument should not be discussed *sui generis* but in companionship with a family of terms that coalesce to give it meaning. *Rationality* and *freedom* are among the most important. Both ideas have enormous consequences for one's view of argument, and both, in turn, are dependent on a view of argument. Chapters 7 and 8 detail these reciprocal influences. Views of rationality and freedom augment the interactional theory, elaborating its political and philosophical context. The interactional theory in turn is a lens for viewing rationality and freedom. It so redefines their conceptual horizons as to sever both constructs from their historical roots. That rationality and freedom should be separated from their Enlightenment histories is the point I want to make here.

Even before argument, rationality, and freedom join forces, we have a guilt-by-association problem. Seeing argument coupled with opposition, we might wonder whether it has fallen in with bad companions. The most prim and proper ideas acquire unsavory reputations running with the wrong crowd. Terms like *conflict*, *competition*, *dissension*, and *strife* certainly look belligerent, especially beside less rowdy terms like *cooperation*, *harmony*, *mutuality*, and *nurturing*. We may seem to have put argument at odds with utopian visions of community based on mutual interests and shared love (Kirkpatrick, 1986) or on harmony with natural direction (Unger, 1975).

The problem is the interactional theory's *contractarian* flavor. Communication uses intersubjectivity, working consensuses, mutual adjustment, emergent cooperative strategies, and accommodation. Conversational repair, epistemic, and deliberative motives involve agreements about rules and procedures. Since the doctrine underlying contractarianism is individualism (Gierke, 1934; Kirkpatrick, 1986), it may seem that we have fallen victim to the disease we set out to cure.

This bad appearance is compounded by the decision to join argument with Enlightenment coinages such as rationality and freedom, which are dependent on the language of individualism. Both ideas conjure up a dichotomy of person and society and a Hobbesian view of human nature. A celebration of conflict and opposition tied to a radical individualism seems rambunctious if not menacing.

Perhaps we can find a less criminogenic environment. We can rescue the social contract from individualism by moving it, lock, stock, and barrel, to a new environment—namely, the interactional theory. The transportation of ideas across field boundaries always involves a degree of transformation (Dunbar, 1985; Willard, 1982, 1983), but there is nothing subtle about the changes needed here. The problem lies in thinking *at all* in terms of a dichotomy or opposition of individual and community (Tocqueville, 1956; Bellah et al., 1985). The interactional theory emphasizes the functional fit of people and groups and the constitutive importance of communication. This view precludes any dichotomy of person and society. It dismisses as myth the state of nature (or any version of the Fall) and visions of society as redemption. It undercuts grandiose pictures of human nature.

Individualism is not a unified camp. Locke's theory is not identical to Hobbes's (though it uses Hobbes's picture of human nature). Rousseau is not interchangeable with Adam Smith or James Mill. But these theories do share a general picture: the sovereign individual forsakes the state of nature (the locus of genuine freedom) for society (*Gesellschaft*, in Tonnies's [1957] terms), thereby becoming the basic unit of analysis (Arieli, 1964; Gierke, 1934; Heilbroner, 1972).

The Enlightenment did not invent individualism. The Sophists saw the natural state as a ceaseless pursuit of predatory self-interest checked only by the raw power of confederations. Plato and Aristotle saw the *polis* as suppressing animal nature by enforcing good habits. This view found its dreariest, most exaggerated voice in Hobbes, who put human relations in the state of nature on a par with starving dogs tussling over a carcass. They are pitted, "each against all"— blood enemies snapping at scarce meat, seeking conquest and domination, wanting the company only of comparative weaklings. Human life was "solitary, poor, nasty, brutish, and short." Enter Leviathan. A big dog stops the fight. The smaller dogs agree to a pact because they cannot kill the big dog and because a pack can more effectively kill outsiders. Rapaciousness still rules but is manifested in countless specific acts, atomic constituents of a bigger machine. Public life becomes (pick your metaphor) a *jungle*, ringing with bestial mayhem, or a *mercantile casbah* in which countless individual acts of greed sum up to social utility.

Rousseau and Locke produced equally unflattering if less grisly portraits. For Rousseau, the need for affiliation *is* the state of nature. People are *social* creatures whose natural gregariousness waxes in communities and wanes in isolation. For Locke, the catalyst that impels the individual toward community is the need to protect property. In both scenarios, sociability stems from weakness: we share life's miseries (Rousseau) and insecurities (Locke). We want autonomy so we transfer our dependence to a necessary abstraction, the "general will."

Rousseau is not concerned as much with explaining *society* as with justifying the idea of the state. Sociability makes the state possible; the press of events makes it necessary. A return to the state of nature is a retreat to privacy and family; the pull of citizenship is away from such comfort. Hence an apologetic for the state—a straightforward political agenda, no hedges or dodges. Quite differently, in Hobbes (and the Whigs, especially Spencer), a political agenda masquerades as anthropology or biology. The state comes in by the back door as nature's creation, the status quo being a natural necessity and natural necessity being the ultimate imprimatur.

Hobbes et al. produced no theories of communication. This is doubtless fortunate. One can imagine Bentham's thoughts about accommodation and coorientation or what Hobbes might have said about interpersonal trust. Not a pretty picture. But these thinkers likely did not set communication aside so much as they failed to consider it at all. If one feels obliged to explain communication, one is not likely to dabble in individualism. Consider, for example, a philosopher who might well have joined explanations of human nature and communication. Yet in Sartre we find a radical individualism spurred by a disregard for communication as the developmental and functional basis of action. Sartre wanted to critique bourgeois morality by establishing a powerful (and compelling) picture of personal responsibility. He achieves this vision by insisting on consciousness as a negativity, an estrangement, a negation of facticity. Reflection pulls ego away from the stream of consciousness into a solitary world, making each person "an absolute choice of self" abandoned in the world, Being-for-itself, engaged with events for which one alone bears responsibility. One is *condemned* to responsibility. Sisyphus had it easy.

It is odd that Sartre would adopt so reified a picture of human nature. But the seeds of this move are planted in his view of negation: Being-for-itself is virtually autistic. The negativity of consciousness assumes the absence of communication and the possibility of a solitary ego unaffected by communication—a reality (presumably with a private language) standing over and against the social world.

Barnes (1967) holds that Sartre does not ignore socialization and cognitive development and that he sees the self as existing in events. This is too charitable. At best, if Sartre can be said to have a communication theory at all, he envisions a mature ego entering conversation intact, its essence unaffected, and achieving freedom only by leaving it. This presumes nothing more complex than an Expressive MDL: ego may need to get ideas across, but ego will not need social comparison, negotiated meanings, or coordinated strategies. Ego is *dichotomized* with the social—the whole point of seeing consciousness as negation.

We all occasionally err (as Russell said of Bergson) in mistaking personal idiosyncracies for universals. Perhaps Sartre mistakes a romantic vision of genius, of isolation and intuitive insight, for consciousness per se. We know that Bohr and Heisenberg, after exhausting arguments with Pauli and other colleagues, arrived at the principles of complementarity and indeterminancy while alone. After many arguments, Heisenberg produced the idea of matrices and Max Born produced the idea of statistical waves of probability while alone (Pagels, 1982). Such cases square with our intuitions about artistic creation and conceptual innovations. So maybe Sartre confuses consciousness per se with *his* consciousness.

The interactional theory does not explain leaps of genius. But it suggests that solitary thought is not negation. Bohr and Heisenberg regarded physics as a *social* enterprise; the Copenhagen group existed in its arguments. Withdrawing from the fray may have given them time to catch up, take stock, and try fresh thinking. Constant argument is hard going. But the need for contemplation and solitude does not support individualism or negative consciousness or impugn the centrality of communication.

The rejection of individualism does not affect our ability to believe in individuals. Dewey might have been replying to Sartre in making his famous distinction between individualism and individuality:

Individuality is at first spontaneous and unshaped; it is a potentiality, a capacity of development. Even so, it is a unique manner of acting in and with a world of objects and persons. It is not something complete in itself, like a closet in a house or a secret drawer in a desk, filled with treasures that are waiting to be bestowed on the world. Since individuality is a distinctive way of feeling the impacts of the world and of showing a preferential bias in response to those impacts, it develops into shape and form only through interaction with actual conditions; it is no more complete in itself than is a painter's tube of paint without relation to the canvas. (1930:168)

The point is to avoid a false opposition of individual to society and thus a reified view of structure. To ignore interaction is to devalue individuality. To see society as "fixed in institutions" is to devalue human effort: "But 'the connection of events' [quoting Emerson] and the 'society of your contemporaries' as formed of moving and multiple associations, are the only means by which the possibilities of individuality can be realized" (1930:170). Withdrawal to a "merely inner world" is a mistake, Dewey says, but there are "subtle forms of retreat, some of which are erected into systems of philosophy" (p. 171).

Constructivism and interactionism are data-driven theories, both presiding over robust research traditions and using their yield to refine ideas. Their picture of communication is not conjured from thin air. It has empirical weight. Conversely, the state of nature and its corollary picture of human nature have never been more than anecdotal. Whether one means prehistoric savagery, childhood, tribal culture, or, like Rousseau, private and family life, the state of nature does not comport with the evidence. For instance, one need not be Chomskyian or Piagetian to deny that childhood is a state of nature: generative mechanisms, whatever their individual permutations, make sociality possible (Delia, 1983). Nor must one veer to the nurture side to claim that communication practices in families are immediately important. The idea of a state of nature requires a polar contrast of two elements that differ in kind: a real social animal versus a mythic beast. Do real horses get their character from their differences from unicorns?

If one cannot take the causal claim seriously, the human nature presumably flowing from it becomes doubtful. Because Hobbes had no communication theory—let alone the idea of different MDLs—he was unable to see that strategies are situationally emergent or that general orientations to interpersonal matters are pragmatically developed.

The atomistic view of social life has the same anecdotal status. The interactionist's claim that organizations exist in and through the activities of their members suggests an interdependence between person and society that the atomic constituent view cannot acknowledge. I have already considered the empirical defects of broad abstractions such as "culture" and "society" (Chapter 1). People are multivalent; society is balkanized into discourse domains. The relationship between individuals and social worlds cannot therefore be a simple, universal one.

Atomism is a worse metaphor now than in Hobbes's day. Our world of "quantum weirdness" (Pagels, 1982), increasing entropy in closed systems, and invisible but real probability waves does not translate easily to the realm of action. To take but one example, one might say that the state of public opinion (a consensus) is a statistical drift, but we do not assess a *disciplinary* consensus by sampling techniques. Human groups and organizations are not closed systems. People are not analogous to atoms: their motives in *particular* situations may not be relevant to whatever random samples of their communities might reveal. If the ebb and flow of opinion in a system is not random, then individual choices are more than expressions of probability waves. Action, Burke insists, is different from motion.

And preferable. Taken seriously by organizational actors, atomism is a debilitating idea. It implies that organizations are indivisible wholes closed to critique and reconstruction; it overlooks situational adaptation and (thus) organizational evolution. As we shall see, freedom is a feature of one's thinking that cannot coexist with atomism. So dichotomizing the individual and society is a mistake, not only because it yields needless disputes but because it is empirically wrong.

Maybe argument is not such a hard case after all. Rid of their shady companions and free of their old neighborhood, rationality and freedom clean up nicely. Perhaps we can discuss both constructs as if they are (1) ideas, not facts of nature; (2) cogent enough not to need mythical states to instantiate them; and (3) sufficiently flexible (and broad) to serve a more complex theoretical agenda.

Rationality

Argument's link to rationality has historically been formalistic, logic being the paradigm case of both. This connection does not hold in the interactional theory. If argument is *interaction*, its reformed connection with rationality is as follows: arguments put a premium on arguers' good will; good will puts a premium on rationality.

The importance of good will is the easiest part of this equation to prove. To value argument is to value conflict; to value conflict is to prize good will. The first premise arises from the way the interactional theory is constructed. The political interests that spark our fascination with argument imply the importance of conflict in organizational life. The power and ambiguity of authority (Chapter 6) imply that opposition is intellectually healthy. In defining argument as interaction based on dissensus and downplaying the argument as serial predication view, we have shifted Argumentation's disciplinary focus. The field-defining aim, *mutatus mutandis*, is to understand, critique, and refine (with the aim of strengthening) the conditions of opposition in organizations and institutions and to study the effects of particular approaches to conflict.

This disciplinary metamorphosis may seem counterproductive. In celebrating disputation, aren't we applauding disputatiousness? There is something disagreeable about disagreements. People do not behave well—or their bad behavior seems more evident—in conflicts. In giving Argumentation a curatorship role toward opposition, we may seem to be building a theory that more resembles a catalog of social pathologies than a compendium of high aspirations. Argumentation should not resemble Criminology. If you think that good will is in short supply, you may be suspicious of any theory so dependent on it.

But socal comparison and idea-testing are paradigm cases of reflective behavior, not pathologies. We equate the examined life with *tested* ideas. And the presence of opponents is not the sole constraint on advocates. Arguing is not merely or essentially compliant behavior. People are constrained by their beliefs, by circumstances, and by rules.

The language of individualism again clouds our thinking. First consider the social side. To prize dissensus goes against an older tradition in Argumentation that values opposition less than the rules that constrain it. Concerned with distinguishing squabbles and tiffs from argument proper (Brockriede, 1975, 1977; Burleson, 1979b, 1980), many scholars emphasize rule-following (Barth and Krabbe, 1982; Barth and Martins, 1982; Naess, 1966; Krabbe, 1987; Mills, 1968; Rescher, 1977b; Smith and Hunsaker, 1972; Toulmin, Rieke, and Janik, 1979; Ulrich, 1985; Walton, 1985). In defining Argumentation as a normative discipline (Wenzel, 1980, 1985), an implicit view of rules-as-discipline operates. The goal is to achieve rules of sufficient clarity and power to render good will unnecessary (Gottlieb, 1968; van Eemeren and Grootendorst, 1984; van Eemeren, Grootendorst, and Kruiger, 1983). A side effect of this focus is a lacuna in the literature: the beliefs, motives, and commitments requisite to sound argument are ignored.

Now consider the individual side. The individualist may reply that nothing but death makes good will unnecessary. Have we but world enough and time, we can subvert any rule, twist any principle to fit our wants. There is, Goodnight (1986) says, "something personal that resists socialization," something that makes us sunshine citizens and summer conformists (see Connolly, 1987). But individualism is too romantic, no better than the exaggerated diminution of personal motives. Dewey again provides the antidote: "To gain an integrated individuality, each of us needs to cultivate his own garden. But there is no fence about this garden: it is no sharply marked off enclosure. Our garden is the world, in the angle at which it touches our own manner of being. By accepting the corporate and industrial world in which we live, and by thus fulfilling the precondition for interaction with it, we, who are also parts of the moving present, create ourselves" (1930:171). The study of organizational life always bloodies the rugged individualist. Motives and intentions are sometimes buried beneath events. Once free of the language of individualism, the issue emerges in clearer focus: any theory that celebrates conflict puts a premium on good will.

It is harder to prove that good will is tied to rationality. One needs special views of both. The view of rationality entailed by the interactional theory yields the needed picture. The drift of my reasoning is that communities are rhetorically constituted, so the processes of conformity and dissent do not *necessarily* differ in every respect or in kind. People do commit themselves to groups; they are willing to do the work, argue the points, and repel invaders because they value their communities. But they also rebel—often "rationally." They dissent but play by the rules. My point is reminiscent of Dewey's: one sign of good will is playing by the rules—which may be why innovators often emphasize continuities between their ideas and conventional wisdom (Gross, 1988; Campbell,1986).

Freedom

A theory of argument is a theory of freedom. Explanations of argument require assumptions about volition and choice. Moreover, freedom is easiest to understand in contexts where it counts most. Arguments are exemplary cases because they involve conflict. Freedom becomes an engaging construct once conflict is seen as a pervasive part of the social fabric yet not the shackled animal warfare envisioned by Hobbes.

To jettison the Enlightenment view is not to substitute an equally exaggerated existential determination of thought or an *innate goodness*. Stupidity, greed, and sloth are as definitively human as rationality. The interactional theory does not dissolve the dichotomy of person and society, it bypasses it. Individuality is a fact; individualism is a discredited doctrine.

In Argumentation, freedom is more a rhetorical flourish than a considered theoretical construct. As Jefferson's heirs, Argumentation scholars feel obliged to affirm the values of the free marketplace—all the while defending theories of decision making whose content is at odds with those proclamations. As we will see, the disciplinary thrust of Argumentation is toward *systems* whose *rules* and *constraints* impel arguers to make good decisions whether they are inclined to or not.

The view of freedom generated by the interactional theory goes against the grain of much recent thinking, which tends to *singularize*, to speak of freedom as a monolithic problem. One thus attributes the crisis of modernity to (say) institutional inflexibility (as if organizations and their conditions of flexibility did not differ), or to false consciousness, or to the epistemic hegemony of expert domains, or to the need for methods that get the benefits of stability yet encourage innovation. We may call it the cult of The Quest. The Grail is a singularized resource transcending the near-infinite particularities one finds in human practices—relativity being the Dark Wood our knight must traverse. The crisis of modernity is a useful expositional device, but questions of freedom (as of rationality) arise on a landscape of multiple contexts and organizations posing problems so variable that The Quest will always fail. The view of freedom defended here comports with many versions of The Quest, but there is no Grail here—only a preference for opposition.

So the interactional theory of argument has similar implications for rationality and freedom. Both are socially constituted yet integral to the processes that form them. Both constructs affect an array of important issues yet are given content by those issues. A sticky circle, this. It will pay to tread lightly.

7

Three Senses of Rationality

The construct *rationality* has as many guises as there are human interests it might serve. It is used to designate a mental faculty, features of texts and expression, and a person's preferences, reflective habits, modes of reasoning, and methods of expression. It is contrasted with faith, experience, emotion, sensation, nondiscursive symbolism, spontaneous or unprincipled behavior, and expressive communication. These uses are so varied that any talk of rationality exposes us to the risk of incommensurability-by-spurious agreement (Fuller, 1982). Our intuitions that there is such a thing as reason and that we are the better off for it can easily get lost in the desiderata of particular theories and the often heated disputes they engender. But we are obliged to enter some of these disputes, for the interactional theory implies a specific picture of rationality. It won't do to say that the theory describes rationality incarnate, leaving it to chance or someone's biases how that assertion will be taken.

Not all rationality theories include argument in their definitions, but virtually all argument theories include rationality in theirs. This is unremarkable if we consider that by endorsing the importance of rationality, we are confirming the intuition that Argumentation's task is to reconstruct the conditions of sound discourse. Despite the variety of rationality theories, the conflicts among them, and the notorious difficulties with fringe cases (Bennett, 1964; Hesse, 1980; Quine, 1969; Krausz and Meiland, 1982; Douglas, 1973; Emmett and MacIntyre, 1970; Benn and Mortimore, 1976), the tie between argument and rationality is intuitively plausible. We would be surprised not to find interfield agreement about the inferiority of at least some clear-cut cases of emotional arousal, unreflective followership, and bureaucratic inertia.

Rationality as an Epideictic Construct

This concern with rationality is doubly unremarkable if we consider the epideictic function rationality theories serve. In calling something "rational," we register approval of motives, actions, texts, discourses, or the fit of means to ends. To praise, Aristotle said, is to recommend. The purpose of epideictic oratory was to single out exemplars for emulation—a view Quintilian turned into a foundational assumption of Western education. Thus Cicero enjoined the young to learn great oratory by studying great orators. This Greco-Roman coupling of rationality with pedagogy has had, we shall see, enormous consequences for rationality.

It may seem objectionable to say that rationality is a way of expressing approval. To make rationality a matter of praise and blame is to make it a *local* matter, for epideictic practices are embedded in particular fields. This smacks of emotivism. Readers persuaded of MacIntyre's (1981) claim that emotivism thrives on relativity may smell a similar fish here. Others may be distressed by what they see as a category mistake: praise and blame have emotional content; to see rationality as epideictic is to blur the most important distinctions the rationality construct is supposed to emphasize—distinctions between reason and emotion or faith, or between fact and value (Brown, 1963; Hick, 1964; Nielsen, 1962, 1974; Nagel, 1954; Russell, 1928, 1948; Santayana, 1954; Walsh, 1947; Whitehead, 1929).

The first objection is implausible. Emotivism is a behavioristic theory; the interactional theory is not. Emotivism takes the Expressive as the paradigm case communicator; the interactional theory does not. The interactional theory predicts that people sometimes behave in ways predicted by emotivism—as the Expressive blurts out feelings—but humans have more complex resources than behaviorism allows, as we shall see in Chapter 8's discussion of freedom. An argument theory, for instance, describes resources upon which people and communities may draw to ensure that their normative judgments are not mere affective expressions.

The second objection is merely a spasm. Even in the heyday of faculty psychology, logic and emotion were thought to mingle. Moreover, this objection is irrelevant, for the interactional theory puts our thinking about rationality onto very different ground. The objection, that is, does not contradict the claim being made here that the terms rationality and irrationality characteristically arise in judgments of someone's thinking, utterance, or decision making. In pedagogical contexts, the terms function as appraisals of reasons or methods for holding or adopting beliefs.

7.1. The Functions of Rationality

The proof of this claim is to ask what rationality theories chiefly do. The Greeks saw rational soul as the basis for distinguishing humans from animals—not just as a zoological/taxonomic nicety but as a rank ordering of life forms. Aristotle further conceived of rationality as a set of potentialities people might or might not achieve. People could be valued by their learned states of capacity (hexes). Subsequent theories extolled consistency, logic, propositional expression, having ordered preferences, and suppressing emotions. The point was to applaud conformity—playing by principled rules (Ryle, 1949). Theories based on Weber's notion of instrumental rationality were ways of explaining and prizing organizational structure and effectiveness, conformity to group values, competent functioning in organizations, the fit of means to ends, and the efficacy of accommodations to environments. The common thread among these theories is that they praise something by calling it rational.[1]

Many writers seize upon Levy-Bruhl's (1910) distinction between logicality and prelogicality (often in attacking it) by focusing on rationality as a comparative construct for understanding the beliefs and actions of other cultures, especially primitive ones (Winch, 1958; Wilson, 1979; Hollis and Lukes, 1982; Lloyd and Gay, 1981). The impetus for this work arises in debates about relativism. If one proves the possibility of translating primitive codes, the relativist is hard pressed to defend incommensurability (Davidson, 1973–74; Hollis and Lukes, 1982). However sound this starting point, primitive practices are sometimes prized for playing the fool to Western Science's straight man. One ennobles one's practices by noticing bizarre or inferior elements in primitive practices:

It is because the sociologist has a wider range of data, has become conscious of the importance of eliminating emotional and evaluative elements in his concepts and has a tradition of enquiry that uses such concepts and provides models of analysis, that he is in a better position than medieval man or primitive man to understand medieval or primitive society. He, after all, makes the attempt to understand other societies. They do not. His wider tolerance, his intellectual curiosity, and his willingness to criticize his own procedures, are his initial advantages over men in other cultures. Other societies to them—but not to him—are bizarre, laughable, and "ununderstandable." (Wilson, 1970:xi–xii)

Make this reasoning too solemn and you have a state of nature theory. As a pragmatic, political matter (aside from its context in the relativism debate), this is dangerous talk. The whigs took it as licensing paternalism, colonialism, and the pillage of inferior cultures. It is also epistemically dangerous. Whatever Wilson's intentions, the rhetorical effect is a backdoor celebration of *our* practices—shifting the debate from *justifying* our practices toward comparing them with inferior ones.

Such inquiry is also a way of prizing instrumental rationality. Gellner (1970) stresses the importance of a society's hopes, ambitions, and Weberian ideal types but as emotional pretenses set apart from the real stuff. In considering Durkheim's thought, Gellner lodges the value of comparative studies in self-critique, a goal shared by many in this tradition (Hesse, 1980; Barnes, 1974, 1977; Douglas, 1975; Bloor, 1976). There is no need to be charitable to the primitive and every reason not to be charitable with ourselves. The conclusion is that "ultimate goals and values do not fit into the instrumental means-ends-means schema of the self-perpetuating circle that characterizes formal rationality" (Wilson, 1970:xvii). The variants of this literature that seek to prove the universality of particular components of Western science or Western accounts of the basic categories of thought (Lukes, 1970, 1982; Hollis, 1970) are straightforwardly evaluative. "The new hunt for the Holy Grail is on," Gellner (1982:181) says with approval. It is not interesting per se to note the differences in standards by which people take things to be true: "Where the relativist sees only differences in these standards for rating reasons as good, the rationalist insists on ranking the standards" (Hollis and Lukes, 1982:11).

My point is not to attack these approaches but to underscore their evaluative component. Their thrust is to elaborate our appreciation of our epistemic institutions by holding them up to the mirror of primitive practices (Geertz, 1987; Marcus and Fischer, 1986). Their point is not to engender deference to the variety and diversity of human practices but to prove that we all use the same basic categories, we use different categories to the same effect, or there are similarities and differences that bear consequences for a particular view of rationality. All three lines are celebratory of one or another feature of our own epistemic enterprises.

Let's say that you still cannot quite accept my claim. Perhaps your objection is as follows: "Rationality theories seem evaluative but needn't be. Let's say rationality is *consistent* expression, nothing more. You're rational if consistent, irrational if inconsistent. I concede that such rationality has good and evil outcomes—which is just my point. Rationality is neither good nor evil; it just *is*." This objection certainly is consistent, but it endorses a trivial position (see Willard, 1983). A rationality deprived of value is an adjective shorn of importance. If consistency gets us morals, ethics, and Auschwitz, then "rationality" is less important than the attributes and circumstances that guide us toward good or bad actions. If Reinhard Heydrich and Mother Theresa share "rationality," their commonality is less important than the additional constructs we need to explain their differences. And why use *rationality* when *consistency* better says what we mean?

This objection aside, I take it that I have proved that rationality is a way of expressing approval. But I may seem to have undercut the importance of my point by admitting that it neither helps nor hurts any particular rationality theory. Weber (1930), after all, distinguished *Wertrational* from *Zweckrationalitat* as different uses of rationality for describing evaluative and instrumental practices. Perhaps the claim that rationality is an evaluative construct is an obvious but trivial point.

Let me capsulize my answer, then elaborate it. In a phrase, the rationality construct has acquired more emotional weight than it ought to have. Proponents of the reason versus faith contrast are more pious and faithful than they should be. Advocates of particular systems sound like ontologists rather than tinkerers with techniques. When techniques become religion and religion becomes ontology, blood pressures rise and the dialogue heats up. Clarity and charity are the first casualties.

It is presumably fitting for disciplines reflectively to consider their practices. When we value things without realizing it, we surrender our autonomy to think about them. When our hopes masquerade as empirical facts and our pieties pass as universals, they put a ceiling on our possibilities. The following reasoning is an example: "The justification for the teaching of argumentation lies in one crucial assumption: *all things being equal, the truth will prevail.* When given a fair chance, the truth should survive, because it's more natural, more attractive, and less contrived than falsehood. Argumentation functions to encourage equal defense of ideas, and hence to propagate truth" (Smith and Hunsaker, 1972:3). Or: "I shall contend that there are tests for whether a belief is objectively rational and that subjectively rational beliefs need not pass them; that there is a minimum score which all beliefs must attain and a maximum score which some must; and that 'good reason' is an objective term, to be applied with increasing warrant as the maximum is approached" (Hollis, 1982:72). The first passage reflects Aristotle's doctrine that truth has a natural tendency to triumph over falsity; the second applauds technology and science as epistemic models. The point of both is to skewer relativists.

An animus for both lines of reasoning is worth nurturing. The natural propensity doctrine can sanction dogmatism and true believership. It underwrites absolutism, intolerance, and suppression. It inspires us to equate conventional wisdom with truth and rationality with conformity. But doctrinaire skepticism is not needed to reject these claims. At least two objections do not depend on a distaste for absolutism.

Both passages in effect restrict rationality to scientific beliefs. The truths that will stack up on Hollis's epistemic thermometer are measurable. But the moral dilemmas and political decisions that concern us in daily life are of a different order. It is not just that they turn on epistemic claims that fall short of scientific standards but that their epistemic claims are hybrids of different fields (Dunbar, 1986; Goodnight, 1982; Riley, Hollihan, and Freadhoff, 1986; Rieke, 1982; Schuetz, 1986; Willard, 1982, 1983; Zarefsky, 1981, 1982), for example, as the abortion controversy taps multiple bodies of knowledge.

The mistake is not in imputing high epistemic standards to science but in depriving ordinary discourse of a construct like rationality. With enough help, encouragement, and institutionalized nurturing, anybody can be "rational." But there is heroism in ordinary life. People sometimes do well in bad conditions. They wrestle with incomplete, ambiguous, and overabundant evidence. They suffer time and resource constraints. They confront problems that outstrip their power to affect events. They vie with Expressive colleagues. They struggle with their own biases and emotions. And out of this miasma they occasionally wrest good decisions.

My point is not that collapsing rationality to science creates a hyperbolic standard (though I do think that some critics use the rationality construct to cloak mere disagreements in loftier terms; it is gratifying to find one's opponent guilty of high crimes). The more important point is that rationality is an appropriate construct for ordinary life. When people succeed in bad conditions, they merit the esteem implied by the term *rationality*. They also merit sustained study.

In addition to not wanting to deprive ordinary discourse of the rationality construct (hyperbolic standards again aside), we want rationality to be an optimally useful idea. Hollis's standard arguably is not. Its effect is to make science the ideal type or exemplar toward which ordinary discourse should aim. This is a misdiagnosis: ordinary discourse is doubtless ineptly disciplined, but the problem of public deliberation arises from politically and epistemically competing claims (Willard, 1982, 1983, 1986; Goodnight, 1980, 1982). Resolving those disputes, or wresting decisions from them, is an art for which we seem to possess no principles. If rationality matters, it ought to affect our deliberations about war and peace, nuclear power safety, environmental protection, social welfare, and law. Whatever the status of claims in natural sciences (Hesse, 1980), the techniques people use to grapple with public issues are artifices to be tinkered with. Their importance lies in their capacity to resolve competing factual claims.

Technique is not the whole or even the main point. Argumentation is hypnotized by technique. Its disciplinary attention is so riveted on particular methods that it has lost the original Greek vision of rationality as a personal achievement. This narrow vision stems from the discipline's historical ties to debate. It is easier to teach debate techniques than the personal traits that promote useful arguments. Doing so disguises the fact that forms of discourse prefer particular lines of argument. An insensitivity to the limits a mode of discourse places on the possibilities within it is the most expensive kind of ignorance. Witness Socolow's (1976:2) claim that "the public [environmental] debate is cloaked in a formality that excludes a large part of what people care most about."

The discipline's fixation with technique also stems from a failure to distinguish between anthropological particulars (specific community practices) and ontological claims about rationality. Empirical portraits of the former get entangled with the piety inspired by the latter. Hence the extreme unction with which some theories are defended (e.g., cost-benefit analysis [Willard, 1982]). A striking feature of rationality theories is their imperialism, their preference for universality and regnancy over local success. As we saw (7.1), rationalists do not want to understand the inner workings of particular rationalities; they want to rank them (Hollis and Lukes, 1982). The interactional theory implies a different view: rationalities are pragmatically linked to communities and contexts; the problem of the public sphere does not lie in its failure to emulate in general any particular discourse domain; nor does the reconstruction of a public discourse imply—Vienna Circle–style—the hegemony of a single commensurating discourse.

Rationality, in one guise or another, is Argumentation's gold standard, the basis for justifying a preference for argument and structured decision making over the competition (feelings, hunches, and intuitions on the cognitive side, raw power and bureaucratic inertia on the sociopolitical side). Our thinking about argument is so inter-twined with assumptions about rationality that it is futile to discuss argument without these values coming into play. It isn't just that one cannot speak of argument in a positivistic value-free language but that one would not want to. If rationality is Argumentation's raison d'être, noticing the epideictic effect of rationality theories is not a trivial point: it underscores the foundations of the discipline's thinking.

7.2. Theories of and about Rationality

A theory *of* rationality explains what rationality is. A theory *about* rationality explains how a particular theory of rationality should be applied—specifying, for example, the objects to which rationality is imputed. Aristotle's view of rational soul is a theory *of* rationality; his formal logic is a theory *about* it. The former describes human nature; the latter instantiates this nature in particular practices. The latter fixes our attention on the horizon of technique, which colors most views of rationality (e.g., Rieke and Sillars, 1984), though these theories are sometimes phrased like theories *of* rationality (e.g., Toulmin, Rieke, and Janik, 1979:13). Rationality has been seen as a feature of talk and text, of coherence or consistency, of fitting means to ends, of having an ordered set of preferences, and of logical form.

It may be wrong to see theories *of* and *about* rationality as related. We do not confuse carpentry with tools or art with technique. Argument scholars have not worked out what the relationships between theories of and about rationality might be. Certainly we might not applaud a particular utterance for being consistent for the same reasons that we applaud a person for being consistent: we applaud expositional consistency in the abstract, but not Reinhard Heydrich's consistency. We applaud students but not Nazis for their ordered preferences. Nonetheless, our preferences for certain theories of rationality are often dictated or biased by our hewing to one or another theory about rationality. We are likely to propose the syllogism as a cognitive model if it is our archetypal rational technique (e.g., McGuire, 1960b, 1981).

Three Senses of Rationality

Our view of argument works best with three senses of rationality working in tandem: (1) *an ontological sense,* a theory *of* rationality, the symbolic interactionist view of rationality as perspective-taking; (2) *an anthropological sense*, a theory *about* rationality as a social fact, as a word fields use to express approval of someone's actions—*irrationality* being used to describe deviant utterance—and as a construct arguers use (the ideals and norms they appeal to) to create, discipline, and evaluate their own actions and those of others; and (3) *a pedagogical sense*, a theory *about* rationality as the normative content of a discipline's self-description to novices. All three of these senses of rationality comport in different ways with our rough intuitions. In attempting to express our intuitions discursively, we might avail ourselves of any or all to define our meaning ostensively.

The three senses are obviously value claims about different phenomena: (1) values sociality and communicative competence; (2) and (3) value conformity. All three senses are necessary to understand the behavior of arguers and the cognitive/social effects of arguments: arguers exemplify rationality as well as talk about it. "Working in tandem" thus means that argumentation critics should consider the differences among the three senses and their varied relationships with the empirical happenings in arguments.

Only sense (1) is a logical entailment of the interactional theory (or so closely intertwined with it that we cannot tell which is antecedent). Senses (2) and (3) are faces of rationality that *cohere* with the theory (and especially with the field theory [Willard, 1982, 1983] I have spun out of it) but are by no stretch conclusions *from* the theory. They are not any the less important for this: as epistemic practices, they may have more pragmatic importance than sense (1). Suffice it to say that (1) is part of the inner workings of the interactional theory.

This difference aside, the three senses of rationality can all be seen developmentally, as evolutionary products whose nature is revealed by their natural histories. A merit of thinking this way is that it underscores the common genealogies of argument and rationality and their near-identical evolutionary tracks. Also thinking in the manner of the natural historian puts us in the right frame of mind for considering the myriad variations on the theme of rationality.

7.3. The Natural History of Two Ideas

Remembering that Darwin did not equate natural selection with any whiggish sense of betterment or progress and resented the use of his name to label a near-creationist view of benevolent natural "rightness" (Gould, 1980), we are nonetheless curious about why a practice and idea like argument has persisted over time. Does it have survival value? Has it achieved a "splendid local adaptation" (Gould, 1977a, 1977b) among other concepts? And what of its close companionship with rationality? Is it accidental, or has it historically enhanced the survivability of both concepts?

These questions take us back to the Greeks and remind us that common ancestors often spawn multiple genealogies. The mollusk is an instructive parallel. There are some five thousand species of the invertebrate division "mollusk," likely descended from common ancestors such as the flatworm. The mollusk's evolutionary history displays no unilinear progress or entelechy toward ideal completion but myriad local adaptations to conditions—ranging from giant clams, squid, and octopi to oysters, mussels, snails, sea cucumbers, urchins, and worms.

The mollusk puts us in the right frame of mind for considering rationality. We would not consider rank ordering the giant clam and the octopus, comparing them as if they were opponents in a metaphysical foot race or competing candidates for God's favor in the great scheme of things. They are different and incomparable solutions to environmental conditions. Equifinality is hot stuff in nature. Rationality is less diverse, but its sundry modern species represent analogous local adaptations to particular conceptual problems. It is both tolerant and plausible to think that the comparative merit of rationality theories—especially the anthropological ones—turns on their uses. The equation of rationality with consistency serves those who, like pigs hunting truffles, want to root contradictions out of discourse; the equation of rationality with propositional utterance serves students of textual analysis; regarding rationality as having an ordered set of preferences serves economists and theorists interested in justice; equating rationality with logical validity serves some logicians; equating rationality with statistical precision serves particular philosophies of science; and so on. It is pointless to speculate about the relative merits of the three classifications introduced here. They do different work. Sense (1) exposes the innards of the interactional theory; sense (2) illuminates particular practices; and sense (3), which is a special case of (2), exposes the pedagogical and socializing uses of rationality.

Naming rationality's near ancestors is easy. Plotting its multiple genealogies is trickier. The Greek view of rational soul as a higher endowment differentiating people from beasts is arguably the common ancestor whose influence is traceable in many linealogies. Aristotle's syllogism, and its function in *episteme*, spawned the practical and dialectical syllogisms, which in turn led to their rhetorical cousin, the enthymeme. Dialectic, transformed from Plato's truth-seeking into a theory of criticism by Aristotle, harnessed the practical syllogism for practical but disciplined conflict. As evolutionary lines, the syllogism and dialectic went their separate ways; but their paths often crossed (e.g., in the scholastics' resurrection of syllogistic exercises).

The Greeks saw a symbiotic relationship between argument and rationality: rationality was argument's necessary conceptual environment and empirical precondition; argument was rationality's chief instrument and empirical symptom. One result of this thinking was the view that rationality was a personal achievement, an outcome of a person's habits and virtues. Rational soul was seen as potentia; a person, by thinking and acting rightly, could achieve *hexes*—states of capacity for thinking and acting rightly; rationality, therefore, was an achievement, a point of pride, something not everybody had the full measure of.

Perhaps the most arresting feature of rationality's multiple evolutionary tracks is the degree to which the personalization of reason has been selected against. For the Greeks, rationality was necessary for distinguishing humans and animals, as in Aristotle's distinction between animal and rational soul. Rationality was the *definiens*, humanity the *definiendum*. The Darwinists—as opposed to Darwin—took the same tack. Contemporary approaches to rationality, shorn of Greek taxonomism and natural historical interests, nonetheless lodge a person's rationality in his or her success in using a system such as logic, thus distinguishing competent from incompetent people, or good ones from bad ones. The system, not the person's achievement, became the focus.

Theories *of* rationality attached themselves to particular accounts of human nature, theories *about* rationality attached themselves to particular practices. Argument has usually been found in the vicinity of the latter, though *rational* argument has virtually always been taken as symptomatic of the former. Like the mollusk, argument and rationality achieved "splendid local adaptations" and are thus found occupying different niches in different conceptual schemes.

7.4. Sense (1): Rationality as perspective-taking

Kant met Darwin in Cassirer's parlor. Since then, the claim that communication is definitive of human nature and of human action has become an ontological commonplace. The point is not just that intersubjectivity and social cognition are vital human practices (Roloff and Berger, 1982; Wegner and Vallacher, 1977; Weimer and Palermo, 1974; Wyer and Carlston, 1980) but that they are paradigmatic of humanness. Having built a view of argument on these assumptions, an ontological sense of rationality follows:

Argument is a paradigm case of intersubjectivity. Intersubjectivity is the paradigm case of rationality. Argument is a paradigm case of rationality.

This does not nominate an anthropological particular as a *definiens* of human nature. It does not tie rationality to traits of utterance (logic, publicness, or criticizability). It does not stipulate that utterance must be consistent, verbal, or pragmatically related to ends. It is not a theory *about* rationality. The interactional theory does not foreclose these anthropological particulars or deprive Argumentation of any particular theory about rationality. It only implies that every view of rationality may succeed in one ecological niche yet fail in another (Willard, 1983).

Nor does Sense (1) require *objectivity*. Intersubjectivity requires public reciprocal intentions; it ties the objectivity of claims to their communicability. But objectivity is a personal accomplishment. It thus belongs among the anthropological senses of rationality and not to claims about the conditions that make these accomplishments possible.

It would be redundant and misleading for the definition to emphasize a Weberian instrumental rationality, redundant because the definition assumes that arguers do not behave randomly, that they have goals (to influence others, to test ideas, to witness for beliefs), misleading because instrumental rationality is not the highest ambition the definition permits.

Sense (1) differs in important ways from the pedagogical sense. My definition of argument does not equate argument with rationality by tacking a normative standard on at the end, as Quintilian did in defining the rhetor as a "good man speaking well." Good people speaking badly and bad people speaking well are occasionally more interesting, so it seems arbitrary to exclude them. I do not want to define argument, as argumentation scholars have for sixty years, as "logical speech" or as "persuasive appeals to a rational audience," or even as "primarily rational appeals" (Mills, 1968). These stipulations depend upon the logic-emotion dichotomy and faculty psychology fashionable in the Enlightenment but dubious in the twentieth century. The conviction-persuasion duality today is a value judgment disguised as a fact about cognition (Willard, 1983). Moreover, such normative definitions tend to exclude interesting aspects of argument from the realm of study: illogical appeals, fallacies, and cheap tricks. The better assumption is that people in conflict situations sometimes use every appeal at their command

and that these are an interesting part of argumentation's field of study. Value judgments should not masquerade as definitions.

So the natural history of argument entails a sense of rationality peculiar to it. A promising candidate is that developed by symbolic interactionists out of Mead's thinking. Mead conceived of mind as an actor's capacity to take the role of the other toward developing actions. He called this ability to calculate the effects of one's actions on others "reflexiveness"—meaning that rational action always entails a reflexive reference to self. Reflexiveness thus inheres in an ongoing adjustment process in which one turns one's own experience back on oneself. The person is "able consciously to adjust himself to that process, in any given social act, in terms of his adjustment to it. Reflexiveness, then, is the essential condition within the social process for the development of mind" (Mead, 1954:134).[2] Mead thus uses Wundt's view of the significant gesture to reconcile what Wundt thought separate: individual consciousness and social structures (Farr, 1981; see also Durkheim, 1938; Schutz, 1962; Weber, 1947).

Rationality inheres in one's future orientation. It represents a "temporary inhibition of action" during which the person calculates outcomes (Meltzer, 1972), the "deliberative inner forum" (what Burke calls the inner parliament), which rehearses intended acts before their performance, evaluates alternatives, and estimates the perspectives of significant others vis-à-vis the intended act.

Mind is thus the capacity to import a social act for predictive purposes. Its core processes are the continual balances we achieve between assimilation and accommodation embodied in the "I-Me" interactions of the social self, the ongoing interplay between impulsive individual lines and the imported definitions, expectations, and probable reactions of others. Thus Mead calls rationality "the highest expression of sociality" (1932:86)—perhaps the same thing Geertz (1962:724) means in saying that "a cultureless human being would probably turn out to be not an intrinsically talented though unfulfilled ape, but a wholly mindless and consequently unworkable monstrosity. Like the cabbage it so much resembles, the Homo Sapiens brain, having arisen within the framework of human culture, would not be viable outside it."

Why insist upon this view? The answer is in three parts. First, it comports with the ethnographic, communication, and sociological evidence (Buss, 1978; Fincham and Jaspars, 1981; Forgas, 1981; Garfinkel, 1964; Goffman, 1974; Goodenough, 1964; Gumperz and Hymes, 1972; Gurvitch, 1971; Harre and Secord, 1972; Kluckhohn, 1961; Moscovici and Farr, 1981; Roloff and Berger, 1982). Second, it coheres with the interactional theory—especially its constructivist side and with its insistence on avoiding the language of individualism. This happy conjunction of the first reason with the second presumably is not accidental. The third reason turns on the normative and interactive character of social science, the fact that descriptions become norms and that observation and insight can cause changes in the phenomena studied. Just as important as the empirical soundness of Mead's view is the fact that we can live with it. As self-portraits go, it is neither van Gogh nor Sargent. For purposes of morale if nothing else, the field must believe that arguers are more than servo-mechanisms for forces or systems (as mediums claim to let the dead speak through them). Arguers are doing something definitive of their humanity—accommodating their private views to the requirements of public justification by entering into a structure of reciprocal intentions with others. In using "rationality" to name this accomplishment, we emphasize its nature as a personal achievement without resorting to Individualism.

This use of rationality comports with our intuitions about responsibility and choice. To equate rationality with conformity to a system is to celebrate both conformity and the system. But citizenship—indeed social life in general—often requires choices among competing rationalities and a tolerant and tentative attitude while working within an institution. A knowledge of how every institution prefers certain conditions and excludes others (Connolly, 1987) helps us choose among rationalities. An appreciation of the distinction between ontological and anthropological senses of rationality may help us adopt the optimum attitudes.

Consistent with Mead's theory of mind, we expect rationality to manifest individual differences consistent with the variations we notice in assimilation, accommodation, and MDLs as well as differences in cognitive development (Kohlberg, 1971). Since the facts about how arguments work are different for different people, we need to see rationality as a phenomenon that is manifested differently according to differences in fields, arguers, subjects, and situations. Put differently, argument instantiates rationality; one's performance in arguments is diagnostic of one's mastery of the competencies associated with communication (Ammon, 1981; Delia, 1983). The links between cognitive attainments, strategic repertoires, and communication performance are plausible inferences from the evidence (Applegate, 1978, 1980; Applegate and Delia, 1980; Argyris, 1964; Benoit, 1981, 1983b; Bernstein, 1974; Burleson, 1981; Clark and Delia, 1976, 1977, 1979; Fillmore, Kempler, and Wang, 1979; Labov and Fanshel, 1977; Mischel, 1971; Hymes, 1979; Dale, 1972). The focus on the relative complexity of MDLs (O'Keefe, 1986) puts more emphasis on the substance of one's beliefs about communication, but this does not require abandoning cognitive complexity. Constructs must somehow translate to particular strategies; the three MDLs explain that translation. Thus it is plausible to expect that rationality will be variously manifested in arguments.

There is, for example, a relationship between construct differentiation and conversational success (Delia, O'Keefe, and O'Keefe, 1982). People differ in the sophistication and detail of their conversational knowledge. Complex people "have elaborate schemata for conversations marked by sensitivity to the structure, form, and process of conversing. . . . They are sophisticated conversationalists with sensitivity to both content and form. They realize that meanings are located not only in the words uttered but also in the context framing those words. They have a greater ability, because of better developed constructs and schemata for conversations, to participate effectively in exchanges and to comprehend more completely and recall their discussions" (Daly, Bell, Glenn, and Lawrence, 1985:31). Owing to differences in how cognitive complexity is measured (O'Keefe and Sypher, 1981), it is unclear whether (and at which stages) conversational success is tied to the abstractness, differentiation, or comprehensiveness of constructs. There is reason to think that differentiation is developmentally first, with abstraction and comprehensiveness coming later (Applegate and Delia, 1980; Burleson, 1980; Delia, Kline, and Burleson, 1979; O'Keefe and Delia, 1979). At any rate, "One can confidently say that the relative overall developmental status of an individual's construct system has been shown to have important consequences for the kinds of communicative strategies the individual employs in regulative, feeling-centered, and persuasive communicative situations; for the sorts of rationales the individual provides; . . . for the quality of the individual's referential communication; for the number of persuasive arguments used and the number of possible reasons given for potential success or failure; and so on" (O'Keefe and Sypher, 1981:85–86). This reinforces the equation of rationality with communication-specific abilities, the expectation that people will differ systematically in their mastery of social skills, and the possibility that rationality consists of skills that can be taught.

7.5. Sense (2) Rationality as an anthropological datum

Having elaborated sense (2) elsewhere (Willard, 1983), I will make only passing mention of it here, flagging *"rationality"* in quotations when I mean it in this sense. Suffice it to say that the diversity of *"rationalities"* and the inconclusiveness of disputes among them should not surprise us. Every "rationality" has its focus and range of convenience and a range of phenomena for which it is inappropriate. Each is open to critique if defended as a universal but has its place in the sun if defended as a local affair. Arbitration among "rationalities" is often impossible. One cannot adjudicate "rationality" claims except as a partisan. There would have to be agreed-upon overarching rules governing the arbitration process—rules whose intellectual authority exceeded the putatively local claims of the competing theories. Davidson's (1973–74) reasoning in getting to the claim that incommensurability between conceptual schemes is impossible illustrates the point. Only theoretical imperialism can authorize the claim that local disputes turn on trivialities or appearances that the arbitrating view transcends.

Argumentation's analytical/critical aims do not require refereeing disputes between "rationalities." The field must not ally itself with any particular "rationality" or play at rank ordering "rationalities," just as we might say that Anthropology should not certify civilizations or that Sociology should not rank order communities. The better program is to study "rationality's" myriad manifestations and to analyze its various uses. The fact of "rationality" is more important than any particular "rationality." To see "rationalities" as local anthropological particulars undercuts their claims to universality but does not impugn their internal prerogatives. Their local purpose is judgment and evaluation. To study these practices is not to endorse local purposes.

Of all biblical admonitions, "judge not" may be the least observed. Judgment is a foundational practice of organizations. Disciplines are unimaginable shorn of their evaluative prerogatives. Expertise is a commodity we license, for we have no other way of measuring it (Haskell, 1984). "Rationality" and "irrationality" are ubiquitous judgments. "Rationality" is a fact, a practice, a word best suited to express approval of someone's discourse; "irrationality" is a term expressing disapproval of or sympathy for someone's incompetence or deviance.

As a practice, "rationality's" natural history inheres in the evolution of organizations. This does not just mean that organizations embody Weberian instrumental "rationality." Organizational theorists have already made this point (Beckhard, 1969; Bennis, 1966; Guest, 1962). The subtler implication is that "rationality" is pivotal to organizational practices. We now speak of complex organizations to emphasize that human organizations have evolved from relatively simple, straightforward aggregations based on simple purposes to immensely complex arrangements founded on complex purposes and practices (Silverman, 1971).

Inter alia, organizations define competence and expertise. They do so to survive, both as a matter of internal quality control and of external justification. Among the components of competence and expertise are a person's fit with an organization's normal practices. Rationality is thus standardization's talisman. It labels one's normalcy or conventional competence with the organization's routines. It is thus tied to the timidity and conservatism we find in organizations as well as being an integral part of an organization's self-justifying rhetoric.

This is another reason why Argumentation should avoid partisanship for particular models. Compliance and facility with etiquettes may be socially valuable attainments, but too much conformity is pathological. Organizations, like people, thrive on change, innovation, and adaptation to conditions. An equation of organizational success with conformity would yield an implausible picture of how organizations thrive.

It merits saying that "irrationality" is an interesting charge, which speaks volumes about the assumptions of the person making it. Some theorists (e.g., Veatch, 1962) have labored to defend "rationality" to authorize their right to judge others irrational. One does want to shout names at the barbarians at the gate.

7.6. Sense (3) Rationality and "rationalities" as pedagogical goals

To praise is to recommend, Aristotle said. "Rationality" thus functions as a pedagogical rationale for particular beliefs and techniques. The disciplines, like all social entities, have a recurring need to socialize initiates, to civilize and housebreak novices to the field's folkways and rules. "Rationality" is often an appropriate label for each field's substantive recommendations to novices. The disciplines for whom "rationality" is a subject matter such as Informal Logic and Argumentation thus manifest a frankly persuasive agenda: they do not merely study "rationality," they advocate particular "rationalities."

I want to discuss "rationality" as a pedagogical goal in two ways—as a natural part of every field's socialization process and as a particular aim of Argumentation. The first focus explains the diversity of anthropological particulars and suggests lines of research for the argument scholar. It is also an important part of Argumentation's pedagogy concerning the diversity of epistemic practices. To ask what a community's standards of "rational" behavior are is perhaps the most interesting question to be asked about it. What do its natives see as sane and insane? This question strikes at the heart of the community's constitution—not only the form of its socialization practices but the substance of what novices are told.

It also exposes the rhetorical constitution of communities, their emotional force, attractiveness, and cohesiveness. Gellner (1970) is mistaken in saying that a group's hopes and ideal types are emotional pretenses, not the real thing. Gellner's "rationality" is pretty stern stuff: "rational" change presumably clanks its way through conventional practices, stripping its gears on anomalies, and grunts its tedious way toward progress. Admittedly, communities often stifle their dreamers, force-fit innovations into conventional molds, and make revolutions look like tame extensions of conventional thinking. Descartes succeeded in emphasizing his continuity with his predecessors; Newton found the going rougher, forcing him to delay publication (Gross, 1988); Darwin made remarkable rhetorical commitments to continuity (Campbell, 1986). But it is still mistaken to downplay the importance of ideals and pretensions. What draws people to a community, gets them committed to its conventions and aims, and makes them love it enough to defend it? Surely hopes as much as accomplishments, dreams as much as achievements, are the rhetorical fuel of going communities. Pretense, not protocol, leads us to extend our reach. Rhetorical trappings can develop lives of their own, becoming a community's motive force for innovation. Healthy groups thus infuse their socialization and pedagogical practices with their hopes and ambitions. A sympathetic description of any group's practices presupposes an understanding of the higher hopes behind them.

So the belief that a group's "rationality" is the centerpiece of its self-definition, a pivotal component of its rhetorical constitution, is a promising starting point. Disciplines socialize novices by stressing the least controversial conventions, norms, and ideal types. Novices do not first meet complex problems; they meet the comfortable paradigm cases (see Chapter 9)—the uncontestably "rational" exemplars. So to know a field of discourse is, *inter alia*, to know the ways it justifies its practices internally and externally and the ways it deals with deviants.

7.7. The Optimism of Argumentation Pedagogy

Argumentation's pedagogical program is founded on a fundamental optimism, a therapeutic proposition that we can improve upon nature, that we can do better than we often do, that decision making can be strengthened and refined. Habermas's idea of claims redeemable through discourse is similarly optimistic though broader in thrust; and the idea of "precization" (van Eemeren and Grootendorst, 1984; Naess, 1966), or variants of Russell's theory of corrections, or what Richards calls the study of misunderstanding and its remedies, are incorrigibly optimistic commitments.

Behind all this is the assumption that nature's raw materials are open to refinement and enhancement. But argument scholars do not really work with nature's raw materials. They use the language of rationality to describe "rationalities," thus overvaluing particular techniques. Debate, not argument, is the organizing model. Debate is more formal than argument; its explicit rule structure gives it an impersonal force lacking in most interactions. If you do not trust people to do the right thing, you put your trust in structures. Hence the cult of debate.

Ehninger's (1970) notion of argument as method captures many of the pedagogical aims around which Argumentation scholars have effected consensus: providing instruction in critical decision making, logical exposition, the analysis of controversies, tests of evidence, ethical responsibilities, social effects of advocacy, and the rules of "rational" procedure. Argumentation, like other disciplines, has codified its stock of knowledge for pedagogy and often labels these basics as "rationality."

Theoretical moves of this sort make us wonder whether "rational decision making" is a myth. Because decision making often does not conform to our expectations, which are colored by the formal debate model, they do not look "rational." The evidence does not get critically weighed; the claims are not fully tested; the judges ignore claims and evidence. The satisficing actor—limited by organizationally constricted vision—almost by definition fails our standard.

7.8. Teaching Rationality

To teach you to fly, I will first teach you the mechanical ins and outs of your craft. You will then master the manipulative techniques for controlling the airplane. Then you will learn the facts of weather, how systems work, how storms move, and so forth. You may think that having mastered these things you are ready to fly, but current thinking in Aviation is that you are only ready to exercise bad judgment. Good technique does not prevent idiocy—the proof being a litany of accidents involving pilots using good techniques but bad judgment. Aviation educators have thus focused on the one variable that might improve the accident record: teaching good judgment. Good judgment is not a matter of flying technique but of *cognitive* habits and techniques for making good decisions. These skills have proved more resistant to teaching than their mechanical cousins.

Argumentation has a parallel problem. Debate techniques are in some respects on a par with basic aviation techniques, and (analogously) as far removed from the personal attributes good decision making requires as aviation techniques are from good judgment. Debate cannot be our sole "rationality." It does exemplify following rules, but debate rules are not the whole story in *any* case and are inappropriate in *some* cases.

But what does one teach if not debate? If arguments get their coherence from the arguers (O'Keefe and Benoit, 1982), what do we train for? What is the pedagogical content of Argumentation? The interactional theory implies that argumentation pedagogy is as much a matter of interpersonal attributes as of techniques. MDLs, the multifunctionality of messages, methods of context adaptation, media choice, role taking, and face protections are not merely topics for improving performance, though they are that; they are personal attainments necessary for benefiting from arguments. It is one thing to say, as Cederblom does, that we should see ourselves as belief-forming processes, not as fixed personalities, and quite another to explain how one does that.

It is in keeping with our theory to claim that argument skills, which we are taking as paradigmatic of rationality (and occasionally of some "rationalities"), are matters of training. A variety of experimenters have succeeded in instructing children in particular communication tasks (Clark, Willihnganz, and O'Dell, 1985; Clark, O'Dell, Willihnganz, 1985; Asher and Wigfield, 1981; Fry, 1966, 1969; Shantz and Wilson, 1972; Whitehurst and Sonnenschein, 1981). Developmental studies report coincidental increases in cognitive and communication sophistication (Flavell et al., 1968; Bearison and Gass, 1979; Bragg, Ostrowski, and Finley, 1973; Meichanbaum and Goodman, 1971). Coding systems have been developed to reflect children's progressively higher levels of accommodation to message recipients (Alvy, 1973; Clark and Delia, 1976, 1977, 1979; Burke and Clark, 1982).

7.9. Runaway Rhetoric: Where Argumentation's Overblown Claims Come From

Argumentation's historical ties to pedagogy have infected its intellectual ecology with a doubly defective rhetoric which has created a hyperbolic standard for designating what can count as "rational" and founded its pedagogy on a confusion of theories *of* and *about* rationality. The result is an exaggerated rhetoric of rationality.

Argumentation historically arose as a skills pedagogy. Theory followed practice: higher-order concepts evolved from the pedagogical repertoire. "Criticism" came to describe pedagogy in thinking, speaking, and listening skills and their putatively more sophisticated uses by critics. But the former has so constrained the latter as to produce a fifty-year tradition of inconsequential work. Our theories find their only audience in the classroom; our criticism speaks only to us. The field seems condemned to underestimate the scope and importance of its principles and their applicability to public and intellectual problems. The horizons of argument criticism are so circumscribed that we define the problem of the public sphere in terms of elementary expositional mistakes, as if we can adjudicate the abortion controversy by fixing fallacies, or the nuclear power debate by correcting inconsistencies.

In our concern to mute the individualism of children by socializing them into the authority structures of discourse communities, to replace their hedonism, narrow-mindedness, and near invincible ignorance with loftier attainments and ambitions, the temptation to serve up accomplished doctrines on silver platters is powerful. But—*tu quoque*—the justification of dialectic is not dialectically achieved. Often it is an argument from Aristotle's authority, or Plato's, or Whateley's, or Habermas's. If rule utilitarianism is dialectic's final justification, what constitutes its proof? If Argumentation's pedagogical rationale is that ordinary discourse falls short of the rules of "rational" discourse, what constitutes evidence for justifying the rules?

Owing to its pedagogical interests and its corollary choice of an audience for its arguments, Argumentation has muddled the justification of dialectic with a different line of reasoning—that critical thinking is better than impulse. Since youthful actions are notoriously more glandular than cognitively driven, no one would doubt this claim—which is just my point. Ehninger and Brockriede (1978:2) say that "a critical decision is based on an interpretation of relevant facts and values." But impulse aside, I should think that every decision, be it good, silly, or evil, is based on interpretations of relevant facts and values. We disagree more about others' interpretations than about whether their decisions are based on nothing. No one would doubt that rule-guided action is better than impulse—but is this an important point for a field to make? With this reasoning, Argumentation will find itself in the position of the theorists who equate "rationality" with having reasons—any reasons being better than no reasons. But can we point to people who act without reasons? More likely, we want to object to their reasons, to say that their reasons are "causes" or that they are inferior to other reasons.

So the reasoning shifts course: critical decisions are communally rather than individually grounded. Thus Ehninger and Brockriede contrast "facts and values" with "desires and prejudices"—the former being intersubjectively confirmable, the latter idiosyncratic. But this does not help. First, as Stich and Nisbett (1984) say, we have to give the rebel his due. We do not want to say that everyone who disagrees with a well-founded consensus is uncritical or insane, though we might believe they are mistaken. Opposition is the dialectical counterpart to authority. Second, prejudices always masquerade as facts; one field's "values" are another's "dogmas." Third, impulse again aside, what would count as uncritical? A jihad? But holy wars are based on authoritative grounds—"rational" interpretations of facts and values intersubjectively confirmed (à la Stich and Nisbett) by a community.

So a celebration of having reasons whatever they are or of abiding by community norms whatever they are is not the point Argumentation wants to make. Pedagogy should suppress impulse, but a general theory of decision making poses more difficult problems. We often want to object to our opponents' reasons or methods—which brings us back to the rule utilitarian's problem of justifying conformity to a rule.

Ehninger and Brockriede ultimately take a pragmatic tack. But their pedagogical values make their argument more doctrinaire than it needs to be. Science is the ideal: "No scientific theory is accepted until it has been tested thoroughly." Now I do not think this claim is true—for, say, the Copernican Revolution, the general theory of relativity, or—perhaps most important—the Darwinian revolution, which was adopted, as Phillip Kitcher says, because of its ability to unite the field of biology, not because of its research, or even because it was correct (Darwin had odd genetic beliefs). It is not that science cannot be a paradigm case of critical decision making but that, owing to our choice of audience, we argue the point in such a way as to undercut it.

A different solution is to argue in a circle. Science is our most consistently successful epistemic enterprise, with dialectic as its basic veridical method; its success proves the value of dialectic: "Success is everywhere a valid—indeed the valid—criterion of methodological appropriateness. . . . There can be no real question that an established method—one which has 'proven itself' over a wide variety of applications within its range of correlative objectives—has solid claims to a presumption in its favor" (Rescher, 1977b). Whether debate has been science's method and whether it has "proven itself" are empirical questions. But Rescher's exposition only looks like an empirical argument. It uses no case-by-case proof of the centrality of debate to science—as opposed, say, to other accounts of scientific method, or as opposed to the research that suggests that debate is not quite what happens (Latour and Woolgar, 1979; Mitroff, 1974). We expect our logics of justification to be more formalized and housebroken than our logics of discovery, but a preference for critical over "uncritical" decisions presupposes success with empirical examples. The rule utilitarian's case is not lost, but it needs case histories.

The Jeffersonian legacy and the pedagogical imperatives in which it is embodied encourage a mechanical, overrationalized view of intellectual evolution. The developmental logic that spawns an idea must be rational before we are willing to call someone's acceptance of the idea rational—rather as if the logic of acceptance must be on a par with the logic of justification (or, horror of horrors, the logic of discovery). Since post hoc analyses can make historical succession seem like logical connection, it is permissible to speak of rational progress. Again Argumentation's choice of audience makes for whiggish claims. Accomplished doctrines on silver platters, today's truths must not be historical accidents or whims. Dialectical inquiry is our version of natural selection. If there is rationality in the structure of a corpus, its corpus dialecti is "rational" debate. But the proof of its rationality is circular.

Pedagogy yields a circumscribed view of decision making. It is uncontroversial that decisions occur in contexts governed by social effects as well as dialectical rules. But it is pedagogically convenient to think that the social aspects of decision making are pathological disintegrations, or at least imperfections, militating against otherwise rational debate. Though we might grant that science has social aspects, we resist seeing them as an integral part of scientific rationality. We likewise restrict our norms of political and social decision making to those features of debate that seem to transcend or bypass individual motives, the pressures of interest groups, vagaries of public opinion, and other manifestations of Burke's "blunt quest of advantage."

Summary

Argument is rational and "rational"—reflexive in Mead's sense and locally sound in communities. Arguments thus merit programmatic research to enhance our understanding of reflexive and conventional action. Their inquisitorial nature makes them unique social enterprises: their etiquette permits demands that character-istically call forth more public evidence about a person's inferences than is common in other interactions. One is more apt to be chal-lenged and thus more likely to anticipate an interlocutor's moves. Hence the political and epistemic importance of justification. Per-haps our justifications sometimes beg the question of how we get our claims. But the anticipation of justification affects how we get and present claims. Arguments are naturally occurring corollaries to research contexts. It's as if we stand back and watch while our subjects frame their hypotheses, select methodological principles appropriate to the hypotheses, use techniques appropriate to both, and conduct their own research act.

Chapter 12's discussion of the position notion capitalizes (as do many theories of decision making) on the seemingly unremarkable fact that arguers want to appear "rational." But *why* do people care about "rational" appearances? The answer developed here is that a hope to appear "rational" is of a piece with other conformities—a pivotal part of a person's identification with a group. "Rationalities" are thus components of the health and pathologies of public dis-courses and vital objects of research, analysis, and criticism. We hit snags only in defending local models as universals. The point is not to defend one model against all comers or to hope for the eventual triumph of a single commensurating system that can adjudicate all disputes. The better goal is to help each perform its task more ef-fectively.

Notes

1. "Nonjustificationist" rationality theories are cases in point. Consider Weimer's (1979:40) claim that "science is a comprehensively critical en-deavor; all its conjectures, including the most fundamental standards and basic positions are always and continually open to criticism. Nothing in science is immune to criticism or justified fideistically, by appeal to au-thority." I think this exaggerates science's immunity to authority appeals, but it illustrates the valuing at the base of Weimer's position: consider the opposite pole to the commitments imputed to science. Rationality is thus our way of valuing science.

2. I am using Mead's thinking selectively. His view of mind as emergent from social processes and his deterministic view of language are unconge-nial; nor do the reflexiveness and rationality constructs need these notions. Strict behaviorism would link social effectiveness to conditioning. But it seems implausible to say that one is rational by virtue of being environ-mentally determined.

8

Freedom

If severance from the Enlightenment proved beneficial to rationality, it is doubly so for freedom. Freedom is especially vulnerable to confusion and sloganizing—much too fragile a construct to thrive inside the individualism debate. The sources of this susceptibility merit a close look, for they weaken Argumentation's most important disciplinary rhetorics—its stances toward political freedom and institutional critique and toward argument as method. My first aim here is to explain how it has come about that these parallel rhetorics do not jibe.

My second aim is to defend the interactional theory as an alternative grounding for freedom. The theory, I believe, is a less toxic environment: it does not so individualize freedom that it contradicts the facts of communication or so corporatize it as to obscure personal responsibility. A focus on the functional interdependencies among people and groups implies that freedom is a feature of one's thinking developed, like other cognitive developments, through communication practices. Where the individualist sees freedom as a pregiven state (if negative freedom is assured, everyone will come to questions of positive freedom with more or less equal equipment), the interactional theory sees freedom as consisting of skills and competencies. The language of competencies, however, is a language of *discipline*, so the question at hand is whether the interactional theory successfully manages the tension between the rhetorics of discipline and of freedom.

The Genesis of a Muddle

Argument and freedom have enjoyed a long symbiosis, a kinship reinforced by each turn in the debate about freedom. Aristotle's view (perpetuated in the otherwise disparate works of Epicureans, Stoics, Augustine, Aquinas, Leibniz, and Locke) conceived of freedom as a suppression of tyrannical internal forces. Unchecked passions enslave us; rationality liberates us. Mill's emphasis on negative freedoms as preconditions of individualism cemented the link between argument and freedom. Thus Jefferson, Rousseau, Lippmann, and Habermas attack despotism for its hostility to dissent and critique. Positive freedom theories focus on one's power and ability to perform an act or class of acts—power being a composite of communication competencies and political and economic clout. Postmodernists define *coercion* by joining force, prohibitions, and sanctions to ideology and false consciousness, manipulative socialization, and propaganda (Habermas, 1973, 1975, 1984; Kelman, 1961), thus focusing on means that gain their effect by circumscribing consumers' knowledge. To conceal is to deprive; to deprive is to enslave.

So whether one is distressed by the tyranny of emotions, institutions, organizations, or governments, one may see argument and freedom joined in a benign circle—each the necessary condition of the other. Liberalism stresses that arguments yield freedom; institutional theories emphasize that arguments need freedom. The former stresses argument's liberating, critical functions; the latter prohibits epistemology-by-jackboot. Every opinion should have an equal chance in the marketplace of ideas: no guns, no censorship, and as much tolerance as possible.

This intellectual tapestry seems manageable at first. We have two clear-cut battle lines and a common ground between them—thesis, antithesis, synthesis. Locke and company are arrayed against Spinoza and company and transcended by the postmodern common ground built upon the concern for institutional critique. The middle ground gets the advantages, but not the flaws, of both extremes.

But compromises among flawed positions do not magically sum up to virtues. The three positions in the individualism debate in fact depend upon three mistakes: (1) *the Existentialist's Mistake*: exaggerated assimilation—imputing too much freedom to humans, exaggerating their aloneness, underestimating the effects of culture, society, milieu, and ideology and—proportionately—the accommodations people make to public codes; this mistake makes us think that social structures have constraining influences only on the weak-willed; (2) *the Hegelian Mistake*: exaggerated accommodation—

imputing too little freedom to humans, undervaluing their cognitive prospects, deliberative instruments, and social arrangements—assuming that actions are epiphenomena of social or organizational structure; and (3) *the Centrist's Mistake*: the postmodern attempt to walk a middle course between individualism and communalism.

We are prone to the *Existentialist's Mistake* when we endorse conformity to rules or, conversely, when we enjoin individuals to be reflective or skeptical about conventions. The former case is pedagogical, a matter of socialization: individualism is the pathology, rule-following the remedy. The latter case is epistemic and moral—an emphasis on individual responsibility for maintaining independence from social norms, beliefs, and conventions. Both positions exaggerate individual autonomy. The pedagogical rationale is sometimes stated as if argument rules are the only "rational" restraints on otherwise free spirits. The matter is a simple choice of behaving willy-nilly or of conforming to principles. Once socialized, people are, however implausibly, expected to be reflective not blind followers. This expectation stems from a preference for individual conscience over community consensus—an enduring metaphor in American literature, for escaping group delusions is what heroes do.

The *Hegelian Mistake* is tempting when we turn our attention to explanations of social and conceptual stability and structure. We underscore an obvious fact—that individualism flies in the face of the structure and stability we see in daily life—and mistakenly take that fact to sanction an existential determination of thought that makes individuals irrelevant to explanations of social processes. We see argument as the logic of a thought system playing itself out.

Both mistakes find their most extreme voices in combat with one another. One overpsychologizes action to refute claims that minds are epiphenomena of social systems. And PCT sometimes paints so individualistic a psychological picture as to preclude the possibility of communication. In weighing opposing positions, we feel the pull of the center—as if by taking the middle road we avoid the pitfalls of the extremes. Thus the *Centrist's Mistake* is tempting: one mixes diluted versions of both extremes to concoct a middle ground between individualism and institutional apologetics. The classic liberal of *On Liberty* is suited up to do battle with *The Organization Man*.

8.1. The Illusion of Middle Ground

The most prominent variation of the postmodern concern for institutional critique, the *reflective acquiescence* position (Chapter 6), asks individuals to conform only to institutions whose epistemic strategies are transparent to them (Connolly, 1987). Discipline and freedom are allies on this account, for reflectively accepted disciplines yield more flexible and better understood decisions. This position is prone to exaggeration and, because it is a middle ground in a flawed debate, a collapse to the individualist side. It puts the onus for critique on the person and thus needlessly reduces the potentiality of organizations for nurturing dissent to matters of individual insight. Three examples typify this middle course.

Connolly (1974) speaks of a person achieving a balance between private and public mandates. A person is "autonomous" insofar as the person's behavior "is informed by his own reflective assessment of his situation." The determinist's point that we are enclosed in systems that mold conduct and circumscribe our self-understanding does not preclude reflective critique and reconstruction: to reflectively assess the ways in which one is determined is to become freer. One "explores routes" to make one's assumptions and actions more open to reflective thinking and thereby to revision. Conventions and habits should cease to be forces acting upon one and become considerations one can accept or modify. "In Dewey's language, he encourages intelligent reflection to enter into the desires, projects, and practices he endorses. Knowing that the very concepts and beliefs he brings to a reconsideration of past habits reflect in part those habits themselves, he seeks to expose himself to alternative modes of classification in the interests of identifying new angles of vision from which he can view and evaluate his acquired habits" (1974:154–55).

Connolly sees the trap in this position, for he knows that the methods and ideas needed for critique do not come from thin air. "Internalization of socially received concepts, beliefs, and norms is a necessary precondition for critical reflection into any particular project or practice: The initial system of concepts and beliefs that help to define us provides the materials out of which we define and comprehend our setting. We must always accept some concepts and beliefs in order to isolate others for critical examination; we must therefore follow some practices unreflectively now so that the source and rationale of others can be considered reflectively" (1974:155).

This reasoning is familiar and plausible. One must suspend judgment on something in order to do anything. Everything is open to doubt in principle, but never in practice, for radical doubt freezes action. Argument principles require suspended judgment to make decision making possible. Similar claims are often made about scientific method. But this is a predicament not a solution. The only a priori measure for identifying constructs that merit suspended disbelief is their disciplinary status. Whether this is a vicious circle is a difficult question, for it is not susceptible to generalizations. Whether anyone (in any imaginable context) has suspended disbelief on just the tragically central assumption that should be doubted is a specific question which depends upon the argumentative conditions, the claims being made, and the positions being taken.

Bernstein (1976) similarly captures the tension between autonomy and social structure along with its political and critical implications. He holds out for the possibility of transforming institutions—a balancing act much like Connolly's. Intellectual criticism, Bernstein argues, may not be sufficient to yield fundamental change. Criticism and critical thinking are fallible; the pull of convention is powerful; social/political institutions resist transformation yet must be transformed to achieve freedom:

> We can recognize that there will be no significant movement toward emancipation unless there is a transformation of social and political practices and institutions. But we must also recognize that human beings are capable of bringing to consciousness the interpretations, evaluations, and standards that they tacitly accept, and can subject them to rational criticism. We are still vastly ignorant of the material conditions necessary for critique to play a role in the transformation of existing forms of social and political reality. But we do know—or ought to know—that if we fail to attempt the project of critique—if we do not seek a depth understanding of existing forms of social and political reality; if we are unwilling to engage in the type of argumentation required for evaluating the conflict of interpretations; if we do not strive to realize the conditions required for practical discourse—then we will surely become less than fully human. (1976:236)

Like Connolly, Bernstein (1983) seeks to institutionalize reflective thinking through a language of criticism.

The Connolly/Bernstein reasoning is reminiscent of Dewey's (1962:32) claim that the problem of constructing a new individualism consonant with the objective (mass, technical, pecuniary) conditions under which we live is "the deepest problem of our times." Appreciating the weaknesses of the Existentialist's Mistake and the Hegelian Mistake, Dewey takes the middle ground—defining the problem as one of formulating a revised individualism to supplant the pioneer individualism of simpler times. To account for the expanding importance of corporate and organizational structures in American life, Dewey proposes that "dominant corporateness" is the hard fact to which the new individualism must accommodate. The influence of organizations is both a cause and symptom of the American tendency to create social structures and to submerge the individual beneath corporate collectivism. "Associations tightly or loosely organized more and more define the opportunities the choices and the actions of individuals (1962:36). In face of this trend, "personal motives hardly count as productive causes in comparison with impersonal forces."

Dewey is neither nostalgic for frontier individualism nor enamored of corporate schemes of collectivist interdependence. Modernity has merely changed the conditions of individualism. The individualism it permits is a kind of insanity: lawlessness, reckless disregard for community, depression, and alienation become the only alternatives in the new corporate interdependence. Habermas (1981) similarly speaks of a "monetarized" (Dewey's influence) and "bureaucratized" (Weber's) outcome from the "colonization of the lifeworld"—by which he means the subordination of the individual to systemic imperatives.

The Existentialist's Mistake and the Hegelian Mistake are not opposite poles on a continuum that contrasts the individual *as given* against social structure *as given*. Dewey sees this contrast as a quaint throwback to a simpler age. It is as mistaken to see individuals as isolated, independent givens as it is to see social structure as impersonal. Following Mead, Dewey equates groups with the ongoing interactions of their members. He sees social structure as consisting in the relations among actors in a group, organization, or society: "And all relations are interactions, not fixed molds. The particular interactions that compose a human society include the give and take of participation, of a sharing that increases, that expands and deepens, the capacity and significance of the interacting factors" (1962, 85). Conformity is an absence of this interplay: "the arrest and benumbing of communication." Thus in denouncing the corporatism of American life, Dewey insists that the corporate organizational mentality is a two-way street: people build it; people buy into it; people can reconstruct it.

Inside the individualism debate, the Connolly/Bernstein/Dewey position is not a middle course but a robust individualism. The goal is a *psychological* freedom that sees through systematically distorted communication and nurtures reflective thinking, dissent, and (thus) critique. Institutional critique aims to expose the organizational features that promote curiosity, reflection, and innovation, but the onus for the search is on the person. The individual chooses among constraints and practices, suspends judgment here to achieve action there, achieves intellectual breakthroughs and advances, circumvents local deadlocks by jettisoning a rule and borrowing another in a manner the community has not thought of. In other words, to explain dissent and intellectual change, we personalize them in a way that pits the individual against the prevailing community. In this way, Barber (1952) establishes as one of science's fundamental norms *individualism*—a "moral preference" for the individual conscience over community authority. Weigh this presumption against Stich and Nisbett's (1984:237) claim that deference to authority is "generally, the right thing to do." The middle ground between these presumptions is not a happy place, so the focus on personal attributes gravitates toward the individualism side.

8.2. The Rhetoric of Discipline Does Not Square with the Rhetoric of Freedom

The idea that the middle ground of a flawed debate muddles otherwise sound proposals has a parallel within Argumentation which further illustrates the influence of individualism. There is a discrepancy between two broad rhetorical postures common to Argumentation—a tension between the two faces of freedom and conventional claims about argument as disciplined discourse. This incongruity is easily overlooked, for it arises in two separate rhetorics.

The rhetoric of freedom is a pivotal feature of the postmodern position. As a social comparison process, argument is a paradigm case of critique. Since critique is an enabling condition of freedom, and political freedom is needed to yield intellectual freedom, argument is an archetypal democratic process. This confederation makes freedom central to Argumentation's disciplinary rationale. We have only to ask why argument interests us to find freedom in the answer. In claiming that arguments yield better decisions and sound criticism, we assume that arguers could proceed in presumptively less acceptable ways. Situations present choices; choices make for disputes; disputes pose further choices. The balancing of such choices is definitive of human action. Speculations on argument thus acquire importance because they contribute to our self-portrait as a species.

This fusion of freedom and argument is institutionalized in Argumentation's pedagogy. Our textbook rhetoric (rooted as much in Greek and Enlightenment thought as in the Frankfort School) makes Argumentation a guardian of freedom, a discipline vested with curatorship of democratic processes. On this view, argument is a guarantor and a litmus test of freedom—the two ideas being so tightly joined as to be procedurally equated. These twin rhetorical stances— the postmodern and the classical—combine to make argument the paradigm case of freedom.

Another strain of thought within Argumentation paints a different picture. A rhetoric of method and discipline suggests that argument is not the paradigm case of freedom. This rhetoric is partly based upon empirical evidence which, as we saw, describes informal arguments of naive actors as rule bound and constrained by the demands of interlocutors. The existence of opposition calls the *tu quoque* possibility into play. And formality is a matter of degree, so comparatively formal arguments are bound by comparatively more explicit argumentation rules.

Coinciding with this empirical picture is the discipline's cautionary rhetoric, drawn largely from Plato's picture of human frailty. People left to their own devices are vague, idiosyncratic, intuitive, lazy, and impulsive, swayed this way and that by their attitudes, prejudices, and pieties. Their choices are not decisions, but dumb brute lunges at narrow self-interest. Argumentation plays the domitrix. It *binds* and *disciplines*. It *subjects* ideas to standards. It *restrains* or *inhibits* impulses. It *systematizes* vague preferences, proposes procedural *rules*, and *institutionalizes* and brings *order* and *coherence* to what might otherwise be random, untutored, and ineffectual. This terminology of bondage presupposes a human nature, a force to be suppressed, an unshackled brute: civilization and its discontents. Argument theory seeks to bind discourse, to *constrain*, *check*, and *correct*. The language of discipline is thus a language of precision and stringency. As Foucault says, "discipline" means "discipline."

So we wrap ourselves in a rhetoric of freedom to lend dignity and worth to our subject, yet there are senses of *freedom* that, as a matter of disciplinary purpose, we seek to suppress. A theory of argument celebrates discipline. As Foucault (1972) predicts, our fascination with discipline inclines us to see disciplines as exemplary epistemic communities.

8.3. The Reflective Acquiescence Rejoinder—Again

Perhaps the reader is not much impressed by this incongruity, for a reply seems readily at hand. Accepting disciplinary constraints is reflective acquiescence. Argument rules are in principle open to critique; constraints reflectively conceived can be reflectively accepted. Thus intellectual discipline is a modest sacrifice for political freedom.

This reasoning is a bit glib, for there are no reasons to suppose that Argumentation escapes in microcosm the flaws of the broader individualism debate. The need to suspend disbelief applies with special force to argument principles, for procedure is often what people in real contexts least want to debate. Rules may be open in principle but not in practice once events gain momentum. And argument principles operate within other disciplines whose principles may have the same halfhearted openness to critique. Whatever their commitments to reflective revision, communities retain the prerogative of rule enforcement. No discipline would concede that novices can take or leave its rules. To open ourselves to critique, as comprehensively critical rationalism (Weimer, 1979) enjoins us to do, does not oblige us to abandon any particular rule or to refrain from enforcing it as long as it stands.

The reasoning behind the rational acquiescence rejoinder might hold that "statements about freedom involve judgments about responsibility." To point to something that constrains us is to state (or imply that one could state) a grievance against those responsible for it (Connolly, 1974:116). Argument rules are open to grievances because they are contrivances rather than natural limits on our abilities. If you are blind, it is wrong to say that your blindness is a constraint on your freedom though it is certainly a constraint on your abilities. But if I blind you, we construe your blindness differently: *I* have done something for which you hold me responsible (Connolly, 1974). We assume that "constraints" are intentional creations (Oppenheim, 1961; Berlin, 1958; Scott, 1970) and that they thereby differ in kind from social forces, folkways, ideologies, mores, and prejudices—these being on a par with being blind through no human agency (Connolly, 1974:162). So we balk at seeing Argumentation as an enemy of freedom: its principles are open to critique—vulnerable to grievances.

This objection only seems plausible; and it involves more than a little arm-waving. For one thing, constructivists do not concede that folkways, ideologies, mores, and prejudices are on a par with being blind through no human agency. Being good individualists, they notice that people are not uniformly slaves to their histories because they are not equally reflective—no Hegelian mistake here. Being good developmentalists, they need not exempt their ancestors from the responsibilities they assume for themselves vis-à-vis their progeny. The distinction, then, between constraints for which we might enter grievances and those for which we cannot, seems contrived.

The same reasoning applies to Habermas's ideal of reflective acquiescence to rules whose operations and assumptions are transparent. As I argued in Chapter 6, it is easy to exaggerate our reflective possibilities: artifice cannot always be distinguished from accident. Consider the question of when or in what circumstances it is "rational" to accept a discipline's knowledge *as* knowledge. Even staunch individualists concede that one's social inheritance figures in the decisions even of reflective persons. One cannot play the continual skeptic: some things must be taken for granted or bracketed. Reflective thinking may thus be a muddled mixture of tradition and critical intentions.

Communities are less immune to this muddle of received wisdom and reflection than individuals, for they have a vested interest in promoting conformity. They perpetuate themselves by strengthening their traditions and conventions. Their histories are reservoirs of stability, reserves to be drawn upon to maintain the status quo. Thus Toulmin's (1972) jurisprudential case law analogy for explaining intellectual change needs a further principle to explain how one transcends case law. The conservative presumption advocates reliance on precedent (Goodnight, 1980) unless conventional wisdom is overturned by an advocate who discharges a burden of proof. But the conservative presumption is not a rationale for piety. One cannot *assume* that one's heritage is a logical production. Fuller (1986) argues that consensus formation may be an accidental phenomenon, "the result of a statistical drift in allegiances, in which the reasons invoked by the individual scientists may have little to do with each other." The point is not that every intellectual inheritance is on a par with social forces, mores, and ideologies but that "rational progress" cannot be *assumed* to be independent of "mere sociology." If *we* cannot distinguish artifice from accident, how can we suppose our ancestors could? *We* make do with temporary expediencies, dubious shortcuts, and enabling assumptions whose defects we bracket, then forget. Why, short of turning Darwin on his head, should we assume any better of our predecessors?

Moreover, the very idea of reflective acquiescence presupposes a metamorphosis of youthful acquiescence into mature reflectiveness that cannot be left vague. The young are expected to accept rules on authority yet later on to achieve reflective acquiescence, the radical unmasking and reconstruction of epistemic grounds. But where does this postmodern butterfly come from? Its cocoon is surely not a discipline, for the purpose of disciplinary life is to get better at disciplinary affairs. If these affairs do not coincide with the needs of critique—the whole point of the critique of modernity is that they rarely do—then Habermas is asking more than the impossible from individuals.

So it won't do to assume that a person's entrance into and perseverance in a discipline automatically qualifies as (or equips one for or predisposes one to) reflective acquiescence. The very idea of "discipline" cuts against reflective acquiescence. The language of discipline is a language of dominion and jurisdiction, of rules, roles, and restraints, and of expertise and specialism. Free spirits need not apply.

8.4. The Rhetoric of Discipline versus the Rhetoric of Political Freedom

Readers sympathetic to counterfactual proposals may be impatient with my reasoning till now and may suspect that I am being willfully obtuse in ignoring solutions to modernity: universal audiences, impartial standpoints of rationality, or Habermasian discourse—all designed to nurture critique. What follows is by no means a full-dress critique of such counterfactuals, but I do think that even the most robust of these proposals is vulnerable to the dissonance between our rhetorics of discipline and of freedom.

Consider Habermas's assumption that discourse—understood as a counterfactual ideal speech situation—is characterized by freedom. When ideal schemes are not merely utopian, their schemers are not completely free to specify just any conditions. Rawls has to keep his original position consistent with his views of rationality and contractarianism. Toulmin's impartial standpoint of rationality must square with his populational account of intellectual growth. And Habermas must assume that Discourse is a possibility presupposed by speech acts seeking understanding. Given the importance of systematically distorted communication in this diagnosis, freedom becomes the pivotal counterfactual.

But it does not follow that redemption through discourse requires *free* discourse. Speech is indexical, so utterances may and should refer to disciplined knowledge as standing behind, vouching for, or authorizing them. It is unremarkable if *A* asks us to accept *X* because *X* comports with a discipline's body of knowledge and conventional methods. So Habermasian discourse requires a sense of disciplined freedom which works against the effects of particular disciplines. This reasoning can be fleshed out by following Habermas's line of thinking.

Habermas is not afraid that the center will not hold but that the center does not exist. Pluralism is an empirical fact. But the case for relativism is inconclusive if one distinguishes between the *psychology* and the *logic* of argument (think: *substance versus form*). Sociological analyses—which show that a particular group at a given time had thus and so beliefs—do not foreclose an abstract analysis of the universal felicity conditions of discourse. There should be a coexistence between empirical analyses of how argument fits into existing normative contexts, going epistemic orders, and the analysis of validity claims which transcend social particularities but which are presupposed in the formal activities of all fields of discourse (Burleson, 1979b; Wenzel, 1980, 1985).

Like Piaget, Habermas joins objectivity, rationality, and knowledge. Objectivity is tied to the publicness of expression; rationality has to do with "how speaking and acting subjects *acquire and use knowledge*" (Habermas, 1984:8). "The rationality of an expression depends on the reliability of the knowledge embodied in it"—which means that we base the rationality of an expression on its susceptibility to criticism and grounding: "An expression satisfies the precondition for rationality if and insofar as it embodies fallible knowledge and therewith has a relation to the objective world (that is, a relation to the facts) and is open to objective judgment. A judgment can be objective if it is undertaken on the basis of a *transsubjective* validity claim that has the same meaning for observers and nonparticipants as it does for the acting subject himself" (Habermas, 1984:9). Utterance thus takes its "rationality" from its fit with the veridical and judgmental standards of going epistemic orders. So far, so Popperian. Claims must be fallible and intersubjective.

But if practices authorize claims, what stands behind practices? What vouches for them beyond the bare fact that they exist? Certainly not a substantive claim if it is to defeat relativity. Enter the ideal speech situation: "The general symmetry conditions that every competent speaker must presuppose are sufficiently satisfied insofar as he intends to enter into argumentation at all" (Habermas, 1984:25).

His critique of Klein is instructive. Argumentation, for Klein, is a process of transforming something collectively invalid into something collectively valid by assessing its fit with a collectivity's trusted ideas. By "collectively valid" Klein, through Habermas, means "only those views that are actually shared by specific groups at specific times; he screens out all internal relations between what is *de facto* accepted as valid and what should have validity in the sense of a claim transcending local, temporal, and social limitations: 'The *valid* and the *questionable* are thus relative to persons and times'" (Habermas, 1984:28). "In restricting 'what is collectively valid' to the convictions that are actually expressed and accepted at a given time and place, Klein puts forward a description of argumentation that foreshortens attempts to convince by an essential dimension" (Habermas, 1984:28). Klein, like Toulmin in this regard, seeks a kind of *consensus gentium*: "I believe that in the systematic analysis of actual argumentation—as in every *empirical analysis*— relatively fixed *regularities* can be found, according to which people argue: precisely the logic of argumentation. And I believe ... that this concept covers much of what is usually understood by the 'rationality of argumentation' " (Klein, 1980:49–50). But this consensualism forecloses the possibility of considering a claim's possibilities of redemption through discourse: "Paradoxical consequences of this kind arise from the attempt to sketch the logic of argumentation *exclusively* from the perspective of the flow of communication processes and to avoid also analyzing consensus-forming processes from the start as the achievement of rationally motivated agreement and as the discursive redemption of validity claims" (1984:30). Habermas does not object to empirical studies of argumentation practices; nor does he foreclose the *consensus gentium* Klein hopes for. "But it does not follow at all from this that we have to renounce concepts of validity analogous to truth, to expunge every counterfactual moment from the concept of validity and to equate validity with context dependent acceptability." Thus, "For me the advantage of Toulmin's approach lies precisely in the fact that he allows for a plurality of validity claims while not denying the critical sense of a validity transcending spatio-temporal and social limitations" (1984:31).

One way of writing Habermas off is to agree with him. The ideal speech situation is counterfactual, but it would be good if everyone accepted it. Our reach should exceed our grasp or what's a metaphor? Discourse is thus an ideal fields should strive for. The core contradiction of capitalism is the private appropriation of public wealth which, at the level of discourse, manifests itself as a suppression of a generalizable interest by particular interests. We cannot achieve rational consensus on public decisions because the public interest has been co-opted by particular communities. So it is a worthy goal to cut through the legitimations of particular domains, to help them transcend their systematically distorted communication not only by exposing their ideologies but by giving them a successor: an original position, an impartial standpoint of rationality, or a redemptive discourse.

We are, in sum, precisely where Connolly, Bernstein, and Dewey left us. And with an added problem, for to see discourse as a normative goal is to radically devalue it. I do not see how a thoroughly socialized academic, steeped in the epistemic folkways and values of a discipline, can say—and mean it—that the counterfactual conditions of discourse are ideals toward which a discipline should strive. The *generalization*, that is, cannot be accepted sincerely. If conflicts between the demands of discipline and discourse arise, they will be concrete matters to be hashed out on the spot. Disciplinary actors might adopt a universal perspective for concrete cases yet hesitate to commit themselves in the abstract (except as an empty posture) to abandon their disciplines. Except, perhaps, for the unction of the advocate, there is no difference between asking disciplinary actors to accept a universal and asking them to accept any other outside idea. Peripheral discourse (Chapters 9 and 11) works best when it starts with concrete cases.

Habermas conceives of freedom in a familiar way: negative freedoms free us from external constraints; these freedoms are necessary preconditions of positive freedom, which frees us for morality and autonomy. But what is a discipline but a system of constraints, rules, regulations, and recipes to guide action? The *point* of disciplines is discipline; their peculiar strength is their ability to foster programmatic work, to nourish scholarship, and to codify knowledge. These merits are tied to mundane bureaucratic functions—the most indispensable being licensing, accreditation, and the bureaucratized assessment of merit. Disciplines, after all, are animated by their practices, the customs, rituals, and folkways that tend, on the whole, to yield certain outcomes. They require socialization; novices gradually acquire credentials for speaking by passing successive tests. They pass Piagetian-like developmental stages toward full enfranchisement. So no discipline could thrive on an egalitarian distribution of the opportunity to speak. Physicists do not attend lectures on cosmology by sophomores; nor do they entertain willingly incursions from other fields. A Ph.D. in Physics or Philosophy is a license to talk physics or philosophy. Too, not all fully enfranchised disciplinary actors are equal, and properly so. Disciplines reserve the prerogative of plebiscitary judgments. Professor Jones is not the intellectual equal of Smith. Smith should get a fuller hearing than Jones because there is a qualitative difference in their work. No discipline would surrender this prerogative.

So to acknowledge the universal is to devalue the particular, unless the acknowledgement is empty. Seeing Habermas's felicity conditions as norms toward which disciplines should strive is empty rhetoric—a way of not taking discourse seriously. When one's horizon of understanding is rooted in a discipline, one can pay lip service to counterfactual norms but turn to one's discipline for actual practices. Or worse, one may acknowledge universal standards yet *take for granted* that one's discipline meets them. Otherwise, to take Habermas's felicity conditions seriously is to establish a liberal presumption (Goodnight, 1980). One stands ready *in principle* to modify or abandon one's discipline.

It might be objected that the supposed tension between ideals of discourse and discipline trades on a pious attitude toward disciplines. One can concede that discipline means discipline but add (as

Foucault and Goodnight would) that disciplines exemplify the erosion of freedom—the expansion of technical control central to the diagnosis of the crisis of modernity. This objection can take two paths: one reader may see it as a call for a Foucaldian subversion; another may see it as a check on an exaggeration. The former reader sees my position here as a straw man; the latter sees it as a failure to appreciate the world's elitist structure, a naive rebuke of the disciplines' lack of general suffrage.

Neither version is right. I favor appreciating the *ambiguity* of discipline (Chapter 9). Disciplines are indispensable yet coercive. They are conventional yet dependent on opposition for epistemic health. This does not play into the jaws of a Foucaldian trap because the interactional theory implies that intellectual stability and change do not always depend on the same people (Chapter 9). The Foucauldian misses the importance of peripheral discourses and the degree to which opposition is imperative to healthy disciplinary life. The latter version of the objection is mistaken if nothing in the interactional theory contradicts elitist or pluralistic elitist claims. One need not genuflect to disciplines, or any particular discipline, to appreciate the tension between Habermas's ideal of a discourse immunized against constraint and the fact that disciplines are founded on constraints.

The Interactional Theory

So our intuitions, feelings, and disciplinary rhetorics about freedom and about discipline do not coincide. The language of individualism has stymied the postmodern program by leaving the idea of critique mysterious. Critique seems to work best as an empty slogan or gesture, for it ultimately requires discipline. Left inside the discourse on individualism, the advocate of critique will have to slug it out, case by concrete case.

Perhaps a change in scenery will help. The Connolly/Bernstein/Dewey position does not *need* to be an individualism: it is the bad neighborhood, not the logic of the position, that leads to the overpersonalizing of critique. The position might be strengthened by a view of dissent as a social, coordinated enterprise. We can still speak of freedom as a cognitive option (8.5 below) and of skepticism as a personal stance. But the translation of personal attributes into effective dissent involves the creation and maintenance of positions (Chapter 12), coalition formation, the creation of subfields, and ongoing disputes with insiders and outsiders (Blume, 1974; Hagstrom, 1965). The language of psychology gives way to the languages of group and organizational communication, social movements, and of positioning.

This shift in thinking does not denigrate leadership. Nor does it imply that rogue intellectuals do not occasionally dissent alone. Its effect, rather, is to enlarge the cast of characters, for solitary dissenters must attract followers. One practical difference between a dissenter and a crackpot, I should think, lies in the size of their following. To put the onus for critique on individuals is to ignore the complex, often divided and subdivided, nature of epistemic communities. The interactional theory focuses on the functional interdependencies among people and groups and thus puts the responsibility for critique on dissident groups, not lone wolves. Copernicus and Lavoisier are exemplars of a bygone era—not ideal types appropriate to current science. The Copenhagen *group* is a better model, for it was much like a debating society (Pagels, 1982) that got "into the spirit of the quantum theory" (Heisenberg, 1952) by ceasing to think in Newtonian terms.

The reader who remains skeptical about the case against individualism may see this claim as a triviality. Having conceded that Connolly, Bernstein, Dewey, and Habermas might easily adopt the interactionist position, am I merely proposing a minor repair of the individualism debate?

The answer lies in the interactional theory's picture of communication—which emphasizes *social comparison, development* and *differences*. Social comparison means that though freedom is a feature of one's thinking, it is a social achievement. Skills and competencies are acquired developmentally, so people possess them as a matter of degree. This means, as Dewey says, the individual is not a given but an achievement. Since competencies are necessary conditions of freedom, freedom is not a given: everyone would *not* be equally free in the absence of legal constraints. It might seem possible to regulate communication but not thought, as though thought is a fixed entity given in equal measure to all. But this distinction ignores developmental differences and understates the degree to which thought is given content and channelized by the working agreements (and, to be sure, the systematic distortions) of public communication.

Assumptions about development and differences also apply to disciplines. Differences in subject matter and purpose aside, epistemic disciplines are not equally mature, stable, cohesive, or deterministic. Some may follow a theory of knowledge that defines epistemic betterment as the successive elaboration of a thought system. "Getting better" means becoming progressively more certain. The quirk in such views is that intellectual progress authorizes increasing closed-mindedness: the immature disciplines are more obliged than their superiors to be open to critique. Here we have the crisis of modernity in its clearest form, for local perfections do not just co-opt public and universal discourses, they delegitimize them.

Success in epistemic disciplines need not be equated with increasing certainty. It is more in keeping with the interactional theory to see a group's epistemic success as involving greater flexibility, adaptability, and cognizance of the interconnections among claims and (thus) of alternative modes of inquiry. If it is a personal virtue to see ourselves as belief-forming processes, this attitude (on the interactionist view) becomes a group virtue par excellence.

The sole claim here is that groups may mimic the virtues of their members, for both public and private virtues are open to deliberation, assessment, and critique. This does not imply that groups are individuals writ large, for group dynamics are not equivalent to individual psychology and public positions are derived from agreements that may or may not reflect any person's psychological perspective. Nor, for the same reasons, are individuals seen as groups writ small. The interactional theory stresses that argument is a public activity dependent upon the reciprocal constraints, inhibitions, and channelizations—we might well call them public virtues—that arguers agree to as they function as language users, players in a conversational game, and, in general, as they exercise their membership in fields of discourse. These fields are expected to differ fundamentally in purpose, cohesiveness, modes of participation, openness, and determinism.

8.5. Freedom and Determinism as Cognitive Options

Inside the view of communication defended here, I want to say that freedom and determinism are largely cognitive options. Notice that inside a communication theory, the reply to my claim is *not* to defend groups as being more powerful than individuals, for the two claims are but different links in the same chain of reasoning. We know by experience that humans vary in their orientations to groups—ranging from glum passivity, sheeplike conformity, or mindless fanaticism to reflective acquiescence, critique, and dissent. Obviously, then—with an enormous variation in degree—to speak of freedom is to speak of personal skills, competencies, motives, and thus of responsibilities. Social entities, conversely, vary in their demands on their members. I may be a true believer in the Flat Earth Society but a rather skeptical and tentative member of the Democratic party.

The reasoning behind my claim that freedom and determinism are largely a cognitive option turns upon a psychology. PCT, as Kelly frames it, is an individualistic theory. It says that public actions flow from subjective understandings. Public choices *reflect* cognitive processes. This is why PCT is better seen as a component of a communication theory. Communication is not solely expressive; it does not require common ground built from accurate representations of speakers' thoughts. It requires only working agreements. Moreover, fitted to the idea of social comparison, PCT's claims acquire an interesting ambiguity, for some of them might easily apply to groups. As Connolly might say, this is an ambiguity to be respected, for it is in some cases plausible to speak of groups as being dogmatic, closed-minded, or prejudiced. This is not a claim of self-similarity, for we almost never speak of people as risky shifting, dividing into subgroups, as lynch persons, as having facilitation effects, or suffering groupthink. I imagine most of those things would be hard to do alone—or at least, like sex and conversation, better done with others.

THE PRINCIPLE OF ELABORATIVE CHOICE.   Kelly (1955) says that people construe events so as to enhance their understanding of them. We select interpretations that enhance our cognitive system: "Whenever a person is confronted with the opportunity for making a choice, he will tend to make that choice in favor of the alternative which seems to provide the best basis for anticipating the ensuing events" (Kelly, 1955:64). This is why Hamlet chose a problematic, unappealing life over the unknown terrors of death: "Whatever the breadth of his viewpoint, it is our assumption that man makes his choice in such a fashion as to enhance his anticipations. If he constricts his field of vision, he can turn his attention toward the clear definition of his system of constructs. If he is willing to tolerate some day-to-day uncertainties, he may broaden his field of vision, and thus hope to extend the predictive range of the system" (1955:65). So either choice—constricted certainty or broadened understanding—may elaborate the person's cognitive system.

In deciding to believe or do something, our thinking is informed, indeed made possible, by the ways our constructs proportion our world, the ways we feel free to move among cognitive options. Constructs are the reference axes by which we make sense of phenomena, the patterns or templates we create to fit over events. Since experience resides in the ways we systematize our past interpretations, our constructs are arranged hierarchically. They form, Kelly says, two-way streets along which one may travel to reach conclusions. In arranging constructs, we are "binding sets of events into convenient bundles which are handy for the person who has to lug them. Events, so bound, become predictable, manageable, and controlled" (1955:126).

The Principle of Elaborative Choice seems similar to Aristotle's claim that "all men by nature desire to know," but Kelly's is a more complex picture. Aristotle envisioned a curious intellect seeking first causes and essences, an intelligence seeking certainty by virtue of a native entelechy. Kelly, conversely, envisions an intellect that might decide to restrict its field of vision rather than extend it. Aristotle's claim is thus partly false on the PCT account. *Not* knowing might be as or more attractive.

EXPLANATION IS A FORM OF DOMINATION. Theories, Kelly says, "are the thinking of men who seek freedom amid swirling events. The theories comprise prior assumptions about certain realms of these events. To the extent that these events may, from these prior assumptions, be construed, predicted, and their relative courses charted, men may exercise control and gain freedom for themselves in the process" (1955:21). For Kelly, this idea has clinical implications. The clinician must understand the parameters of freedom a patient defines for himself to understand the anxiety the patient would experience if the cognitive system were threatened:

A construct is threatening when it is itself an element in a next higher-order construct which is, in turn, incompatible with other higher order constructs upon which a person is dependent. . . . Death, of course, is incompatible with living, at least in the minds of most people. There are people, however, who do not see death and life as incompatible. One may see death as an entrance to a phase of life beyond the River Styx . . . [or] as a vestibule through which transmigration of the soul takes place. If death is incompatible with the construction system . . . then the like elements in the context of death are threats. (1955:166)

We may wonder why fanatics appear not to find death threatening while their victims often do, why some social systems are able to encourage their populations toward martyrdom while others look aghast at, say, Iran's fountain of blood, Jonestown, or Masada. PCT draws our attention to the shape of cognitive systems for which death jeopardizes fewer elements than a dishonorable life. It also highlights the less dramatic reasons why we cling to old ideas in the face of new ones: "One maintains his construct system by clarifying it. . . . This means, among other things, that one controls his system by maintaining a clear identification of the elements which the system excludes as well as those which it includes. The moment one finds himself becoming involved in any way with the excluded elements, . . . he becomes aware of the onset of incompatibility and sees these new clutching associations as threats. Like a wounded animal, he faces his enemy" (1955:167).

Our open-mindedness, in sum, is proportional to our confidence. We fear ideas that jeopardize favored interpretations; we interpret events in such a way as to perpetuate our present interpretations; and we embrace ideas that seem to strengthen our favored cognitive ways.

A theory binds or determines the events subordinated to it: "It is not determined by the events themselves; it is determined by the superordinating point of view of the theorist. Yet it must conform to events in order to predict them" (1955:19). Behavior is thus experimental: one's constructs must conform to events. The assumption here is that the person evolves hierarchically arranged construct systems. Constructs can be ordinally related because one construct can subsume another as one of its elements either by extending the cleavage intended by the other or by abstracting across the other's cleavage line: "The construct *good vs. bad* may subsume, respectively, among other things, the two ends of the *intelligent-stupid* dimension. In this sense, 'good' would include all "intelligent" things plus some things which fall outside the range of convenience of the *intelligent vs. stupid* construct. 'Bad' would include all the 'stupid' things plus some others which are neither 'intelligent' or 'stupid.'" (1955:57). Kelly's example of abstracting across the *intelligent vs. stupid* cleavage line is an *evaluative vs. descriptive* construct. The *intelligent vs. stupid* construct is subsumed as a dimension, identified as evaluative and thus contrasted with "descriptive" constructs. In this way constructs are systematized hierarchically as we order our experience. These hierarchies may be more or less complex depending in part upon the construed importance of the events which fall within the system's range of convenience.

So determinism is the control of a superordinate construct over its elements. We are liberated from the domination of circumstances to the extent that we are able to construe them. Or we enslave ourselves with our own ideas: "Since determinism characterizes the control that a construct exercises over its subordinate elements, freedom characterizes its independence of those elements. Determinism and freedom are then inseparable, for that which determines another is, by the same token, free of the other. Determinism and freedom are opposite sides of the same coin—two aspects of the same relationship" (1955:21).

However cogent the objections to self-similarity may be, people often see thought systems as analogous to a person's cognitive system. Hence the freedom and determinism of disciplined knowledge: the truth shall make us free. But this parallel does not hold up. Social knowledge depends upon negotiated agreements and compromises. Where we attribute cognitive dissonance to a person who holds incompatible beliefs, we would not say the same of groups, for disagreements become apparent in the clash of positions and are not on a par with a contradiction held by an individual. And while bodies of knowledge can be and are regarded as systems, they are not psychological systems (Chapter 9). The interactional theory, for instance, suggests that no matter how holistically we view cognitive systems (and we have reviewed reasons for doubting Quine's holism), its public cousin differs in kind. Holism is a *tactic*, a way of curating positions. It is an attitude some advocates have about their positions vis-à-vis the rest of the world.[1]

8.6. The Determinism of the Taken-for-Granted

Poincare says that the most dangerous hypotheses are the tacit, unconscious ones: "Because we make them without knowing it, we are unable to abandon them" (1952:151). Kelly puts it that unexamined assumptions are hostages we give to fortune. We set the measures of our own freedom or determination by the level at which we establish our convictions. If we base our lives on inflexible convictions about temporary matters, we become victims of circumstances. But if we are reflective about our points of view, "if our prior convictions are cast into principles rather than rigid rules, we will be more able and apt to choose alternatives that lead to personal freedom" (Kelly, 1955:21–22). Thus, Dewey says, freedom "consists in a trend of conduct that causes choices to be more diversified and flexible, more plastic and cognizant of their own meaning, while it enlarges the range of their unimpeded operation" (1960:280).

These claims by a mathematician, a psychologist, and a philosopher place an increasing emphasis on the social—Dewey being the most sociological, for he advocates a "jealous and unremitting care for the influence of social institutions upon the attitudes of curiosity, inquiry, weighing, and testing of ideas" (1960:286). This is a plausible position if we find it easy to imagine that groups, in various ways, may help and hinder curiosity and inquiry. There is irony in this, for Dewey is defending much the same position as Foucault: social institutions hinder us by relegating assumptions to the background, yet, ironically, this implicitizing effect is also among the chief benefits of social life. We cannot keep everything in mind at once, so other people perform a valuable reassurance function: they confirm the tacit, underwrite the implicit, reinforce normalcy, and otherwise confirm that certain assumptions need not be opened to question. They keep our skeptical workload manageable, for normalcy validates the unsaid. This irony is not a problem to be defeated so much as a permanent tension between the needs to act and to assume. Since this tension cuts across numberless contexts and subjects, it explains the variations we find in life—the "splendid local adaptations" as Gould says.

Our ordering and arranging of our own freedom is arguably the most interesting and revealing thing we do. Our subjugation by a despotic government might be lamentable, but not especially interesting as a picture of human nature. The more intriguing phenomenon is our self-imposed limits, the conceptions we have of ourselves and our world that lead us to freedom or bondage. This is why the views of Fromm, Orwell, and Shaw are more interesting than that of Aldous Huxley. Huxley takes behaviorism seriously. His work is a passionate brief against mind control, but it exaggerates the power of conditioning and proportionately underestimates our ability to resist outside control. Fromm had the deeper terror that people escape from freedom, that they surrender their autonomy, because they cannot bear its responsibilities. Choices foreclosed are evil; choices foregone are tragic.

Orwell and Shaw remind us not to underestimate the power of greed, stupidity, and cowardice. Theirs is a picture much like Thoreau's. Our surrender to the polity resembles a mindlessness, not the mindlessness of the fanatic but of the automaton, the toy soldiers marching in file. Behold the marine, said Thoreau, such a *thing* as governments make. Shaw and Kelly would reply: behold a thing who was once a person. The straitjacketed, crippling conventions and delimiting etiquettes of societies are as comforting as they are despotic. Freedom can seem like a kind of suicide. Hamlet's soliloquy thus resembles Big Brother's reassurances: better to stay with the evils we know than to fly to troubles we know not of. As Pogo says, "We have met the enemy, and he is us."

8.7. Elitism and the Ideology of Involvement

This rationale for reflective thinking is a familiar and, as far as I know, uncontroversial position. But it is an easily confused idea. Argumentation theorists who do not see the effects of individualism on their work are likely to muddle the rationale in two ways. They may tie it to a preference for political activism, an ideology of involvement which equates the surrender of personal freedom with estrangement from political life. And they may interpret reflective thinking within the context of exaggerated claims about "rational" acquiescence. They are prone to these mistakes because they are accustomed to singularizing the question of the individual's relation to society. They thus see the difference between a person's relations to specific groups and to mass society as principally a matter of scale. The interactional theory predicts that one's relations even to particular groups may differ in kind.

The debate about elitism, pluralism, and "democratic elitism" (Bachrach, 1966) never spilled over into the disciplines concerned with argument and critical thinking. The pedagogical rationale of these disciplines is couched in the language of mass democracy: in a free society, "decisions are based on the *consent* of the governed. The rational process of decision-making should be operant among the public if the public is to fulfill its role responsibly" (Smith and Hunsaker, 1972:12–13). Argumentation principles are thus remedies of nonreason in mass democracy (Eisenberg and Ilardo, 1980; Olshewsky, 1983).

These theorists are not confined to the mass democratic position. Their theories do not *entail* nonelitist rationales. One might easily take the position that argument theories are elite language games. The masses are apathetic, disengaged, ignorant, and often easily manipulated by the elites who dominate public organizations (Dye and Zeigler, 1978). Mass political life has effects that emanate into the elite groups that exercise power—positions taken in the mass public may tie our hands even in private—but its central function is as a legitimizing ritual. The only democratic requirement is that the ranks of the elites be open to anyone who has mastered the disciplines thought to be entry requirements (Dahl, 1956, 1958, 1961, 1967). Jefferson's "natural aristocracy" must be superseded by the idea of discipline. With this priviso, the pedagogical rationale is intact. Argumentation principles are the keys to the kingdom—*phronesis* in pinstripes.

Argument theorists do not take this position—partly because elitism does not jibe with the egalitarian rhetoric that often drives Argumentation's pedagogical rationale (Chapter 7). Because they see themselves dispensing *suffrage* (argument skills being the competencies of citizenship), argument scholars peg their theories at the lowest common denominator. Simplicity makes for equal opportunity. And theories addressed to students reflect their audience: argument principles are seen as remedies to passivity, apathy, and ignorance. They are packaged in a missionary rhetoric which proselytizes for political involvement. The trope is indolence: Mencken's "great unwashed" escapes from freedom, shuns the political arena, wallows in lethargy or cussedness, and succumbs to "the forces of nonreason" (Ehninger and Brockriede, 1978:3). Freedom as the effect of reflective thinking becomes an either-or proposition measured by political involvement.

This picture starts with a plausible premise—who can defend the forces of nonreason?—and increments its way to empty posturing. Whatever its success as a sales pitch for "rationality," the ideology of involvement is a flimsy position.

We might not like to think that the estranged citizen has *concluded* rather than lapsed into alienation, but one *can* reason one's way to estrangement. One might decide—and not irrationally—that the impersonal size and scope of organizational life justifies estrangement as much as involvement, that political participation is an illusion, a hollow ritual which has the effect of intensifying the self-righteousness of power holders. In a bureaucratic context, which replaces motives with rules, skepticism can degenerate to impotent cynicism as policies (not decisions) are incrementally imposed (not deliberated). Perhaps once things come to votes, outcomes don't matter.

Somewhat differently, the citizen in a complex, specialized world might plausibly decide that his or her personal involvement is redundant. Try this thought experiment. Imagine that the critical thinking movement is radically successful. Every adult—no exceptions even in the remotest villages—is cognitively enfranchised for full intellectual participation. Would we want to hear everyone out, or to avoid redundancy would we still speak of public opinion in the aggregate? Would we conclude that this ideal pedagogical completion justified mass democracy? I doubt it. Conceding the most extravagant scenario, deliberative excellences do not translate into subject matter expertise.

I will not belabor the second source of confusion, the exaggeration of reflective acquiescence. But lest the reader doubt that argument theorists inflate their expectations of citizens, I offer the following example. This explanation of public responsibility, I submit, is typical—both in its vagueness and in the simplicity it imputes to public issues. Smith and Hunsaker hold that responsible decision making has several essential elements:

(1) a knowledge of the problem; (2) a knowledge of how the problem relates to other problems in the society; (3) a knowledge of the various arguments leading to the decisions to be made; (4) a critical ability to assess those arguments well enough to reach the wisest decision. Surely the elements do not always operate in enough cases. But whenever we teach a citizen to

evaluate situations in terms of rational and good reasons, we improve our societal systems. . . .

At the end of the 1970 congressional campaign Senator Edmund Muskie concluded that "public debate is the heartbeat of the democratic process." (1972:13)

In fibrillation, perhaps: no single elite, let alone a mass public, could meet these standards. This is more than harmless pedagogical arm-waving: it is empirically mistaken. Criteria (1) and (2) are, regardless of the question at hand, the property of specialists. Criteria (3) and (4) are presumably attributes of public decision makers, though the Greco-Roman model of *phronesis* in which the generalist gains enough command of specialized knowledge as to render wise decisions, is surely a vast exaggeration of the abilities even if a well-trained elite—which is why public decision makers in fact specialize.

It is always a mistake, I think, to confuse reflective thinking with omniscience. The idea that freedom and determinism are features of our thinking is susceptible to inflation when muddled with pedagogical rationales and inflated expectations about reflective acquiescence to communities. I trust that it is clear that the above reasoning does not absolve the public of responsibility. My claim, rather, is that argument theorists start off on the wrong foot. Broad claims about public responsibility—when the responsibilities would defeat even the best of an elite—put the whole discourse about the public on the wrong ground. In tracing the mistakes in this move, we have everywhere seen the effects of the language of individualism—the image of a lone individual wresting freedom from a deadening society. In that image lies the deepest mistake, for it obscures the social nature of reflection and the layers of social life in which political meanings are formed and (thus) in which responsibilities are defined.

8.8. False Consciousness

It might seem that an emphasis on self-imposed constraints contradicts the notion of false consciousness rooted in ideology. Certainly *Wissensoziologie*, the Franco-German sociology of knowledge associated with Marx, Mannheim, Durkheim, and Pareto, proposed an existential determination of thought (*Seinsverbundenheit des Wissens*) that precluded the conclusion that freedom and determinism are features of our thinking. But sociologies of knowledge have moved far from their *Wissensoziologie* origins (Curtis and Petras,

1970). One need not propose an existential determination of thought to assert that a social milieu affects individuals.

Nor should one, for it overdraws the scope of "irrationality." The notion of the collective unconscious emphasized the dependence of group life on impulsive, irrational factors, what Mannheim called an "emotional-unconscious undercurrent" that assured the continuous epistemic orientations of group life. This presumed a psychoanalytic model in which the subconscious was a force. Since collective unconsciousness is *ex hypothesi* false consciousness, the theorist assumes a position of special privilege, as in the case of the *Eighteenth Brumaire* and the *Manifesto* in which false consciousness (presumably) causes workers stubbornly to resist their best interests. Groups thus acquire stability from this masking of "real" conditions. Beyond the obvious objection that this reasoning only presumes that intellectuals do not share the facts of group affiliation, class interests, and (thus) false consciousness, it suffers from serious conceptual difficulties. The reasoning behind the position rules out an adequate explanation of how one can recognize the brute existence of the subconscious, how someone can throw off false consciousness, how multivalence, changing allegiances, and conceptual change within groups are possible, and how epistemic disagreements are resolved.

Perhaps the least plausible assumption, but the most necessary for the success of *Wissensoziologie*, was Mannheim's "free-floating intellectuals." They were putatively beyond the laws of group life, unbonded to ideologies and social ties. They thus embodied *Wissensoziologie*'s answer to the objections besetting it. But the position was faulty. *Wissensoziologie* proposed so powerful a determinism that it seemed impossible that intellectuals could be exempt from it.

The free-floating intellectual has parallels in the concern for critique. Critics who want criticism to serve as a roving touchstone of rationality, a portable arbiter of interfield disputes, are laying claim for themselves to a position which is at least similar. People in particular fields, the reasoning goes, are blinded by their immersion in their discourses; a view from outside yields a clarity denied to those "possessed by a discourse." Some elite theorists likewise describe elites in terms much like Mannheim's. Because elites seem socioeconomically similar, the temptation is to see them comfortably ensconced atop the class struggle, their aloofness permitting a clearness of vision denied others.

A sociology of knowledge need not suffer these defects if based upon a less powerful and pervasive determinism. It can acknowledge that people sometimes surrender their freedom and act against their interests *and* that they do not always do these things, that they can rise to critique, that they can change groups. One can, in sum, *have* a sociology of knowledge while still believing that we are as determined as we choose to be. This conclusion is even easier to reach if one's organizing question is not the relation of individual to community.

8.9. A Revised Stance

Claims about freedom inevitably enter a discourse on argumentation at two points. They arise first in Lippmann-like claims about the necessity of negative freedoms. Arguments *need* an absence of constraint. Such claims are the essential condition of Argumentation's *political* rationale. But the political rationale alone is not enough, for argument scholars want to say that argument *yields* freedom as well as needs it. A thing does not become important because it needs freedom but because it yields freedom. Moreover, guns are just one sort of restriction. Persuasion and subtle influence may be more coercive. Ideas and emotions harvest more loyalty than physical force. Blind followership is a more powerful impediment to the marketplace of ideas than censorship. So the idea that Argumentation could get by with a simple plea for political protection deprives argument of importance and begs important questions. Argumentation's *pedagogical* rationale thus involves claims about positive freedom as an outcome of argument.

If the pedagogical rationale is indispensable, we should consider its fit with the political rationale. The entropy principle says that we spend energy to make energy. Do we also expend freedom to forge it? In considering the place of argument in political life, we may think of it as a generator that transforms one kind of freedom into another—with costs. Argument's fuel is negative freedom; its output is positive freedom; if it is subject to entropy, it consumes at least as much as it produces. So, just as we do not confuse a generator with the power it yields, we must not equate argument with freedom, or indeed brandish any slogans of the "lifesblood of freedom" variety. The language of argument is one of constraints, rules, and inhibitions. Argument does not work if people fail to play by the rules. Argument, to stay with our metaphor, is the conversational system in harness—doing useful work.

Since discipline has costs, groups may ask whether argument is worth its price. Such questions turn on specific utilitarian calculi—not with abstract questions of the merits of communal life. So seen, the question is easily affirmed: the ride is worth the admission price, for there is no other carnival in town. To acknowledge the necessity of discipline is not to relinquish one's skeptical prerogatives or to deny that the price of intellectual freedom may be the loss of other freedoms. In putting our faith in opposition, we conclude that critique is a duty even while conceding that we cannot embrace freedom absolutely. In the sociopolitical sphere, entropy is a manageable expense *if* arguments yield intellectual freedom. As the claims in Chapter 5 about the epistemic effects of arguments were modest ones, studded with caveats about possible sources of interference, our claims about the freedom generated by arguments should reflect the same care. Social comparison serves epistemic functions, but it is a weak and fragile process often compromised by (among other things) ideology and incompetence.

Summary

Individualism puts the onus for critique on individuals—with so exaggerated a picture of reflective acquiescence that it obscures the interdependencies necessary for the formation of dissident groups. This spawns a dubious view of critique, for it underestimates critique's dependence on discipline and the degree to which the social conditions necessary for discipline cut against broad claims about freedom. The interactional theory ties its vision of the possibilities of critique to its empirical picture of argument. It thus poses as a problem what the individualist takes for granted: can freedom coexist with the idea of discipline?

This question reveals that Argumentation is founded on a paradox, for it sells discipline packaged in a rhetoric of freedom. It seeks to democratize political power, but uses a rhetoric of mass political participation that glances off the surface, for the key to political power is specialism and discipline. Thus it is important to avoid inflated claims about freedom, especially ones conjoining argument and freedom. This chapter has sought a position that will inhibit such claims. Within the interactional theory, argument both constrains and liberates. Negative freedom is a precondition of opposition, positive freedom its potential outcome.

Allied with this picture of argument as liberation is a more modest picture of reflective acquiescence. Having objected to exaggerated pictures of reflective acquiescence—because they put impossible demands on individuals—we have substituted a faith in opposition per se. This move does not relieve individuals of the responsibility for critique, but it casts those duties in social terms, for critique is fueled by the opposition made possible by competing groups.

Notes

1. The conflict between individualism and collectivism branches out to other disputes, for instance that between methodological "holists" (e.g., Hegel, Gellner, and Mandelbaum) and "individualists" (e.g., Hayek, Popper, and Watkins). Here too the middle road seems attractive. Dray (1967:58) claims that the two positions are not as far apart as they seem: "In spite of their insistence that what they put forward is a methodological doctrine which is merely supported by metaphysical considerations, it seems clear that what interests methodological individualists most is the related ontological claim that human beings are the 'ultimate constituents' of the social world." By contrast, Dray says, though holists are attacked for flirting with metaphysical notions, they are most concerned with upholding "the logical respectability of using holistic collective concepts and macroscopic laws, if need be." Each position can accept claims from the other. Perhaps Dewey's view that individuality is coextensive with social groups—that they exist in a dialectical relationship—captures the truth in both positions. But the fact that differences between individualists and holists may be bridgeable does not detract from the decision to avoid the language of the debate.

PART III

Argumentation as a Discipline
Introduction

In fitting the interactional theory into Argumentation's conceptual ecology, two different paths might be taken: expansion or multiplication. The former involves expanding a single construct: *Argument* once meant "serial predication" but now *also* means "claiming and reasoning in general" *and* "interaction," and so on, or shaping the new elements to fit the single construct. The latter involves enlarging the sphere of relevance surrounding a construct, creating new or refined relevancies to other constructs, and, in general, redefining or refining a discourse for describing a range of phenomena.

Expansion and multiplication embody different strategies and topics. The two paths force the defender of a theory onto unique argumentative ground, thereby dictating the *position* one must take (Chapter 12). To argue that argument as interaction is an *addition* to a single dominant construct does not simply require that the interactional theory be defended differently; it demands substantive changes in the theory, for example, that utterance be defined in terms of the logical methods currently available for analyzing claim-reason complexes.

Moreover, to insist upon integrating argument as interaction with the prevailing argument as CRC model requires an untenable view of disciplinary structure and discourse—namely, that Argumentation is a thought system, each element of which is logically related to a regnant or organizing construct, "argument." Chapter 9 makes explicit the picture of discipline and disciplined discourse entailed by the theory. In the foreground of that portrait is the discipline as a rhetorically constituted community, not a thought system.

Nor are expansion and multiplication methodologically innocuous. The former aims for a single dominant method, such as logic; the latter prefers multiple methods chosen for their suitability to particular questions and problems (Delia, O'Keefe, and O'Keefe, 1982). Argument as interaction admits of a range of questions and problems for which a variety of methods are appropriate, for example, interaction analysis, ethnographic and naturalistic observation, interviews and free-response data collection, and various self-report scaling techniques.

I trust it is now clear why I have taken pains to avoid the disputes about "what can count as argument." Though one might want to expand a single construct for any number of reasons, the issue at hand is how the interactional theory should be construed. The purpose of the chapters to follow is to make a case for multiplication over expansion.[1]

Chapter 10 argues that unclarities and needless disputes may arise when disciplines take the expansionist route as a method to achieve the advantages of multiplication. Informal Logic has taken the expansionist route—stretching the fallacy notion to include a variety of important phenomena. I believe, however, that the fallacy construct is better kept narrow and that there are more precise labels for the faults informal logicians want to call fallacies. In other words, the multiplication route would better serve Informal Logic's interests.

My aim is not to lecture informal logicians with wagging finger but to underscore some striking parallels between how expansionist reasoning works for the "fallacy" and "argument" constructs and to emphasize one methodological option available to Argumentation scholars guided by the interactional theory. Chapter 11 thus advocates that Argumentation take the same path—multiplication rather than expansion—and for the same reasons. The interactional view of argument need not be seen as an expansion of a single, unitary construct but as an enlargement of a sphere of relevance. This choice is a conclusion to be drawn from the picture of disciplinary discourse implied by the theory.

The degree to which argument as CRC should be stretched or narrowed has been extensively discussed and needs no reiteration here (Burleson, 1979a, 1980; Cox and Willard, 1982; Kneupper, 1978, 1979). Suffice it to say that these debates often come down to questions of the degree to which new phenomena can be molded to accommodate to the old model. This requirement often takes scholars far afield from the ground that interests them. For instance, if one makes "inference" a sense of argument (Hample, 1978, 1979b, 1980, 1981), one may have to adopt cumbersome conventions (public-private distinctions or radical devaluations of the message) not as integral moves in one's work but as justifications of idiosyncratic uses of the term *argument*. Unnecessary difficulties ensue. One can instead opt to widen the sphere of relevance, which requires only that one prove a connection between argument and inference.

If one wants to say that intentionality is relevant to messages and, therefore, that deconstruction is irrelevant to Argumentation's project, the optimal course would not be to claim that intentions are messages. One might end up with a theory of communication as solely expressive not because one wanted to defend that view but because one has been imprecise about the connections between messages and intentions. Conversely, if one wants to say that logic must be expanded to include indexical expressions (Bar-Hillel, 1964) or token reflexive words (Reichenbach, 1940), then the debate about whether a unitary entity must be expanded is appropriate to the point one wants to make.[2]

Chapter 12 is devoted to elaborating two methodological upshots of the interactional theory—its views of "positions" and "situations." These allied constructs may prove to be useful rubrics for uniting what may seem to some readers an unduly loose amalgam of methods. It is one thing to say that a broad theory makes for multiple methods and quite another to say how one integrates multiple methods. Though the discussion in Chapter 12 by no means exhausts the methodological possibilities of the interactional theory, it may suffice to convince the reader that argument as interaction is a manageable subject matter. It will doubtless enrage, or at least appall, anyone hewing to the doctrine that "once method is determined, all the rest is mere plumbing."[3]

And that, unfortunately, will have to do for now. Methods exist in the doing. The final test of the interactional theory will be whether the bare outline presented here stimulates useful research.

Notes

1. I am not arguing the inferiority of construct expansion in principle. The suitability of either option depends on one's goals. If one is concerned with drawing complex, fine-grained connections among phenomena, one may adopt expansion as an expositional preference. I thus adopt multiple meanings of the term *argument field* (Willard, 1983, 1988) to account for the variety among and connections between social organizations. Nor do I

place much stock in the particular labels, *multiplication* and *expansion*. Other labels might serve as well.

2. This may be a bad example. As rational enterprises go, Logic is more a company town than the social sciences are. Its core constructs may be indistinguishable from the discipline's sphere of relevance. Perhaps my distinction between the two paths cannot be too hard and fast respecting narrowly circumscribed ecologies. Nonetheless, Logic *was* evaluating the inclusion of matters hitherto excluded, yet the debate often centered on the specific inclusion of indexical expressions or token reflexive words in a language. That the debate most often centered on the inclusion of new phenomena under a preexisting construct justifies my classifying it as a construct expansion rather than multiplication. If I am wrong about this, it would not necessarily undercut the distinction vis-à-vis a more diffuse discipline such as Argumentation.

3. This principle, stated as natural (or at least University of Chicago) law appears in Ellen Wondra's introduction to the august Bibfeldt Lecture, 1987.

9

Disciplined Discourse

Every theory of argument carries an implicit vision of the disciplined inquiry appropriate to it. By simplifying, narrowing, and focusing—or complicating, broadening, and blurring—its constructs, an argument theory suggests methods and disciplines germane to the empirical reality it describes. The burden of this chapter is to clarify the picture of disciplines and disciplinary discourse implied by the interactional theory. Seeing disciplines as spheres of relevance—rather than as thought systems organized around narrow constructs—is an important part of this picture.

Disciplines as Complex Formations

The view of discipline flowing from the interactional theory is a fuzzy package. A discipline is (at least) a community, a practical tradition, a problem focus, a text milieu or *corpus*, and a creative grammar or rhetoric. The fuzziness sets in when we try to explain relationships among these factors. Some of this nebulousness may be correctable, but the interactional theory suggests that fuzziness is often a fact. Respecting fuzziness as a fact prohibits isolating these factors to fit one's convenience or interest—for instance, restricting scientific fields to conceptual, not sociological or organizational factors (Darden and Maul, 1977:44). The interactional theory implies the interdependency of conceptual and social factors.

Admittedly, this interdependency raises difficulties. The connectedness of ideas to activities and people is easy to brandish as a slogan but harder to explain. Theorists who stress this connectedness may seem to have fallen into a tar pit and to be chiding others for not following suit. Nonetheless, the interactional theory suggests that argument processes within communities (which may be unavailable to even the most imaginative hermeneutic engagement with texts) affect interpretations of ideas and thus steer intellectual change. Joined with Foucault's (1977) claim that discursive formations are "retrospective projections" on the past, the claim that fields are constituted by their communication practices implies that human disciplines cannot be reduced to purely conceptual domains.

9.1. The Ambiguity of "Discipline"

The term *discipline* may be inherently equivocal. In popular parlance it designates personal virtues or competencies (as we speak of a performer's discipline or an athlete's development) as well as a society's punishments and corrections. Thus it seems unremarkable to speak of arguments as imposing discipline upon arguers and of formal deliberations as being rule governed. *Discipline* is also used to designate professional guilds, academic associations and traditions, conceptual systems, text-milieus, a loose shorthand for an intellectual field's activities, or a strictly defined technical term for classifying argument fields (Toulmin, 1972).

These usages have a vague but genuine common theme. Obviously, the athlete, violinist, and biologist are each disciplined, even if the details of their disciplines differ. So many of these stipulative and empirical definitions are not mutually exclusive. To say that disciplines are distinguished by their testing procedures (Fuller and Willard, 1987) does not detract from the claim that they are also political entities, bureaucratic conveniences, and vehicles for the suppression of ideas (Popper, 1982; Foucault, 1977). To say that a discipline is a creative grammar is not to deny that it is also a community of flesh and blood people.

Obviously discipline is an omnibus of mixed feelings about our rational enterprises. On one hand, disciplines are loosely knit professional associations that nurture research traditions, protect long-term projects, and package knowledge for pedagogy. We esteem "disciplined" work—its rigor, care, and attention to detail; its need to survive critical tests. On the other hand, disciplines are enmeshed in bureaucratic structures (academic departments, professions, guilds, and the like). Discipline may be a kind of blindness, a channelizing, a narrowing, analogous to—pick your metaphor—a snail's shell, heavy protective devices to be dragged along, or bulwarks, unmovable ramparts to repel invaders and conserve resources. With either metaphor, they are social structures that incline toward conservatism, incrementalism, preservation, and glacial change. As a biochemist says, "Disciplines are political institutions that demarcate areas of academic territory, allocate the privileges and responsibilities of expertise, and structure claims on resources" (Kohler, 1982:1). When peoples' *professional* stakes in disciplines are tied to maintenance of stability and tradition (nobody wants hard-won skills and expert knowledge to become obsolete [Cohen, 1985]), or when disciplines keep their borders closed to idea importation, then disciplines can be said to exert an inertial drag on ideas (Jordanova, 1986; Popper, 1982) .

9.2. Disciplines as Spaces and Rhetorics

To acknowledge the merits of these competing views is to appreciate the ambivalence, hostility, and respect intellectuals have felt toward disciplines. We must accommodate to all three. Toward that end we can say that a discipline is

1. A *community*—an organization animated by the actions of flesh-and-blood people. At worst, we might speak of a collective like-mindedness enforced by equations of "rationality" with conformity and of conventional wisdom with truth. At best, we might speak of a collectivity founded on reflectively shared values whose mutual criticism performs valuable functions in the development of ideas (Pagels, 1982; Watson, 1968).
2. A *practical tradition*—an amalgam of real, historically bound practices. At worst, we might speak of a set of trusted methods that form the outer horizons of acceptable ideas; favored instruments become ends in themselves. At best, we might speak of practices, including dialectics, which have borne up under sustained scrutiny.
3. A *problem focus*—a shared stock of puzzles and interests. At worst, we might speak of the community as construing its problems as narrowly as possible so as to maximize the fit between its techniques and its relevant phenomena, and, less honorably, to keep its reading load down. At best, we might say that the community extends or defines its concepts and procedures reflectively appreciative of the costs of both moves; a core value of "discipline" is the clear formulation of questions.

4. A *text milieu*—a *corpus*, a "literature" deemed relevant to the community; in the worst case we might speak of a doctrine of true faith, the authority of history, the logical ancestry of current practices and (thus) the litmus test of the "rationality" of proposals; in the best case we might speak of a reflectively acquired trust in the community's consensus.
5. A *creative grammar*—logics of discovery and of justification; logics for making distinctions, stating relationships and consequences, demarcating constructs and locating them in systems. This last idea—that of creative grammar—merits elaboration, for it bears consequences for the methodological choices implied by the interactional theory.

Foucault (1972:32) says that the unity of a discourse inheres "not so much in the permanence and uniqueness of an object as on the space in which various objects emerge and are continuously transformed." He calls this space a grammar. We might also call it a "rhetoric" (Brockriede, 1982; McCloskey, 1985; Nelson, 1987a, 1987b). Discourses have principles for grouping and reorganizing concepts plus enunciative strategies, ways of ordering inferences, successive implications, and descriptions and of specifying the spatial distributions these elements cover.[1] Natural history in the seventeenth and eighteenth centuries differed from that of the sixteenth not just by using new constructs and changing the meanings of old ones. The more consequential change affected the arrangement of statements, their succession in particular wholes:

It was the way in which one wrote down what one observed and, by means of a series of statements, recreated a perceptual process; it was the relation and interplay of subordinations between describing, articulating into distinctive features, characterizing, and classifying; it was the reciprocal position of particular observations and general principles; it was the system of dependence between what one learnt, what one saw, what one deduced, what one accepted as probable, and what one postulated. In the seventeenth and eighteenth centuries Natural History was not simply a form of knowledge that gave a new definition to concepts like "genus" or "character," and which introduced new concepts like "natural classification" or "mammal;" above all it was a set of rules for arranging statements in a series, an obligatory set of schemata of dependence, of order, and of successions, in which the recurrent elements that may have value as concepts were distributed. (Foucault, 1972:57)

The "space" needed for the unity of a discourse thus arises in regularities of utterance. Utterance implies audience. Regularities of utterance require points of coalescence in a segment of a population's attention. "Audience" thus implies a "principle of attention" (Willard, 1983). Ideas and advocates get a hearing from those who pay attention to them. Paying attention is a foundational disciplinary act. And this, in turn, implies that regularities of utterance may differ at different points in a discipline. One's "point" or "position" in a discipline (to come full circle) is definable in terms of the audience currently attending to one's claims, or to which one addresses one's claims, and the authoritative evidence to which one appeals.

9.3. Peripheral Discourse

Disciplines are more than just packages of ideas with "isms" tacked on; they are communities held together by centrifugal force. If they are professionally entrenched, they may also be conserved by the bureaucratic inertia of the profession and of the university. If we see an intellectual ecology as a circle, with its paradigm cases at the center and fringe cases at the periphery,[2] it is easy to imagine that innovative ideas arise at the outer edges, at the points of overlap, intersection, and cross-pollination with other disciplines—just where we find constructs like argument, decision making, and "rationality."

Organizations are both centrifugal and centripetal. The paradigm cases stay home in the capital; the warriors are stationed at the remote outposts. *Out there*, on the borders of alien states, is where ideas mingle, cross-pollinate, and produce hybrids. Disciplines with wide spheres of relevance are ones with open borders—open to outside influence. They barter at least some purity for novelty.

Innovation is at least sometimes centripetal. Constructs gravitate to the outer boundaries of disciplines, partly because of their increasing complexity. The expansion of the fallacy construct (Chapter 10) is a case in point. The "argument" construct is another. Argument was once seen as equivalent to logic—as formal relations among empty symbols or as serial predication. Objections to the simplicity and restrictiveness of this view stimulated an evolution facilitated by the importation of ideas: social factors, fields of discourse, attitudes, beliefs, and modes of expression became important. By the late 1970s, the language of social interaction, conversation, and attribution had been widely adopted (Brockriede, 1972, 1985; Burleson, 1979a; Hample, 1979b, 1980; Kneupper, 1980). Each new factor brought its own ramifications and family of concepts, thus proliferating Argumentation's links to other disciplines and increasing the complexity at its outer boundaries.

Giving normal science its due, conceding that intellectual growth does occur at the conventional center of disciplines, and *not* claiming that peripheral discourse is exclusively "revolutionary" while discourse at the center is exclusively "evolutionary," one can nonetheless say that disciplines often evolve in the activities of *peripheral* scholars—so called because they are not looking inward to the paradigm cases that have historically united their disciplines. Their disaffection may stem from their discipline's inability to solve its own problems, from boredom with those problems or, as Kuhn says, from a fascination with new puzzles. Their move to the periphery may be a quick dash after a novel construct or a permanent relocation inside a new audience (see Holton, 1973; Mulkay, 1979; Mulkay, Gilbert, and Woolgar, 1975; Whitley, 1974; Woolgar, 1976).

Chomsky revived linguistics by importing ideas and methods indebted to Wittgenstein.[3] The Eve Hypothesis in Anthropology arose from methods and findings imported from Genetics. Plate Tectonics bogged down in Geology until confirming evidence arrived from Oceanography during the International Geophysical Year. Heisenberg and Born used the idea of matrices to achieve a breakthrough in Physics. Toulmin imported the sociological concept of "fields," a jurisprudential model, and a populational evolutionary model into Logic to transcend the narrowness he hoped to correct. Aside from whatever effect this scheme had inside Logic, its effects in Argumentation were revolutionary. The importation of an economic model of rationality into the fields studying decision making created Cost-Benefit Analysis—and a genuine revolution.

9.4. Disciplines Are Not Systems

Given the audience segmentation described above, Quine's (1953) doctrine that knowledge meets experience as a corporate whole is mistaken in a critical way. The effects of developments at a field's periphery may not radiate inward so much as outward to other fields. Misunderstandings may make an inward radiation spurious. Corrections may be delayed—bogged down in the size of the literature. The field's paradigm cases might remain unaffected by (and their guardians innocent of) developments at the outer edges. Relations between actors at the center and at the periphery may become more professional than Popperian. This supports Kuhn's "Planck Hypothesis" that ideas gradually pass from favor not from refutation but because their proponents die off.

The best test of an idea cannot be its effect on the current institutionalization of ideas but how well it stands up to criticism in the long run. If this claim seems incoherent—if you think that how an idea stands up to criticism is essentially a matter of its fit with the current institutionalizations of ideas—then the problem of explaining conceptual innovation may seem insurmountable. The problem lies in thinking—à la Quine's holism—that every element in a conceptual ecology must mesh with every other element, like the gears in a watch.

New ideas do not achieve their niches by a happy consonance with *everything* in a system. Given the size, scope, and literary density of (say) Symbolic Interactionism, how could one notice and successfully communicate a holistic consonance? If an Argumentation researcher were to report that atmosphere effects obtain in syllogisms proceeding from religious major premises but not from secular humanist major premises, how quickly might we know the implications of this finding for the beliefs that Argumentation is a normative discipline and that arguments from authority are fallacious when undertaken to bypass criticism, and the like?

It is better to think of new ideas as getting a toehold here, a tenuous perch there, because they jibe with local elements of an ecology. This is one reason why fields of discourse should not be seen as "thought *systems*." The system metaphor may apply to narrow disciplines, though the "position" construct (Chapter 12) seems better suited to the care small groups take in organizing ideas. But the system metaphor—or any version of Quinian corporate wholeness— does not fit large-scale disciplines or professions. Big fields have publishing organs (journals, book series, and the like) that persist regardless of the material available to fill them. Publishing abhors a vacuum. They may thus publish an array of material whose fit with a prevailing paradigm or with one of a number of competing paradigms is vague, ambiguous, and essentially contestable.

The sphere of relevance idea makes for a broader critical stance and a more empirically sound explanation of how ideas are judged. If our empirical picture of argument is right, the shape of a discipline is as much an *effect* as a cause of innovation.

9.5. The Debate Fallacy

Disciplinary disputes are sometimes seen as rational scenes: clearly designated advocates make their cases to a common, unified, and clear-cut audience of judges. This picture is an idealization, of course, but that makes it all the more influential in attempts to define the "rational" activities inside going social orders (Rescher, 1977b; Toulmin, 1972; Tracy, 1975; Weimer, 1979). The defect in this picture—call it the "debate fallacy"—is that it confounds differences in scale. Clear-cut debate may be possible in small communities, but disputes within large, diffuse professions and disciplines may be protracted, muddled affairs with indeterminate outcomes.

One explanation of this cloudiness turns upon differences within a large audience—its "segmentation," to appropriate a term from advertising and marketing. The intuitive idea is that overhomogenized views of mass audiences result in advertising and marketing errors. Audiences are rarely of a single mind. Small groups might be homogeneous, but larger ones are fragmented into subaudiences. When we find such segmentation, it is plausible to think that different disciplinary actors are not occupying the same argumentative ground, not taking equivalent "positions."

Peripheral ideas are not by definition revolutionary, but it is plausible to think that revolutionary ideas get their first and perhaps clearest formulations in small peripheral communities. Otherwise they might get lost in the clamor of competing voices of a bigger field's mass communications. They acquire influence by getting attention. As their audience grows, they may supplant predecessor ideas either by refuting or subverting them or simply by becoming the focal point of a statistical drift in public opinion.

The latter is, I think, more common than and is often thought to be demonstrably inferior to the former. Thus *Weltanschauungen* theorists are sometimes said to endorse mob psychology or celebrate fashion over "rationality." But this is mere posturing: a disciplined consensus is not equivalent to the mood of the crowd at a political rally. Nor are all disciplined consensuses alike. Moreover, the accusation requires an indifference to evidence: to claim that a discipline's state of consensus reduces to mob psychology or fashion is to acquire a burden of proof that, as far as I know, no rationalist has discharged. To claim (or assume) that explanations of intellectual change reduce to a simple contrast of "rational" versus "sociological" processes implies a command of empirical evidence bearing on both sides.

Perhaps we can attack this question on a less sweeping horizon by considering the conceptual change in Argumentation's ecology entailed by the interactional theory. The most glaring effect is that the interactional theory does not refute or subvert conventional models such as the CRC or serial predication. It is not radical conceptual change.

Radical conceptual change requires subversion of parts if not the whole of a preceding grammar. "Quantum weirdness" (Pagels, 1982) subverts our Newtonian intuitions about the world—not only by proposing invisible entities (Planck's constant, space-time transformations, electrons, photons, quarks, and, more recently, chaos and superstrings) but by proposing fundamentally different relations. In Newton's world, $3 \times 5 = 5 \times 3 = 15$; but, after Heisenberg, Dirac, and Born, this need not be true in matrices depending on the order of calculation. After de Broglie, Schrödinger, and Born, we posit invisible waves of probability by focusing on *our representations*. Thus the Copenhagen Interpretation was a new grammar, born in Bohr's decision to ignore conflicts with classical physics and in Heisenberg's decision to quit worrying about what atoms *looked like* and to focus on what they did (Pagels, 1982; Heisenberg, 1952).

Though this subversion of a previous grammar might seem to support the rationalist's case, there is a parallel story to be told. One can also see this shift as a discourse deviation, moving from one segment of an audience to another—in the case of the quantum revolution, a relatively small international group. Peripheral groups, of course, may seek influence in broader disciplines and professions, which explains why many innovations are at first disguised (or sincerely defended) as consonant with prevailing views (Gross, 1988). Once the disguise is penetrated or abandoned, it ceases to insulate the new idea from criticism at the discipline's core. Or the core itself may dissolve and transform as a working majority of disciplinary actors move into the new domain. Thus Quantum Mechanics shifted radically to the periphery, separated from Newtonian Mechanics, and over time reemerged at the center of Physics.

Does the argument-as-interaction model analogously subvert the whole of a preceding grammar? It might seem so; one notices a conspicuous absence of harmonizing disguises. The decision that disputes about what can *count as argument* are uninteresting is an avoidance, not an adaptation to the definitional disputes idiomatic to core discourses. The interactional model enjoins us to weigh the factors relevant to an argument's operations, however broad this sphere of relevance may be. It thus radically subordinates the claim-reason model, formal analysis, and the objectification of texts to its broader social scientific program. Toulmin's claim-warrant-backing-date model—argumentation's prevailing paradigm case—functions here as a pedagogical device and occasional analytic instrument but not as an interesting case of "argument."

But subversion of a grammar implies that a single generative mechanism is changed; and this need not happen with the interactional theory. The interactional model does not refute its predecessors: the CRC model is not transformed; mutations of serial predication have not arisen. The interactional theory, quite differently, bypasses the sphere of relevance established by Logic to concoct a view of the communications relevant to interaction. Whether the CRC might be repositioned inside the theory is a separate question.

It may clarify matters to speak more concretely to the nature of a *sphere of relevance*. My reasoning is that disciplines are, among other things, substantive domains—packages of constructs, conceptual assemblages, intellectual ecologies. We may thus speak of a discipline's sphere of relevance—its range of germane subjects, ideas, problems, and methods. This range is not necessarily equivalent to the compressed circle of the discipline's paradigm cases, its agreed-upon core. It is more a penumbra of connections at the outer boundaries of an ecology, its fuzzy cases, its controversial intersections with other fields. Relevance is not equivalent to endorsement. Claims can be relevant but false or bad. One might admit that psychology plays a role in logical reasoning but as a spoiler or contaminant. Or one might say that psychology is irrelevant to logic. The former move gives psychology a niche in the ecology; the latter denies it one. The sphere of relevance inheres in the occupied niches—in the ideas that have achieved local adaptation.

The analogy between cognitive organization and field ecologies (Chapter 1) comes into play here. The interactional theory puts a premium on opposition. A plausible inference from this is that people should stay open-minded because contact with new ideas provides more grist for the cognitive mills. So too with organizations. Happiness, contentment, and internal agreement are sometimes pathological—especially to disciplines because they depend on opposition for growth. So the gist of Chapter 11's reasoning is that "discipline" need not mean narrowness, especially in a social science. The discourse that often arises when peripheral groups try to integrate their ideas into mainstream thinking—when they seek to stretch the paradigm cases to admit new ideas—is a legitimizing, rationalizing discourse that does not always work to the advantage either of the new ideas or of the paradigm cases.

Summary

My point is not to insist on a single view of disciplines. We have observed systematic differences among people, organizations, and the ways communication is constituted. Subject matter differences may enforce additional differences. Given its interest in the social constitution of knowledge, Argumentation should be especially appreciative of such variations.

To assert that Argumentation is a discipline, or that it should be seen as a particular sort of discipline, is neither to commend nor to disparage the idea of discipline but to notice the vision of disciplined discourse the interactional theory entails. Inside the theory, a discipline must be a community, animated by the arguments and discourse of its members, a practical tradition, a problem focus, a text milieu, and a grammar or rhetoric. The least congenial position is to see disciplines as thought systems and thus to expect a holism or Quinian corporateness. Nor is the "argument" (as CRC) a regnant construct into which all new constructs must fit. The sphere of relevance surrounding the subjects of argument, decision making, and opposition is a broad one. My preference is to think of a sphere of relevance surrounding the mode of interaction that interests us and to make that sphere as broad as it needs to be.

The next chapter is a case in point. Expansions of the fallacy construct are inferior to multiplying the sphere of relevance surrounding it. Chapter 11 continues this theme vis-à-vis Argumentation per se.

Notes

1. For Foucault, the term *discourses* is close enough to what I mean by "field" or to what the Rhetoric of Inquiry calls "a rhetoric" that differences can be ignored here. Although I believe that Foucault's view of grammars is an appreciable contribution to "the archaeology of knowledge," I am less sure that the companionship between the interactional theory of argument and his broader program is as congenial. His organizing problem is a radical devaluation of transcendental reason. The dependence of reason on local grammars is one move in this scheme. The importance of substantive differences across domains *seems* underplayed in this argument. I do not know whether Foucault meant to create a tension between creative grammars and substance, but if he did, I want no part of it.

2. My reasoning here is different from that of Black (1970:12; see also O'Keefe, 1982), who reserves clarity for the paradigm cases and imputes "looseness" to the fringe cases (in Logic). Logic, in this case, is a poor case in point, for most cases of interfield importation involve not single constructs but positions (Chapter 12) or families of constructs. Not everything in a peripheral discourse needs be "loose" or "borderline" in any sense. Peripheral discourse deviates from the paradigm cases in some sense but not every sense. Also, the claim that fuzziness is a fact might be taken to concede clarity to paradigm cases. But fuzziness as fact challenges the appropriateness of paradigm cases—inappropriate clarity being inferior to almost any alternative.

3. I owe this example to Barbara J. O'Keefe.

10

Fallacy Theory

I advocate that Argumentation scholars use *fallacy* as a narrow term of art whose source of authority is logic and **not** as an all-encompassing term for every condemnation critics might wish to make. This claim does not stem from a preference for narrow versus broad definitions (I argue below that recent fallacy models are only apparently broad) but from the belief that *fallacy* is an inappropriate label for moral, procedural, and relational defects. These flaws may be condemnable, but the *fallacy* label misstates the authority behind such condemnations.

I address this claim to Argumentation, not Informal Logic.[1] Only informal logicians can judge the effect of my claims inside their field. But work in Argumentation and Informal Logic has lately exhibited striking interconnections and interdependences, so there may be merit in considering the implications of the interactional theory for the theory of fallacies and for the conditions in which it should be imported into Argumentation. For Argumentation, the fallacy idea is doubly engaging—as a methodological resource available to the interactional theory and as a parallel case (to "argument") for proving the merits of multiplication over construct expansion.

The Case for Multiplication

The question at hand is whether we favor multiplication (expanding the sphere of relevance surrounding a construct) over expansion (enlarging or extending a single construct). This chapter argues that multiplication is the better course—as dictated by the interactional theory and by events inside Informal Logic. Part of its superiority stems from defects in taking the expansionist route. Let us consider these defects first.

10.1. Two Views of Fallacy

If one focuses exclusively on expansion, a simple choice presents itself: the fallacy construct may be expanded to include every sort of mistake arguers make or narrowed to include only logical errors. Expanding the construct, as Kelly says, will broaden its explanatory power at the price of vagueness; narrowing the construct will make it more precise but constricted.

Etymological and usage considerations do not help us decide. Common parlance and most dictionaries countenance both usages. Characteristically, *fallacy* first refers to deceit, fraud, guile, trickery, or deceptive appearance, and secondarily to narrower, distinctively logical meanings, invalid inferences, errors in reasoning, and logical mistakes (*Webster's Ninth New Collegiate; Webster's 20th Century, Unabridged*).

Nor does precedent guide our choice. Argumentation theorists have historically seen their subject matter as an applied logic. They thus appropriated the narrow view or "Standard Treatment" (Hamblin, 1970) as a corollary to their approaches to criticism and to the normative content of their subject matter. Their source of authority was Logic. But Logic now presents a dual face—the informal logicians having broken ranks with the formalists to create a separate field (Blair and Johnson, 1980). Despite internal disputes, Informal Logic has organized itself around a sufficiently coherent agenda of problems and procedures to be called a research tradition, field, or discipline. Central to this agenda is the expansionist program— broadening *fallacy* to include moral, procedural, and interactional failings: "It is *reasoners* who commit fallacies—arguments in themselves usually are not fallacious" (Kahane, 1980:36). It is now commonplace to hear that fallacies belong as much or more to Psychology than to Logic (Massey, 1981; Copi, 1978; Fearnside and Holther, 1959).

This new field evolved less from defects in the narrow view of fallacies than from an expanding range of interests. The problem was not that logical errors should not be exposed or that logical instruments are inadequate for this purpose. Logic's *narrowness* was objectionable: it was inapplicable to the ordinary situated discourse of daily life. Thus Toulmin lamented Logic's strain toward autonomy. In questioning the Aristotelian aim that Logic seek to become a formal science, Toulmin set the stage for the revolution in Informal Logic: "How far logic *can* hope to be a formal science, and yet retain the possibility of being applied in the critical assessment of actual arguments will be a central question for us" (1964:3). Following Toulmin's lead, argument scholars in many disciplines hold that logic is too narrow to be a field-defining paradigm. Taken as a regnant model of discourse, logic ignores intentionality, social contexts, and personal relationships. Thus Johnson and Blair appropriate a telling passage from Wittgenstein: "What is the use of studying philosophy if all that it does for you is enable you to talk with some plausibility about some abstruse questions of logic, etc., and it does not improve your thinking about the important questions of everyday life?"

Their objection is to the outer boundaries of Logic's ecology. The point is not that logical concepts fail in their self-defined tasks but that these concepts are too narrow to illuminate and evaluate ordinary discourse. The birth of Informal Logic was a Kuhnian revolution. A group's disaffection with traditional puzzles and its search for greener (in this case broader) pastures led its scholars toward Logic's periphery to expand their studies to include phenomena hitherto left to Psychology, Sociology, or Communication.

But as we shall see, the benefits of multiplication cannot be acquired through expansion of single constructs. Multiplication, because it implies bigger families of constructs, prefers narrow definitions as a rule. Inside the interactional theory, then, I advocate reserving *fallacy* to designate a narrow range of discourse problems, logical mistakes—a range of phenomena different from "procedural errors" or "moral failings," or (to take the most radical case) "resorting to persuasion."[2] This decision does not prohibit the criticism of moral and procedural errors. It clarifies them by removing the patina of logical rigor from moral and political judgments. The expansionist path, conversely, asks a single construct to bear too much weight. Moreover, complaints about Logic's prospects as Argumentation's organizing paradigm do not speak to the merits of a narrow view of fallacies. They bear on questions such as whether logic's *disciplinary purposes* are appropriate to Argumentation. They do not prohibit the conclusion that logic is one instrument among many in an arsenal whose diversity reflects the breadth and complexity of the phenomenon. One can examine discourse to expose its logical structure and to uncover logical mistakes without foregoing other options. It is thus plausible for a discipline which has decided that logic cannot be its organizing paradigm to nonetheless consider whether a distinctively logical view of fallacies might be clearer than more expansive uses of the construct.

It is appropriate now to consider more concretely how and why the expansionist program goes wrong and the multiplication project does not. The place to start is with an obvious offshoot of the interactional theory, that judgments are indexical to anthropologically based bodies of thought.

10.2. Sources of Authority

To condemn someone for violating a rule puts a premium on the rule and the assumptions behind it. Behind every fallacy stands a rule. Behind every rule stands a body of assumptions which authorize our regarding the rule as binding. And behind every body of assumptions stands a community consensus which legitimates—gives authority to—the rule and its backing. Argumentation scholars and informal logicians do not appeal to law as a rule's source of authority. They speak, rather, of a rule's force of "rationality"—meaning that they presume that they could justify any condemnations if challenged.

If I accuse you of a logical mistake, I expect Logic to guarantee my claims. Just as we think that a tree's resilience is in its roots, our very sense of what a fallacy is and how we should think about it stems from the authority we accord to Logic. If you challenge me, then, my accusation is as strong as my fit with the facts of Logic.

The problem arises if I accuse you of a more complex error—one that is not simply a logical mistake. Say I accuse you of a moral deficiency, a procedural error, or a relational defect. What will the source of authority of my condemnation be? Certainly not a theory of argument. Informal logicians do not achieve their broad view of fallacies on the basis of a definition of argument but from the broader range of interests mentioned above. Their view of argument is as a set of linked propositions, an "identifiable set of propositions" (Walton, 1985:27; Hamblin, 1970; Woods and Walton, 1976, 1977, 1978; Brody, 1973; Barry, 1976; Munson, 1976; Johnson and Blair, 1983; Fogelin, 1978). But their view of *fallacies* is more ethical or procedural. Suppressing evidence, guilt by association, and name calling are moral and skill defects.

My point is not that informal logicians err in not getting their view of fallacies from their view of argument. The interactional theory does not clearly yield a theory of fallacies either. The theory suggests that the analysis and criticism of arguments will draw on principles from a range of fields and from bodies of assumptions having no clear relation to one another (e.g., ethics, organizational and procedural theories, politics, and jurisprudence). The problem is to be as clear as possible about the sources of authority presumptively licensing one's claims. Differentiating threads of authority is sometimes complex and difficult—a problematic worthy of a discipline's sustained attention and appropriate to Argumentation's subject matter. Under the aegis of our theory, the focus is on the sources of authority and jurisdictional ranges of particular judgments.

There is a surface resemblance between theoretical moves made in this book and the informal logicians' expansionist move. I use a definition of argument to justify an expansive sense of what counts as argument utterance and claim that we should regard all communications occurring in an argument as relevant to argument analysis. The grounds for this decision turn on the lack of principled methods for excluding particular communications. It might seem that this broad view of utterance dictates a broad view of fallacies. Yet while one can (say) derive a relevance rule from the structure of conversation (Grice, 1975), it is not clear that one can justify a rule standing behind a fallacy on the basis of one's picture of argument. The internal logic of the interactional theory dictates a broad view of utterance, but it does not specify what should count as a fallacy. Moreover, this move does not *define utterance*. Rather, it designates a range of communications relevant to argument.

Some fallacies are rooted in Ethics and Political Science. The reasons for condemning loaded terms, ambiguity, vagueness, popularity, slippery slope, etc., are more ethical or political than logical. If one concedes (as most informal logicians do) that one can have a valid but unsound argument (Kahane, 1971:3–26), one will lodge fallaciousness not in the structure of utterance but in pragmatic excesses. Unexaggerated, the slippery slope is unobjectionable, even essential (say) for arguing certain defenses of the First Amendment. So too the *Ad Verecundiam*: Authority appeals are not in principle mistaken but are wrong when used to shut off inquiry. And similarly, it is one's intentions, not the vagueness of one's claims per se that are condemnable. Ambiguity and vagueness are inevitable—and in some cases (e.g., diplomacy, negotiations) preferable. And we condemn the suppression of evidence not by pointing to logical rules but to political utilitarian claims that evidence suppression works out badly. The authority of our judgment comes from the historical evidence, the disciplinary province of History, or from utilitarian reasoning.

If the rules behind fallacies draw their authority from ethical or political principles, the practice of not distinguishing between intentional and unintentional fallacies seems mistaken. As a pragmatic political matter, it is hard to imagine the grounds for putting the conscious suppression of evidence on a moral par with ignorance.

So every *fallacy* presupposes a body of thought and a community to vouch for it. I trust that most readers will concede that strictly logical fallacies can be traced clearly enough to Logic. But what of the broader array of errors informal logicians now study? Does the attempt to make these new interests fit onto the fallacy construct— the expansionist program—create problems that the multiplication route avoids?

10.3. Defenses of (the Broad View of) Fallacy Are (Broadly) Fallacious

I have argued that the broad view of fallacies encompasses moral and procedural (rather than logical) failings. The *labels* have a logical ring, but the particulars differ in kind: "A fallacy is . . . a deceptive and misleading tactic used intentionally or accidentally by an advocate, which may have the effect of deluding an opponent or onlooker. . . . It creates an illusion based on deception. Unless fallacies are detected and exposed, the arguments in which they occur assume a *false air of legitimacy*. Once the inner workings of a fallacy are revealed, the illusion of proof and the false air of legitimacy vanish" (Eisenberg and Ilardo, 1980:83). Similarly: "Fallacies are arguments that are persuasive yet unsound. Their persuasiveness comes from their superficial resemblance to sound arguments; this similarity lends them an air of plausibility" (Toulmin, Rieke, and Janik, 1979:158). So the advertiser who dresses an actor in a medical smock and stands him or her in a laboratory to extol the virtues of a product errs because of a spurious resemblance to sound argument. We stoop to such advertising because we hope that the actor will be perceived as a physician. It is presumptively sound to believe a medical claim on a physician's authority, so we hope to cash in on the presumption of authority. The crime, then, is in the bogus resemblance.

No one would doubt that this is deceptive communication. But the argument theorist might be tempted to use fallacy theory in an equally deceptive way: to give fallacies Latin names—making them sound like diseases, defects in discourse as concrete as anatomical parts. The language of disease and diagnosis makes fallacy hunting seem scientific. The *appearance* is that a science is vouching for our condemnations—a resemblance at least as spurious as the advertiser's. "It's a relief," Norman Cousins said, "to finally know the name of your disease, as if in giving it a name you set aside other fears and confront a known foe." Carnap did call logic "spiritual hygiene." So the game is afoot: like medical detectives, we will hunt *Ad Baculum* infections, *Ad Misericordiam* parasites, and the *Herpes Ad*

Hominem. Moral, value, and procedural judgments thus masquerade as logical entailments creating the illusion that the certitudes and rigors of Logic authorize one's judgments. We can call this practice "sweetening the well."

A second fallacy—hasty generalization—also occasionally arises in fallacy theory. The typical defense of the *Ad Populum* starts with an extreme case—the textbook exemplar being Hitler—and then generalizes to emotional appeals per se. Though we might wonder whether Hitler can be a standard example of anything, the typical textbook treatment uses Hitler to exemplify emotional and popular appeals. The most extreme cases of emotional manipulation (in Copi's case, snob appeals and bandwagon techniques) are taken to stand for the class.

10.4. Not All Fallacies (Broadly Construed) Are Always Fallacious

This is a bromide. Few informal logicians would dispute it; most have defended it and wrestled with its exceptions. The claim is at least as old as Whateley (1836:196), who, respecting the Sportsman's Defense, argued that the *Argumentum Ad Hominem* could sometimes be sound. Toulmin, Rieke, and Janik (1979:157) put it that "arguments that are fallacious in one context may prove to be quite solid in another context. So we shall not be able to identify any intrinsically fallacious forms of argument." This is a remarkable claim in a field whose textbooks contain *lists* of fallacies.

THE ARGUMENTUM AD HOMINEM. The *Ad Hominem* has at least two guises: it refers to adapting one's message to another person (and thus to persuasion per se) and, quite differently, to attacking another person. The former use prohibits persuasion (and perhaps dialectic). The latter, however, is the more common meaning, so it is the best starting place.

My claims are these: (1) it is confusing to call the *Ad Hominem* a fallacy; as fallacy theorists actually defend it, the *Ad Hominem* symptomizes personal frailties and relational defects; it is irrelevant to the logic of utterance; (2) there are some cases in which the evaluation of speakers and their claims cannot be prudently separated; and so (3) all the fallacy really says is that the advocate should be sure that an attack on a person is relevant—a point that can be made more precisely outside fallacy theory because the standards for determining relevancy are exterior to it. To collapse all three of these claims into one, the interactional view permits the inference that whether the *Ad Hominem* is fallacious depends on a deep description of the particular encounter in which it arises. As Kahane (1971:28) says, with some understatement, "It's often quite hard to decide whether an attack on a man is fallacious or not."

Walton (1985) distinguishes the "circumstantial" Ad Hominem from its "abusive" cousin. The problem, he says, is that Ad Hominems are sometimes valid objections not to a claim studied in vacuuo but to a claim someone in particular makes. It is sometimes valid to attack people for not practicing what they preach. Say that I am a libertine priest. If I ask you to take my advice on my authority, but don't myself follow the advice, you are justified in thinking that my morals undermine my logic. They undermine my *authority*— which is why you were supposed to follow my advice. So too the stockbroker: If I advise you to buy stock X while I am dumping X, you are justified in doubting my logic because you doubt my probity. As a consultant, my logic is no better than my goodwill. Moreover, it is sometimes pertinent, indeed the main point to say that people are not practicing what they preach, as in Patrick Henry's Stamp Act Speech (March 23, 1775): "Suffer not yourself to be betrayed with a kiss. Ask yourselves how the gracious reception of our petition comports with those warlike preparations."

The ideology behind the Ad Hominem is formalism: the arguments on paper should speak for themselves divorced from interpersonal judgments. The Ad Hominem, properly speaking, is a failure of relevance: "We reject what someone says on the irrelevant ground that *he* is in no position to say it" (Mackie, 1964:177). This makes the most sense with easy examples, for instance, the smoking parent who enjoins the child to refrain from smoking; the fallacy theorist who tells the child that the parent's hypocrisy does not undermine the logic of the utterance. One can in principle evaluate claims and speakers separately.

This is too simple. Our picture of argument as interaction depicts a coordinated social enterprise in which more than the relationships among statements may be at stake. Dissensus can affect relationships as well as ideas. Since the structure of a relationship can be part of the truth conditions of a claim, tensions between what one says and what one does can be analytically relevant. Smoking is not solely a health issue but a complex package of social traditions, self-image, and parental identification. It is counterintuitive to ask the child to *ignore* the relationship between the parent's behavior and the claim.

There are clear-cut cases in which the link between a speaker and a claim is relevant, for example, arguments about relationships would contain self-referential claims as well as claims about a relationship. Still other claims are logically (which in this case is to say properly) tied to *ethos*. In a world built on expertise (Haskell, 1984), the probative link between speakers and their statements is routine, unexceptional (as when physicians speak to patients, architects and engineers to civic planners, physicists speak of nuclear power safety, and generals speak of military matters).

Ethos has traditionally been thought of as a general evaluation relevant to a whole utterance. A president's ethos, we would say, affects the citizens' evaluations of his or her communications—ethos and speech being singular, undifferentiated, global terms. But people do differentiate between their evaluations of speakers and of their messages; and their messages are not received as globalities. The drug addict and the alcoholic are not condemned as hypocrites when they confess their weaknesses while enjoining others to avoid drugs and alcohol. The criminal who speaks from behind bars to dissuade children from crime is not seen as a hypocrite. These people have an ethos vis-à-vis *these* persuasive messages that exempts them from the requirement of practicing what they preach.

This is still another reason why Argumentation scholars have erred in ignoring ethos (Chapter 6). The historical legacy, largely Aristotle's, has held that ethos and logos differ in kind and are thus analytically separable. The contemporary world's dependence on expertise undermines this belief—as do the tricky cases in which expertise intermingles with bias, as in the case of the general who has genuine military expertise but a proportionate promilitary bias, or the nuclear physicist who has the consultant's vested interest in the industry's growth but undoubted credentials to speak about nuclear safety.

THE ARGUMENT FROM AUTHORITY.   My claims here are that (1) it is mistaken to call authority appeals fallacies; as a rule, arguing from authority is a presumptively sound procedure; (2) fallacy theorists undercut their own case by mislabelling the argument from authority as a fallacy; and (3) the errors fallacy theorists want to prohibit are not exhibited in the talk: they are bad attitudes, not logical errors. What the fallacy theorists want to defend is open-mindedness, the spirit of free debate and inquiry; they want to prohibit attempts to stifle inquiry and impede debate. These are uncontestedly valuable goals, but they are better defended on their own merits than as features of a fallacy theory.

Seeing the argument from authority as a fallacy was originally an anti-Scholastic move and was justified as Bacon's new science left church hegemony in epistemological matters wrecked in its wake. Hence the spirit of Huxley's 1870 sermon: "Every great advance in natural knowledge has involved the absolute rejection of authority."

The scientist, Huxley said, "absolutely refuses to acknowledge authority." "What are among the moral convictions most fondly held by barbarous and semi-barbarous people? They are convictions that authority is the soundest basis of belief." So this fallacy has a political history. It was an anti-Catholic move necessary in its time. Given the reemergence of fundamentalism in the late twentieth century, it is perhaps not irrelevant today. Hence the more contemporary view: "That a view is held by certain people is also in general irrelevant to its truth, so that appeals to authority are usually examples of *ignorantio elenchi*. Cases in which the authority appealed to can be independently shown to be an authority in the sense of being likely to be well-informed about the point at issue are exceptions" (Mackie, 1964:177). I take issue with every statement in this passage. Religious sects *do* attempt to shut inquiry down, but I nonetheless believe that, in the modern context, each of Mackie's claims is defective.

I think it is mistaken, in our consensualist context, to say that an appeal to authority, even a mistaken one, is a fallacy. The appeal to authority not only is not a fallacy but is arguably the paradigm case of "rational" procedure (Stich and Nisbett, 1984; Haskell, 1984). The fact that a claim is believed by certain people is not in principle irrelevant to its truth. Is the consensus of physicists and engineers irrelevant to issues of nuclear safety? Is it plausible to think that, despite the consensus among experts, dice throws have cumulative odds, the solar system has hard boundaries, or the sun orbits the earth? If we want to know whether a proposed bridge is safe, whether to launch the space shuttle, whether our indigestion is cancer, or whether recombinate DNA research is a health threat, we acquiesce to the expert: we consult authorities because it is presumptively prudent to do so.

So it is plausible to think that Mackie's second claim is defective: occasions when we find genuine authorities are not "exceptions." As Kuhn says, our world is balkanized into interpretive communities, which are checks against rampant individualism (in the sense that I am not free "rationally" to believe just anything; if I want to be "rational," I am obliged to enter a social matrix of rights and obligations and to defer to a community's expertise).

What fallacy theorists really want is to prohibit religious dogmatism: "Appeals to authority become fallacious at the point where authority is invoked as *the last word* on a given topic. The opinion of that authority is taken as closing off discussion. . . . No further evidence is considered; the authority's opinion has settled the matter once and for all." Lest we doubt that it is the Scholastic mind-set the authors object to, note their example: "As Aristotle assures us, the stuff of which heavenly bodies are made is not subject to change" (Toulmin, Rieke, and Janik, 1979:171).

This closure has nothing to do with logic. Here is an arguer whose dogmatism makes for intolerance and a devaluing of debate and inquiry. The arguer has a personal frailty, a bad attitude toward inquiry and toward the interlocutor. If people flee arguments this way, they doubtless merit censure. But is it right to call this behavior fallacious? Toulmin, Rieke, and Janik (1979:171) say that "fallacies are arguments that are persuasive yet unsound. Their persuasiveness comes from their *superficial resemblance to sound arguments*" (emphasis added). But how does this square with their example? A pious genuflection to Aristotle does not resemble a sound argument—at least in most intellectual circles; *nor is it persuasive in intention or effect*. The brute uncooperativeness in the example is the *opposite* of an attempt to persuade: the speaker is retreating from interaction. It is difficult to imagine our being persuaded by this—unless we already believe Aristotle to be the last word on the subject—which, again, would be the opposite of persuasion. The authors thus end up prohibiting a caricature: "Appeals to authority become fallacious only when expert opinion is invoked in an argument precisely to stifle inquiry rather than to illuminate the issue in question" (p. 172). Aside from the question of how we are to label the advocate who introduces expert evidence *to win* rather than to illuminate—a problem to which I shall soon turn—the authors clearly want to prohibit a bad attitude toward inquiry. They undercut their case by misnaming it. They do not proscribe authority appeals so much as a Habermasian/Rortyian transgression, the condemnation of which we can best justify by pointing to the values of "keeping the conversation going."

AD POPULUM AND AD MISERICORDIAM. These two fallacies are defensible stated as matters of degree but morally objectionable stated as categorical imperatives.

Ballard (1972; see Copi, 1978) defines *Ad Populum* as any attempt to use "emotively based" persuasive techniques to arouse the enthusiasm, approval, and desires of a multitude. The term *multitude* tells a story: Ballard abhors pandering to the mob; he fears grandiloquent orators manipulating the "great unwashed" or sheeplike nonleaders mouthing the crowd's pieties, saluting its shibboleths, and pandering to its prejudices. If we cut through the hasty generalization and straw man in Ballard's presentation, we find, I think, a general antipathy for persuasion. In principle, adapting to an audience's opinions (which Aristotle says is the signal characteristic of persuasion) is wrong.

But surely this is a matter of degree—otherwise Ballard would by implication prohibit dialectic. Getting one's interlocutor to accept one's premises by working with the interlocutor's premises has been the definitive dialectical move since Socrates—and this, Aristotle says, it shares with persuasion. This process of working with and adapting premises has lately been thought to be definitive of scientific reasoning (Barth and Krabbe, 1982; Bernstein, 1982; Nelson, MeGill, and McCloskey, 1987; Rescher, 1970, 1973, 1977a, 1977b; Weimer, 1979).

Aside from pragmatic objections such as that going social orders cannot function without persuasion, I do think that Ballard's reasoning, indeed any reasoning that proscribes persuasion, encourages true believership and dogmatism. People should not be encouraged to believe that they know the truth. It underwrites bad behavior from jihads and inquisitions to the sorts of actions fallacy theorists want to prohibit. Consider the reasoning by which it is said to be wrong to shut off inquiry (p. 228). Ballard's argument, I should think, encourages us to search for absolutes in our beliefs. It underwrites just the attitude toward inquiry fallacy theorists hope to proscribe.

The *Ad Populum* stems from an exaggerated version of audience adaptation. One gloss of the fallacy is Walton's (who is attacking it): "Such an argument is directed to a specific group of actual persons rather than being an attempt to argue from true premises. . . . The fallacy here would be that of throwing concern for the truth aside in favor of an outright partisan process of trying to convince by utilizing whatever assumptions, no matter how outrageous, that one's target audience seems prepared to tolerate" (1985:30). Advertising has historically been the case in point for such reasoning. But it is important to see that the reasoning also applies to *public rationales*. Decision makers cannot always make their public rationales match the pragmatic genesis of their decisions. Nor in all cases should they. Diplomacy, defense, and negotiations require at least some adaptation to public niceties. For such discourse, it may not matter that public and private rationales differ *if* the entailments of the public rationale radiate inward to the private decision-making sphere. At any rate, the fallacy applies to public rationales in general and *seems* to draw its authority from distinctively political arguments concerning secrecy.

Walton's definition begins with the supposed opposition to truth I have already described as the fallacy's center. Then the definition progressively narrows. It is unclear whether one would object in principle to audience adaptation but quite clear that using *any* assumption "however outrageous" is unacceptable. But this is hyperbolic. If one concedes that the fallacy is a matter of degree, isn't it fallacious to exemplify the fallacy with its most exaggerated case? If it is not a matter of degree, the reference to opinions "however outrageous" is unnecessary; it would be wrong to adapt even to plausible audience premises.

10.5. The Broad View Is Not Really Broad

We have returned to musing on Toulmin, Rieke, and Janik's (1979) claim that we cannot identify "any intrinsically fallacious forms of argument." The evidence is accumulating that whatever it is that makes an appeal fallacious is something other than its propositional form—its logic—and thus that the language of fallacy theory may be inappropriate to the moral and procedural principles fallacy theorists want to defend.

The pattern discerned in the above fallacies is a narrowing movement: broad labels are introduced with clear-cut, extreme examples. Because these are often caricatures, the fallacy rule gets studded with caveats and exceptions. In accounting for exceptions, the fallacy rule gets winnowed down, narrowed, or softened—typically to the relevancy rule. Kahane's (1971:27–28) treatment of the *Ad Hominem* exemplifies this narrowing process. We start with a definition—"an attack on the man"— move to a clear-cut, extreme example, viz., Senator Randolph's famous "a small band of bra-less bubbleheads," and *then*, considering exceptions, collapse the fallacy to a failure of relevance: "It's often quite hard to decide whether an attack on a man is fallacious or not. In particular we need to assess the *relevance* of the attack to the issue at hand" (Kahane, 1971:27–28). At the finish line, then, the mode of argument is less important than the question of relevance.

So an initially categorical claim transposes into something else. There is nothing in principle wrong with the *Ad Verecundiam*, but there are objections to blind followership, or being wrong, or being mistaken; and *Guilt by Association* is not in principle wrong; it is fallacious when the advocate has the facts wrong (see Johnson and Blair, 1983:82–84). So too with the *Red Herring, Straw Man*, the *Appeal to Tradition* (the principle of presumption being a somewhat difficult objection to any categorical version), *Hasty Generalization* (see Ulrich, 1985:119), and the *Slippery Slope* (Govier, 1982b:303).

The point is not that one should tolerate morally doubtful persuasive strategies but that fallacy theory does not have the resources for authorizing condemnations of such strategies. The source of authority is Ethics, a political theory, or a community's values. What fallacy theorists have done is decide, rightly, that an array of extra-

or nonlogical phenomena (such as the factors discussed here) are interesting and thus that the fallacy rubric can be broadened to include these phenomena. Their mistake lies with the second step.

If I am right about how fallacies get whittled down, the informal logicians' reformations of the fallacy construct are only apparently broad. They actually collapse to four prescriptions: be relevant, be right, be open-minded and tolerant, and keep the conversation going.

What are the sources of authority of these rules? As Grice (1975) reminds us, "relevance" is a normative expectation of coordinated social action—a rule arising from the structure of conversation itself. As field theory (Willard, 1983) implies, "be right" is an epistemic function of particular discourse domains since standards for deciding the correctness of claims inhere in the veridical and judgmental practices of particular fields. Open-mindedness and tolerance have advocates and critics among philosophers, sociologists, social critics, and political scientists. Within disciplines, both qualities are perhaps less valued than they are as political ideals. As a general prohibition of censorship, however, both principles are found in many fields. Finally, there are the arguments of Habermas and Rorty about keeping the conversation going—not as a logical matter but as a political and (arguably) moral claim having social and political effects. We have moved very far from the sphere of ideas suggested by the term *fallacy*.

10.6. The Limits of Circumstance

> Beware a pursuit of the superhuman;
> it leads to an indiscriminate
> contempt for the human.
> —Devil to Don Juan, *Man and Superman*

One can always improve on events. "Recollected in tranquility," as Coleridge says, every action is deficient, every actor blind to something. Our lives are mired in circumstance and grasped by particulars: perpetual nescience inside dreams of omniscience. Our dismal kismet is that to act is later to be contrite. The best-intentioned, optimally reflective arguer is, for all that, *situated*— which is to say blinded, continually vulnerable to second guessing. In a world of limitless literatures, evidence suppression is a powerful case in point. If we find anything of importance a speaker fails to mention, a forgotten or unknown example, the charge will stick. If we hold people accountable for the whole world, anything they say can be turned into a fallacy.

Our picture of argument should make us more charitable, less judgmental. Empirically, arguments are "guided by context-relevant intentions and beliefs produced by schemes of interpretation" (Delia, O'Keefe, and O'Keefe, 1982:155). The strategies within them are bound to the arguers' intentions and thus inevitably based on context-bound beliefs. "Since actions reflect a person's beliefs about an unfolding situation, actions are characterized by emergence. . . . Present action permits validation or modification of interpretive schemes; future choices will reflect the success or failure of the present choice. In this way, every act collapses past, present, and future; and thus every act emerges from a new past into a new future" (1982:156).

Fallacy theory, appropriate as it is to the dissection of texts, puts hyperbolic demands on phenomena for which it is inappropriate, for example, interaction, relationships, and motives. Consider the case of propaganda. On one hand, we enjoin advocates to argue truthfully. On the other, we demand that they present counterarguments and evidence. But how tolerant can and must a person be who is speaking truthfully? Is one obliged only to acknowledge that another side exists, or to defend that other side with the same zeal one brings to "the truth?" The former answer prohibits propaganda—something we can do without fallacy theory. The latter answer prohibits advocacy. If we advocate a "concern for the truth" (as Copi and Kahane do), are we not moving full circle against the fallacy theorists' brief against propaganda? If I know the truth, why am I obliged to give full play to the opposition?

Diseases are sometimes as definable by their cures as by their genesis. One thus discusses treatment regimens without knowing why they succeed or fail. We are in a parallel situation here. Arguments, we decided, are real empirical happenings. They—and the fact that they are continually possible—are the most effective antidote to propaganda. This is why every propaganda machine tries to muzzle its opposition. Propaganda is notoriously hard to define, but the suppression of opposition is almost universally thought to be definitive of propagandistic regimes.

The proof that arguments correct propaganda lies in our empirical knowledge of what happens in them. Claims are challenged, motives are questioned, examples and evidence are demanded. Arguments are not always successful, but they are the least congenial environment for propaganda. How do we discover that public rationales *have* entailments except by virtue of a developing opposition? And doesn't that same opposition exert the pressure toward making one's public stance *applicable* to one's private practices?

This consideration should discredit any proposal to prohibit advocacy. Just as we would err in killing a fever, circumventing the body's natural defense mechanism, we would go wrong in proscribing even the most committed and zealous advocacy. The point is not that a single advocate present both sides of a controversy but that his or her claims be tested against opposition from others.

The prohibition of advocacy is admittedly a *reductio*. Most fallacy theorists doubtless want to inhibit not prohibit advocacy. Their point is to bring the language of restraint, constraint, restriction, and inhibition into argument practices. They want to keep us honest and ensure that the game is played fairly. And perhaps this means that the disciplinary boundaries between Informal Logic and Argumentation are best dissolved. Argumentation's historic concern has been with *disciplined* controversy; Informal Logic's recent concern is with inhibiting the worst extremes in controversy—a potentially happy marriage if ever there was one. But this common disciplinary content has no bearing on the present claim that it is a mistake to stretch the fallacy concept.

A decision to regulate rather than to suppress appeals to different rules with different sources of authority. The regulative rules constitute much of Argumentation's traditional subject matter; considerations of their scope and force have been staples of the field's activities; recent approaches have tied normative claims about argument rules to empirical studies of their outcomes. The Volstead Act had a moral tone; repeal rang pragmatically.

10.7. Fallacy Theory Need Not Be Condemnatory

In considering the transportation of fallacy theory from its place of origin to another discipline, we need not feel constrained to accept any or every feature of the theory. Interfield borrowing is as much a matter of transformation as of transportation (Willard, 1982, 1983). Within Informal Logic, the thrust of fallacy theory is pedagogical; transported into Argumentation, it may turn critical. Fallacy theory anywhere in the vicinity of critics should be an object of alarm.

That is, we should be alarmed by the practice of using the label *criticism* to lend undue dignity and epistemic stature to critical claims. Fallacy theory's similar tendency to *appear* as disinterested, technical appraisal might further underwrite outrageous practices by lending an air of plausibility and legitimacy to claims that would not otherwise survive scrutiny.

Argumentation theorists need not think of fallacies in inhibitory terms. It is permissible to conceptualize the rules standing behind each fallacy more as *topoi* than as restrictions. In this way, the corpus (the body of arguments, explanations, examples, and defenses—in a phrase, the literature) behind each fallacy may be seen as a resource anyone might use in pressing one's case. So viewed, the fallacies are ammunition—or better, weapons—at the arguer's disposal.

Seeing fallacies as *topoi* also returns us full circle to the subject of good will. We shall probably have to admit that arguers should see the rules—fallacy as well as ethical and procedural—as constraints upon their actions as well as argumentative resources.

At first it seems plausible to say that arguers need not see these rules as constraints on their actions because wired into the very structure of the encounter is a *tu quoque* possibility—live by the *Ad verecundiam*, die by the *Ad Verecundiam*. Here we are led to think of the *tu quoque* not as an argument (or possible fallacy, as it is in some systems) but as an empirical fact. The brute reality of opposition hard-solders the *tu quoque* onto every attack we make.

The weakness of this proposal might become apparent in particular unequal relationships. Remember that the interactional theory does not presuppose that arguers engage one another at parity. Though arguments require a minimum of parity to be called arguments at all, inequalities of status, skill, and knowledge surely affect their outcomes. For ill-matched interlocutors, our thinking of the *tu quoque* as an empirical fact may be empty rhetoric. The arguer who lacks the status, skill, or knowledge to capitalize on empirical *tu quoque* possibilities can only in the abstract be said to have those possibilities.

So arguments and the opposition they symptomize cannot overcome bad will. But they do enforce good will by a contractarian effect. If ethical, procedural, or fallacy rules are *topoi*, they are equally available to disputants. Just as presidents occasionally choke on their own rhetoric, find their private moves constrained by their public commitments, so other arguers may find themselves bound by the unforeseen outcomes of their choices. To dip into a rule pool is to contract with one's interlocutor for equal access. Thus, while enforced good will seems like a contradiction in terms, it is an obvious outcome of seeing communication as a public, cooperative venture and of seeing opposition as integral to organizational health.

Summary

We are at Argumentation's periphery, noticing intersections with another discipline—Informal Logic—and considering ways to import one of the latter's constructs. The interactional theory defines our optimum disciplinary use of the fallacy construct—namely as a relatively narrow designation of logical mistakes whose source of authority is Logic. Other terms are better suited to label procedural and interpersonal errors and (thus) the sources of authority for critical judgments. This narrows the term perhaps more than informal logicians want to narrow their field, but the breadth of the term is not the best way to justify broadening Informal Logic's borders. Nor is a broad sense of fallacy helpful to Argumentation theorists who want to know how fallacy theory fits into argument criticism.

This chapter is not a critique of Informal Logic. In saying that some actions falling within the ambit of fallacy rules are not condemnable, I am repeating a point often stressed by fallacy theorists. The claim that fallacy theory collapses to general rules ("be right," "be relevant," etc.) is now commonplace. Indeed, the writing of this chapter preceded by only months a special issue of *Argumentation* devoted to fallacy theory. There, Johnson (1987:247) insists that "there are three basic fallacies: irrelevant reason, hasty conclusion, and problematic premise." Fogelin and Duggan (1987:255) similarly note that "we sometimes call things fallacious which are not instances of arguing at all." And—in an analysis strikingly similar in effect to the one in this chapter—Hintikka (1987) urges that Aristotle's so-called fallacies are often procedural defects, not logical mistakes. This, he says, augurs for seeing fallacies as residing in "information-seeking questioning processes." Ignoring this true location of fallacies, Hintikka argues, is a "colossal mistake, a super fallacy worth the title of this paper ['The Fallacy of Fallacies']."

In claiming to address only Argumentation and that many of my points have been explicitly made by informal logicians, I am not raising a shield against critique from informal logicians. At least two claims made in this chapter, though addressed to Argumentation, are not innocuous inside Informal Logic. The claim that some informal logicians have a muddled attitude toward *persuasion*, that their reasoning sometimes presumes an antipathy for persuasion that is justifiable only by focusing on outrageous cases, implies that fallacy theory needs to be more concrete and explicit about the kinds of persuasion it wants to prohibit. And the claim (10.5) that fallacy lists seem to start big, then whittle each fallacy down to more careful claims, often to the relevancy rule, strikes at the heart of fallacy theory's *rhetorical posture*. The question of what fallacy theory would look like if each list started with the concrete examples, not with the general labels, seems to me to be a fundamental one—affecting the rhetorical strategies available to the discipline's pedagogy.

Notes

1. In considering Argumentation and Informal Logic side by side, I intend no turf-tending. Neither discipline is sufficiently mature to claim epistemic hegemonies over particular topics. The borders between them are nebulous, though scholars from professions as diverse as Communication and Philosophy may occasionally feel different tugs of tradition and employ different enunciative styles. Nonetheless, if redefinition of Informal Logic's expansionist program into a multiplication of its sphere of relevance is accepted, it is obvious that the two disciplines' spheres of relevance are intermingled, perhaps indistinguishable. This might mean that they are just different research traditions (Laudan, 1977) ultimately unifiable in their common concern with opposition and decision making. Their merger might signal the emergence of a new field, which I elsewhere (Willard, 1987c) call "Epistemics."

2. Seeing fallacies as logical mistakes does not preclude, for example, seeing rule violations as fallacies. Fallacies may be seen as "speech acts which hinder in any way the resolution of a dispute in a critical discussion" (van Eemeren and Grootendorst, 1987:284). Anything that frustrates *resolution* is a fallacy. I would not posit resolution as the sine qua non of argument, but this does not prohibit defining rule violations as fallacies. The law, for example, meets the criterion I have established, namely, that the source of authority for a condemnation be clear. Ultimately, though, I do not see the point in calling rule violations or obstructions of resolution "fallacies" when one can call them "rule violations" or "obstructions."

11

Argumentation's Sphere of Relevance

This chapter pursues two claims. First, researchers and critics should assume that a broad sphere of relevance surrounds argument. This claim continues with the case for multiplication over expansion and parallels Chapter 10's brief against expanding the fallacy construct. Second, the interactional theory entails multiple methods, for it emphasizes individual differences in language and language behavior, communication competencies, situations, and communities. Argumentation can best meet its epistemic, analytical, and critical purposes by proceeding along a broad front, its research and criticism pursuing multiple goals and employing multiple methods.

Argumentation's Sphere of Relevance

The interactional theory does not expand the argument construct in the way informal logicians have enlarged the fallacy construct. Instead the theory enlarges the context in which the construct is discussed. It broadens Argumentation's sphere of relevance—the array of phenomena empirically related to argument, opposition, and decision making. The theory is a package of crisscrossing, functionally related phenomena: personal perspectives and repertoires, inference, creative and strategic grammars, messages, text milieus, situations, and fields of discourse.

This enlarged sphere of relevance may be the source of misgivings.

The reader may be sympathetic to the idea of argument as inter-action but afraid that the subject has become unwieldy. Theories that simplify, circumscribe, and isolate constructs seem precise and determinate. Theories that complicate, broaden, and blur families of constructs court multiple methods in broad, fuzzy contexts. The interactional theory is clearly of the latter sort: the compressed narrowness of applied logic is replaced by a focus on interaction which enlarges the scope, breadth, and differentiation of Argumentation's concerns.

Still, breadth of vision is worth some fuzziness. Perhaps the reader can be convinced that indeterminacy is a tolerable price for a disciplinary self-definition that does justice to argument's embeddedness in social life, its connectedness to other social phenomena. The case for the sphere of relevance idea is instantiated in the claim that Argumentation should proportion its subject matter to fit the complexity and variety of the phenomena associated with argument and to multiply argument's connections with other constructs when appropriate.

11.1. Fuzziness as Eschatology

To start, let's cast the reader's misgivings in a strong form—both because some people hold this view and because the exaggeration exposes the link between our view of disciplinary discourse (Chapter 9) and the defense of pluralism and insistence on individual differences in this chapter. Later these qualms can be put in a less theatrical form as a concern for circumscribing scholarly attention and obligations.

Argumentation's loss of precision may seem to presage a disintegration—the discipline falling prey to the relativity and intellectual entropy endemic to the crisis of modernity. What was once a clear-cut, determinant, distinctively logical field has expanded to include what may seem to be an unmanageable array of factors.

Scholars of the objectivist bent might liken this expansion to an explosion.[1] The center has not held; the core has reached critical mass; particles are shooting outward, scattering randomly. Explosion and entropy, they might say, are the physical order of things. Our universe is expanding and with it our universes of knowledge. Discourse has divided and multiplied, spawning myriad subspecialties which themselves move toward subdivision. Disciplines start as small research traditions (Lauden 1977, 1984), then expand to a point where the originating core recedes from visibility. The proposal to expand Argumentation's sphere of relevance thus seems alarming. Heraclitus is back, in quantum drag.

Disciplines *have* multiplied and *are* increasingly subdivided into specialties. But—to loiter only momentarily inside this metaphor— increasing complexity does not make for entropy in open systems. Even inside this metaphor, intellectual communities are open systems because they live by communication. Their growth is orthogenetic. They become increasingly complex by exploiting the developmental options open to individuals: social comparison, communication, and importation of ideas. Kelly's organization corollary, remember, suggests that regnant constructs can unite hitherto discrete constructs. Higher-order explanations evolve to subsume apparently incompatible lower-order ones. Maxwell's electromagnetic theory unified electricity and magnetism; Einstein unified space and time; grand unified field theories may soon conjoin explanations of strong nuclear force with weak and electromagnetic force. So epistemic change (in this case, multiplication) is not necessarily analogous to explosion even inside the physical metaphor. The interactional model, as we have seen, avoids the dichotomies of the individualism debate. It arguably unifies as much as it disintegrates.

Its hyperbole aside, the concern for disciplinary determinacy may prompt the mistaken conclusion that to adopt the interactional theory is to expand the construct "argument" (hitherto a logical construct referring to CRCs or serial predications)—the effect being that this construct accumulates still another meaning, interaction. This mistake arises if one thinks about a discipline as a thought system ruled by a single regnant construct. Once again, expansion seems to be the only route—and in this case a bad one. But the effect of the interactional theory is *multiplication*, and we have already considered reasons not to see disciplines as thought systems.

I have paused inside this metaphor only for the benefit of the reader who is loath to leave it. The physical metaphor is a vestigial remnant of Aristotle's hierarchy of knowledge and of the Vienna Circle's hope that the language of physics might be a universal commensurating discourse. On a mirror of nature account (Rorty, 1979), knowledge takes its shape from the reality it reflects. But the interactional theory suggests the inappropriateness of this metaphor— not merely that it is too theatrical or exaggerated but that it does not jibe with the realities of communication.

So a general angst about relativity and specialization (or the mistaken conclusion that we are debating the expansion of the CRC or serial predication model) is not an appropriate or coherent stance for considering the disciplinability of the argument construct. Still, one can be willing to jettison the mirror of nature yet want as much precision and determinacy as possible. To set aside an extravagant trepidation is not to allay the reader's fear that argument has been set inside too broad an intellectual tapestry. The idea of a sphere of relevance may still seem inimical to the very idea of discipline.

11.2. The Narrowness Objection: "Discipline" Means "Circumscribe"

The reader's misgivings might be cast in the form of a concern for disciplinary coherence—an interest in keeping a subject matter manageable. The objection—let's call it the "narrowness objection"—can be stated as follows: The idea of a sphere of relevance goes against the grain of the very idea of discipline. The sphere of relevance suggests illimitability and porous disciplinary borders. But disciplines exist to narrow and define subjects, to make coherent questions possible. This constriction makes for precision and determinacy—which is why disciplines and their boundaries are indispensable for intellectual growth. This objection will not wither for want of allies. Consider but one special case, Hamlyn's (1971:4–5) assessment of the fit of Piagetian developmentalism into Philosophy. Because Piaget's views have philosophical implications, Hamlyn believes that philosophers may need to distinguish in Piaget's thought what is acceptable (*qua* Philosophy) and what is not:

This will involve asking which questions are genuinely philosophical and which are not. . . . Questions about the conditions which are normally necessary if one is to be said to have a certain form of understanding are different from questions about the origins of that form of understanding. I have also suggested that the former kind of question is a genuinely philosophical one. (pp. 4–5)

The mixture of philosophical and empirical issues involves in each case a muddle . . . the philosophical and psychological questions which are at stake are different from each other, and . . . there are no grounds for the belief that philosophical questions can be answered by appeal to empirical evidence or vice versa. (p. 19)

Philosophy *qua* discipline poses questions of a particular sort. Ideas *should* be circumscribed. The point of discipline is to sacrifice breadth for clarity; strict import regulations are thus appropriate.

My point is not to squabble with Hamlyn. His claim refers to Philosophy; philosophers must evaluate it. But his position resembles the ground actors anywhere might occupy in applying the narrowness objection to their disciplines. That we seldom find theorists in the natural and social sciences occupying this ground does not refute the narrowness objection, but it suggests that the equation of discipline with narrowness may often be a local political phenomenon.

But epistemic provincialism is not the only objection to the equation of discipline with narrowness. The claims to follow are that the equation unduly values normal science, that it is an unnecessarily timid way to think about intellectual progress, that it presupposes an overdetermined view of the text milieu, and that social sciences in principle should not close their borders. Apart from these concerns, I shall contend that arguments, as described by the interactional theory, are too complex to be adequately represented by narrow models. After all, the advocate of the narrowness objection must have an alternative view of argument in mind—something more determinate and concise. All of these claims flow from the picture of disciplinary discourse implied by the interactional theory (Chapter 9).

11.3. Defects of the Narrowness Objection

First, the narrowness objection restricts intellectual growth to normal science, which has the side effect of forcing one who notices "abnormal" conceptual change to defend a revolutionary or irrationality hypothesis, appropriate or not. The objection obscures the effects of idea importation and border discourse and thus makes for autistic disciplines (Willard, 1983). A field's decisions about importing ideas establish its social contracts for discourse with other fields—its options for taking and exerting influence across field boundaries.

Second, a social science in principle should not close its borders (Willard, 1983). Conceptual ecologies in such fields are "intermestic" (a political scientist's term denoting the interdependency of a nation's domestic and foreign policies). Implications are conceptual gypsies: weak allegiances, frequent border crossings (Geertz, 1980). Their world is not carved up like academic departments. As we have seen (Chapter 9), the importance of peripheral discourse lies in its potential for circumventing a field's intransigent disputes or moribund traditions (Cohen, 1985).

Third, to insist too much on boundaries is an unnecessarily timid way to think about disciplines. Kelly's principle of elaborative choice says that we construe things so as to enhance the extension or definition of our cognitive systems. A system is extended when its range of convenience is increased, when it admits of rendering more events meaningful; its definition is enhanced when it becomes more ex-plicit and clear-cut. We choose breadth at the expense of detail and precision or detail and focus at the price of narrowness. Both are costly but not in the same currency. In either case, whenever one has the opportunity for making a choice, one will "tend to make that choice in favor of the alternative that seems to provide the best basis for anticipating the ensuing events" (Kelly, 1955:64). Since communities exist in and through the activities of their members, the parallel between cognitive systems and communal ecologies comes into play here.

But unlike individuals, disciplines benefit from a division of labor and can move along multiple fronts simultaneously. Some people work at clarification, making premises explicit, and correcting con-ceptual problems; others, usually at the periphery, emphasize elabo-ration, innovation, and accommodation to new ideas; and still others proceed with narrow research programs, leaving theoretical concerns to others. These disparate activities have different strengths and weaknesses: the clarifiers are deliberately narrow and conventional; peripheral actors may be imaginative but untidy; and researchers in compact traditions are specialized, competent, and narrow. Disci-plinary health is conserved by the *interplay* among these activities—a robust opposition between them being a growth imperative for complex communities. The dominance of each activity will wax and wane over time, but the long-term survival of each is necessary to the health of the ecosystem.

The introduction of a broad theory into a healthy community will (if it catches on) call all three activities into play. Their interplay puts new ideas to multiple tests and interpretations—some pulling in different directions. Extension and elaboration thus may be si-multaneous movements in comparatively complex fields. The ten-sion between them ensures that Argumentation will achieve as much determinacy as possible while doing justice to argument's sphere of relevance. This is not a warranty of coherence, but it does enable disciplines not to judge new ideas by their breadth. Fields, so defined, do not need narrowly circumscribed subjects to produce clear questions; they need only nurture their clarifiers and research traditions.

This picture of competing activities within disciplines flows from the interactional theory: if arguments are *interactions,* and disci-plines are animated by these activities, then disciplines are com-munities. Communities by definition may be segmented into subcommunities just as any audience can be subdivided into interest groups. In contrast, the preference for narrowness stems from seeing disciplines as text milieus, which itself arises from seeing argument as serial predication. Serial predications are *things* embodied in tangible artifacts, viz., texts; one thus looks for "rational" progress in the texts. But this search (the interactional theory implies) sets one up to be duped by Foucauldian deceptions or post hoc rationalizations if one emphasizes texts over activities. This contrast both displays the difference between the interactional and CRC or serial predication models and underscores the inadequacy of the latter for explaining intellectual change.

Argument Analysis

Just as Linguistics must discard the "fiction of a homogeneous speech community" (Carroll, 1979; Delia, 1983) and universalist views of competence to account for individual differences, argumentation under the aegis of the interactional theory anticipates individual differences in communicative and argumentative competencies, situations, positions, messages, and communal methods for defining contexts and pursuing goals. This does not just imply the appropriateness of multiple methods; it implies that methods should not be defended as universals and that many methods that are inadequate as universals nonetheless have uses as local procedures.

11.4. Formalism

I start with a case the reader who has stayed with me this far is most likely concerned about. If your thinking is still dominated by a preference for single methods, you may wonder if the interactional theory supplants formal analysis with interaction analysis. Perhaps by looking at the reformed position of formalism in the theory, I can undercut the grounds of your question. The gist of what follows is that formal analysis has a place in the theory as a way of explicating utterance and analyzing positions. Some logical tools fit this program. Since logical analyses are reductionist, we need to specify this fit.

When argument scholars speak of the "demise of formalism," they do not mean that utterance lacks analyzable form or that consistency or the arrangement of terms are irrelevant or useless. They mean, rather, that a general philosophical view about the relationships among fields has been discarded. The paradigm in question is Aristotle's schematizing of levels of knowledge in which Logic stands at the apex as an a priori, ahistorical, and nonempirical science of pure form—logical form being isomorphic of being as such. Now add a hefty dose of monism: logic, knowledge, and ontology are *formally* one. If syllogistic form is isomorphic of being as such, we should find looser, weaker versions of it in psychology (the practical syllogism), discourse (the dialectical syllogism), and communication (the enthymeme). Their materials are opinions (*doxa*), not certainties, and not just the opinions of the most enlightened but of everyone relevant to an occasion. Argumentation, this reasoning goes, is an applied logic. It—or any study of the lower modes of reasoning—cannot contribute to the higher level of analysis. Logical form is a biological fact—fundamental to the constitution of mind—and a normative ideal toward which the weaker versions should aim.

A vagueness in Aristotle's system is the relationship between form and matter. *De Anima*'s famous (and I think thoroughly materialist) image of the signet ring stamping its impression on wax does not translate to *discourse*. Aristotle knew that the apodeictic syllogism had to consist of empty symbols to be true, that its form did not guarantee the truth of its premises. Formally valid serials could have false conclusions. One has to be a monistic materialist, I suppose, not to see this as a lacuna. But in the inferior domains, nothing but the citizens' good intellectual habits guaranteed the truth of premises.

That last sentence may seem wrong. Aristotle *had* a theory of opposition. He held that groups made better decisions than solitary thinkers because individuals' vices and virtues complemented one another in groups: your virtues make up for my vices, and vice versa. His theory of dialectic thus emphasized cooperative criticism. But because he saw argument as serial predication, the opposition was in the ideas, not the people and practices. Indeed, his proposal that individual vices and virtues become complementary in groups implies that group life *should* undercut opposition (Willard and Hynes, 1988).

Formalism lived long and prospered: Thomism, the Renaissance revival of Pythagorean mathematics and Euclidian geometry, Copernicus, Kepler, Descartes, Leibniz, Galileo—and still later, Frege's axioms and Russell and Whitehead's *Principia*. The Vienna Circle's proposal that physics constituted the language of nature (and therefore of the unified sciences) was an analogous program.

An offhand remark by Hume stimulated one offshoot, the problem of induction (Katz, 1962; Kneale, 1949; Kyburg and Nagel, 1963; Swain, 1969). Induction, let's say, is not deduction. Inductive serials have psychological premises, which may or may not be suppressed; their conclusions are merely probable (Russell, 1948; Wisdom, 1952; Reichenbach, 1940); inductive serials involve presuppositions

(Burks, 1953) and thus cannot be entailments (Feigl, 1961); and they are field-dependent (Toulmin, 1968; Strawson, 1958). These factors singly or in tandem are problematic as intrusions on form. They undercut the hope that form might guarantee substance.

A parallel movement in Psychology adopted Aristotle's practical syllogism as a cognitive model to study the ways formal reasoning got contaminated by emotions, wishful thinking, atmosphere effects, and conversion errors (Begg and Denny, 1969; Chapman and Chapman, 1959; Feather, 1964; Guilford, 1967; McGuire, 1960b; Sells, 1936; Simpson and Johnson, 1966; Wyer, 1974a, 1974b, 1975). Like their cousins in Argumentation, the contaminant studies take it for granted that inference is logical and regard motivational elements as adjuncts to, or components fitted onto, or as general environments of essentially logical processes. Since such studies rarely tap their subjects' ordinary ways of thinking or their views of the experimental situation, they may only mean that people forced in artificial contexts to employ unfamiliar inferential and expositional techniques often make errors.

The demise of formalism, in sum, is a surrender of Aristotle's hierarchy and of the idea that any particular form is the basis of inference and utterance. Logical mistakes should still concern us; models of inference, exposition, and decision making still have formal implications; but the diversity of communication processes, differences in MDLs, and differences in situations mean that argumentation is no longer an applied (or inferior) logic straining toward perfection. That people can consciously adopt (or unreflectively succumb to) any number of models suggests both the complexity and the ambiguity of arguments as social happenings and the creativity, flexibility, and occasional ingeniousness (or mindless passivity) of arguers. The discipline's need to accommodate to a multiplicity of models reflects this complexity and diversity.

11.5. Multiplicity of Models

The view of disciplines developed here emphasizes the necessity of a division of labor. The broader the sphere of relevance, the more expansive the landscape of issues. If individual differences are to be respected, Argumentation should avoid single models either as discipline-defining universals (in the sense that one might hold the CRC to be Argumentation's field-defining object of interest) or single models of aspects of argument (e.g., as one might propose single models of inference, organization, or decision making). Many models have local successes, which a general theory of argument must respect. And many models are sometimes defended as the best, or most typical, or ideal, which a general theory must resist. The advantages of valuing multiple models are readily seen in three topic domains pertinent to the interactional theory: inference, organization, and decision making.

First, one can find subjects who can be taught to use any cognitive model that has been used to describe inference. If they are asked specifically enough, you will get subjects to use ANOVAs (Kelley, 1967, 1971, 1972) or syllogistic reasoning (McGuire, 1960b). The famous Doodlebug problem transports us into a world whose causality is topsy turvy; the rules have to be learned from scratch. People can in fact learn the new causalities and reason with them. No single model of inference can account for the variations people contrive. There are many proposals: associationism, gestalt theory, impression formation, attribution theory, and PCT. Aristotle's practical syllogism is the most persistent (e.g., McGuire, 1960b). Recent applications of quantum mechanics to brain structure (Harth, 1986) suggest that people think differently not only because they use different models or procedures but because their brains develop differently. Harth's point is that the brain is adaptable, has considerable randomness in cell connections and electrical discharges, and thus shapes itself to experience. Because communication practices vary, the brain's basic ways of processing information may evolve differently. Thus "neural Darwinism" (Edelman, 1988) predicts variations in brain patterns and connections. Moreover, an adaptability that makes brains unique should also yield systematic individual differences in choice: people will vary in their adeptness at using new cognitive procedures.

The same variability that makes it impossible to create a single cognitive model permeates other research domains. Certainly successor theories occasionally correct the mistakes of their predecessors. But much of the movement from model to model reflects the measurement of different realities.

As we shall see in "The Balkanization," the study of organizations has been a succession of conflicting models: Taylorism, rational bureaucracy, the human relations and human resources models, open systems theory, the interpretive model, radical functionalism, and others. These models were derived from observations of different organizations, and organizations can still be found to match any of them. Organizations are built on implicit value structures (Smircich, 1983a, 1983b, 1985), organizational cultures (Frost et al., 1985), and environments that differ from those even of similar organizations. No single model of organization could subsume such diversity. The test of organizational models is not of their generality but of their fit with particular cases.

Similarly, decision making is pluralistic in a significant sense: it does not have just a history of successive explanations but a current plethora of models, each supported by evidence. The models include the analycentric, bureaucratic, technocratic, authoritarian, democratic, disciplined, brainstorming, and quality circles. Decision makers apparently follow different implicit values and procedural assumptions as well as explicit rules and folkways. No universal model will include all variations, so no single model of anything—and especially not a piecemeal assembly of putatively universal models—can explain the empirical genesis of decisions.

These three domains have in common a multiplicity of models involving scenarios, systems, or institutions people may enter. This pluralism reflects analogous historical experiences: general models succumb to obdurate individual differences and variability across situations. MDLs symptomize individual differences in communication constituting assumptions, so we expect to find some people clinging to cognitive models set in concrete and others displaying versatility and flexibility. Respecting complex communicators, we surely want to know if there are situational features that encourage their flexibility and call forth particular models.

The search for general models in the psychological, organizational, and decision-making domains reflects a desire to avoid getting bogged down in the idiosyncrasies of situations. But the degree to which situations call forth communication practices needs underscoring. The rational bureaucratic model of organizations may *seek* to transcend all situations, but healthy organizations live in their particular adaptations. Just as we might imagine that some situations would call for Expressive behavior even from Rhetoricals, we know that even the strictest bureaucracies occasionally accommodate to personal development or compassionate goals.

Are there features generic to arguments that lead Conventionals to use particular cognitive and decision-making models? What constrains the Rhetorical in adopting points of view? How does the relative flexibility and inflexibility of arguers to shift procedures and adapt to events affect the ongoing interaction? Does opposition bring out the worst in Expressives (which might otherwise remain hidden or innocuous)? And a different question: Does opposition bring out the worst in Rhetoricals? Is the Conventional best suited to argument (meaning, do arguments work best when recipes are not too rhetorically followed)? Posing such questions we see that one organizing purpose of argument studies is to enrich our stock of knowledge about communication. Another purpose is to complement organizational studies. The unity between Argumentation and organizational studies is thus a central theme of "The Balkanization."

There used to be—perhaps there still is—a division among research traditions in Communication: *source*-centered, *audience*-centered, and *message*-centered theories focused respectively on persuasive strategies, the psychology of persuasion, and texts. Aristotle is occasionally mentioned as the father of all three. His treatments of rhetoric are analogous, at different points in his work, to the Sophist's cookbook rhetorics, contemporary psychologies of persuasion, and logical textual analyses. The imputation of all three to the same rhetorical system permits the inference that they are not mutually exclusive. They may be de facto exclusive—which is unsatisfactory when researchers in one domain regard phenomena in the others as fixed effects (Jackson and Jacobs, 1981b). But these three foci were at least originally held together by a discipline-founding picture: a speaker delivers a speech to an audience. The three foci were but different stances or lenses for the study and analysis of the founding picture.

That founding picture has been lost, for there are now many theories that do not define their positions in the discipline by their stance vis-à-vis a single phenomenon. Group and organizational communication studies, mass communication, journalism, and public relations all see speeches as one among many vehicles communicators might employ. The interactional theory likewise allows for multiple vehicles chosen for multiple motives with multiple effects. Its concern is with an emergent, collaborative form of interaction for which a distinction between speakers and audiences or an insistence on the act as the discipline's organizing unit of analysis are not appropriate.

11.6. Historical and Structural Biases

Criticism often poses the problem of recreating events. The interactional theory seems to intensify this problem. Even the most generous reader may wonder if indeterminacy has not gotten the better of our descriptive methods. Once again, though, it is important that a plausible reservation not get out of hand. Inflated expectations about descriptive possibilities will heighten fears of indeterminacy. The historical kinship between Rhetorical Criticism and History may give the reader an idealized picture of descriptive determinacy beside which the interactional theory looks unduly fuzzy. But this is a spurious contrast. My point is not that every historian (in History or Rhetorical Criticism) hews to a naive caricature of positivistic precision and exactitude, or that historians cannot use the argument-as-interaction model but that, viewed through the lens of the interactional theory, the naive historical view is inappropriate to Argumentation's disciplinary interests.

Even in formalism's heyday, few Argumentation scholars analyzed serial predications as interesting in their own right. This fact is worth underscoring by way of refuting the narrowness objection. Even the scholars who have defended narrow constructs have painted with broad strokes. They would have the rhetorical critic presiding over a differentiated mass of pieces: the situation, the psychology of the arguers, their public utterances, and their social effects. These are the big pieces that must be dismantled to be understood. Situations consist of perceptions and events; psychology consists of thus and so processes, traits, and states; and utterances are composed of the relations among premises and among units of meaningful utterance. And each of these smaller units can again be subdivided. Then one puts the pieces together, like a puzzle; selecting a theory of situations, a psychological theory, a logic, and a social or historical theory, one patches together an account of an event. The fit between these pieces is not a matter of their empirical relations in situations but of their abstract theoretical consistencies.

Notice the *historical* and *structural* biases. We want to fix a historically real event, to give it objectivity, nail it down, get the facts right. Freeze-dried life. The structural bias is that we see the parts building toward the whole, not in idiosyncratic or random ways but by an orderliness akin to teleology.

So we should avoid an exaggerated contrast between the interactional theory's indeterminacy and the naive historicist's "determinacy." But the suspicious reader may smell a straw man: most argument scholars long ago conceded that the *Weltanschauungen* theorists get the better of the positivists on the theory-embeddedness of observation. History as interpretation is now a mainstream idea.

Just so. What has happened here is a deexaggeration of the reader's qualms about indeterminacy. *Mutatis mutandis*, the reader's more modestly put reservation is that the interactional theory's emphasis on emergence and transformation requires that all description be seen as an artifice for freezing ongoing projects. But this outcome, as far as I can see, puts the interactional theory squarely within mainstream thinking about interpretive criticism.

A more serious reservation—and one I cannot entirely dispel—is that the interactional theory, because of its stress on individual and situational variation, is not as useful in illuminating particular cases as we might wish. Most of us are interested in argument, because we see criticism as an important human possibility and because we care about its political effects. In our daydreams, at least, we see criticism as bringing an ideally completed theory of communication to bear on a situation—to illuminate the situation by using the theory. And consistent with that, we often hope that particular studies will buttress and clarify a general theory. But the clearer these expectations become, the more difficult they are to fulfill. Both assume, to one degree or another, that argument is a single process that is more or less constant across arguers, fields, and situations.

The interactional theory undercuts this claim. It describes non-trivial differences in peoples' accommodations to social demands, in their MDLs, in the projects they pursue in arguments, in situations, and in the very facts of communication. The theory suggests that strategy and tactics are as emergent as—and dependent on communication constituting assumptions—as person perception and definitions of situation. Opposition is itself emergent, contingent on the communication constituting factors affecting everything else. Single models of argument's constituents are thus implausible. Carroll's (1979:15–16) view of competence puts the general point nicely:

It seems necessary to extend the notion of competence to describe a whole range of competencies (with emphasis on the plural), not only those having to do with implicit knowledge of language rules, but also those having to do with the characteristic abilities of speakers (or writers) to use their linguistic knowledge to produce effective communications, to retrieve particular types of linguistic knowledge when called for, or to adapt . . . to the demands of different occasions. There are different classes of language rules, for example, phonological, syntactic, lexico-semantic, orthographic, and sociolinguistic. Likewise, there may be diverse kinds of communication tasks with respect to which individuals differ in their characteristic approaches, modes of adaptation, and capabilities of performance.

The point is not *just* Feyerabend's hope to let a thousand flowers bloom. Perhaps pluralism (or tolerance) should be an end in itself in disciplines, but the important point is that methods must be matched to phenomena. The analyst needs at least as much flexibility as situated arguers do. The interactional theory predicts interpersonal differences as well as variations in the situational features which arguers construe to call for particular responses. Only a multiplicity of models will reflect these variations. Whether this creates an unmanageably complex position remains to be seen—to be tested, that is, by the discipline's division of labor.

11.7. Message Analysis

Argumentation is often said to be a "normative" field (Ehninger, 1970; Ehninger and Brockriede, 1978; Wenzel, 1980). This once meant that Argumentation was a "distinctively philosophical entertainment" (Natanson, 1965:10) concerned with argument as such rather than with particular arguments. More recently, this focus has transformed into a concern for argument as procedure (Wenzel, 1980, 1985), a focus on standards of conduct, rules, or recipes (van Eemeren and Grootendorst, 1984) capable of yielding optimal deliberative outcomes.

One would think from all this that Argumentation's orientation to communication would resemble the Conventional MDL. Yet despite the centrality of normative models, the implicit theory of communication behind many argument theories is not the Conventional but the Expressive MDL. "The basic paradigm of Communication can be expressed in the single question: who said what through what medium for what purpose, despite what distractions, with what results?" (Jensen, 1981:5; see also Copi, 1978; Crossley and Wilson, 1979; Eisenberg and Ilardo, 1980; Ennis, 1969; Fearnside and Holther, 1959; Fogelin, 1978; Freeley, 1981; Hamblin, 1970; Hample, 1980, 1981; Kahane, 1971; and most of the essays in Miller and Nilsen, 1966). Using a less dated communication model than Jensen's, yet a more explicit commitment to normative models, Ehninger and Brockriede (1978:222) achieve the same vision: "How can debaters and judges nudge the transaction in the direction of achieving the goals of debate: cooperative investigation, critical method, and wise decisions? On a specific level, debaters can speak or write as clearly as they can. . . . They can do this for most judges by selecting words that say what they want to say as precisely, simply, specifically, concretely, nontechnically, and familiarly as they can find." Or, finally: "A judgment of a speaker's argumentation that is based on his incorrect formulation of his intention or on the incorrect interpretation of his words may in itself be not unreasonable or irrational, but it is an *irrelevant* judgment because it does not relate to the speaker's actual point of view" (van Eemeren, Grootendorst, and Kruiger, 1984:24). We might thus speak of "precization" (Naess, 1966) in much the same way Russell thought of the theory of corrections. This assumes that the only relationship between a rationale and someone's intentions is correctness or incorrectness—indeed, that the point of speech is either to get one's ideas across or to disguise them.

On this view, how do we analyze an argument? We disassemble it. We lay out its constituent parts. The parts of serial predications are terms, premises, and their arrangement. The substance of the terms and premises has an unclear fit with this scheme, though formal rigor is thought to prevent gross reasoning errors. The resultant picture is of ordinary discourse straining toward perfection, reaching toward but falling short of logical perfection. The relation of these pieces to a speaker is straightforward: the predication either succeeds or fails in expressing or disguising the speaker's views.

This confirms and underwrites the Expressive's view of communication. Language is seen as a vehicle for reporting inner states, even when it is seen as creating and sustaining relationships (e.g., Sproule, 1980:38–43). Argumentation texts do not see clarity as a model or theoretical construct appropriate to particular problems but as a fundamental organizing value (Smith and Hunsaker, 1972; Thompson, 1971; Ehninger and Brockriede, 1978; Freeley, 1981; Jensen, 1981). As textbook content, this doctrine arises as a full-fledged theory of discourse that codifies the Expressive's basic assumptions about the possibilities, operations, and ends of discourse and, intentionally or not, stamps them with the imprimatur of a discipline.

This is a perplexing result. It is plausible to think that Expressives are handicapped, that they can profit only minimally from arguments and from social comparison. Expressiveness surely makes for diminished prospects in situations and in life. This disability is exacerbated by a pedagogy centered on expression. As a disciplinary value, the Expressive MDL yields a literal-mindedness that undercuts the usefulness of ideas and of opposition. One would expect Expressives to see metaphors as expressions of a particular reality, not as ways of tying ideas together to make innovations possible. Correspondingly, one would expect disciplines committed to the Expressive MDL to take their metaphors literally. Argumentation raises this literalness to an art form.

We often speak metaphorically of thought as if it were analogous to public processes, for example, Burke's "inner parliament," "we're debating the matter," "inner conversation," "private monologue," and the like. Such loose metaphors may be valuable if not taken literally or concretely. The "inner parliament" is an entry point to a general way of thinking about the relationship between opposition and inference. It underscores the balances individuals achieve between competing interests and how they resolve conflicts by subsuming them beneath larger frames of reference. Some models permit the expression of factors that other models ignore. Seeing humans as "limited capacity information systems" (March and Simon, 1958; March and Olsen, 1976; Nisbett and Ross, 1980), for example, has allowed a clearer discussion of the constraints on inference than previous models.[2]

But speaking this way does not require taking the "inner parliament" literally. Individuals do accommodate to *sets* of competing interests, but to envision mind as a cacophony of competing voices, like a parliament, makes it resemble hallucinatory schizophrenia. Harold Kelley's suggestion that people do ANOVAs would be preposterous if taken literally to mean that humans universally categorize either "in cell" or "across cells" to attribute internal states to others or that ANOVAs are automatic responses—as if a robotic brain rasps metallically, "stimulus object present; begin ANOVA routines."

No model has captured the field's attention—or been taken so literally—as Toulmin's (1964) model of argument. And no practice better illustrates the claim that Argumentation uses the Expressive model than that of identifying the warrant (W) in the model as an "inferential Leap" (Ehninger and Brockriede, 1978). It assumes that a claim (C) is linked to evidence (E) by someone's mental leap—the W being someone's motivations, beliefs, or attitudes about the relationship between C and E. If C is a rationale, however, its logical connections are to a position, not the logical premises argument analysts would intuitively identify as connected to C. Indeed, there is no place for the position idea in the model.

Purely logical analyses of texts can get around these problems by ignoring intentionality and indexicality. This ultimately *equates* utterance with intention: "An argument is *successfully communicated* when the person hearing or reading the argument correctly grasps the argument which the arguer has actually put forward" (Wilson, 1980:391). In effect the Expressive MDL is given a textual guise: the intentions are in the text; one hermeneutically brackets the author. Or one infers the author from textual evidence, as in the case of interpretations of rationales. But the study of rationales—as politically or logically interesting and as appropriate to Argumentation's disciplinary concerns as it may be—does not illuminate the creative, strategic processes central to arguments.

Summary

Why do we find arguments interesting? They are important components of decision making and therefore politically important. They are methods of social comparison and learning and so are cognitively important. They are deliberative methods, which makes them sociologically and politically important. And they are judgmental processes so they are epistemically important. Corresponding to these diverse interests are a variety of empirical happenings taken to instantiate argument's political, cognitive, sociological, and epistemic importance as well as methods of research and analysis deemed appropriate to these happenings.

Why do we find arguments puzzling? They are emergent processes, so they resist freeze-framing. They are social processes, so they involve a complex of personal perspectives and repertoires, inference, creative and strategic grammars, as well as messages, texts, text milieus, situations, organizations, and discourse fields. They are functional processes, though their effects are sometimes hard to pin down. They raise, in sum, a complicated agenda of questions.

This broad tapestry of objects and methods makes for a broad sphere of relevance surrounding argument, decision making, and the subject of opposition in general. As a social science, Argumentation studies the phenomena relevant to the empirical processes of argument, no matter how untidy and fuzzy the resulting package may be.

I have tried in this chapter to complete the parallel with Informal Logic: Argumentation should not attempt with the argument construct what informal logicians have attempted with the fallacy construct. Indeed, the interactional theory should not be evaluated on such terms, for the interactional model is not an expansion of the argument as CRC: it differs in kind.

Notes

1. Argumentation's enduring disciplinary style is embodied in a preference for concreteness. The thingness of serial predicative logic, the objectification of form in argument diagrams, and even the conventional way of describing motives (as warrants fitted onto units of meaningful utterance) symptomize this physicalist bias. This bias may be of a piece with the Expressive MDL I impute to the discipline in general.

2. I owe this example to Barbara J. O'Keefe.

12

![decorative bar]

Positions

The claim that arguments have epistemic effects is premised on the belief that arguments force people onto public courts and into conventional contracts. This emphasis on the public arena and on the deliberative frame appropriate to it suggests the need for an analytical construct for understanding a person's public stances, messages, private beliefs, and strategic repertoires and the coherences between them. This chapter proposes the "position" as a construct that may meet these needs.

Common Ground versus Working Consensus

Rhetorical theorists often speak of *common ground* as a precondition and effect of communication. This is an individualistic idea, for it supposes a sharing of private worlds. Burke's *consubstantiality* thus ties persuasion to a sharing of belief: common substance is a resource we use to achieve still more commonality. The Expressive MDL takes this common ground literally. Thus theologians such as Buber and Jaspers distinguish *authentic* from *inauthentic* communication by virtue of the former's expressive accuracy.

My reasoning in this chapter works in the opposite way, and may be seen by some as an advocacy of inauthentic communication. The idea of authenticity is useful for some purposes (if you and I are discussing our relationship, the accuracy of self-representations may be relevant), but it is inappropriate to most public communication. Indeed I do not believe that communication requires common ground except, of course, on the Expressive MDL. Public discourse often turns on perceptions of common *interest*, but these perceptions are better captured by the position construct.

12.1. Conventional Contracts

What does it mean to say that arguments force arguers onto the public court? To argue is to "go public," so arguers are not utterly free agents. They abide by social conventions; they must accept (and live with) *public* meanings. Public discourse requires a "working consensus" (Goffman, 1959) which arises from the meanings speakers commit themselves to. Working agreements may not correspond to the speakers' private intentions and beliefs; indeed they can acquire lives of their own. In complex arguments (Chapter 2), "participants become committed to certain wants and beliefs whether they intend this or not. For example, in making an evaluation a speaker can be held accountable for having assumed the requisite degree of expertise whether she realizes it or not" (Jacobs, 1987:234). To argue within a field is to agree to abide by the rules.

To adopt a position is to become vulnerable for its outcomes. A politician who says, "busing is an issue of local autonomy," may be disguising the reasons and assumptions behind the claim because they are too dangerous to articulate publicly. "Local autonomy" is thus camouflage for "keep white schools white," a claim the speaker cannot explicitly make. The audience understands the subterfuge and assumes (because of the speaker's ethos) that publicly acceptable reasons are being substituted. But this tactic may draw the speaker into an unwanted dispute about the constitutional basis of local autonomy. Having boarded the roller coaster, one is obliged to finish the ride.

Our acknowledgment of our vulnerability to argument passes us from the subjective to the intersubjective. This recognition is on a par with the jurisdictional decision we make in deciding that a matter that we hitherto reserved as solely a matter of private judgment is justifiably a matter of law. In ceding it to the law's venue, we make it public property. In the passage from the private to the public domain our ideas cease to be truisms and become argumentative claims. Once we acknowledge that we are playing on the public court, we rehearse our defenses (McGuire, 1964; McGuire and Millman, 1965). More than any other kind of interaction, except, perhaps, clinical ones, arguments force us to take the role of the other, to weigh our claims and consider their links to evidence and other claims and to impose a rigor upon our methods of communicating our beliefs. We realize that we are playing by intersubjectively validated rules, not by our private preferences (Goffman, 1963, 1969, 1971).

Even to say that a person decides to play on the public court is too simple. Just as organizational communication theorists hold that every formal structure has a counterpart informal structure, so it is that the decision to go public may involve choices among several courts—some more formal and public than others. The public turf is not a single plot like "the commons" in economic theory. It is rather more analogous to countless truck gardens.

Short of jurisprudential rules having the force of law, something obliges us to abide by the rules even when they restrict our personal freedom. I argue below that our hope to appear "rational" symptomizes our alignments with social orders. Yet a more familiar picture is also part of the equation: Rousseau's reasoning, whatever its merits as a political theory, is pertinent to the social contract presupposed by every argument. However altruistic or Christian or moral we may be, we also obey the rules—and pay the price of doing so—because others do. We play by the rules of argument at least because we expect the other guy to play by the rules. We both want to play the game. The point of the rules lies in the accommodations we make for joint action (van Eemeren and Grootendorst, 1984; Jackson, 1985; Habermas, 1984), or in the scripts we follow (Benoit, 1981, 1983; Abelson, 1976; Trapp, 1982), or, as Giddens (1979) says, in the regularization of the interdependency between people and groups.

Complex arguments may not turn on a single contract, but instead, like real estate deals, involve layers of commitments. Nothing in the contract to argue, for instance, enjoins us to be civil. Nor does the decision to argue by itself prohibit lying, cheating, and evasion. The threat of scrutiny embodied in the presence of an interlocutor who might catch us may restrain our worst impulses: Deterrence, criminologists say, is proportional to the perceived risk of apprehension. But it is also plausible that we refrain from lying, etc., because we subscribe to codes—standards of professionalism, the Ten Commandments, or Ann Landers's Ten Rules for Happy Marriage.

I am not taking a deterministic view of positions and rules. The claim that actors gravitate into public processes and are thus forced into this or that outcome doesn't cut against the belief that people are able to manipulate the public system. The capacity of humans to distort and adapt rules to wants and circumstances is breathtaking but not limitless. The Christian entrepreneur whose morals are flexible enough to accommodate to a Survivalist model of the business world (yielding an ethics red in tooth and claw) has achieved a tidy separation of domains. The cognitive and strategic advantages of such compartmentalization are considerable, as in the case of the government that condemns terrorism as a violation of international law and morality, yet proclaims international law and morality a "hollow myth" when the International Court finds against it in another suit. But we do see people called to account; the *tu quoque* is a serious weapon, especially for the press.

12.2. Zones of Accountability

Apart from not reading public accountability as a deterministic idea, there is an advantage in not seeing it as a hermeneutic proposal. Arguers often justifiably insist on being held to account only for their intentions, not for every meaning someone wrings out of a claim. The arguers in Example 4.2 (Chapter 4) might refuse to abide by national statistical evidence because their utterances are addressed to each other and no one else and because their private purposes are legitimate. Likewise, *C* in Example 4.1 would refuse to be held accountable for a literal reading of "an FTE is an FTE." In a private conversation, *C* is accountable to *T*—the person addressed—not to every imaginable addressee. The ongoing maintenance of a position is a way of constraining messages. Since messages are indefinitely describable (O'Keefe, 1988), one's position is a way of defining one's zone of accountability.

More public utterances put speakers in a broader interpretive zone of accountability. We commonsensically expect diplomats and politicians to be sensitive to the nuances of language and the pitfalls or impossibilities of translation. We expect speakers to take care that their intentions are as clear as they want them to be. Witness the *contretemps* surrounding Alexander Haig's statement ("I'm in charge here") following an assassination attempt on the president. The claim was interpreted by the press as an egomaniacal claim, a power grab. But there is a more plausible reading: avoidably ambiguous message construction. Haig might justifiably claim that he intended to reassure the public at a critical time—to send the message "someone's in charge; this is a contained crisis, nothing to panic about." If one thinks like a career military officer, "I'm in charge here" means that "I" take responsibility for what happens (surely a good thing in general and a noble thing in generals); "here" means "where I'm standing," "where I happen to be." For a military careerist and chief of staff concerned daily with executive operations, power and authority reside in roles, not places. Unfortunately, "here" also meant the White House—perhaps our most definitive symbol of national power and authority. Haig may have forgotten the difference between his taken-for-granted way of seeing the location of power and how outsiders see it. Presidential authority is operationally but not symbolically irrelevant to place.

"Taking the role of the Fourth Estate" is a prerequisite of any but the most reckless mass communications. And taking the press's perspective ought to be relatively easy. I cannot prove that journalists, by disciplinary heritage, are prone to an Expressive MDL, though Journalism may be the only profession that *claims* to be Expressive. The picture is of an obdurate reality, positivistically describable, to be depicted accurately or inaccurately (Bok, 1983; Cater, 1959; Commission on Freedom of the Press, 1947; Gerald, 1963; Hulteng, 1985). The ethics codes, for example, stress timeliness, accuracy, and clarity (Article 2, Code of Broadcast News Ethics, Radio Television News Directors Association); journalists are seen as "carriers of information" whose main duty is "to serve the truth" and whose definitive mark of professionalism is "objectivity" (Code of Ethics, Society of Professional Journalists, Sigma Delta Chi). The standard objective questions (Is it fair, accurate, and complete? [Metzler, 1986] Is it true or false? What does it conceal?) symptomize an implicit theory of communication—one rather at odds with the Conventional or Rhetorical strategies people of interest to the press may employ.

The cognitive effects of public compliance are an important issue, but they are irrelevant to the importance of going public. Just as conformity to etiquette may change our private beliefs, as public compliance with laws may change private rejections of the laws' goals, obeying the rules of argument may affect how we see our own beliefs. Doubts about a system's usefulness are brought into the open; forced social comparison occurs; though we may defend our system at all costs, we cannot avoid seeing it as a commodity in the social system—seeing it vis-à-vis the beliefs of others. Yet people also adopt masks: users of Rhetorical MDLs adopt personae; people in all walks of life can and do cynically manipulate public facades, folkways, and standards to their personal advantage. The public court guarantees nothing about one's sincerity or morals, though it may enhance the risks of getting caught. At any rate, "going public" may or may not have private cognitive implications; it always has public implications.

This idea of a zone of accountability—even in its broader guise in mass communication—is not a hermeneutic realm. In a pluralistic society, speakers cannot be accountable for *every* meaning someone might conceivably assign to their utterances. Paleontology is not accountable for the funny twists creation scientists might give their claims and evidence; and as the U.S. Supreme Court has just held, textbook writers are not responsible for offending fundamentalists. It is plausible to assume that jurisdictional decisions involve choosing among segments of "the public"—selecting the authoritative domains that seem appropriate for authorizing our claims.

12.3. Position Defined

The construct *position* may serve as a loose rubric for uniting the multiple questions arguments raise, though it by no means exhausts the range of questions argument theorists pose or fully explains the social, cognitive, and epistemic functions and effects of arguments. The position notion is a way of avoiding false oppositions of individuals with the fields of discourse in which they move and of illuminating the effects of one on the other.

As far as I know, *position* rarely functions as a technical term. Argumentation texts often speak loosely of a debater's or lawyer's position (see, e.g., Wilson, 1980), or of legal briefs as argumentative stances, but they seem to prefer other terms as objects of analysis such as the brief, the case, and the proposal. The brief is a sustained, structured defense of a claim; the case is a unified coalition of briefs organized around a proposal; and a proposal is an explicit structure of changes. All three are documents available for sustained scrutiny. In what follows, position is not equated with brief, case, or proposal, though all may function as emblematic of or occasionally equivalent to an advocate's position. Thus traditional methods for analyzing (and attacking) briefs, cases, and proposals may well be entry points to an advocate's position.

One technical usage of *position* is pertinent: in marketing and advertising, *positioning* refers to the strategic decisions one makes to differentiate one's product from the competition. One can manufacture a product sufficiently unique to appeal to a select group and thereby to avoid direct confrontation with entrenched competitors. Or one can create a new cognitive niche in the consumer's mind for an existing product: Lysol languished as a "disinfectant" but achieved a 50 percent market share as a "household cleanser" (Kleppner, 1979). *Positioning* in this usage is a marketing strategy—a surrogate for "audience analysis" and "audience adaptation" (Smith and Lusch, 1976). It includes the analysis and adaptations of research data to build strategically useful audience profiles, which, in turn, serve as the bases for the creation of persuasive messages directed at particular segments of an audience.[1] *Segmenting*, remember, refers to differentiations within an audience (Maggard, 1976; Percy, 1976).

Consulting *Roget's*, one finds synonyms for *position* grouped *geographically* (locality, location, place, site), *personally* (attitude, opinion, belief, view), *strategically* (post, situation, circumstances, predicament, posture), and *honorifically*, as in one's social position (consequence, prestige, status). The first three senses are obviously apropos: we naturally speak of arguers occupying particular ground, or of "President Reagan's position on Nicaragua" not as equivalent to particular messages but as standing for a constellation of public statements perhaps emblematic of his private commitments, and of an arguer's posture, situation, or predicament rather as if they were analogous to what military folk call "occupied ground." Notice the consonance of the geographic and strategic (and even honorific) senses of *position* with the marketing/advertising verb *positioning*.

In the context of the geographic, strategic, and personal meanings of *position*, the argument scholar can see the term as a construct with two distinguishable but compatible references. The differences in meaning can be ignored for certain purposes yet must be enforced for others. Thus *position* refers to two distinct but related phenomena: (1) a public stance, posture, or perspective; and (2) a personal stance, one's analysis of the coherence between one's beliefs, attitudes, and intentions and one's public messages or public stance. We may call these position$_1$ and position$_2$.

Examples of position$_1$ arise in the ways we characterize peoples' perspectives, points of view, attitudes, and stances. To say, "Reagan is a conservative," is to imply the existence of a constellation of describable beliefs, attitudes, or tendencies. More specifically, "Reagan opposes the Sandinistas" implies that his perspective includes beliefs X through N; he advocates thus and so policies; and he is likely to react in this or that way to certain proposals. Such imputations may or may not be episodic, but they are always dispositional (Warr and Knapper, 1968). We also notice position$_1$ in artfully contrived documents such as the *State Department White Paper on Communist Infiltration in Vietnam* or a litigant's brief in a legal proceeding.

Position$_2$ is closer to *positioning*. One is *translating* one's intentions into messages and strategies. One is discovering and analyzing, à la Aristotle, "the available means of persuasion." One is considering the connections between one's beliefs and one's actions. In such usages, the language of strategy and tactics, artifice and craft, cooperates with the language of commitment and accountability. Position$_2$ may thus be taken to be the analytic moves one makes either to create specific messages or to achieve a position$_1$.

Position$_2$ refers to an analytical construct—a coherence pattern discerned by the argument scholar or by the naive actor. In using the construct, both are analyzing the fit between elements of one's private beliefs and strategic repertoire and one's public stance or messages. My position$_2$ is not equivalent to my "point of view"; nor is it synonymous with my public statements. Position$_2$ does not correspond to a unit of interaction, thought, or meaningful utterance. Rather, it is a coherence one creates between public and private claims.[2]

My views on the subject of Nicaragua are a mishmash of vague attitudes and beliefs, perhaps so simple that (on the predictions of cognitive dissonance or balance theories) if I like (dislike) Reagan I will approve (disapprove) of aid to the Contras. Such simple cojudgment and cognitive vagueness may prove satisfactory—perhaps forever if nothing happens to spur housecleaning. But we spruce things up for company. A question ("What do you think of the Contras?") may force me to shuffle through my ideas, rearranging and straightening up—creating, as Kelly says, a cognitive "system" as well as a public performance in the process. In answering any question, even in idle chit-chat, I want to seem "rational" and intelligent. However I answer the question, further questions may follow—forcing me to clear up at least enough of the clutter to make coherent conversational moves. My "rationality" may be "bounded" (March and Simon, 1958; March and Olsen, 1976). I will satisfice till pressed, discharge the burden of rejoinder sufficiently but not optimally. Or my "rationality" may be a facade (Goffman, 1959, 1961a, 1961b, 1963, 1964). In both cases, the conversation may be important enough to keep me careful even if the topic is not important enough to warrant the effort of a complete system overhaul. Like housecleaning, I will stuff things away where the company won't look— if I am sure they won't look too hard.

The pivotal assumption in this scenario—and one that often passes as unremarkable among argument theorists—is that I want to appear "rational." The importance of this desire is often overlooked because argument theorists focus on rules rather than motives. Yet we have seen consistently that argument is dependent upon, yet cannot guarantee, good will. This prompted the skepticism with which this book began: if argument is so easily subverted and cannot guarantee the existence of the good will it requires, then argument may itself be an empty facade. Hence the spirit of the organizational scholars who see "rationality" as a facade (Conrad,

1985) and thus decision making as an organizational myth (March and Simon, 1965; March and Olsen, 1976; Westerlund and Sjostrand, 1979) or "garbage can" (March, 1970). But all of this ignores the more basic question: *Why* do I hope to seem "rational?"

Recall the view of "rationality" (Chapter 7) said to flow from the interactional theory. One's "rationality" in a community is one's sanity, competence, and predictability—one's authenticity as a native, one's bona fides as a group member. Hence the intrinsic conservatism of community norms and the need for peripheral discourse to achieve innovation and change. In the context of these claims, my hope to appear "rational" is explicable: if I identify (Kelman, 1961) with a community, pin my identity to it and my self-worth to my success in it, my hope to seem "rational" may symptomize nothing more complex than a hope for acceptance and status. Securing identification (as opposed to negative sanctions) is generally thought by persuasion scholars to be the most powerful method by which social orders solve the good will problem. So even though arguments do not guarantee good will, the communities in which they occur provide something almost as good: the hope to appear "rational."

12.4. Institutional Intentionality

The importance of intentionality has been underscored (Chapter 4). In some cases, or for certain questions, it is essential to know what a speaker means to be saying. We thus speak of a person's position$_1$ as a constellation of private beliefs and public actions. But the relation between utterances and an individual's beliefs is not always a central, and is sometimes a misleading, idea. Ours is the age of the spokesperson; many messages are not from people but from institutions. The spokesperson thus works with and from positions that are group creations (e.g., press releases, CEO statements, public relations documents, White Papers, and the like). One's private opinions may be irrelevant; they are understood to be standing on their own or to be group accomplishments (and thus matters of group responsibility). One who focuses exclusively on the connection between messages and private beliefs (because one sees communication as Expressive) will thus occasionally distort the nature of rhetorical events.

Even when personal motives are relevant, the rhetorical maneuvers may arise from a position$_2$ of considerable complexity. Consider the recent spectacle of the secretary of state distancing himself from the events surrounding the Iran arms deal. To appear simultaneously honorable, ignorant of a major policy initiative, yet competent as secretary of state is tricky going. To see the secretary's statements as expressions of his mental contents—and not as strategic productions fashioned out of a position—is to put too simple a face on a breathtaking rhetorical accomplishment.

12.5. Positions and MDLs

Since arguments do not function the same ways for people of different complexity, we should expect systematic differences in both positions among users of Expressive, Conventional, and Rhetorical MDLs. Expressives will have primitive positions contrasted to Conventionals and Rhetoricals. Since they see communication as a process in which people express what they think or feel and thus see messages as ways of making known one's thoughts, Expressives will either get their meaning across or disguise it. Their "analysis" would thus assess whether a message got a point across or kept something disguised successfully. The Expressive sees no difference between the two senses of position. Argumentation based on the Expressive MDL likewise sees the accuracy of the correspondence between private beliefs and public statements as a core problematic. I see it as a comparatively rudimentary problem among an array of questions. A Rhetorical MDL might yield a message at variance with or irrelevant to the speaker's private substantive beliefs: one might advocate aid to the Contras even if one does not privately believe in it. But rhetorically contrived messages are *not* unrelated to the speaker's *analysis* of the relationships between plans and practices, beliefs and claims, situational features and lines of action.

Message creation is a process in which, among other things, one translates one's thoughts and strategic repertoire into message strategies. This translation requires a creative theory analogous to a Chomskyian generative grammar, the sparsest instance of which is the Expressive MDL. Expressives characteristically fail to distinguish between thought and expression. When stimulated, they respond. The situation provokes thoughts and feelings; the purpose of communication is to dump those thoughts and feelings out. Since Expressives assume that other people produce messages in the same way, there is no reason to think of communication rhetorically. Though the Expressive might understand that a Rhetorical message is better in a situation, she or he lacks the knowledge about communication necessary for systematically altering a message in the service of achieving effects (O'Keefe and McCornack, 1987). We thus expect to find idiosyncratic and subjective semantic and pragmatic connections between the Expressive's messages and their contexts and among elements within Expressive messages. O'Keefe's (Chapter 1) question ("Why did the speaker say this *now?*") thus has a clear-cut, almost S-R behavioristic answer vis-à-vis the Expressive: an event causes a mental state; the speaker then says what she or he is thinking. To the question, "why did the speaker say *this?*" our answer is that the common thread that unites or thematizes the elements of an Expressive message consists of "whatever is on the speaker's mind" (O'Keefe, 1986:9).

The Conventional, conversely, sees him or herself engaged in a cooperative enterprise—using the recipes, playing by the rules. In analyzing the coherence between beliefs and public statements, the Conventional would be concerned with conventional fit as well as with intersubjective confirmation. The Conventional position$_2$, then, might have the assessment of persuasive effectiveness as one analytical goal, observing etiquette as another, and fit with conventional wisdom as still another.

The Rhetorical sees communication as a creative, negotiative process from which social selves and situations emerge. This view of the relationship of message and context is the mirror opposite of the Expressive's. It also differs markedly from the Conventional's view of context as given. The Rhetorical sees messages as creating "contexts"—leaving it to the interactionally achieved "architecture of intersubjectivity" (Rommetveit, 1980, 1974; see Chapter 4 here) to anchor meaning (O'Keefe, 1986:11–12). Since messages are ambiguous, communication is seen as a coordination problem: "The fundamental message function is negotiation. Since ways of speaking create selves and situations and since ways of speaking are (by assumption) freely selected by message producers, the context of communication becomes, rather than an anchor for meaning, a resource that is interactionally managed and strategically exploited" (p. 12). So what is needed is consensus: the Rhetorical has to get an interlocutor to act in the same play.

There is a parallel between what O'Keefe says of Rhetorical MDLs and the position developed in Chapter 9 about disciplinary stability and change. The people, beliefs, practices, and contexts that yield conservation and conservatism, stability and fixity, may differ from the people, beliefs, practices, and contexts that yield intellectual adaptation and innovation. A Conventional MDL makes it plausible to think that an intellectual ecology maintains stability as a matter of following recipes and conventional acquiescence. Conventional discourse creates conventional stability. Rhetorical discourse creates adaptation and change.

Toulmin (1972) wants to explain conceptual stability and change in a language common to both, thereby exposing the "rationality" common to both. He goes wrong, I think, in posing this question outside the framework of a theory of communication. But as "The Balkanization" argues, he also goes wrong in assuming that stability and change arise from the activities of the same populations. Yet a theory of intellectual change must surely require a picture of what people do to create change. If we see both stability and change as inhering in discourse strategies, it is plausible to think that the Conventional language appropriate to the former may be inadequate to explain the Rhetorical processes common to the latter. When conceptual changes are not logical implications derivable from the structure of a community's current knowledge, they are likely adaptations blown in from the periphery. Plausibly, such innovations are made possible by the creation of new contexts, new connections among constructs, rather than conventional adaptations of existing contexts.

Oddly, this same point arises in discussions of texts because texts are often taken to instantiate a field's current intellectual ecology and thus to embody the "rationality" in the field's intellectual change. The MDL notion implies that we should not seek a single theory of intellectual stability and change, for we will not find field actors using messages (and thus arguing) in universal ways. What follows, therefore, is an exposition along two tracks: a thesis about how Argumentation theorists and critics should see texts and a thesis concerning the centrality of performance in intellectual stability and change.

12.6. Relation of Positions to Texts

In some cases—not all, to be sure—the messages of Expressives, Conventionals, and Rhetoricals may look alike. There may be no clue to the speaker's position in a text taken as a record of an utterance. Pedagogy, for example, no matter how rhetorical or conventional it may be, often *looks* Expressive. Obviously, the three MDLs are models the analyst might follow in giving meaning to such bare messages. Because traditional Argumentation theories have been premised on the Expressive model, they have promoted a tendency for analysts to be satisfied with texts. And this, in turn, may explain why the intellectual coherence and "rationality" of bodies of knowledge are so often thought to inhere in the coherence within and among texts.

The status of texts as objects of research has been disputed since the early 1970s. Some disputes turn on the status of texts not as literary objects but as historical records (Willard, 1983). The fact that *documents* are occasionally (or for certain purposes) equivalent to positions$_1$ fuels the belief that logical analyses of texts can yield interesting results. The fact that documents are occasionally (and for certain purposes) unrelated either to positions$_1$ or positions$_2$ lends ammunition to the charge that texts should be studied halfheartedly if at all and that textual exegesis may be irrelevant to what arguments in fact accomplish. The dispute was fueled by an unfortunately narrow (and Expressive) view of texts. Texts either are or are not accurate records of what someone said; they either are or are not accurate expressions of their creator's thinking; they have thus and so effects on audiences; and so on. In other words, the dispute bundled a view of texts as Expressive messages with a proportionately simple view of historical records and a too unidimensional sense of intentionality.

What now seems clear, but did not then, is that the terms *text*, *document*, and *message* represent different analytical moves, require different methods, and occasionally refer to different empirical phenomena. Also, texts and documents—speech transcripts as well as legal briefs, position papers, and essays—might be created, analyzed, and used by Expressives, Conventionals, or Rhetoricals. Their sophistication and intersubjective effectiveness should thus correspond to the developmental attainments of their creators. The three MDLs, O'Keefe predicts, should display developmental succession, that is, there will be a "logically necessary order" both to their acquisition and to their functional utility for generating effective messages, especially in difficult communication situations (O'Keefe and McCornack, 1987:73). The Rhetorical MDL capitalizes on conventional knowledge not to infer action from a context but to create a context. Thus the Rhetorical cannot function without mastery of the Conventional system. The Conventional MDL likewise exploits a mastery of the Expressive system "to generate expressions that count as actions in given contexts" (p. 72).

Legal briefs are thus written with the expectation that they will undergo sustained, hostile scrutiny. Since there are systematic differences in peoples' abilities to represent the intersubjective expectations and possibilities in an analytical context, we expect briefs, position papers, and any other formalized or doctrinal statements to vary. The Expressive will be as clear as possible; the Conventional will be as conventionally sound, polite, and fair as possible; and the Rhetorical will try to create a way of perceiving (and possible dodges as opposition heats up).

For the Conventional and Rhetorical, texts need not be corporeal, objective givens against which ephemeral human interpretations are butted. The choice need not be between the "concreteness" of texts versus the variability of peoples' points of view. The Rhetorical, for example, may see a text as a strategic resource of great flexibility. "The Rhetorical design logic makes information about the subtleties of verbal behavior constantly relevant to the process of message planning and interpretation: knowledge of the ways in which communicative choice and language style convey character, attitude, and definitions of the situation is systematically exploited" (O'Keefe, 1986). Thus textual analyses may not reveal the positional moves someone has or has not made. Although a logical disassembly of a text or document may have value for certain purposes, it is of limited utility for understanding arguments.

The logic of positions is not equivalent to the logic of texts. Though some texts are rightly taken to exemplify a position, we most comfortably think of "Smith's position" as something Smith has and is responsible for. Smith's text might not be a replica of his position. Intervening variables might include Smith's creative ability, audience analysis—including accuracy of perception, the transformation of intentions to strategies, and Smith's MDL. A Conventional or Rhetorical interlocutor might use a text's logic to constrain Smith's position (e.g., by appealing to consistency). One might strategically frame a text (or utterance) with this possibility in mind. An Expressive might not be able to adapt to and capitalize upon such potential. Attempts at constraint do not always succeed: hermeneutic scholars point to the breadth of interpretations possible in texts. With enough weasel words, one can waffle on some public issues indefinitely.

To restate this reasoning with respect to intellectual change, one might see knowledge structures as possibilities or as constraints (or both). One might prefer, for example, to reason conventionally as long as the use of current recipes keeps one on interesting ground. But if one is struck by ambiguities in a prevailing system and the latitudes in reasoning these seem to permit, one might take prevailing knowledge to be a stock of materials ready to be adapted to particular needs. As one becomes fascinated by local as opposed to discipline-central needs and interests, one's flexibility and adaptiveness may push one away from the conventional interpretive center.

12.7. Situations

As with texts, a discussion of situations can also follow parallel tracks. On one level, the interactional theory has consequences for how critics ought to view situations (Chapter 3). On another level, if arguments have epistemic effects and it is thereby appropriate to think of them as foundational to a discipline's stability and innovation, then the circumstances in which they arise bear consequences for explanations of discipline.

Argumentation theorists have debated the nature of situations as if a single account, fitted to a single rhetorical theory, could be found. Early treatments held situations to be relatively fixed fabrics of constraints, possibilities, and exigencies (Bitzer, 1968). Corrections to that view emphasized the interpretive activities of actors "in" situations (Willard, 1982, 1983). The definition of situation was thus a psychological and negotiative process.

The revised view had two weaknesses: it was overpsychologized (it did not seem to allow for situations themselves to have constraints and demands independent of the arguers' perspectives), and it tended to explain differences in definitions of situation by the wastebasket construct "psychological differences." The first mistake was an odd one because it stemmed from undervaluing the constraints and possibilities in communication processes. Exaggerated individualism always undervalues communication. Taken literally the revised view precluded communication. The second mistake was more natural: if one is attacking exaggerated social determinism, one wallows in psychological differences.

The systematic differences in MDLs offer a better explanation. Positions and situations are of a piece and may be expected to parallel the relative complexity of design logics. The Rhetorical MDL, we have seen, is the most complex: it subsumes knowledge of conventional means to achieve goals while recognizing that situational features are emergent within the unfolding process of communication. The Rhetorical does not see selves and situations as given in a conventional system of rules and does not see meaning as fixed in messages by their form and context. Selves, situations, and meanings are all matters of negotiation: "The potential of language to evoke roles and structure context is exploited through the manipulation of stylistic variation in language and explicit contextualizing elaborations of messages. The same attention to the details of message construction is devoted to message interpretation, leading to more careful listening and depth interpretation of intentions, motives, and character" (O'Keefe and McCornack, 1987:72). Expressives see situations as fixed structures of constraints, positions as stable and obdurate, messages as fixed structures of meaning, and other people as stable (and similar to themselves). Conventionals see the situation as given but look for the rules, roles, and relations relevant to their projects and observe the proprieties and follow the recipes for adapting their projects to the expectations of others. Rhetoricals attempt to negotiate shared definitions that make their projects possible.

Argumentation scholars go wrong in seeking a single, universal sense of what situations are—a mistake inherited from rhetorical critics who get their view of situations from History. If your thinking about situations *starts* with a historical descriptive model, you will see situations as describable structures (or if you are swayed by Goffman, as stages and sets on and against which actors play out their lines). You will see criticism as a search for thick description to permit links to the other *pieces*: actors' psychologies, actions, and effects.

Under the regime of the interactional theory, what does "thick description" mean? You would have to know enough about a situation to diagnose expressive communications. Since context irrelevancy is an important symptom, one would have to know that a claim is irrelevant. Your description would further have to specify the ways in which the arguers' positions constitute the situation. The situation is not a stage on which the positions rest or a container in which they function but an integral part of them—just as one could not describe a situation without describing the coherence relations the actors have contrived. Positions are not the only components of situations, but they are central to them.

Given the centrality of positions to situations, it makes sense to say that different situations call for different actions. The nature of tasks in situations may differ depending on their representation in a position (see Delia, 1983; Applegate, 1978). Seeing situations in terms of the complexity of a person's representation of goals and obstacles in a position is an important part of seeing differences among the MDLs. People who have more differentiated and integrated cognitive systems may be able to seize upon "the relevant situational variables that will lead to more successful outcomes. As B. J. O'Keefe has argued, social cognition is organized around personal and social purposes, and people may evaluate others in terms of 'rough and ready' assessments that are important to achieving their practical aims" (Willihnganz, 1987:168). Some situations call forth purely conventional responses—as in the simplest kinds of arguments distinguished in Chapter 2. "Let's go to dinner" may be treated as a request; conversational troubles may need remedy;

someone may need comforting; complexes of multiple goals may need balancing; ideas may need testing; and so on.

The Rhetorical, rather differently, has it both ways. Positions are components of situations; situations are components of positions. Both elements are negotiated, mutually accommodated achievements emergent from interaction. Since the goal of argument might be to solve a problem, the Rhetorical options may include reconstruing the situation, the position, or both. Since impediments to problem solving or decision making may include matters of expression, the Rhetorical may see language as a flexible resource, open to reformulation and refinement. Discourse thus has the potential to transcend its starting point.

There remains an unclear fit between situational elements, MDLs, and the messages communicators in fact produce. How and why are certain situational variables interpreted as calling for this or that strategy? Are there recurring features of situations that call for (say) Expressive communications even from Conventionals and Rhetoricals? And presuming that we can answer these questions, will we then know how to distinguish between an expressive message produced by an Expressive and one produced by a Conventional or Rhetorical? The position idea may be a point of leverage for addressing such questions because it is a way of specifying important aspects of a person's definition of a situation.

Summary

So we have recast our thinking about intellectual stability and change. On our account, stability is often Conventional; innovation is (at least in its beginnings) often Rhetorical. Whereas many scholars attempt to explain stability and change as though they are opposing activities in the same audience, I have chosen to see audiences as segmented. Pressures for change may thus manifest themselves in the creation of new subcommunities often lying at a field's periphery. If the peripheral views radiate inward, pressures for conventionalizing them will intensify—which may explain why "rational progress" is often a Foucauldian deceptive history. The grounds of innovation, I submit, are to be found in epistemic practices—argument being foremost among them.

This explanation—an admittedly cursory defense of the "position" construct—will have to do for now. Obviously, such an epistemic explanation will play a prominent role in consideration of the structure, function, and effects of discourse fields. But a full dress defense must await the successor volume.

Notes

1. What may seem disagreeable about "positioning" is its lack of emphasis on personal commitment, belief, and responsibility. It seems to be pure instrumental rationality—unfettered strategy, amoral analysis. But the advertiser might plausibly object that positioning in a particular case is (or is not) restrained by *another* position, a moral stance, a professional code. Positions are instrumental, but they do not exist in a vacuum.

2. I owe this line of reasoning and especially the definition of position$_2$, to Barbara J. O'Keefe.

Bibliography

Abbreviations

APSR	=	*American Political Science Review*
APQ	=	*American Philosophical Quarterly*
ASQ	=	*Administrative Science Quarterly*
ASR	=	*American Sociological Review*
CD	=	*Child Development*
CM	=	*Communication Monographs*
CSSJ	=	*Central States Speech Journal*
HCR	=	*Human Communication Research*
ILN	=	*Informal Logic Newsletter*
JAR	=	*Journal of Advertising Research*
JAFA	=	*Journal of the American Forensic Association*
JASP	=	*Journal of Abnormal and Social Psychology*
JEP	=	*Journal of Experimental Psychology*
JESP	=	*Journal of Experimental Social Psychology*
JP	=	*Journal of Personality*
JPL	=	*The Journal of Philosophical Logic*
JPSP	=	*Journal of Personality and Social Psychology*
JSP	=	*Journal of Social Psychology*
JSPR	=	*Journal of Social and Personal Relationships*
JTSB	=	*Journal for the Theory of Social Behavior*
LA	=	*Logique et Analyse*
MSRCD	=	*Monographs of the Society for Research in Child Development*
POQ	=	*Public Opinion Quarterly*
PPR	=	*Philosophy and Phenomenological Research*

PQ = *Philosophical Quarterly*
P&R = *Philosophy and Rhetoric*
PR = *Psychological Review*
PS = *Philosophy of Science*
PSS = *Philosophy of the Social Sciences*
QJS = *Quarterly Journal of Speech*
SCA = Speech Communication Association
SE = *Social Epistemology*
SM = *Speech Monographs*
SSCJ = *Southern Speech Communication Journal*
SSS = *Social Studies of Science*
WJSC = *Western Journal of Speech Communication*

Abelson, R. P. 1976. "Script Processing in Attitude Formation and Decision-Making." In J. Carroll and J. Payne, eds., *Cognition and Social Behavior.* Erlbaum.

Abelson, R. 1960–61. "In Defense of Formal Logic." *PPR* 21:333–46.

Abrahamsson, B. 1977. *Bureaucracy or Participation.* Sage.

Adams, K. L. 1983. "Negotiating Social Conflict in Varying Relational Contexts." In Zarefsky, Sillars, and Rhodes.

———. 1985. "Communication as Negotiation: A Study of Strategic Interaction in Social Relationships." Ph.D. dissertation, University of Utah.

Ajzen, I. 1977. "Intuitive Theories of Events and the Effects of Base Rate Information on Prediction." *JASP* 35:303–14.

Allen, G. 1985. *The Importance of the Past.* SUNY.

Allen, T. H. 1978. *New Methods in Social Science Research.* Praeger.

Allison, G. T. 1971. *The Essence of Decision.* Little, Brown.

Allport, F. H. 1933. *Institutional Behavior.* University of North Carolina Press.

Altman, I., and D. A. Taylor. 1973. *Social Penetration.* Holt.

Alvy, K. T. 1973. "The Development of Listener Adapted Communications in Grade-School Children from Different Social Class Backgrounds." *Genetic Psychology* 87:33–104.

Ammon, P. 1981. "Communication Skills and Communicative Competence: A Neo-Piagetian Process-Structural View." In Dickson.

Anderson, J. E. 1979. *Public Policy-Making,* 2d ed. Holt.

Andrews, J. R. 1983. *The Practice of Rhetorical Criticism.* Macmillan.

Anscombe, G. E. M. 1959. *Intention.* Oxford.

Antaki, C. 1981. *The Psychology of Ordinary Explanations of Human Behavior.* Academic.

Applegate, J. L. 1978. "Four Investigations of the Relationship between Social Cognitive Development and Person-Centered Regulative and Interpersonal Communication." Ph.D. dissertation, University of Illinois.

———. 1980. "Person- and Position-Centered Teacher Communication in a Day Care Center." In N. K. Denzin, ed., *Studies in Symbolic Interaction,* vol. 3. JAI.

Applegate, J. L., and J. G. Delia. 1980. "Person-Centered Speech, Psychological Development, and the Contexts of Language Usage." In R. St. Clair and H. Giles, eds., *The Social and Psychological Contexts of Language*. Erlbaum.

Archer, M. S. 1982. "Morphogenesis versus Structuration: On Combining Structure and Action." *British J. Sociology* 33:455–83.

Arendt, H. 1958. "What Was Authority." In C. Friedrich, ed., *Nomos*. Harvard University Press.

Argyle, M., and M. Henderson. 1984. "The Rules of Friendship." *JSPR* 1:211–37.

Argyris, C. 1957. *Personality and Organization*. Harper.

——. 1964. *Integrating the Individual and the Organization*. Wiley.

Arieli, Y. 1964. *Individualism and Nationalism in American Ideology*. Harvard University Press.

Aron, R. 1950. "Social Structure and the Ruling Class." *British J. Sociology* 1:1–17, 126–44.

Aronson, E., J. A. Turner, and J. M. Carlsmith. 1963. "Communicator Credibility and Communication Discrepancy as Determinants of Opinion Change." *JASP* 67:31–36.

Asch, S. E. 1946. "Forming Impressions of Personality." *JASP* 41:258–90.

Asher, S. R., and A. Wigfield. 1981. "Training Referential Communication Skills." In Dickson.

Ashworth, P. D. 1979. *Social Interaction and Consciousness*. Wiley.

Athay, M., and J. M. Darley. 1981. "Toward an Interaction-Centered Theory of Personality." In N. Cantor and J. K. Kihlstrom, eds., *Personality, Cognition, and Social Interaction*. Erlbaum.

Aune, J. A. 1979. "The Contributions of Habermas to Rhetorical Validity." *JAFA* 16:104–11.

Austin, J. L. 1975. *How to Do Things with Words*. 2d ed. Harvard University Press.

Ayer, A. J. 1956. *The Problem of Knowledge*. Macmillan.

Bachrach, P. 1967. *The Theory of Democratic Elitism*. Little, Brown.

Ball, D. W. 1967. "An Abortion Clinic Ethnography." *Social Problems* 14:293–301.

Ballard, K. E. 1972. *Study Guide for Copi: Introduction to Logic*. 4th ed. Macmillan.

Balthrop, V. W. 1980. "Argument as Linguistic Opportunity: A Search for Form and Function." In Rhodes and Newell.

——. 1982. "Argumentation and the Critical Stance: A Methodological Approach." In Cox and Willard.

Barber, B. 1952. *Science and the Social Order*. Free Press.

Bar-Hillel, Y. 1964. "Indexical Expressions." *Mind* 63:359–79.

——, ed. 1971. *Pragmatics of Natural Language*. Reidel.

Barker, E. M. 1981. *Everyday Reasoning*. Prentice-Hall.

Barnes, B. 1974. *Scientific Knowledge and Sociological Theory*. Routledge.

——. 1976. "Natural Rationality: A Neglected Topic in the Social Sciences." *PSS* 6:115–26.

——. 1977. *Interests and the Growth of Knowledge*. Routledge.

Barnes, H. E. 1967. *An Existentialist Ethics*. Vintage.

Baron, J. 1985. *Rationality and Intelligence*. Cambridge University Press.

Baron, R. S., and N. Miller. 1969. "Credibility, Distraction, and Counter-argument in a Forewarning Situation." *Proceedings, 77th Convention of the American Psychological Association* 4:411–12.

Barry, V. E. 1976. *Practical Logic.* Holt.

Barth, E. M. 1972. *Evaluaties.* Van Gorcum. [From van Eemeren, Grooten-dorst, and Kriuger, 1987.]

Barth, E. M., and E. C. W. Krabbe. 1982. *From Axiom to Dialogue.* De Gruyter.

Barth, E. M., and J. L. Martins. 1982. *Argumentation.* Benjamins.

Bartley, W. W. 1963. *The Retreat to Commitment.* Knopf.

Bay, C. 1958. *The Structure of Freedom.* Stanford University Press.

Baynes, K., J. Bohman, and T. McCarthy. 1987. *After Philosophy.* MIT Press.

Bearison, D. J., and S. T. Gass. 1979. "Hypothetical and Practical Reasoning: Children's Persuasive Appeals in Different Social Contexts." *CD* 50:901–3.

Beckhard, R. 1969. *Organization Development.* Addison-Wesley.

Begg, I., and J. P. Denny. 1969. "Empirical Reconciliation of Atmosphere and Conversion Interpretations of Syllogistic Reasoning Errors." *JEP* 81:351–54.

Bellah, R. N., et al. 1985. *Habits of the Heart.* University of California Press.

Bem, D. 1972. "Self Perception Theory." In L. Berkowitz, ed., *Advances in Experimental Social Psychology.* Vol. 6. Academic.

Benedict, R. 1934. *Patterns of Culture.* Houghton Mifflin.

Benhabib, S. 1986. *Critique, Norm, and Utopia.* Columbia University Press.

Benn, S. I., and G. W. Mortimore, eds. 1976. *Rationality and the Social Sciences.* Methuen.

Bennett, J. 1964. *Rationality.* Routledge.

Bennis, W. G. 1966. *Changing Organizations.* McGraw-Hill.

Benson, J. K. 1973. "The Analysis of Bureaucratic-Professional Conflict: Functional versus Dialectical Approaches." *Sociological Quarterly* 15:376–94.

———. 1977. "Organizations: A Dialectical View." *ASQ* 22:1–21.

Bentley, A. F. 1926. *Relativity in Man and Society.* Putnam.

Benoit, P. J. 1981. "The Use of Argument by Pre-School Children: The Emergent Production of Rules for Winning Arguments." In Ziegelmueller and Rhodes.

———. 1982 "The Naive Actor's Concept of Argument." Paper for the SCA, Louisville, Ky.

———. 1983a. "Characteristics of Arguing from a Social Actor's Perspective." In Zarefsky, Sillars, and Rhodes.

———. 1983b. "Extended Arguments in Children's Discourse." *JAFA* 20:72–89.

———. 1985. "Strategies for Threatening Face: Mitigating and Aggravating Bids and Rejections." In Cox, Sillars, and Walker.

Benoit, W. L., and P. J. Benoit. 1987. "Everyday Practices of Naive Social Actors." In Wenzel.

Berger, C. R. 1979. "Beyond Initial Interaction: Uncertainty, Understanding, and the Development of Interpersonal Relationships." In H. Giles and R. N. St. Clair, eds., *Language and Social Psychology*. Blackwell.

Berger, C. R., and J. J. Bradac. 1982. *Language and Social Knowledge*. Arnold.

Berger, C. R., and R. Calabrese. 1975. "Some Explorations in Initial Interaction and Beyond: Toward a Developmental Theory of Interpersonal Communication." *HCR* 1:99–112.

Berger, C. R., and W. Douglas. 1981. "Studies in Interpersonal Epistemology: III. Anticipated Interaction, Self-Monitoring, and Observational Context Selection." *CM* 48:183–96.

Berger, C. R., and K. A. Kellerman. 1983. "To Ask or Not To Ask: Is That a Question?" In R. Bostrom, ed., *Communication Yearbook 7*. Sage.

Berger, C. R., et al. 1977. "Interpersonal Relationship Levels and Interpersonal Attraction." In B. Ruben, ed., *Communication Yearbook 1*. Transaction/ICA.

Berger, P., B. Berger, and H. Kellner. 1973. *The Homeless Mind*. Vintage.

Berger, P. L., and T. Luckmann. 1966. *The Social Construction of Reality*. Doubleday.

Berlin, I. 1958. *Two Concepts of Liberty*. Clarendon.

Berlinsky, D. J. 1976. *On Systems Analysis*. MIT Press.

Bernstein, B. 1974. *Theoretical Studies towards a Sociology of Language*. Schocken.

Bernstein, J. 1982. *Science Observed*. Basic Books.

Bernstein, R. J. 1976. *The Restructuring of Social and Political Theory*. University of Pennsylvania Press.

———. 1983. *Beyond Objectivism and Relativism*. University of Pennsylvania Press.

Bersheid, E., and E. Walster. 1974. "Physical Attractiveness." In L. Berkowitz, ed., *Advances in Experimental Social Psychology*, Vol. 7. Academic.

Biddle, B. J. 1979. *Role Theory*. Academic.

Bierstedt, R. 1950. "An Analysis of Social Power." *ASR* 15:730–38.

———. 1954. "The Problem of Authority." In M. Berger, T. Abel, and C. H. Page, eds., *Freedom and Control in Modern Society*. van Norstrand.

Bigge, M. L. 1971. *Positive Relativism*. Harper & Row.

Bitzer, L. F. 1959. "Aristotle's Enthymeme Revisited." *QJS* 45:399–408.

———. 1968. "The Rhetorical Situation." *P&R* 1:1–14.

———. 1978. "Rhetoric and Public Knowledge." In D. Burkes, ed., *Rhetoric, Philosophy, and Literature*. Purdue University Press.

Black, M. 1970. *Margins of Precision*. Cornell University Press.

Blair, J. A., and R. H. Johnson, eds. 1980. *Informal Logic*. Edgepress.

Blanshard, B. 1962. *Reason and Analysis*. Open Court.

Blau, P. M. 1955. *The Dynamics of Bureaucracy*. University of Chicago Press.

———. 1964. *Exchange and Power in Social Life*. Wiley.

Bleiberg, S., and L. Churchill. 1975. "Notes on Confrontation in Conversation." *J. Psycholinguistic Research* 4:273–78.

Bloor, D. 1976. *Knowledge and Social Imagery*. Routledge.

Blum, J. P., and J. J. Gumperz. 1972. "Some Social Determinants of Verbal Behavior." In Gumperz and Hymes.

Blume, S. S. 1974. *Toward a Political Sociology of Science*. Free Press.

Blumer, H. 1969. *Symbolic Interactionism*. Prentice-Hall.

Blumenberg, H. 1983. *The Legitimacy of the Modern Age*. MIT Press.

Bok, S. 1983. *Secrets*. Pantheon.

Bordieu, P. 1978. *Outline of a Theory of Practice*. Cambridge University Press.

Borger, R., and F. Cioffi, eds. 1970. *Explanation in the Behavioural Sciences*. Cambridge University Press.

Borgida, E., and R. E. Nisbett. 1977. "The Differential Impact of Abstract vs. Concrete Information on Decisions." *J. Applied Social Psychol.* 7:258–71.

Bottomore, T. B. 1966. *Elites and Society*. Penguin.

Bragg, B. W. E., M. V. Ostrowski, and G. E. Finley. 1973. "The Effects of Birth Order and Age of Target on Use of Persuasive Techniques." *CD* 44:351–54.

Brenneis, D. 1987. "Dramatic Gestures: The Fiji Indian *Pancayat* as Therapeutic Discourse." *IPRA Papers in Pragmatics* 1:55–78.

Brock, T. C. 1968. "Communication Discrepancy and Intent to Persuade as Determinants of Counterargument." *JESP* 3:296–309.

Brock, T. C., and J. Blackwood. 1962. "Dissonance Reduction, Social Comparison, and Modification of Other's Opinion." *JASP* 65:319–24.

Brockriede, W. E. 1972. "Arguers as Lovers." *P&R* 5:1–11.

———. 1974. "Rhetorical Criticism as Argument." *QJS* 60:165–74.

———. 1975. "Where Is Argument?" *JAFA* 11:179–82.

———. 1977. "Characteristics of Arguments and Arguing." *JAFA* 13:129–32.

———. 1982. "Arguing about Human Understanding." *CM* 49:137–47.

———. 1985. "Constructs, Experience, and Argument." *QJS* 71:151–63.

Brody, B. A. 1973. *Logic*. Prentice-Hall.

Bromley, D. B. 1977. *Personality Description in Ordinary Language*. Wiley.

Bronson, W. 1975. "Developments in Behavior with Age-Mates during the Second Year of Life." In M. Lewis and L. Rosenblum, eds., *Friendship and Peer Relations*. Wiley.

Brown, P., and S. Levinson. 1978. "Universals in Language Usage: Politeness Phenomena." In E. N. Goody, ed., *Questions and Politeness*. Cambridge University Press.

Brown, S. C., ed. 1979. *Philosophical Disputes in the Social Sciences*. Harvester.

Brown, R. H. 1987. "Reason as Rhetorical: On Relations among Epistemology, Discourse, and Practice." In Nelson, MeGill, and McCloskey.

Brown, R. R. 1963. *Explanation in Social Science*. Aldine.

Bruner, J. S., and R. Tagiuri. 1954. "The Perception of People." In G. Lindzey, ed., *Handbook of Social Psychology*. Addison-Wesley.

Brunsson, N. 1982. "The Irrationality of Action and Action Rationality: Decisions, Ideologies, and Organizational Actions." *J. Management Studies* 19:29–44.

Bryant, D. C. 1973. *Rhetorical Dimensions of Criticism*. Louisiana State University Press.

Burgess, P. 1970. "The Rhetoric of Moral Conflict: Two Critical Dimensions." *QJS* 56:120–30.

Burgoon, J. K., and J. L. Hale. 1984. "The Fundamental Topoi of Relational Communication." *CM* 51:193–214.

Burke, J. A., and R. A. Clark. 1982. "An Assessment of Methodological Options for Investigating the Development of Persuasive Skills across Childhood." *CSSJ* 33:437–45.

Burke, K. 1950. *A Rhetoric of Motives*. Prentice-Hall.

Burks, A. W. 1953. "The Presuppositional Theory of Induction." *PS* 20:177–97.

Burleson, B. R. 1979a. "On the Analysis and Criticism of Arguments: Some Theoretical and Methodological Considerations." *JAFA* 15:137–47.

———. 1979b. "On the Foundations of Rationality: Toulmin, Habermas, and the a Priori of Reason." *JAFA* 16:112–27.

———. 1980. "The Place of Nondiscursive Symbolism, Formal Characterizations, and Hermeneutics in Argument Analysis and Criticism." *JAFA* 16:222–31.

———. 1981. "A Cognitive-Developmental Perspective on Social Reasoning Processes." *WJSP* 45:133–47.

———. 1982. "The Development of Comforting Communication Skills in Childhood and Early Adolescence." *CD* 53:1578–88.

Buss, A. R. 1978. "Causes and Reasons in Attribution Theory." *JPSP* 36:1311–22.

Buss, A. H. 1961. *The Psychology of Aggression*. Wiley.

Byrne, D. 1969. "Attitudes and Attraction." In L. Berkowitz, ed., *Advances in Experimental Social Psychology*. Vol. 4. Academic.

———. 1971. *The Attraction Paradigm*. Academic.

Campbell, J. A. 1986. "Scientific Revolution and the Grammar of Culture: The Case of Darwin's *Origin*." *QJS* 72:351–76.

Carlson, L. 1982. *Dialogue Games*. Reidel.

Carroll, J. B. 1979. "Psychometric Approaches to the Study of Language Abilities." In C. J. Fillmore, D. Kempler, and W. S-Y. Wang, eds., *Individual Differences in Language Ability and Language Behavior*. Academic.

Cater, D. 1959. *The Fourth Branch of Government*. Houghton Mifflin.

Cavanaugh, M. A. 1987. "One-Eyed Social Movements: Rethinking Issues in Rationality and Society." *PSS* 17:147–72.

Cederblom, J. 1986. "Willingness to Reason as an Attitude toward Oneself." Paper for the International Conference on Argumentation, University of Amsterdam, the Netherlands.

Chaiken, S. 1979. "Communicator Physical Attractiveness and Persuasion." *JPSP* 37:1387–97.

Chapman, L. J., and J. P. Chapman. 1959. "Atmosphere Effect Reexamined." *JEP* 58:220–26.

Cialdini, R. B. 1971. "Attitudinal Advocacy in the Verbal Conditioner." *JPSP* 17:350–58.

Cialdini, R. B., et al. 1973. "Attitudinal Politics: The Strategy of Moderation." *JPSP* 25:100–108.

Cialdini, R. B., and R. E. Petty. 1981. "Anticipatory Opinion Shifts." In R. E. Petty, T. M. Ostrom, and T. C. Brock, eds., *Cognitive Responses in Persuasion*. Erlbaum.

Cicourel, A. V. 1970. "Basic and Normative Rules in the Negotiation of Status and Role." In Dreitzel.

————. 1974. *Cognitive Sociology*. Free Press.

Clark, R. A., and J. G. Delia. 1976. "The Development of Functional Persuasive Skills in Childhood and Early Adolescence." *CD* 47:1008–14.

————. 1977. "Cognitive Complexity, Social Perspective-Taking, and Functional Persuasive Skills in Second- to Ninth-Grade Children." *HCR* 3:128–34.

————. 1979. "Topoi and Rhetorical Competence." *QJS* 65:187–206.

Clark, R. A., L. L. O'Dell, and S. Willihnganz. 1985. "The Development of Compromise as an Alternative to Persuasion." University of Illinois Press.

————. In Press. "Children's Use of Strategies to Protect Feelings When Responding to a Request." *CD*.

Clark, R. A., S. Willihnganz, and L. L. O'Dell. 1985. "The Impact of Instruction in Protecting Feelings When Responding to a Request." *Communication Education* 34:47–56.

————. 1986. "Training Fourth Graders in Compromising and Persuasive Strategies." Unpublished Ms. University of Illinois.

Cohen, I. B. 1985. *Revolution in Science*. Harvard University Press.

Cohen, M. D., J. G. March, and J. P. Olsen. 1972. "A Garbage Can Model of Organizational Choice." *ASQ*. 17:1–25.

Cole, M., and S. Scribner. 1974. *Culture and Thought*. Wiley.

Collin, F. 1985. *Theory and Understanding*. Blackwell.

Commission on Freedom of the Press. 1947. *A Free and Responsible Press*. University of Chicago Press.

Commission on the Space Shuttle Challenger Accident. 1986. *Report of the Presidential Commission on the Space Shuttle Challenger Accident*. Government Printing Office.

Connolly, W. E. 1974. *The Terms of Political Discourse*. Heath.

————. 1987. *Politics and Ambiguity*. University of Wisconsin Press.

Conrad, C. 1985. *Strategic Organizational Communication*. Holt.

Cook, T. D. 1969. "Competence, Counterarguing and Attitude Change." *JP* 37:342–58.

Copi, I. 1978. *Introduction to Logic*. 5th ed. Macmillan.

Cox, J. R. 1987. "Cultural Memory and Public Moral Argument." Van Zelst Lecture in Communication, Northwestern University.

Cox, J. R., M. O. Sillars, and G. B. Walker, eds. 1985. *Argument and Social Practice*. SCA.

Cox, J. R., and C. A. Willard, eds. 1982. *Advances in Argumentation Theory and Research*. Southern Illinois University Press.

Craig, R. T., and K. Tracy. 1983. *Conversational Coherence*. Sage.

Crawshay-Williams, R. 1957. *Methods and Criteria of Reasoning*. Routledge.

Crockett, W. H. 1965. "Cognitive Complexity and Impression Formation."

In B. A. Maher, ed., *Progress in Experimental Personality Research*, Vol. 2. Academic.

———. 1977. "Impressions and Attributions: Nature, Organization, and Implications for Action." Paper for the American Psychological Association.

———. 1984. "The Organization Corollary." In J. C. Mancuso and J. R. Adams-Weber, eds., *Systems of Personal Constructs*. Praeger.

Cronen, V. E., and N. Mihevc. 1972. "Evaluation of Deductive Argument: A Process Analysis." *SM* 39:124–31.

Crossley, D. J., and P. A. Wilson. 1979. *How to Argue*. Random House.

Curtis, J. E., and J. W. Petras. 1970. "Introduction." In J. E. Curtis and J. W. Petras, eds., *The Sociology of Knowledge*. Praeger.

Dahl, R. A. 1956. *A Preface to Democratic Theory*. University of Chicago Press.

———. 1958. "A Critique of the Ruling Elite Model." *APSR* 52:463–69.

———. 1961. *Who Governs?* Yale University Press.

———. 1967. *Pluralist Democracy in the United States*. Rand McNally.

Dale, P. E. 1972. *Language Development*. Dryden Press.

Daly, J. A., R. A. Bell, P. J. Glenn, and S. Lawrence. 1985. "Conceptualizing Conversational Complexity." *HCR* 12:30–53.

Danto, A. C. 1966. "Freedom and Forbearance." In K. Lehrer, ed., *Freedom and Determinism*. Random House.

Darden, L., and N. Maull. 1977. "Interfield Theories." *PS* 44:43–64.

Davidson, D. 1968. "Actions, Reasons and Causes." In A. R. White, ed., *The Philosophy of Action*. Oxford University Press.

———. 1973–74. "On the Very Idea of A Conceptual Scheme." *Proceedings and Addresses of the American Philosophical Association* 45:5–20.

Davis, P. J., and R. Hersh. 1987. "Rhetoric and Mathematics." In Nelson, McGill, and McCloskey.

Deaux, K. K. 1968. "Variations in Warning, Information Preference, and Anticipatory Attitude Change." *JPSP* 9:157–61.

Delia, J. G. 1970. "The Logic Fallacy, Cognitive Theory, and the Enthymeme: A Search for the Foundations of Reasoned Discourse." *QJS* 56:140–48.

———. 1972. "Dialects and the Effects of Stereotypes on Interpersonal Attraction and Cognitive Processes in Impression Formation." *QJS* 58:285–297.

———. 1974. "Attitude toward the Disclosure of Self-Attributions and the Complexity of Interpersonal Constructs." *SM* 41: 119–26.

———. 1976a. "Change of Meaning Processes in Impression Formation." *CM* 43:142–57.

———. 1976b. "A Constructivist Analysis of the Concept of Credibility." *QJS* 62:361–75.

———. 1976c. "Change of Meaning Processes in Impression Formation." *CM* 43:142–57.

———. 1977. "Constructivism and the Study of Human Communication." *QJS* 63:66–83.

———. 1980. "Cognitive Structure and Meaning Structure: Recent Constructivist Research." Paper for the SCA, New York.

―――. 1983. "Social Psychology, Competency, and Individual Differences in Communicative Action." *Journal of Language and Social Psychology*. 2:207–18.

Delia, J. G., and R. A. Clark. 1977. "Cognitive Complexity, Social Perception and the Development of Listener-Adapted Communication in Six-, Eight-, Ten-, and Twelve-year-old Boys." *CM* 44:326–45.

Delia, J. G., R. A. Clark, and D. E. Switzer. 1974. "Cognitive Complexity and Impression Formation in Informal Social Interaction." *SM* 41:299–308.

―――. 1979. "The Content of Informal Conversations as a Function of Interactants' Interpersonal Cognitive Complexity." *CM* 46:274–81.

Delia, J. G., and W. H. Crockett. 1973. "Social Schemas, Cognitive Complexity, and the Learning of Social Structures." *JP* 41:413–29.

Delia, J. G., W. H. Crockett, A. N. Press, and D. J. O'Keefe. 1975. "The Dependency of Interpersonal Evaluations on Context-Relevant Beliefs about the Other." *SM* 42:10–19.

Delia, J. G., and L. Grossberg. 1977. "Interpretation and Evidence." *WJSC* 41:32–42.

Delia, J. G., S. L. Kline, and B. R. Burleson. 1979. "The Development of Persuasive Communication Strategies in Kindergartners through Twelfth-Graders." *CM* 46:241–56.

Delia, J. G., and B. J. O'Keefe. 1979. "Constructivism: The Development of Communication in Children." In E. Wartella, ed., *Children Communicating*. Sage.

Delia, J. G., and D. J. O'Keefe. 1977. "The Relation of Theory and Analysis in Explanations of Belief Salience: Conditioning, Displacement, and Constructivist Accounts." *CM* 44:166–69.

Delia, J. G., B. J. O'Keefe, and D. J. O'Keefe. 1982. "The Constructivist Approach to Communication." In F. E. X. Dance, ed., *Human Communication Theory*. Harper & Row.

Dembo, L. S., ed. 1968. *Criticism*. University of Wisconsin Press.

Denzin, N. K. 1970. "Rules of Conduct and Study of Deviant Behavior: Some Notes on the Social Relationship." In McCall.

Dewey, J. 1946. *Problems of Men*. Philosophical Library.

―――. 1954. *The Public and Its Problems*. Swallow.

―――. 1960. *On Experience, Nature, and Freedom*. Bobbs-Merrill.

―――. 1962. *Individualism Old and New*. Capricorn.

Dickson, W. P., ed. 1981. *Childrens' Oral Communication Skills*. Academic.

Dixon, K. 1980. *The Sociology of Belief*. Routledge.

Domhoff, G. W. 1967. *Who Rules America?* Prentice-Hall.

―――. 1971. *The Higher Circles*. Vintage.

―――. 1972. *Fat Cats and Democrats*. Prentice-Hall.

―――. 1978. *The Powers That Be*. Vintage.

Douglas, M., ed. 1973. *Rules and Meanings*. Penguin.

―――. 1975. *Implicit Meanings*. Routledge.

―――. 1986. *How Institutions Think*. Syracuse University Press.

Dray, W. H. 1967. "Holism and Individualism in History and Social Science." In P. Edwards, ed., *The Encyclopedia of Philosophy*. Vol. 3. Macmillan.

Dreitzel, H. P., ed. 1970. *Recent Sociology 2*. Macmillan.

Duck, S. W. 1973. *Personal Relationships and Personal Constructs*. Wiley.

———. 1982. "A Topography of Relationship Disengagement and Dissolution." In S. W. Duck, ed., *Personal Relationships 4*. Academic.

Dunbar, N. R. 1986. "Laetrile: A Case Study of a Public Controversy." *JAFA* 22:196–211.

Duranti, A. 1986. "The Audience as Co-Author." In A. Duranti and D. Brenneis eds., *The Audience as Co-Author*. Special Issue of *Text* 6.

———. 1987. "Translocutionary Acts: Toward a Cross-Cultural Theory of Speech Acts." Paper for the International Pragmatics Conference, Antwerp, Belgium.

Durkheim, E. 1938. *The Rules of Sociological Method*. University of Chicago Press.

Dye, T. R. 1976. *Who's Running America?* Prentice-Hall.

Dye, T. R., and H. L. Zeigler. 1978. *The Irony of Democracy*, 4th ed. Wadsworth.

Edelman, G. M. 1987. *Neural Darwinism*. Basic Books.

Eemeren, F. H. van. 1987. "Argumentation Studies' Five Estates." In Wenzel.

Eemeren, F. H. van, and R. Grootendorst. 1984. *Speech Acts in Argumentative Discussions*. Foris.

———. 1987. "Fallacies in Pragma-Dialectical Perspective." *Argumentation* 1:283–302.

———. In press. "A Pragma-Dialectical Perspective on Norms." In R. Meier, ed., *Norms in Argumentation*. Foris.

Eemeren, F. H. van, R. Grootendorst, and T. Kruiger. 1984. *The Study of Argumentation*. Irvington.

———. 1987. *Handbook of Argumentation Theory*. Foris.

Eemeren, F. H, van, R. Grootendorst, J. A. Blair, and C. A. Willard, eds. 1987. *Argumentation: Across the Lines of Discipline*. Foris.

Ehninger, D. 1970. "Argument as Method: Its Nature, Its Limitations, and Its Uses." *SM* 37:101–10.

Ehninger, D., and W. Brockriede. 1978. *Decision by Debate*. 2d ed., Harper.

Eisenberg, A. M., and J. A. Ilardo. 1980. *Argument*. 2d ed. Prentice-Hall.

Eliot, T. S. 1928. *The Sacred Wood*. 2d ed. Methuen.

Emerson, J. 1970a. "Behavior in Private Places: Definitions of Reality in Gynecological Examinations." In Dreitzel.

———. 1970b. "Nothing Unusual Is Happening." In T. Shibutani, ed., *Human Nature and Collective Behavior*. Prentice-Hall.

Emmett, D., and A. MacIntyre, eds. 1970. *Sociological Theory and Philosophical Analysis*. Macmillan.

Engel, S. M. 1976. *With Good Reason*. St. Martin's.

Ennis, R. H. 1969. *Ordinary Logic*. Prentice-Hall.

Ericcson, K. A., and H. A. Simon. 1980. "Self Reports as Data." *PR* 87:215–51.

Ermann, M. D., and R. J. Lundman, eds. 1978. *Corporate and Governmental Deviance*. Oxford University Press.

Ervin-Tripp, S. M. 1987. "The Negotiation of Requests in American Families." Paper for the International Pragmatics Conference, Antwerp, Belgium.

Ewen, S. 1976. *Captains of Consciousness*. McGraw-Hill.

Ewing, A. C. 1942. *Reason and Intuition*. Oxford University Press.

Farr, R. 1981. "The Social Origins of the Human Mind: A Historical Note." In J. P. Forgas, ed., *Social Cognition*. Academic.

Farrell, T. B. 1976. "Knowledge, Consensus, and Rhetorical Theory." *QJS* 62:1–14.

Farrell, T. B., and G. T. Goodnight. 1981. "Accidental Rhetoric: The Root Metaphors of Three Mile Island." *CM* 48:271–300.

Fearnside, W. W., and W. B. Holther. 1959. *Fallacy*. Prentice-Hall.

Feather, N. T. 1964. "Acceptance and Rejection of Arguments in Relation to Attitude Strength, Critical Ability, and Intolerance of Inconsistency." *JASP* 69:127–36.

Feigl, H. 1961. "On the Vindication of Induction." *PS* 28:212–16.

Festinger, L. 1954. "A Theory of Social Comparison Processes." *HR* 7:117–40.

———. 1957. *A Theory of Cognitive Dissonance*. Harper & Row.

———. 1964. *Conflict, Decision, and Dissonance*. Stanford University Press.

Festinger, L., and J. M. Carlsmith. 1959. "Cognitive Consequences of Forced Compliance." *JASP* 63:203–10.

Feynman, R. P. 1988. "An Outsider's Inside View of the Challenger Inquiry." *Physics Today*, February 1988.

Fillmore, C. J., D. Kempler, and W. S-Y. Wang, eds. 1979. *Individual Differences in Language Ability and Language Behavior*. Academic.

Fincham, F., and J. Jaspars. 1981. "Responsibility Attribution." In L. Berkowitz, ed., *Advances in Experimental Social Psychology*. Vol. 14. Academic.

Finocchiaro, M. A. 1981. "Fallacies and the Evaluation of Reasoning." *APQ* 18:13–22.

———. 1987. "Six Types of Fallaciousness: Toward a Realistic Theory of Logical Criticism." *Argumentation* 1:263–82.

Fischoff, B. 1976. "Attribution Theory and Judgment under Uncertainty." In J. H. Harvey, W. J. Ickes, and J. W. Hagen, eds., *New Directions in Attribution Research*. Erlbaum.

Fisher, W. R. 1980. "Rhetorical Fiction and the Presidency." *QJS* 66:119–26.

———. 1984. "Narration as a Human Communication Paradigm: The Case of Public Moral Argument." *CM* 51:1–22.

Fiske, S. T., and S. E. Taylor. 1984. *Social Cognition*. Addison-Wesley.

Flathman, R. 1980. *The Practice of Political Authority*. University of Chicago Press.

Flavell, J. H., et al. 1968. *Role-Taking and Communication Skills in Children*. Wiley.

Foerster, Norman. 1928. *American Criticism*. Houghton Mifflin.

Fogelin, R. J. 1978. *Understanding Arguments*. Harcourt.

Fogelin, R. J., and T. J. Duggan. 1987. "Fallacies." *Argumentation* 1:255–62.

Forester, J. 1985. *Critical Theory and Public Life*. MIT Press.

Forgas, J. P. 1979. *Social Episodes*. Academic.

———. ed. 1981. *Social Cognition*. Academic.

Foucault, M. 1972. *The Archaeology of Knowledge*. Harper.

———. 1977. *Discipline and Punish*. Random House.

Freeley, A. J. 1981. *Argumentation and Debate*. 3d ed., Wadsworth.

Freeman, D. 1983. *Margaret Mead and Samoa*. Harvard University Press.

Freidson, E. 1984. "Are Professions Necessary?" In T. Haskell, ed., *The Authority of Experts*. Indiana University Press.

From, F. 1971. *Perception of Other People*. Columbia University Press.

Frost, P. J., et al., eds. 1985. *Organizational Culture*. Sage.

Fry, C. L. 1966. "Training Children to Communicate to Listeners." *CD* 37:674–85.

———. 1969. "Training Children to Communicate to Listeners Who Have Varying Listener Requirements." *J. Genetic Psychol.* 114:153–66.

Fuller, S. 1983. "In Defense of Incommensurability." 7th Regional Conference on the History and Philosophy of Science, University of Colorado.

———. 1986. "Consensus and Validation in Science: A Problem Paper for PSA 1986." Paper for the Philosophy of Science Association.

———. 1987. "*Social Epistemology*: A Statement of Purpose." *SE* 1:1–4.

Fuller, S., and C. A. Willard. 1987. "In Defense of Relativism: Rescuing Incommensurability from the Self-Excepting Fallacy." In F. H. van Eemeren, R. Grootendorst, J. A. Blair, and C. A. Willard, eds., *Argumentation: Perspectives and Approaches*. Foris.

Galbraith, J. K. 1973. *Economics and the Public Purpose*. Houghton Mifflin.

Garfinkel, A. 1981. *Forms of Explanation*. Yale University Press.

Garfinkel, H. 1962. "Commonsense Knowledge of Social Structures: The Documentary Method of Interpretation." In J. M. Scher, ed., *Theories of the Mind*. Free Press.

———. 1964. "Studies of the Routine Grounds of Everyday Activities." *Social Problems* 11:225–50.

———. 1967. *Studies in Ethnomethodology*. Prentice-Hall.

Garfinkel, H., and H. Sacks. 1970. "On Formal Structures of Practical Actions." In J. C. McKinney and E. Tiryakian, eds., *Theoretical Sociology*. Appleton.

Garvey, C. 1977. "Contingent Queries." In M. Lewis and L. A. Rosenblum, eds., *Interaction, Conversation, and the Development of Language*. Wiley.

Geertz, C. 1962. "The Growth of Culture and the Evolution of Mind." In J. M. Sher, ed., *Theories of the Mind*. Free Press.

———. 1973. *The Interpretation of Cultures*. Basic Books.

———. 1980. "Blurred Genres." *American Scholar* 49:165–77.

———. 1985. *Local Knowledge*. Basic Books.

———. 1988. *Works and Lives*. Stanford University Press.

Gellner, E. 1970 "Concepts and Society." In Wilson.

———. 1982 "Relativism and Universals." In Hollis and Lukes.

Gerald, J. E. 1963. *The Social Responsibility of the Press*. University of Minnesota Press.

Gibbs, J. 1966. "The Sociology of Law and Normative Phenomena." *ASR* 31:315–25.

Giddens, A. 1976. *New Rules of Sociological Method*. Basic Books.

———. 1977. *Studies in Social and Political Theory*. Basic Books.

———. 1979. *Central Problems in Social Theory*. University of California Press.

———. 1981. *A Contemporary Critique of Historical Materialism*. University of California Press.

Gieryn, T. F., and A. E. Figert. 1986. "Scientists Protect Their Cognitive Authority." In G. Boehme and N. Stehr, eds., *The Knowledge Society*. Reidel.

Gierke, O. 1934. *Natural Law and the Theory of Society, 1500 to 1800*. Cambridge University Press.

Gillig, P. M., and A. G. Greenwald. 1974. "Is It Time to Lay the Sleeper Effect to Rest?" *JPSP* 29:132–39.

Gilligan, C. 1982. *In a Different Voice*. Harvard University Press.

Ginsberg, B. 1986. *The Captive Public*. Basic Books.

Glaser, B., and A. Strauss. 1964. "Awareness Contexts and Social Interaction." *ASR* 29:669–79.

———. 1967. *The Discovery of Grounded Theory*. Aldine.

Goethals, G. R., and R. E. Nelson. 1973. "Similarity in the Influence Process: The Belief-Value Distinction." *JPSP* 25:117–22.

Goffman, E. 1959. *The Presentation of Self in Everyday Life*. Anchor.

———. 1961a. *Encounters*. Bobbs-Merrill.

———. 1961b. *Asylums*. Doubleday.

———. 1963. *Behavior in Public Places*. Free Press.

———. 1964. *Stigma*. Prentice-Hall.

———. 1967. *Interaction Ritual*. Doubleday.

———. 1969. *Strategic Interaction*. University of Pennsylvania Press.

———. 1971. *Relations in Public*. Basic Books.

———. 1974. *Frame Analysis*. Harper & Row.

Gomme, A. 1966. *Attitudes to Criticism*. Southern Illinois University Press.

Goodenough, W. H. 1964. "Cultural Anthropology and Linguistics." In D. Hymes, ed., *Language in Culture and Society*. Harper.

Goodnight, G. T. 1980. "The Liberal and Conservative Presumptions: On Political Philosophy and the Foundation of Public Argument." In Rhodes and Newell.

———. 1982. "The Personal, Technical, and Public Spheres of Argument: A Speculative Inquiry Into the Art of Public Deliberation." *JAFA* 18:214–27.

———. 1986. "Ronald Reagan's Re-Formulation of the Rhetoric of War: Analysis of the 'Zero Option,' 'Evil Empire,' and 'Star Wars' Addresses." *QJS* 72:390–414.

———. 1987. "Generational Argument." In van Eemeren, Grootendorst, Blair, and Willard.

Goodwin, C., and M. H. Goodwin. 1987. "Concurrent Operations on Talk:

Notes on the Interactive Organization of Assessments." *IPRA Papers in Pragmatics* 1:1–54.

Gottlieb, G. 1968. *The Logic of Choice*. Macmillan.

Gould, S. J. 1977a. *Ever Since Darwin*. Norton.

———. 1977b. *Ontogeny and Phylogeny*. Harvard University Press.

———. 1980. *The Panda's Thumb*. Norton.

———. 1981. *The Mismeasure of Man*. Norton.

Gouldner, A. 1982. *The Dialectic of Ideology and Technology*. Oxford University Press.

Gouran, D. S. 1985. "A Critical Summary of Research on the Role of Argument in Decision-Making Groups." In Cox, Sillars, and Walker.

———. 1987. "The Failure of Argument in Decisions Leading to the Challenger Disaster: A Two-Level Analysis." In Wenzel.

Govier, T. 1981. "Worries about the Tu Quoque as a Fallacy." *ILN* 3:2–4.

———. 1982a. "Who Says There Are No Fallacies?" *ILN* 5:2.

———. 1982b. "What's Wrong with Slippery Slope Arguments?" *Canadian J. Philosophy* 12:303–16.

Graham, L. 1981. *Between Science and Values*. Columbia University Press.

Green, M. J. 1972. *The Closed Enterprise System*. Grossman.

Greenberg, B. S., and G. R. Miller. 1966. "The Effects of Low-Credible Sources on Message Acceptance." *SM* 33:127–36.

Greenberg, B. S., and P. H. Tannenbaum. 1961. "The Effects of Bylines on Attitude Change." *Journalism Quarterly* 38:535–37.

Greenwald, A. G. 1968. "Cognitive Learning, Cognitive Response to Persuasion, and to Attitude Change." In A. G. Greenwald, T. C. Brock, and T. M. Ostrom, eds., *Psychological Foundations of Attitudes*. Academic.

Gregg, R. 1981. "Rhetoric and Knowing: The Search for Perspective." *CSSJ* 32:133–44.

Grice, H. P. 1957. "Meaning." *Philosophical Review* 66:377–88.

———. 1975. "Logic and Conversation." In P. Cole and J. Morgan, eds., *Syntax and Semantics. Vol. 3: Speech Acts*. Academic.

Gross, A. G. 1988. "On The Shoulders of Giants: Seventeenth Century Optics as an Argument Field." *QJS* 74:1–17.

Grootendorst, R. 1987. "Everyday Argumentation from a Speech Act Perspective." In Wenzel.

Grunfield, J. 1986. *Changing Rational Standards*. University Press of America.

Grunig, J. E. 1975. "Some Consistent Types of Employee Publics." *Public Relations Review* 1:17–36.

———. 1978. "Accuracy of Communication from an External Public to Employees in a Formal Organization." *HCR* 5:40–53.

Grusky, O., and G. A. Miller. 1981. *The Sociology of Organizations*. 2d ed. Free Press.

Guest, R. 1962. *Organizational Change*. Dorsey.

Guilford, J. P. 1967. *The Nature of Human Intelligence*. McGraw-Hill.

Gumperz, J. J. 1972. "Introduction." In Gumperz and Hymes.

Gumperz, J. J., and D. Hymes, eds. 1972. *Directions in Sociolinguistics*. Holt.

Gurvitch, G. 1971. *The Social Frameworks of Knowledge*. Blackwell.

Haan, N., E. Aerts, and B. Cooper. 1985. *On Moral Grounds*. New York University Press.

Habermas, J. 1970. "Toward a Theory of Communicative Competence." In Dreitzel.

————. 1971. *Knowledge and Practice*. Beacon.

————. 1973. *Theory and Practice*. Beacon.

————. 1975. *Legitimation Crises*. Beacon.

————. 1979. *Communication and the Evolution of Society*. Beacon.

————. 1984. *The Theory of Communicative Action, I*. Beacon.

Hagstrom, W. O. 1965. *The Scientific Community*. Basic Books.

Hamblin, C. L. 1970. *Fallacies*. Methuen.

Hamlyn, D. W. 1971. "Epistemology and Conceptual Development." In T. Mischel, ed., *Cognitive Development and Epistemology*. Academic.

Hample, D. 1977a. "Testing a Model of Value Argument and Evidence." *CM* 44:106–20.

————. 1977b. "The Toulmin Model and the Syllogism." *JAFA* 14:1–9.

————. 1978. "Predicting Immediate Belief Change and Adherence to Argument Claims." *CM* 45:219–28.

————. 1979a. "Motives in Law: An Adaptation of Legal Realism." *JAFA* 15:156–68.

————. 1979b. "Predicting Belief and Belief Change Using a Cognitive Theory of Argument and Evidence." *CM* 46:142–46.

————. 1980. "A Cognitive View of Argument." *JAFA* 16:151–58.

————. 1981. "The Cognitive Context of Argument." *WJSC* 45:148–58.

————. 1984. "On the Use of Self-Reports." *JAFA* 20:140–53.

Hancher, M. 1979. "The Classification of Cooperative Illocutionary Acts." *Language in Society* 8:1–14.

Hanson, N. R. 1958. *Patterns of Discovery*. Cambridge University Press.

Hanson, R. L. 1985. *The Democratic Imagination in America*. Princeton University Press.

Hardwig, J. 1973. "The Achievement of Moral Rationality." *P&R* 6:171–85.

Harre, R. 1981. "Rituals, Rhetoric, and Social Cognitions." In J. P. Forgas, ed., *Social Cognition*. Academic.

Harre, R., and P. F. Secord. 1972. *The Explanation of Social Behavior*. Blackwell.

Harth, E. 1983. *Windows on the Mind*. Morrow.

Harvey, O. J. 1962. "Personality Factors in Resolution of Conceptual Incongruities." *Sociometry* 25:36–352.

Harvey, O. J., and W. F. Clapp. 1965. "Hope, Expectancy, and Reactions to the Unexpected." *JPSP* 2:45–52.

Harvey, O. J., H. H. Kelley, and M. M. Shapiro. 1957. "Reactions to Unfavorable Evaluations of the Self Made by Other Persons." *JP* 25:398–411.

Haskell, T. L., ed. 1984. *The Authority of Experts*. Indiana University Press.

Hass, R. G. 1972. "Resisting Persuasion and Examining Message Content: The Effects of Source Credibility and Recipient Commitment on Counterargument Production." Ph.D. dissertation, Duke University.

————. 1975. "Persuasion or Moderation? Two Experiments on Anticipatory Belief Change." *JPSP* 31:1155–62.

————. 1981. "To Say or Not to Say? And if so, When?" In N. C. Weissberg, ed., *Basic and Current Studies in Social Psychology*. Holt.

Hass, R. G., and D. E. Linder. 1972. "Counterargument Availability and the Effects of Message Structure on Persuasion." *JPSP* 23:219–33.

Hass, R. G., R. Mann, and R. Stevens. 1977. "Anticipatory Changes Within the Latitude of Acceptance." Unpublished Ms. [Quoted in Petty, Ostrom, and Brock.]

Hauerwas, S. 1981. *A Community of Character*. Notre Dame University Press.

Hearn, F. 1985. *Reason and Freedom in Sociological Thought*. Allen and Unwin.

Heider, F. 1958. *The Psychology of Interpersonal Relations*. Wiley.

Heilbroner, R. L. 1972. *The Worldly Philosophers*. 4th ed., Rev. Simon and Schuster.

Heisenberg, W. 1952. *Philosophic Problems of Nuclear Science*. Pantheon.

Henninger, M., and R. S. Wyer. 1976. "The Recognition and Elimination of Inconsistencies among Syllogistically Related Beliefs: Some New Light on the 'Socratic Effect'." *JPSP* 34:680–93.

Hesse, M. 1980. *Revolutions and Reconstructions in the Philosophy of Science*. Harvester.

Hick, J. 1964. *Faith and the Philosophers*. Macmillan.

————. 1985. *Problems of Religious Pluralism*. St. Martin's.

Hintikka, J. 1962. *Knowledge and Belief*. Cornell University Press.

————. 1979. "Information Seeking Dialogues." *Erkenntnis* 38:355–68.

————. 1987. "The Fallacy of Fallacies." *Argumentation* 1:211–38.

Hintikka, J., and E. Saarinen. 1979. "Information Seeking Dialogues: Some of Their Logical Properties." *Studia Logica* 38:355–63.

Hoaglund, J. 1987. "Critical Thinking." Paper for *Argumentation et Signification, Centre Culturel International de Cerisy-La-Salle*, Cerisy-La-Salle, France.

Hogwood, B. W., and B. G. Peters. 1985. *The Pathology of Public Policy*. Oxford University Press.

Holdcroft, D. 1978. *Words and Deeds*. Clarendon.

Hollis, M. 1970. "The Limits of Irrationality." In Wilson.

————. 1982. "The Social Destruction of Reality." In Hollis and Lukes.

Hollis, M., and S. Lukes, eds. 1982. *Rationality and Relativism*. MIT Press.

Holton, G. 1973. *Thematic Origins of Scientific Thought*. Harvard University Press.

Hook, S. 1940. *Reason, Social Myths, and Democracy*. Humanities.

Hovland C. I., E. H. Campbell, and T. Brock. 1957. "The Effects of 'Commitment' on Opinion Change Following Communication." In C. I. Hovland, ed., *Order of Presentation in Persuasion*. Yale University Press.

Hulteng, J. L. 1985. *The Messenger's Motives*. 2d ed. Prentice-Hall.

Hunter, F. 1953. *Community Power Structure*. University of North Carolina Press.

Hymes, D. 1972. "Models of the Interaction of Language and Social Life." In Gumperz and Hymes.

———. 1974. *Foundations in Sociolinguistics.* University of Pennsylvania Press.

———. 1979. "Sapir, Competence, Voices." In Fillmore, Kempler, and Wang.

Ice, R. 1987. "Presumption as Problematic in Group Decision-Making: The Case of the Space Shuttle." In Wenzel.

Iseminger, G. 1980. "Is Relevance Necessary for Validity?" *Mind* 89:196–213.

Jackson, S. A. 1985. "What Can Speech Acts Do for Argumentation?" In Cox, Sillars, and Walker.

———. 1986. "Building a Case for Claims about Discourse Structure." In D. G. Ellis and W. A. Donohue, eds., *Contemporary Issues in Language and Discourse Processes.* Erlbaum.

———. 1987. "Rational and Pragmatic Aspects of Argument." In van Eemeren, Grootendorst, Blair, and Willard.

Jackson, S. A., and S. Jacobs. 1980. "Structure of Conversational Argument: Pragmatic Bases for the Enthymeme." *QJS* 66:251–65.

———. 1981a. "The Collaborative Production of Proposals in Conversational Argument and Persuasion: A Study of Disagreement Resolution." *JAFA* 18:77–90.

———. 1981b. "Message: An Unexamined Variable in Communication Research." Paper for the Nebraska Conference in Conversational Analysis.

———. 1987. "Conversational Relevance: Three Experiments on Pragmatic Connectedness in Conversation." In M. L. McLaughlin, ed., *Communication Yearbook 10.* Sage.

Jackson, S., et al. 1986. "Characterizing Ordinary Argument: Substantive and Methodological Issues." *JAFA* 23:42–57.

Jacobs, S. 1983. "When Worlds Collide: An Application of Field Theory to Rhetorical Conflict." In Zarefsky, Sillars, and Ganer.

———. 1982. "The Rhetoric of Witnessing and Heckling." Ph.D. dissertation, University of Illinois.

———. 1985. "Language." In M. L. Knapp and G. R. Miller, eds., *Handbook of Interpersonal Communication.* Sage.

———. 1986. "How to Make an Argument from Example in Discourse Analysis." In D. G. Ellis and W. A. Donohue, eds., *Contemporary Issues in Language and Discourse Processes.* Erlbaum.

———. 1987. "The Management of Disagreement in Conversation." In van Eemeren, Grootendorst, Blair, and Willard.

Jacobs, S., and S. A. Jackson. 1981. "Argument as a Natural Category: The Routine Grounds for Arguing in Natural Conversation." *WJSC* 45:118–32.

———. 1982. "Conversational Argument: A Discourse Analytic Approach." In Cox and Willard.

———. 1983. "Strategy and Structure in Conversational Influence Attempts." *CM* 50:285–304.

———. In press. "Building a Model of Conversational Argument." In B.

Dervin, L. Grossberg, B. J. O'Keefe, and E. Wartella, eds., *Rethinking Communication*. Sage. Citations are to prepublication Ms.

Janis, I. L. 1982. *Groupthink*. Houghton Mifflin.

Janis, I. L., and B. T. King. 1954. "The Influence of Role-Playing on Opinion-Change." *JASP* 49:211–18.

Jehenson, R. 1973. "A Phenomenological Approach to the Study of Formal Organization." In G. H. Psathas, ed., *Phenomenological Sociology*. Wiley.

Jellison, J. M., and J. Mills. 1969. "Effects of Public Commitment upon Opinions." *JESP* 5:340–46.

Jensen, J. V. 1981. *Argumentation*. van Nostrand.

Jervis, R. 1976. *Perceptions and Misperceptions in Foreign Policy*. Princeton University Press.

Johnson, R. H. 1987. "The Blaze of Her Splendors: Suggestions about Revitalizing Fallacy Theory." *Argumentation* 1:239–54.

Johnson, R. H., and J. A. Blair, 1983. *Logical Self Defense*. 2d ed. McGraw-Hill.

———. 1980. "The Recent Development of Informal Logic." In Blair and Johnson.

Johnstone, H. W., Jr. 1959. *Philosophy and Argument*. Pennsylvania State University Press.

———. 1970. "Philosophy and *Argumentum Ad Hominem* Revisited." *Revue Internationale de Philosophie* 24:107–16.

———. 1978. *Validity and Rhetoric in Philosophical Argument*. Dialogue Press of Man and World.

Jones, E. E., et al., eds. 1972. *Attribution*. General Learning.

Jones, E. E., and K. E. Davis, 1965. "From Acts to Dispositions: The Attribution Process in Person Perception." In L. Berkowitz, ed., *Advances in Experimental Social Psychology*. Vol. 2. Academic.

Jones, E. E., and H. B. Gerard. 1967. *Foundations of Social Psychology*. Wiley.

Jones, R. A., and J. W. Brehm, 1967. "Attitudinal Effects of Communicator Attractiveness When One Chooses to Listen." *JPSP* 6:64–70.

———. 1970. "Persuasiveness of One- and Two-Sided Communications as a Function of Awareness That There Are Two Sides." *JESP* 6:47–56.

Jordanova, L. J., ed. 1986. *Languages of Nature*. Rutgers University Press.

Kahane, H. 1971. *Logic and Contemporary Rhetoric*. Wadsworth.

———. 1980. "The Nature and Classification of Fallacies." In Blair and Johnson.

Kane, B. 1986. *Free Will and Values*. SUNY Press.

Kariel, H. 1961. *The Decline of American Pluralism*. Stanford University Press.

Katz, E., and P. F. Lazarsfield. 1964. *Personal Influence*. Free Press.

Katz, J. J. 1962. *The Problem of Induction and Its Solution*. University of Chicago Press.

Kauffeld, F. J. 1987. "Rhetoric and Practical Necessity." In Wenzel.

Keller, S. 1963. *Beyond the Ruling Class*. Random House.

Kelley, H. H. 1950. "The Warm-Cold Variable in First Impressions of Persons." *JP* 18:431–39.

———. 1967. "Attribution Theory in Social Psychology." In D. Levine, ed.,

Nebraska Symposium on Motivation. Vol. 15. University of Nebraska Press.
———. 1971. *Attribution in Social Interaction*. General Learning.
———. 1972. "Causal Schemata and the Attribution Process." In Jones et al.
Kelly, G. A. 1955. *A Theory of Personality*. Norton.
Kelman, H. 1961. "Processes of Opinion Change." *POQ* 25:58–78.
Kemp, R. V. 1977. "Controversy in Scientific Research and Tactics of Communication." *Sociological Review* 25:515–34.
Kenny, M. 1986. *Biotechnology*. Yale University Press.
Kiesler, C. A., and S. B. Kiesler, 1969. *Conformity*. Addison-Wesley.
King, B. T., and I. L. Janis. 1956. "Comparison of the Effectiveness of Improvised versus Non-Improvised Role-Playing in Producing Opinion Change." *HR* 9:177–86.
Kirkpatrick, F. G. 1986. *Community*. Georgetown University Press.
Klein, W. 1980. "Argumentation und Argument." *Zeitschrift fur Literaturwissenschaft und Linguistik* 38/39:9–50 [from Habermas, 1984].
Kleppner, O. 1979. *Advertising Procedure*. 7th ed. Prentice-Hall.
Kline, S. L. 1979. "Toward a Contemporary Linguistic Interpretation of the Concept of Stasis." *JAFA* 16:95–103.
Kluckhohn, C. 1961. "Notes on Some Anthropological Aspects of Communication." *American Anthropologist* 63:895–910.
———. 1962. *Culture and Behavior*. Free Press.
Kneale, W. 1949. *Probability and Induction*. Oxford University Press.
Kneupper, C. W. 1978. "On Argument and Diagrams." *JAFA* 14:181–86.
———. 1979. "Paradigms and Problems: Alternative Constructivist/Interactionist Implications for Argumentation Theory." *JAFA* 15:220–27.
———. 1980. "Rhetoric, Argument, and Social Reality: A Social Constructivist View." *JAFA* 173–81.
Kohlberg, L. 1971. "From Is to Ought: How to Commit the Naturalistic Fallacy and Get Away with It in the Study of Moral Development." In T. Mishel, ed., *Cognitive Development and Epistemology*. Academic.
Kohler, R. E. 1982. *From Medical Chemistry to Biochemistry*. Cambridge University Press.
Kohn, A. 1987. *False Prophets*. Blackwell.
Kolko, G. 1962. *Wealth and Power in America*. Praeger.
Kovesi, J. 1967. *Moral Notions*. Routledge & Kegan Paul.
Krabbe, E. C. W. 1987. "Naess's Dichotomy of Tenability and Relevance." In van Eemeren, Grootendorst, Blair, and Willard.
Krausz, M., and J. W. Meiland, eds. 1982. *Relativism*. Notre Dame University Press.
Kreckel, M. 1981. *Communicative Acts and Shared Knowledge in Natural Discourse*. Academic.
Krehbiel, K. 1984. "Unanimous Consent Agreements: Going Along in the Senate." *J. Politics* 48:541–64.
Kuhn, T. S. 1970. *The Structure of Scientific Revolutions*. 2d ed. University of Chicago Press.
Kyburg, H. E., and E. Nagel, eds. 1963. *Induction*. Wesleyan University Press.
Labov, W., and D. Fanshel, 1977. *Therapeutic Discourse*. Academic.

Lachman, R., J. L. Lachman, and E. C. Butterfield. 1979. *Cognitive Psychology and Information Processing*. Erlbaum.

Laing, R. D., H. Phillipson, and A. R. Lee. 1972. *Interpersonal Perception*. Harper & Row.

Latour, B., and S. Woolgar, 1979. *Laboratory Life*. Sage.

Laudan, L. 1977. *Progress and Its Problems*. University of California Press.

———. 1984. *Science and Values*. University of California Press.

Lee, A. M. 1966. *Multivalent Man*. Braziller.

Leff, M. C. 1987. "Modern Sophistic and the Unity of Rhetoric." In Nelson, MeGill, and McCloskey.

Lehman, David. 1984. "John Ashbery: The Pleasures of Poetry." *New York Times Magazine*, December 16, 1984, p. 62.

Lenski, G. 1966. *Power and Privilege*. McGraw-Hill.

Lentricchia, F. 1983. *Criticism and Social Change*. University of Chicago Press.

Levine, D. N. 1985. *The Flight from Ambiguity*. University of Chicago Press.

Levinson, S. 1983. *Pragmatics*. Cambridge University Press.

Levy-Bruhl, L. 1910. *Les fonctions mentales dans les societies inferieures*. Alcan.

Lewis, D. K. 1969. *Convention*. Harvard University Press.

Linton, R. 1945. *The Cultural Background of Personality*. Appleton-Century-Crofts.

Lippmann, W. 1955. *Essays in the Public Philosophy*. Little, Brown.

———. 1963. "The Dilemma of Liberal Democracy." In C. Rossiter and J. Lare, eds., *The Essential Lippmann*. Vintage.

———. 1965. *Public Opinion*. Free Press.

Livesley, W. J., and D. B. Bromley, 1973. *Person Perception in Childhood and Adolescence*. Wiley.

Lloyd, B., and J. Gay, eds. 1981. *Universals of Human Thought*. Cambridge University Press.

Locke, J. 1952. *The Second Treatise of Government*. Bobbs-Merrill.

Lowery, S. A., and M. L. DeFleur. 1988. *Milestones in Mass Communication Research*. 2d ed. Longman.

Lukes, S. 1970. "Some Problems about Rationality." In Wilson.

———. 1977. *Essays in Social Theory*. Columbia University Press.

———. 1982. "Relativism in Its Place." In Hollis and Lukes.

MacCormick, E. R. 1985. *A Cognitive Theory of Metaphor*. MIT Press.

MacIntyre, A. 1959. *Difficulties of Christian Belief*. Philosophical Library.

———. 1970. "The Idea of a Social Science." In Wilson.

———. 1981. *After Virtue*. Notre Dame University Press.

Mackie, J. L. 1964. "Self Refutation:: A Formal Analysis." *PQ* 14:193–203.

Maggard, J. P. 1976. "Positioning Revisited." *J. Marketing* 63–66.

Mair, J. M. M. 1970. "Psychologists Are Human Too." In D. Bannister, ed., *Perspectives in Personal Construct Theory*. Academic.

March, J. G. 1962. "The Business Firm as a Political Coalition." *J. Politics* 24:662–78.

———, ed. 1965. *The Handbook of Organizations*. Rand-McNally.

———. 1970. "The Technology of Foolishness." In March and Olsen.

March, J. G., and J. P. Olsen, eds. 1976. *Ambiguity and Choice in Organizations*. Universitetsforlaget.

March, J. G., and H. A. Simon. 1958. *Organizations*. Wiley.

———. 1965. "The Concept of Rationality." In D. Singer, ed., *Human Behavior and International Politics*. Rand-McNally.

Marcoups, P. H., and R. Bassoul. 1962. "Juex de mirrors et sociologie de la connaissance d'autrui." *Cahiers Internationaux de Sociologie* 32:43–60.

Marcus, G. E., and M. M. J. Fischer, 1986. *Anthropology as Cultural Critique*. University of Chicago Press.

Massey, G. J. 1981. "The Fallacy behind Fallacies." *Midwest Studies in Philosophy* 6:489–500.

Mayer, J. E. 1957. "The Self-Restraint of Friends." *Social Forces* 35:230–38.

McCall, G. J., ed. 1970. *Social Relationships*. Aldine.

McCall, G. J., et al. 1970. "A Collaborative Overview of Social Relationships." In McCall.

McCall, M. M. 1970. "Boundary Rules in Relationships and Encounters." In McCall.

McCarthy, T. 1982. *The Critical Theory of Jurgen Habermas*. MIT Press.

McCloskey, D. N. 1985. *The Rhetoric of Economics*. University of Wisconsin Press.

McGee, M. C., and J. R. Lyne. 1987. "What Are Nice Folks Like You Doing in a Place Like This? Some Entailments of Treating Knowledge Claims Rhetorically." In Nelson, MeGill, and McCloskey.

McGuire, W. J. 1960a. "Direct and Indirect Persuasive Effects of Dissonance Producing Messages." *JASP* 60:354–58.

———. 1960b. "A Syllogistic Analysis of Cognitive Relationships." In M. J. Rosenberg, ed., *Attitude Organization and Change*. Yale University Press.

———. 1964. "Inducing Resistance to Persuasion: Some Contemporary Approaches." In L. Berkowitz, ed., *Advances in Experimental Social Psychology*. Vol. 1. Academic.

———. 1966. "Current Status of Cognitive Consistency Theories." In S. Feldman, ed., *Cognitive Consistency*. Academic.

———. 1981. "The Probabilogical Model of Cognitive Structure and Attitude Change." In Petty, Ostrom, and Brock.

McGuire, W. J., and S. Millman. 1965. "Anticipatory Belief Lowering Following Forewarning of a Persuasive Attack." *JPSP* 2:471–79.

McGuire, W. J., and D. Papageorgis. 1961. "The Relative Efficacy of Various Types of Prior Belief Defense in Producing Immunity against Persuasion." *JASP* 62:327–37.

McKerrow, R. E. 1980. "Argument Communities: A Quest for Distinctions." In Rhodes and Newell.

McLaughlin, M. L. 1984. *Conversation*. Sage.

McLaughlin, M. L., M. Cody, and H. O'Hair. 1983. "The Management of Failure Events: Some Contextual Determinants of Accounting Behavior." *HCR* 9:208–24.

McLaughlin, M. L., M. Cody, and N. E. Rosenstein. 1983. "Account Sequences in Conversations between Strangers." *CM* 50:102–25.

McPhee, J. A. 1986. *Rising from the Plains.* Farrar, Strauss, Giroux.

Mead, G. H. 1932. *Philosophy of the Present.* Open Court.

———. 1954. *Mind, Self, and Society.* University of Chicago Press.

Meichenbaum, D. H., and J. Goodman. 1971. "Training Impulsive Children to Talk to Themselves: A Means of Developing Self-Control." *J. Abnormal Psychology* 77:115–26.

Meltzer, B. N. 1972. "Mead's Social Psychology." In J. G. Manis and B. N. Meltzer, eds., *Symbolic Interaction.* 2d ed. Allyn and Bacon.

Mencken, H. L. 1955. "On Being an American." In J. T. Farrell, ed., *Prejudices.* Vintage.

Metzler, K. 1986. *Newsgathering.* 2d ed., Prentice-Hall.

Miller, G. R. 1973. "Counterattitudinal Advocacy: A Current Appraisal." In D. Mortenson and K. Sereno, eds., *Advances in Communication Research.* Harper & Row.

Miller, G. R., and T. R. Nilsen, eds. 1966. *Perspectives on Argumentation.* Scott Foresman.

Mills, C. W. 1956. *The Power Elite.* Oxford University Press.

Mills, G. E. 1968. *Reason in Controversy.* 2d ed. Allyn and Bacon.

Mischel, T., ed. 1971. *Cognitive Development and Epistemology.* Academic.

Mitroff, I. I. 1974a. *The Subjective Side of Science.* Elsevier.

———. 1974b. "Norms and Counternorms in a Select Group of Apollo Moon Scientists: A Case Study in the Ambivalence of Scientists." *ASR* 57:167–75.

Monroe, R. 1967. "Renewal of a Public Philosophy: Role of Teachers of Speech." *Speech Teacher* 16:38–46.

Moscovici, S., and R. Farr, eds. 1981. *Social Representation.* Cambridge University Press.

Morris, R. T. 1956. "A Typology of Norms." *ASR* 21:610–13.

Mulkay, M. 1976a. "Norms and Ideology in Science." *Social Science Information* 15:637–56.

———. 1976b. "The Mediating Role of the Scientific Elite." *SSS* 6:445–70.

———. 1979. *Science and the Sociology of Knowledge.* Allen & Unwin.

———. 1980. "The Sociology of Science in the West." *Current Sociology* 28:1–184.

Mulkay, M., G. N. Gilbert, and S. Woolgar. 1975. "Problem Areas and Research Networks in Science." *Sociology* 9:187–203.

Munson, R. 1976. *The Way of Words.* Houghton Mifflin.

Munz, P. 1986. *Our Knowledge of the Growth of Knowledge.* Routledge.

Nadal, M. V. 1976. *Corporations and Political Accountability.* Heath.

Nagal, T. 1986. *The View from Nowhere.* Oxford University Press.

Naess, A. 1966. *Communication and Argument.* Allen & Unwin.

Nagel, E. 1954. *Sovereign Reason.* Free Press.

Natanson, M. 1965. "The Claims of Immediacy." In M. Natanson and H. W. Johnstone, Jr., eds., *Philosophy, Rhetoric, and Argumentation.* Pennsylvania State University Press.

Nelkin, D. 1975. "The Political Impact of Technical Expertise." *SSS* 5:35–54.

Nelson, J. S. 1987a. "Stories of Science and Politics: Some Rhetorics of Political Research." In Nelson, MeGill, and McCloskey.

———. 1987b. "Seven Rhetorics of Inquiry." In Nelson, MeGill, and McCloskey.

Nelson, J. S., A. MeGill, and D. N. McCloskey, eds. 1987. *The Rhetoric of the Human Sciences.* University of Wisconsin Press.

Neustadt, R. E., and E. R. May. 1986. *Thinking in Time.* Free Press.

Newcomb, T. M. 1947. "Autistic Hostility and Social Reality." *Human Relations* 1:69–87.

Newell, S. E., and K. L. Adams. 1985. "Social Confrontation in Relationships of Varying Degrees of Intimacy." In Cox, Sillars, and Walker.

Newell, S. E., and R. K. Stuttman. 1983. "Interpersonal Disagreement: The Study of Social Confrontation." In Zarefsky, Sillars, and Rhodes.

Newton-Smith, W. 1981. *The Rationality of Science.* Routledge.

Nidorf, L. J., and W. H. Crockett, 1965. "Cognitive Complexity and the Integration of Conflicting Information in Written Impressions." *JSP* 66:165–69.

Nielsen, K. 1962. "Appealing to Reason." *Inquiry* 5:65–85.

———. 1974. "Rationality and Relativism." *Philosophy of the Social Sciences* 4:313–31.

Nimmo, D., and J. E. Combs. 1983. *Mediated Political Realities.* Longman.

Nisbett, R., and L. Ross, 1980. *Human Inference.* Prentice-Hall.

Nisbett, R., and T. D. Wilson, 1977a. "The Halo Effect: Evidence for Unconscious Alteration of Judgments." *JASP* 35:250–56.

———. 1977b. "Telling More Than We Can Know: Verbal Reports on Mental Processes." *PR* 84:231–59.

Norman, R. 1976. "When What Is Said Is Important: A Comparison of Expert and Attractive Sources." *JESP* 12:294–300.

O'Keefe, B. J. 1985. "The Functional Integration of Communication Concepts: Evidence for Individual Differences in Reasoning about Communication." Paper for the SCA, Denver.

———. 1986. "The Logic of Message Design: Evidence for Individual Differences in Reasoning about Communication." *CM* in press. [My citations are to prepublication Ms.]

O'Keefe, B. J., and P. J. Benoit, 1982. "Children's Arguments." In Cox and Willard.

O'Keefe, B. J., and J. G. Delia. 1978. "Construct Comprehensiveness and Cognitive Complexity." *Perceptual and Motor Skills* 46:548–50.

———. 1979. "Construct Comprehensiveness and Cognitive Complexity as Predictors of the Number and Strategic Adaptation of Arguments and Appeals in a Persuasive Message." *CM* 46:231–40.

———. 1982. "Impression Formation and Message Production." In M. Roloff and C. R. Berger, eds., *Social Cognition and Communication.* Sage.

———. 1983. "Psychological and Interactional Dimensions of Communicative Development." In H. Giles, R. St. Clair, and M. Hewstone, eds., *Language and the Paradigms of Social Psychology.* Erlbaum.

O'Keefe, B. J., J. G. Delia, and D. J. O'Keefe. 1977. "Construct Individuality,

Cognitive Complexity, and the Formation and Remembering of Interpersonal Impressions." *Social Behavior and Personality* 5:229–40.

———. 1980. "Interaction Analysis and the Analysis of Interactional Organization." In N. K. Denzin, ed., *Studies in Symbolic Interaction.* JAI.

O'Keefe, B. J., and S. A. McCornack. 1987. "Message Design Logic and Message Goal Structure: Effects on Perceptions of Message Quality in Regulative Communication Situations." *HCR* 14:68–92.

O'Keefe, B. J., and G. J. Shepherd, 1985. "The Pursuit of Multiple Objectives in Face-to-Face Persuasive Interactions: Effects of Construct Differentiation on Message Organization." Unpublished Ms., University of Illinois.

———. 1986. "Content and Structure of Impressions Formed during Face-to-Face Persuasive Interactions: Effects of Perceiver's Construct Differentiation and Target's Message Strategies." Unpublished Ms., University of Illinois.

O'Keefe, D. J. 1977. "Two Concepts of Argument." *JAFA* 13:121–28.

———. 1979. "Ethnomethodology." *JTSB* 9:187–219.

———. 1980. "The Relationship of Attitudes and Behavior: A Constructivist Analysis." In D. P. Cushman and R. D. McPhee, eds., *Message-Attitude Behavior Relationship.* Academic.

———. 1982. "The Concepts of Argument and Arguing." In Cox and Willard.

———. 1988. "Describing Messages." Paper for the SCA, Boston.

O'Keefe, D. J., and J. G. Delia. 1981. "Construct Differentiation and the Relationship of Attitudes and Behavioral Intentions." *CM* 48: 146–57

O'Keefe, D. J., and H. E. Sypher. 1981. "Cognitive Complexity Measures and the Relationship of Cognitive Complexity to Communication: A Critical Review." *HCR* 8:72–92.

Olsen, M., ed. 1970. *Power in Societies.* Macmillan.

Olshewsky, T. M. 1983. *Good Reasons and Persuasive Force.* University Press of America.

O'Neill, B. C. 1972. "Conventions and Illocutionary Force." *Philosophical Quarterly* 22:215–33.

Oppenheim, F. 1961. *Dimensions of Freedom.* St. Martin's.

Osgood, C. E., and P. H. Tannenbaum. 1955. "The Principle of Congruity in the Prediction of Attitude Change." *PR* 62:42–55.

Osterhouse, R. A., and T. C. Brock. 1970. "Distraction Increases Yielding to Propaganda by Inhibiting Counterarguing." *JPSP* 15:344–58.

Ozick, C. 1987. "Science and Letters: God's Work—and Ours." *New York Times Book Review*, September 27, p. 3.

Pagels, H. R. 1982. *The Cosmic Code.* Bantam.

Papageorgis, D. 1967. "Anticipation of Exposure to Persuasive Messages and Belief Change." *JPSP* 5:490–96.

———. 1968. "Warning and Persuasion." *Psychological Bulletin* 70:271–82.

Papageorgis, D., and W. McGuire. 1961. "The Generality of Immunity to Persuasion by Pre-Exposure to Weakened Counterarguments." *JASP* 62:475–81.

Percy, L. 1976. "How Market Segmentation Guides Advertising Strategy." *JAR* 16:11–22.

Perrow, C. 1979. *Complex Organizations.* 2d ed. Scott Foresman.

Perelman, C., and L. Olbrechts-Tyteca. 1969. *The New Rhetoric.* Notre Dame University Press.

Peters, D. P., and S. J. Ceci, 1982. "Peer Review Practices of Psychological Journals: The Fate of Published Articles, Submitted Again." *Behavioral and Brain Sciences* 5:187–255.

Pettigrew, A. M. 1979. "On Studying Organizational Cultures." *ASQ* 24:570–81.

Petty, R. E., and J. T. Cacioppo. 1977. "Forewarning, Cognitive Responding, and Resistance to Persuasion." *JPSP* 35:645–55.

———. 1979. "Issue Involvement Can Increase or Decrease Persuasion by Enhancing Message-Relevant Cognitive Responses." *JPSP* 37:1915–26.

———. 1981. *Attitudes and Persuasion.* Brown.

———. 1984. "The Effects of Involvement on Responses to Argument Quantity and Quality: Central and Peripheral Routes to Persuasion." *JPSP* 46:69–81.

Petty, R. E., J. T. Cacioppo, and R. Goldman. 1981. "Personal Involvement as a Determinant of Argument-Based Persuasion." *JPSP* 41:847–55.

Petty, R. E., and R. B. Cialdini. 1976. "The Role of Argumentation in Lasting Attitude Polarization." [Ms. cited in Cialdini and Petty, 1981.]

Petty, R. E., T. M. Ostrom, and T. C. Brock, eds. 1984. *Cognitive Responses in Persuasion.* Erlbaum.

Phillipsen, G. 1975. "Speaking 'Like a Man' in Teamsterville: Culture Patterns of Role Enactment in an Urban Neighborhood." *QJS* 61:13–22.

Planalp, S. 1985. "Relational Schemata: A Test of Alternative Forms of Relational Knowledge as Guides to Communication." *HCR* 12:3–29.

Planalp, S., and J. M. Honeycutt. 1985. "Events That Increase Uncertainty in Personal Relationships." *HCR* 11:593–604.

Poincare, H. 1952. *Science and Hypothesis.* Dover.

Poole, M. S., D. R. Seibold, and R. D. McPhee. 1985. "Group Decision-Making as a Structuration Process." *QJS* 71:74–102.

Popper, K. R. 1963. *Conjectures and Refutations.* Routledge.

———. 1972. *Objective Knowledge.* Clarendon.

———. 1982. *Realism and the Aim of Science.* Rowman and Littlefield.

Press, A. N., W. H. Crockett, and J. G. Delia. 1975. "Effects of Cognitive Complexity and of Perceiver's Set upon the Organization of Impressions." *JPSP* 32:865–72.

Press, A. N., and P. S. Rosencrantz. 1969. "Cognitive Complexity and the Learning of Balanced and Unbalanced Social Structures." *JP* 37:541–53.

Prewitt, K., and A. Stone. 1973. *The Ruling Elites.* Harper & Row.

Psathas, G. 1972. "Ethnomethods and Phenomenology." In J. Manis and B. Meltzer, eds., *Symbolic Interaction.* 2d ed. Allyn and Bacon.

Putnam, R. D. 1976. *The Comparative Study of Political Elites.* Prentice-Hall.

Quine, W. V. O. 1953. *From a Logical Point of View.* 2d ed. Harper.

———. 1960. *Word and Object.* Wiley.

———. 1969. *Ontological Relativity and Other Essays.* Columbia University Press.

Ranson S., B. Hinings, and R. Greenwood. 1980. "The Structuring of Organizational Structures." *ASQ* 25:1–17.

Ravetz, J. 1971. *Scientific Knowledge and Its Social Problems*. Clarendon.

Redner, H. 1987. "Pathologies of Science." *SE* 1:215–47.

Reichenbach, H. 1940. "On the Justification of Induction." *J. Philosophy* 37:97–103.

Rescher, N. 1970. *Scientific Explanation*. Free Press.

———. 1973. *The Primacy of Practice*. Oxford University Press.

———. 1977a. *Methodological Pragmatism*. Oxford University Press.

———. 1977b. *Dialectics*. SUNY Press.

———. 1978. "Philosophical Disagreement: An Essay towards Orientational Pluralism in Metaphilosophy." *Review of Metaphysics* 32:217–51.

Rhodes, J., and S. Newell, eds. 1980. *Proceedings of the [First] SCA/AFA Conference on Argumentation*. SCA.

Richards, B. 1971. "Searle on Meaning and Speech Acts." *Foundations of Language* 7:519–38.

Rieke, R. D. 1982. "Argumentation in the Legal Process." In Cox and Willard.

Rieke, R. D., and M. O. Sillars. 1984. *Argumentation and the Decision-Making Process*. 2d ed. Scott Foresman.

Riley, P., T. A. Hollihan, and Freadhoff. 1987. "Argument in the Law: The Special Case of the Small Claims Court." In F. H. van Eemeren, R. Grootendorst, J. A. Blair, and C. A. Willard, eds., *Argumentation: Analysis and Practices*. Foris.

Roloff, M. E., and C. R. Berger, eds. 1982. *Social Cognition and Communication*. Sage.

Romer, D. 1979. "Distraction, Counterarguing, and the Internalization of Attitude Change." *European J. Social Psychology* 9:1–18.

Rommetveit, R. 1974. *On Message Structure*. Wiley.

———. 1978. "On Negative Rationalism in Scholarly Studies of Verbal Communication and Dynamic Residuals in the Construction of Human Intersubjectivity." In M. Brenner, P. Marsh, and M. Brenner, eds., *The Social Contexts of Method*. Croom Helm.

———. 1980. "On The 'Meanings' of Acts and What Is Meant and Made Known by What Is Said in a Pluralistic Social World." In M. Brenner, ed., *The Structure of Action*. St. Martin's.

Rorty, R. 1979. *Philosophy and the Mirror of Nature*. Princeton University Press.

———. 1987. "Science as Solidarity." In Nelson, MeGill, and McCloskey.

Rosaldo, R. 1987. "Where Objectivity Lies: The Rhetoric of Anthropology." In Nelson, MeGill, and McClosky.

Rose, A. M. 1967. *The Power Structure*. Oxford University Press.

Rosen, N. A., and R. S. Wyer. 1972. "Some Further Evidence for the 'Socratic Effect' Using a Subjective Probability Model of Cognitive Organization." *JPSP* 24:420–24.

Ross, L. 1977. "The Intuitive Psychologist and His Shortcomings: Distortions in the Attribution Process." In L. Berkowitz, ed., *Advances in Experimental Social Psychology*. Vol. 6. Academic.

Ryle, G. 1949. *The Concept of Mind*. Hutchinson.

———. 1959. "Philosophical Arguments." In A. J. Ayer, ed., *Logical Positivism*. Free Press.

Rubin, R. B. 1977. "The Role of Context in Information Seeking and Impression Formation." *CM* 44:81–90.

———. 1979. "The Effect of Context on Information Seeking across the Span of Initial Interaction." *Communication Quarterly* 27:13–20.

Rudwick, M. J. S. 1985. *The Great Devonian Controversy*. University of Chicago Press.

Russell, B. 1928. *Skeptical Essays*. Norton.

———. 1948. *Human Knowledge*. Simon and Schuster.

Salhins, M. 1976. *Culture and Practical Reason*. University of Chicago Press.

Sampson, A. 1973. *The Sovereign State of ITT*. Stein and Day.

Santayana, G. 1954. *The Life of Reason*. Vol 1. Scribner's.

Schank, R., and R. Abelson. 1977. *Scripts, Plans, Goals, and Understanding*. Erlbaum.

Schatz, M. 1978. "The Relationship between Cognitive Processes and the Development of Communication Skills." In B. Keasey, ed., *Nebraska Symposium on Motivation*. Vol 20. University of Nebraska Press.

Schatz, M., and R. Gelman. 1973. "The Development of Communication Skills: Modifications in the Speech of Young Children as a Function of Listener." *MSRCD* 38:1–38.

Scheff, T. J. 1967a. "A Theory of Social Coordination Applicable to Mixed-Motive Games." *Sociometry* 30:215–34.

———. 1967b. "Toward a Sociological Model of Consensus." *ASR* 32:32–46.

———. 1970. "On the Concepts of Identity and Social Relationship." In T. Shibutani, ed., *Human Nature and Collective Behavior*. Prentice-Hall.

Scheflen, A. E. 1973. *Communicational Structure*. Indiana University Press.

———. 1974. *How Behavior Means*. Anchor.

Schegloff, E., G. Jefferson, and H. Sacks. 1977. "The Preference for Self-Correction in the Organization of Repair in Conversation." *Language* 53:361–82.

Schelling, T. C. 1948. *Toward a Theory of Strategy for International Conflict*. Rand.

Schenkein, J., ed. 1978. *Studies in the Organization of Conversational Interaction*. Academic.

Schiller, H. I. 1969. *Mass Communications and American Empire*. Kelley.

Schneider, D. J. 1973. "Implicit Personality Theory: A Review." *Psychological Bulletin* 79:294–309.

Schuetz, J. 1986. "Overlays of Argument in Legislative Process." *JAFA* 22:223–34.

Schultz, B. 1983. "Argumentativeness: Its Role in Leadership Perception and Group Communication." In Zarefsky, Sillars, and Rhodes.

Schutz, A. 1945a. "Some Leading Concepts of Phenomenology." *Social Research* 12:77–97.

———. 1945b. "On Multiple Realities." *PPR* 5:533–75.

———. 1951. "Choosing among Projects of Action." *PPR* 12:161–84.

———. 1953. "Common Sense and Scientific Interpretation of Human Action." *PPR* 14:1–37.

———. 1962. *Collected Papers I.* M. Natanson, ed. Nijhoff.

Scott, K. J. 1970. "Liberty, License, and Not Being Free." In A. de Crespigny and A. Wertheimer, eds., *Contemporary Political Theory.* Atherton.

Scott, R. L. 1967. "On Viewing Rhetoric as Epistemic." *CSSJ* 27:9–16.

———. 1976. "On Viewing Rhetoric as Epistemic: Ten Years Later. *CSSJ* 37:258–66.

Scriven, M. 1980. "The Philosophical and Pragmatic Significance of Informal Logic." In Blair and Johnson.

Searle, J. R. 1969. *Speech Acts.* Cambridge University Press.

———. 1974. "Chomsky's Revolution in Linguistics." In G. Harmon, ed., *On Noam Chomsky.* Doubleday.

———. 1975. "Indirect Speech Acts." In P. Cole and J. L. Morgan, eds., *Syntax and Semantics. Vol. 3: Speech Acts.* Academic.

———. 1979. *Expression and Meaning.* Cambridge University Press.

Sears, D. O. 1967. "Social Anxiety, Opinion Structure, and Opinion Change." *JPSP* 7:142–51.

Sells, S. B. 1936. "The Atmosphere Effect: An Experimental Study of Reasoning." *Archives of Psychology,* No. 200.

Selman, R. L. 1980. *The Growth of Interpersonal Understanding.* Academic.

Sennett, R. 1980. *Authority.* Vintage.

Seth, A., and R. B. Haldane. 1883. *Essays in Philosophical Criticism.* Longmans Green.

Settle, T., I. C. Jarvie, and J. Agassi. 1974. "Towards a Theory of Openness to Criticism." *PSS* 4:83–90.

Shantz, C. U., and K. Wilson. 1972. "Training Communication Skills in Young Children." *CD* 43:693–98.

Shatz, M., and R. Gelman. 1973. "The Development of Communication Skills: Modification in the Speech of Young Children as a Function of Listener." *MSRCD* 38, Serial No. 152.

Shibutani, T. 1962. "Reference Groups and Social Control." In A. Rose, ed., *Human Behavior and Social Processes.* Houghton Mifflin.

Shoeck, H., and J. Wiggins, eds. 1961. *Relativism and the Study of Man.* van Nostrand.

Shweder, R. A., and R. A. LeVine. 1984. *Culture Theory.* Cambridge University Press.

Sillars, A. L. 1982. "Attribution and Communication: Are People 'Naive Scientists' or Just Naive?" In Roloff and Berger.

Sillars, M. O. 1981. "Religious Argument as a Field." In Ziegelmueller and Rhodes.

Silverman, D. 1971. *The Theory of Organizations.* Basic Books.

Simon, H. A. 1976. *Administrative Behavior.* 3d ed. Free Press.

Simpson, M. E., and D. M. Johnson. 1966. "Atmosphere and Conversion Errors in Syllogistic Reasoning." *JEP* 72:197–200.

Smircich, L. 1983a. "Concepts of Culture and Organizational Analysis." *ASQ* 28:339–58.

———. 1983b. "Organizations as Shared Meanings." In L. R. Pondy, et al., eds., *Organizational Symbolism*. JAI.

———. 1985. "Is the Concept of Culture a Paradigm for Understanding Organizations and Ourselves?" In P. J. Frost, et al., eds., *Organizational Culture*. Sage.

Smith, C. R., and D. M. Hunsaker. 1972. *The Bases of Argument*. Bobbs-Merrill.

Smith, R. E., and R. F. Lusch. 1976. "How Advertising Can Position a Brand." *JAR* 37–43.

Snyder, M., and T. C. Monson. 1975. "Persons, Situations, and the Control of Social Behavior." *JPSP* 32:637–44.

Snyder, M., and W. B. Swann. 1976. "When Actions Reflect Attitudes: The Politics of Impression Management." *JPSP* 34:1034–42.

Socolow, R. H. 1976. "Failures of Discourse: Obstacles to the Integration of Environmental Values into Natural Resource Policy." In Tribe, Schelling, and Voss.

Solomon, R. C. 1977. *The Passions*. Anchor.

Sproule, J. M. 1980. *Argument*. McGraw-Hill.

Stich, S., and R. Nisbett. 1984. "Expertise, Justification, and the Psychology of Inductive Reasoning." In Haskell.

Stokes, R., and J. P. Hewitt. 1976. "Aligning Actions." *ASR* 41:838–49.

Stout, J. 1981. *The Flight from Authority*. Notre Dame University Press.

Strawson, P. F. 1958. "On Justifying Induction." *Philosophical Studies* 9:20–21.

———. 1959. *Individuals*. Methuen.

Streeck, J. 1980. "Speech Acts in Interaction: A Critique of Searle." *Discourse Processes* 3:133–54.

Stubbs, M. 1983. "May I Have That in Writing, Please? Some Neglected Topics in Speech Act Theory." *J. Pragmatics* 7:479–94.

Swain, M., ed. 1969. *Induction, Acceptance, and Rational Belief*. Reidel.

Swanson, D. L. 1977a. "A Reflective View of the Epistemology of Critical Inquiry." *CM* 44:207–19.

———. 1977b. "The Requirements of Critical Justification." *CM* 44:306–20.

Tagiuri, R., R. R. Blake, and J. S. Bruner. 1953. "Some Determinants of the Perception of Positive and Negative Feelings in Others." *JASP* 48:585–92.

Taubes, G. 1986. *Nobel Dreams*. Random House.

Thomas, W., and D. Thomas. 1928. *The Child in America*. Knopf.

Thompson, W. N. 1971. *Modern Argumentation and Debate*. Harper.

Tocqueville, A. de. 1956. *Democracy in America*. Mentor.

Tomko, T. N., and R. H. Ennis. 1980. "Evaluation of Informal Logic Competence." In Blair and Johnson.

Tonnies, F. 1957. *Community and Society*. Michigan State University Press.

Torrence, E. P. 1957. "Group Decision-Making and Disagreement." *Social Forces* 35:314–18.

Toulmin, S. E. 1964. *The Uses of Argument*. Cambridge University Press.

———. 1972. *Human Understanding*. Princeton University Press.

————. 1976. *Knowing and Acting*. Macmillan.

Toulmin, S. E., R. Rieke, and A. Janik. 1979. *An Introduction to Reasoning*. Macmillan.

Tracy, D. 1975. *Blessed Rage for Order*. Seabury.

Trapp, R. 1983. "Generic Characteristics of Argumentation in Everyday Discourse." In Zarefsky, Sillars, and Rhodes.

Trapp, R., and P. J. Benoit. 1985. "On Clarifying the Assumptions of an Interactional View of Argument." Paper for the Central States Speech Association, Indianapolis.

Trapp, R., and N. Hoff. 1985. "A Model of Serial Argument in Interpersonal Relationships." *JAFA* 22:1–11.

Tribe, L. H., C. S. Schelling, and J. Voss, eds. 1976. *When Values Conflict*. Ballinger.

Trigg, R. 1973. *Reason and Commitment*. Cambridge University Press.

Turner, R. G. 1977. "Self Consciousness and Anticipatory Belief Change." *Personality and Social Psychology Bulletin* 3:438–41.

Turner, R. H. 1962. "Role-Taking: Process versus Conformity." In A. M. Rose, ed., *Human Behavior and Social Processes*. Houghton Mifflin.

Turner, S. 1980. *Sociological Explanation as Translation*. Cambridge University Press.

Ulrich, W. R. 1985. "In Defense of The Fallacy." In Cox, Sillars, and Walker.

Unger, R. M. 1975. *Knowledge and Politics*. Free Press.

Vatz, R. E. 1973. "The Myth of the Rhetorical Situation." *P&R* 6:154–61.

Veatch, H. B. 1962. *Rational Man*. Indiana University Press.

Vertzberger, Y. Y. I. 1984. *Misperceptions in Foreign Policy Making*. Westview.

————. 1986. "Foreign Policy Decisionmakers as Practical-Intuitive Historians: Applied History and Its Shortcomings." *International Studies Quarterly* 30:223–47.

Wallace, K. R. 1963. "The Substance of Rhetoric: Good Reasons." *QJS* 49:239–49.

————. 1970. *Understanding Discourse*. Louisiana State University Press.

Walsh, W. H. 1947. *Reason and Experience*. Oxford University Press.

Walton, D. N. 1979. "Philosophical Basis of Relatedness Logic." *Philosophical Studies* 29:75–89.

————. 1980. "Why Is the *Ad Populum* a Fallacy?" *P&R* 13:264–78.

————. 1982. *Topical Relevance in Argumentation*. Benjamins.

————. 1983. "Enthymemes." *LA* 103–4:395–410.

————. 1985. *Arguer's Position*. Greenwood Press.

Warr, P. B., and C. Knapper. 1968. *The Perception of People and Events*. Wiley.

Watkins, J. W. N. 1970. "Imperfect Rationality." In R. Borger and F. Cioffi, eds., *Explanations in the Behavioral Sciences*. Cambridge University Press.

Watson, J. D. 1968. *The Double Helix*. Signet.

Watts, W. A., and L. E. Holt. 1970. "Logical Relationships among Beliefs and Timing as Factors in Persuasion." *JPSP* 16:571–82.

―――. 1979. "Persistence of Opinion Change Induced under Conditions of Forewarning and Distraction." *JPSP* 37:778–89.

Weber, M. 1930. *The Protestant Ethic and the Spirit of Capitalism.* Allen and Unwin.

―――. 1947. *The Theory of Social and Economic Organization.* Glencoe.

Wegner, D. M., and T. Giuliano. 1982. "The Forms of Social Awareness." In W. J. Ickes and E. S. Knowles, eds., *Personality, Roles, and Social Behavior.* Springer-Verlag.

Wegner, D. M., and R. R. Vallacher. 1977. *Implicit Psychology.* Oxford University Press.

Weick, K. E. 1969. *The Social Psychology of Organizing.* Addison-Wesley.

Weimer, W. B. 1979. *Notes on the Methodology of Scientific Research.* Erlbaum.

―――. 1984. "Why All Knowing Is Rhetorical." *JAFA* 20:63–71.

Weimer, W. B., and D. S. Palermo, eds. 1974. *Cognition and Symbolic Processes.* Erlbaum.

Wells, G. L., et al. 1977. "Anticipated Discussion of Interpretation Eliminates Actor-Observer Differences in the Attribution of Causality." *Sociometry* 40:247–53.

Wenzel, J. W. 1979. "Jurgen Habermas and the Dialectical Perspective on Argumentation." *JAFA* 16:83–94.

―――. 1980. "Perspectives on Argument." In Rhodes and Newell.

―――. 1985. "Toward a Normative Theory of Argumentation: Van Eemeren and Grootendorst's Code of Conduct for Rational Discussions." In Cox, Sillars, and Walker.

―――. ed. 1987. *Argument and Critical Practices.* SCA.

―――. In press. "Norms of Argument: A Rhetorical Explanation." In R. Meier, ed., *Norms in Argumentation.* Foris.

Werner, H. 1948. *Comparative Psychology of Mental Development.* International University Press.

Westerlund, G., and S. Sjostrand. 1979. *Organizational Myths.* Harper.

Whately, R. 1836. *Elements of Logic.* Jackson.

Whitehead, A. N. 1929. *The Function of Reason.* Princeton University Press.

Whitehurst, G. J., and S. Sonnenschein. 1981. "The Development of Informative Messages in Referential Communication: Knowing When versus Knowing How." In Dickson.

Whitley, R., ed. 1974. *Social Processes and Scientific Development.* Routledge.

―――. 1984. *The Intellectual and Social Organization of the Sciences.* Clarendon.

Willard, C. A. 1976. "On the Utility of Descriptive Diagrams for the Analysis and Criticism of Arguments." *CM* 43:308–19.

―――. 1978a. "A Reformulation of the Concept of Argument: The Constructivist/Interactionist Foundations of a Sociology of Argument." *JAFA* 14:121–40.

―――. 1978b. "Argument as Nondiscursive Symbolism." *JAFA* 14:187–93.

―――. 1981. "The Status of the Non-discursiveness Thesis." *JAFA* 17:190–214.

————. 1982. "Argument Fields." In Cox and Willard.

————. 1983. *Argumentation and the Social Grounds of Knowledge.* University of Alabama Press.

————. 1985a. "Cassandra's Heirs." In Cox, Sillars, and Walker.

————. 1985b. "The Science of Values and the Values of Science." In Cox, Sillars, and Walker.

————. 1987a. "Valuing Dissensus." In van Eemeren, Grootendorst, Blair, and Willard.

————. 1987b. "The Language of Individualism." Paper for the Conference on Public Discourse, Northwestern University.

————. 1987c. "Argumentation et le principes social du reconnaissance." Paper for *Argumentation et Signification, Centre Culturel International de Cerisy-La-Salle,* France.

————. 1987d. "Peer Response to Redner." *SE* 1:278–81.

————. 1988. "The Balkanization of Knowledge and the Problem of the Public Sphere." Ms., Department of Communication, University of Louisville.

————. In press. "Argument as a Social Enterprise." In R. Meier, ed., *Norms in Argumentation.* Foris.

Willard, C. A., and T. J. Hynes. 1988. *Valuing Dissensus.* Ms., University of Louisville.

Williams, R. 1981. *Culture.* Fontana.

Willihnganz, S. C. 1987. "Impact of Individual Differences in Social Cognition and Message Strategy Use on Perceptions of Social Support and Job Satisfaction in Nurses." Ph.D. dissertation, University of Illinois.

Wilson, B. A. 1980. *The Anatomy of Argument.* University Press of America.

Wilson, B. R., ed. 1979. *Rationality.* Blackwell.

Wilson, T. P. 1970. "Normative and Interpretive Paradigms in Sociology." In J. D. Douglas, ed., *Understanding Everyday Life.* Aldine.

Winch, P. 1958. *The Idea of a Social Science and Its Relation to Philosophy.* Routledge.

Wisdom, J. 1952. *Foundations of Inference in the Natural Sciences.* Methuen.

Wolff, R. P. 1968. *The Poverty of Liberalism.* Beacon.

————. 1969. *Critique of Pure Tolerance.* Beacon.

Woods, J., and D. Walton. 1974. "Argumentum Ad Vericundiam." *P&R* 7:135–53.

————. 1975. "Petitio Principii." *Synthese* 31:107–27.

————. 1976. "Fallaciousness without Invalidity?" *P&R* 9:52–54.

————. 1977. "Towards a Theory of Argument." *Metaphilosophy* 8:298–315.

————. 1978. "Arresting Circles in Formal Dialogues." *JPL* 7:73–90.

————. 1979. "Laws of Thought and Epistemic Proofs." *Idealistic Studies* 9:55–65.

————. 1982. *Argument: The Logic of the Fallacies.* McGraw-Hill.

Woolgar, S. 1976. "The Identification and Definition of Scientific Collectivities." In G. Lemaine, ed., *Perspectives on the Emergence of Scientific Disciplines.* Aldine.

Wyer, R. S. 1974a. *Cognitive Organization and Change*. Erlbaum.

———. 1974b. "Some Implications of the 'Socratic Effect' for Alternative Models of Cognitive Consistency." *JP* 42:399–419.

———. 1975. "The Role of Probabilistic and Syllogistic Reasoning in Cognitive Organization and Social Inference." In M. Kaplan and S. Schwartz, eds., *Human Judgment and Decision Processes*. Academic.

Wyer, R. S., and D. Carlston. 1979. *Social Cognition, Inference, and Attribution*. Erlbaum.

Yingling, J. M., and R. Trapp. 1985. "Toward a Developmental Perspective on Argumentative Competence." In Cox, Sillars, and Walker.

Zarefsky, D. 1980. "Process, Product, or Point of View?" In Rhodes and Newell.

———. 1981. " 'Reasonableness' in Public Policy Argument: Fields as Institutions." In Ziegelmueller and Rhodes.

———. 1982. "Persistent Questions in the Theory of Argument Fields." *JAFA* 18:191–203.

Zarefsky, D., M. O. Sillars, and J. Rhodes, eds. 1983. *Argument in Transition*. SCA.

Ziegelmueller, G., and J. Rhodes, eds. 1981. *Dimensions of Argument*. SCA.

Ziller, R. C. 1955. "Scales of Judgment: A Determinant of the Accuracy of Group Decisions." *HR* 8:153–64.

Ziman, J. 1968. *Public Knowledge*. Cambridge University Press.

Zimbardo, P. G., et al. 1965. "Communicator Effectiveness in Producing Public Conformity and Private Attitude Change." *JP* 33:233–55.

Zimmerman, D. H. In press. "On Conversation: The Conversation Analytic Perspective." In J. A. Anderson, ed., *Communication Yearbook 11*. Sage.

Index

Abelson, R. P., 41, 259
Abortion dispute, 100
Abrahamsson, B., 18
Academe: as discourse domain, 74. *See also* Argument field
Accommodation, 2, 14, 17, 19, 20, 26–28, 62, 116, 118, 144, 165, 171, 177–78, 252, 259
Account sequencing, 88. *See also* Agreement
Accountability. *See* Zones of accountability
Acquiescence, reflective, 183–86. *See also* Critique
Acts, communicative, 51, 71, 72–73, 80, 83, 90. *See also* SAT
Adams, K. L., 88
Adjacency pairs, 46–47. *See also* Conversation
Adorno, T. W., 28
Advertising, 13, 108–109, 216, 231, 262, 274. *See also* Segmentation
Agassi, J., 118, 125
Agreement, preference for, 42–43, 59, 85–89, 115, 123–27, 149. *See also* Opposition. *Cf.* Dialectical motive
Ajzen, I., 22, 41
Allport, F. H., 28
Altman, I., 49

Alvy, K. T., 171
Ambiguity, 89, 96, 142
Ammon, P., 165
Amsterdam School, 37. *See also* Eemeren, F. H. van
Analysis, units of, 23–30
Analytic Philosophy, discipline of, 41
ANOVAs, 248, 255
Anscombe, G. E. M., 55
Anthropology, profession of, 167, 214
Applegate, J. E., 21, 35, 62, 165, 166, 272
Aquinas, T., 177
Arendt, H., 132, 138
Arguing, 13, 61, 69, 71, 78–81, 92, 97–98
Argument, 1–8, 42–49, 91, 104, 110; and agreement, 49; ambiguity and evasion in, 89, 93; analysis, 245; and anxiety, 116; and authority, 134–35; and children, 101, 104, 113; cognitive development, 8, 76; and common ground, 257; as communication, 38, 92; competencies, 62; complex, 43–45, 52, 61, 63, 66, 259; claims as acts, 73; and Conventional MDL, 95, 107; conversational regulation/repair, 46, 102; cooperative activity, 40, 54, 61; and culture, 83; and debate, 44, 170; and democracy, 114, 198; as disciplined thought, 2; and discursive claims, 101;

Argument, *continued*
and dissensus, 53; emergent process, 67–90; enthymemes, 102; and ethos, 131–43; and Expressive MDL, 95, 99, 107, 255, 257; as epistemic, 52, 112–30; and field-based procedural rules, 52; fuzzy construct, 101; and illocutionary force, 98; impersonal nature of, 16; individualism, 144; and inference, 105–107; and Informal Logic, 206; as interaction, 42–66, 105, 140; interdisciplinary construct, 3; and intersubjectivity, 48; models of, 255; naturally occurring, 42–43, 45, 46, 53, 54, 102; and organizations, 17, 88; parity in, 50–52; and perspective-taking, 62; and persuasion, 109; and preference for agreement, 123; private and public, 108; prolepsis in, 51; and propositional logic, 100; psychology and logic, 186–87; and rationality, 148–150; and reciprocity of perspectives, 48; rehearsal, 107; restraints upon, 202; and Rhetorical MDL, 95, 99, 106, 107; and rule structure, 8, 43, 45, 81, 258–60; and science, 173; and relationships, 84–85; and SAT, 97; and silence, 97–98; and syllogisms, 101; symbolic nature of, 16; and tentativeness, 118–23; and textual studies, 106–108; and truth conditions, 24; and turn-taking, 43–44, 102; Utterance, 91–111; as a value, 118; versus fights, 85–87. *See also* CRC
Argumentation, discipline of, 4, 8, 91, 104, 109, 127, 136, 149, 152, 158–59, 168, 182–83, 205–208, 214–15, 216–22, 235, 238, 239–56; and debate, 158, 253; and freedom, 150; as normative discipline, 74–75, 149, 215, 253; organizing interests of, 11–12; pedagogy, 169–74, 202; and rationality, 149; and skepticism, 29–30. *See also* Discipline
Argument field (discourse domain, social domain), 11, 17, 24, 25, 29, 37, 52, 59, 105, 108, 117, 129, 153, 157, 160, 165, 187, 192, 201, 210, 213, 214, 215, 218, 219, 233, 239; as unit of analysis, ix, 207, 209–210, 262. *See also* Discipline; Disciplined: discourse; Profession
Argyris, C., 39, 124, 140, 165
Arieli, Y., 144

Aristotle, 8, 15, 25, 31, 65, 75, 101, 105, 117, 127, 129, 132, 134, 139–44, 153, 154, 157, 159, 161, 162, 168, 172, 177, 192, 222, 228–31, 241, 245, 246, 247, 248, 250, 263
Aron, R., 5
Aronson, E. J., 133
Artificial intelligence, 76
Asch, S. E., 22
Asher, S. R., 171
Ashworth, P. D., 22
Assimilation, 14, 17, 20, 22, 165, 177
Associationism, 248
Athay, M., 72
Atmosphere effects, 247
Atomism, 147–48
Attention, principle of, 213. *See also* Audience; Segmentation
Attitude theory, 118–19. *See also* Behaviorism
Attribution, 53, 213, 248
Audience, 120–21, 212–13, 215, 216; analysis, 88, 262–63. *See also* Positioning; Segmentation
Augustine, 177
Auschwitz, 156
Austin, J. L., 55, 69, 81
Authenticity, 257–58
Authoritarian Personality, The, 28
Authority, 16, 24, 131–42, 172, 220, 221, 223–25, 261; argument from, 215, 224, 226, 228–30; deference to, 13, 134–35, 137–38, 182; and ethos, 142; and modernity, 138–41; sources of, 223–25. *See also* Credibility; Ethos; Expertise; Fallacy
Aviation, discipline of, 170–71
Ayer, A. J., 127

Bachrach, P., 17, 140, 198
Background awarenesses, 52, 104. *See also* Indexicality; Intersubjectivity
Bacon, F., 228
Ball, D. W., 61
Ballard, K. E., 230, 231
Balthrop, V. W., 91, 108, 128
Balzac, H., 5
Barber, B., 182
Bar-Hillel, Y., 207
Barker, E. M., 41, 61, 74, 132
Barnes, H. E., 146, 155
Baron, R. S., 133

28, 232; *Ad Populum,* 230–32; *Ad Misericordiam,* 225, 230–32; *Ad Verecundiam,* 224, 232
Fanaticism, 117, 188, 130. *See also* Zealousness. *Cf.* Good will
Fanshel, D., 72, 165
Farr, R., 39, 164
Farrell, T. B., 128
Fearnside, W. W., 221, 253
Feather, N. T., 247
Feedback, 107, 113
Feigl, H., 247
Festinger, L., 113, 130, 135, 140
Feyerabend, P., 252
Feynman, R. P., 125
Figert, A. E., 135
Filmore, C. J., 62, 165
Fincham, F., 164
Finley, G. E., 171
Fischer, M. M. J., 25, 155
Fisher, W. R., 108, 128
Fiske, S. T., 136
Flathman, R., 139
Flavell, J. H., 171
Fogelin, R. J., 132, 223, 237, 253
Forester, J., 113
Forgas, J. P., 48, 49, 164
Formalism, 14–16, 91, 148, 245–55
Form-Matter relationship, Aristotle's, 246
Foucault, M., 139, 140, 183, 189, 210, 219, 273. *See also* Critique
Foundationalism, 131, 138–40
Fragmentation corollary, 20. *See also* PCT
Freadhoff, K. D., 157
Freedom, 9, 176–204; and Argumentation, 150; as cognitive option, 192–96; versus discipline, 176, 182–90; first amendment, 224; negative and positive, 176, 177, 189, 202; and modernity, 150; press, 261
Freeley, A., 74, 253, 254
Freeman, D., 135
Frege, G., 246
Freidson, E., 137
Friendship, 84–85, 88
From, F., 48
Fromm, E., 28, 197
Frost, P. J., 18, 248
Fry, C. L., 171
Fuller, S., 7, 8, 37, 128, 152, 185, 210
Fuzziness as a fact, 101, 104, 209, 218, 219, 240–45

Galbraith, J. K., 5
Galileo, 246
Game metaphor, 16–17, 68, 81, 192–98
Garfinkel, H., 49, 52, 56, 164
Gass, S. T., 171
Gay, J., 154
Geertz, C., 16, 24, 25, 37, 155, 164
Gellner, E., 38, 104, 155, 169, 204
Generalized other, 17. *See also* CSI; Mead, G. H.
Genetic epistemology, 21. *See also* Piaget, J.
Genetics, discipline of, 214
Geology, profession of, 214
Gerald, J. E., 261
Gerard, H. B., 119, 133
Gesellschaft, 144
Gestalt theory, 248
Giddens, A., 38, 39, 259
Gierke, O., 144
Gieryn, T. F., 135
Gilbert, G. N., 214
Gillig, P. M., 133
Ginsberg, B., 24
Giuliano, T., 22
Glenn, P. J., 166
Goal: conflict, 31–32; structure of speech acts, 47
Goethals, G. R., 136
Goffman, E., 16, 28, 48, 54, 64, 72, 95, 136, 164, 258, 259, 264, 271
Goldman, R., 141
Goodenough, W. H., 25, 164
Goodman, J., 171
Goodnight, G. T., 30, 43, 68, 126, 139, 149, 157, 158, 185, 189
Good will (open-mindedness, tolerance), 2, 3, 116–23, 130, 148–50, 233, 234, 236, 264–65. *See also* Dialectical motive; Opposition. *Cf.* Fanaticism; Truth
Goodwin, C., 71
Goodwin, M. H., 71
Gottlieb, G., 108, 149
Gould, S. J., 160, 197
Gouran, D. S., 125
Govier, T., 232. *See also* Fallacy
Grammar, 31, 46, 57, 62; disciplines as creative, 209–13, 216–17, 219, 239, 256; and message strategies, 266–68
Green, M. J., 5
Greenberg, B. S., 133

102, 104–105, 111, 186, 207, 208. *See also* Enthymeme; Ethnomethodology

Individualism, 9–10, 37–40, 75, 130, 139, 142, 144–45, 178; debate about, 9, 10, 28, 37–40, 69, 116, 148–50, 176, 180–82

Individuality corollary, 20. *See also* PCT

Induction, problem of, 246–47

Inference (cognitive processes, reasoning, rehearsal, thinking), 15, 18, 19, 21, 105–108, 123, 175, 206–207, 247, 248

Informal Logic, discipline of, 3, 8, 14, 37, 104, 136, 168, 206, 220, 221, 235–38

Inner Parliament, 254–55. *See also* Inference

Innoculation, 63

Innovation, 213, 215, 243, 265, 268, 270, 271. *See also* Progress

Institutions, 72–73, 81, 105, 147. *See also* Argument field; SAT

Intentionality, 99, 106–107, 207, 222, 255, 265, 270; institutional (organizational), 265–66. *See also* Enthymeme; Indexicality; PCT

Interactional, theory of argument, 27, 91–93, 105, 140, 189–204; and cognitive development, 113; and ethos, 139; and organizations, 147; and rationality, 158

Interfield: borrowing of ideas, 213–15, 218, 235, 268; discourse, 7, 8, 9; theories, 8. *See also* Innovation; Peripheral discourse; Progress

Interpersonal: impressions and communication, 21; rules, 43

Interpretive: model of organizations, 248; schemes, 21–22, 53, 56, 57–58, 59–61, 78

Intersubjectivity (coorientation), 21, 37, 41, 45, 47–54, 57, 67, 69, 70–72, 74, 79, 83, 97, 118, 123, 144, 162–63, 173, 187, 258–59, 267, 269. *See also* Enthymeme; Relationship

Iran, 126, 194, 265

Irrationality, 160, 167, 168, 201, 243

Jackson, S. A., 8, 43, 46, 47, 59, 72, 80, 95, 102, 124, 250, 259

Jacobs, S., 43, 53, 59, 80, 124, 258

James, H., 68

Janik, A., 149, 159, 225, 226, 230, 232

Janis, I. L., 5, 124, 125, 140

Jarvie, I. C., 118, 125

Jaspers, J., 164

Jaspers, K., 257

Jefferson, T., 4, 5, 174, 177, 198

Jehenson, R., 39

Jellison, J. M., 122

Jensen, J. V., 132, 253, 254

Jervis, R., 64

Johnson, D. M., 247

Johnson, S., 121

Johnson, R. E., 37, 221, 222, 223, 232, 237. *See also* Fallacy

Johnstone, H. E., 2, 114, 128

Jones, E. E., 22, 119, 131, 133, 136

Jones, R. A., 135

Jonestown, 194

Jordanova, L. J., 210

Journalism, 29, 73, 250, 260–62; and MDLs, 261–62

Journalists, Society of Professional (Sigma Delta Chi), 261

Judicial: argument, 8, 223; settings, 74

Jurisdiction, public, 258–59

Jurisprudence, 105, 120; as metaphor, 44, 52, 185, 214

Kahane, H., 37, 74, 132, 221, 224, 227, 232, 234, 253

Kant, I., 162

Katz, E., 134

Katz, J. J., 246

Kauffeld, F. J., 68, 69, 70

Keller, S., 5

Kelley, H. H., 84, 127

Kellner, H., 139

Kelly, G. A., 18, 19, 22, 41, 65, 84, 85, 106, 193, 194, 195, 196, 221, 241, 243–44, 248, 255, 264. *See also* PCT

Kelman, H., 28, 132, 135, 177, 265

Kempler, D., 165

Kenny, M., 6, 135

Kepler, J., 246

Kiesler, C. A., 140

Kiesler, S. B., 140

King, B. T., 140

Kirkpatrick, F. G., 143, 144

Kitcher, P., 173

Klein, W., 187–88

Kleppner, O., 262

Kline, S. L., 62, 166

Kluckhohn, C., 24, 164

Knapper, C., 53, 263

Organization corollary, 18, 241. *See also* PCT

Organization Man, The, 178

Organizations, 12, 38, 88, 147, 167–68, 180, 181, 198, 199, 209, 213, 248–50; argument in, 88; preference for agreement versus opposition in, 123–27, 148–50, 179; as processes, 17; and rationality, 167–68; theories of, 259

Organizing schemes, 59; social nature of, 60. *See also* Constructivism

Orthogenetic principle, 20, 32, 113, 241. *See also* Competence

Orwell, G., 197

Osgood, C. E., 135

Ostrowski, M. V., 171

Ostrum, T. M., 140

Pagels, H. R., 137, 146, 190, 211, 216, 217

Paleontology, discipline of, 262

Palermo, D. S., 162

Paradigm case, 99–100, 111, 163, 169, 182–83, 213, 214, 217, 218, 219. *See also* Enthymeme; Textbook writing

Pareto, V., 39, 200

Parity in argument, 50–52, 236

Partial inclusion, 28

Pascal, Turbo, 76

Pauli, W., 146

PCT (Personal Construct Theory), 18–21, 38, 192–96, 248; CSI, 40; and individualism, 178. *See also* Constructivism; Freedom

Pedagogy, 8, 14, 74–75, 80, 114, 160, 161, 163, 178, 182, 198, 210, 217, 235; and rationality, 153, 159–60, 168, 171–74; Argumentation, 169–74, 202, 254–55

Percy, L., 262

Peripheral discourse, 37, 189, 190, 213–15, 265. *See also* Interfield; Positioning; Segmentation

Perlocutionary force, 47. *See also* SAT

Perrow, C., 5

Personal Construct Theory. *See* PCT

Perspective-taking: in argument, 62; as rationality, 162–66. *See also* Competence; Intersubjectivity; Relationship

Persuasion, 31, 102, 108–11, 120, 122, 131–34, 163, 166, 168, 222, 228, 230–31, 250, 263, 265

Peters, B. G., 2, 140

Peters, D. P., 135

Petras, J. W., 200

Petty, R. E., 115, 122, 123, 136, 140, 141

Phillipsen, G., 101

Phillipson, H., 49, 54

Philosophy, profession of, 189, 238, 242

Physical metaphor, 240–42, 246

Physics, 73, 82, 116, 189, 214, 217, 229, 247. *See also* Quantum Mechanics

Piaget, J., 14, 20, 21, 27, 45, 125, 147, 187, 242

Planalp, S., 61

Planck Hypothesis, 214

Plato, 129, 144, 161, 172, 183

Platonic, 127

Platonic universals, 55

Pluralism, 186, 190, 198, 240, 261–62. *See also* Elites

Pluralism, theoretical, 10, 247–50, 252

Pogo, 197

Poincare, H., 196

Political: effects of criticism, 252; freedom, 176, 186; ideology of involvement, 198–200

Political Science, profession of, 3, 224, 232

Politics, 1, 120, 223, 224

Politics and Ambiguity, 142

Popper, K. R., 9, 38, 74, 204, 210

Position (coherence between thought and action, public rationale), 10, 12, 13, 19, 24, 63, 64, 66, 67, 82, 88, 112, 117, 122, 123, 190, 191, 196, 205, 207, 213, 215, 216, 231, 245, 253, 255, 257–74; two kinds of, 263–64; legal briefs, 269–70; and MDLs, 254–55, 266–68; and texts, 268–73. *See also* Moderation effect

Positioning, 262–63, 274. *See also* Advertising; Position

Positivism, 134–35, 159

Postmodernism, 142, 176, 177–78, 182, 185, 190. *See also* Critique

Power Elite, 17. *See also* Elites

Powerlessness, 5, 6

Practical tradition, 209, 211. *See also* Discipline

Precization, 170, 253

Press, A. N., 136

Presumption, 30, 43, 59, 68–69, 124, 125, 126, 182, 185, 189, 228–29, 232

Prewitt, K., 5

Primitive cultures, 154–55
Principia Mathematica, 246
Private versus public: effects of argument, 15; kinds of argument, 108
Problem focus, 211. *See also* Discipline
Profession, 111, 210–11, 215, 216. *See also* Anthropology; Communication; Philosophy; Physics; Psychology; Sociology. *Cf.* Discipline
Progress, epistemic, 125, 141, 160, 169, 185, 191–92, 243, 268, 270. *See also* Ecological metaphor; Importation of ideas; Innovation; Interfield; Jurisprudence; Whiggishness
Prolepsis, 51. *See also* Enthymeme
Propaganda, 234. *See also* Fallacy
Propositional logic and argument, 100. *See also* Informal Logic; Logic
Psychological: freedom, 181, 191–97; processes (*see* inference); preferences, 123–24; structure of argument, 8; system (*see* Cognitive, systems); view of argument, 105; terms, 105
Psychology: profession of, 14, 221, 222; and logic of argument, 186, 187, 192, 193–97, 218, 247
Public: compliance, 261; discourse, 3, 11, 24, 115, 157; effects of going, 122–23; and private argument, 15, 38–39; and rationality, 175; relations, 39, 250, 265; utterances and commitment to position, 122
Public sphere, 9–10, 141–42
Publishing, 215
Putman, R. D., 5

Quantity maxim, 102–104
Quantum Mechanics (physics), 146, 190, 214, 216, 217, 248; discipline of, 217. *See also* Copenhagen; Physics
Quine, W. V. O., 7, 22, 23, 69, 100, 152, 196, 214
Quintilian, 153, 163

Radio Television News Directors Association, 261
Range corollary, 20. *See also* PCT
Ranson, S., 39
Rational: bureaucratic model of organizations, 248–49; desire to appear, 264–65; judgment and ethos, 131, 135

Rationale, public. *See* Position
Rationalism, critical, 125, 184
Rationality, 9, 29, 100, 114–15, 143, 148–50, 212, 213, 215, 268, 269; as anthropological datum, 131, 159–60, 166–68; bounded, 23, 102, 123, 170, 264; and decisions, 5; and cognitive development, 165; as consistency, 156; ecological sense, 161–63; and emotivism, 153; as epideictic construct, 153–54; as garbage can or facade, 264–65; history of, 160–62; instrumental, 154, 156, 163, 167; ontological sense, 159–60; and organizations, 167; pedagogy, 159–60, 170–71; as perspective-taking, 162–66; and public discourse, 175; and reflexiveness, 164; rhetoric of, 4–6, 171–74; theories of and about, 159. *See also* Dialectical motive; Theatrical metaphor
Ratzinger, Cardinal, 10
Ravetz, J., 135
Rawls, J., 186
Reagan, R., 7, 13, 77, 99, 111, 263, 264
Reason-giving, 62, 92–93, 100
Reciprocity of perspectives, 48, 57–58
Redner, H., 6, 135
Reflective acquiescence, 113, 114, 139–40, 178–86, 192, 199, 203. *See also* Habermas, J.
Reflexivity, 58; and rationality, 164–66, 173, 174
Rehearsal, 107, 122–23. *See also* CSI; Inference
Reichenbach, H., 207, 246
Relationship, 23, 47–50, 52, 54–56, 69, 71, 72, 84–85, 97, 101, 222, 227–28, 234. *See also* Intersubjectivity
Relativism, 139, 154–55, 186
Relativity, 3, 10, 11, 117, 118, 141, 151, 153
Relevance, 232–33, 237. *See also* Fallacy
Rescher, N., 2, 44, 149, 173, 215, 231
Research tradition, 104, 109, 135, 221, 238, 240, 244. *See also* Discipline; Peripheral discourse
Retrospective-prospective sense of occurrence, 58, 89, 93, 124
Revolution, 214, 215, 216, 222. *Cf.* Evolution
Rhetoric: as adaptation and accommo-

Rhetoric, *continued*
dation, 28; in constitution of communities, 169, 206; discipline of, 14, 127; of discipline versus rhetoric of freedom, 182, 186; as epistemic, 37, 127–29; as grammar, 212–13; of science, 127; self-justifying, 168–69, 171–74; situation, 73–75
Rhetorical Criticism, discipline of, 250–55, 272
Rhetorical MDL, 32, 34–35, 37, 44, 50, 53, 59, 95, 99–100, 106, 114–116, 249, 261, 266–68. *See also* MDL
Richards, B., 69
Rieke, R. D., 8, 74, 132, 149, 157, 159, 225, 226, 230, 232
Riley, P., 157
Ritualistic View, 128
Rockwell, N., 114
Roloff, M. E., 162, 164
Rommetveit, R., 46, 51, 52, 70, 226
Rorty, R., 126, 233, 241
Rose, A. M., 5
Rosen, N. A., 122
Rosenstein, N. E., 88
Ross, L., 18, 22, 254
Rousseau, J. J., 144, 145, 147, 177, 259
Rubin, R. B., 65
Rules, 37, 54–57, 61, 68–70, 72–74, 81, 82, 144, 149, 154, 171, 178, 183, 184, 235, 236, 258–60. *See also* Conversation; Discipline
Rule utilitarianism, 171–74, 224
Russell, B., 146, 153, 169, 246, 253
Ryle, G., 56, 154

Santayana, G., 153
Sartre, J.-P., 145–46
SAT (Speech Act Theory), 33, 37, 47, 52, 64–73, 78, 80–82, 97, 111
Satisficing, 23, 102, 123, 170, 264. *See also* Rationality
Saussure, F. de, 41
Saying and maintaining, 63
Scheff, T. J., 48, 53, 54
Scheflen, A. E., 47, 70
Scheler, M., 39
Schelling, C. S., 5
Schelling, T. C., 49
Schrödinger, E., 217
Schuetz, J., 157
Schultz, B., 87

Schutz, A., 18, 48, 52, 56, 164
Science, 44, 74, 157, 161, 173–74, 178, 209, 231; bashing of, 6; as legitimator, 225. *See also* Critical rationalism; Rhetoric: of science
Scott, K. J., 184
Scott, R. L., 127, 128
Searle, J. R., 13, 33, 47, 52, 68, 70, 71, 72, 80, 89
Sears, D. O., 123
Secord, P. F., 164
Segmentation, 216, 217, 262, 273. *See also* Advertising; Audience; Division of labor; Peripheral discourse; Positioning
Self-similarity, 39–40, 193, 195
Sells, S. B., 247
Sennett, R., 139
Serial predication, 8, 15, 61, 91, 92, 94, 99–100, 103, 110, 112, 149, 205, 213, 216, 217, 241, 245, 246, 253–54. *See also* CRC
Settle, T., 118, 125
Shantz, C. U., 171
Shapiro, M. M., 84
Shaw, G. B., 197
Shepard, G. J., 31
Shibutani, T., 55
Shweder, R. A., 24
Sillars, A. L., 131, 132
Sillars, M. O., 74, 159
Silverman, D., 167
Simmering down, 83, 84–85, 124. *See also* Relationship
Simon, H. A., 5, 23, 125, 254
Simpson, M. E., 247
Sisyphus, 146
Situation, 68, 72–75, 136, 165, 207, 222, 239, 247, 249, 251–52, 271–73. *See also* Definition of situation
Sjostrand, S., 265
Skepticism, 4–7, 29–30
Slippery slope, 224, 232. *See also* Fallacy
Smircich, L., 248
Smith, A., 144
Smith, C. R., 149, 156, 198, 254
Smith, R. E., 262
Snyder, M., 123
Social: entities as units of analysis, 23–24; and encounters, 49; nature of communication, 70, 147; nature of organiz-

322 / Index

ing schemes, 60; reality, 22; forces and individualism, 75; structure, 68, 75–77, 250

Social comparison, 10, 112–13, 127, 149, 183, 191, 203, 241; and MDLs, 130, 254, 261; in interactional theory, 190

Sociality corollary, 20. *See also* PCT

Socialization, 17, 28, 76, 113, 168–69, 171, 189. *See also* Cognitive: development

Social judgment theory, 119

Social sciences, 18, 165, 243–44, 256

Sociologic, 63–65. *See also* PCT

Sociology, 154–55; literature, 9; of Knowledge, 3, 128; profession of, 167, 222; of Science, 3, 128, 209

Socolow, R. H., 158

Socrates, 15, 88, 120, 231

Socratic effect, 122–23

Sonnenschein, S., 171

Sophists, 144

Sorokin, P. A., 39

Space Shuttle *Challenger*, 125–27

Specialism, 137, 200. *See also* Authority; Ethos; Expertise

Speech Acts, 68; and economy, 102

Speech Act Theory. *See* SAT

Spencer, H., 114, 145. *See also* Darwinists; Ecological metaphor

Sphere of relevance, 98, 205–207, 209–19, 220–23, 236–37, 239–56

Spinoza, B., 177

Spokesperson, 265. *See also* Position

Sproule, J. M., 132, 254

State of nature, 145, 147. *See also* Enlightenment thought

Stein, G., 89

Stich, S., 135, 137, 138, 173, 229

Stoics, 177

Stone, A., 5

Strategic repertoire, 21, 62, 70, 165

Strategy, 31, 115

Strawson, P. F., 247

Streeck, J., 47, 52, 71, 72

Stubbs, M., 52

Stuttman, R. K., 88

Style, as integral to substance, 37, 128

Subjective understanding, and PCT, 193

Subjectivism, 20

Supreme Court, U.S., 262

Surrender, and accommodation, 28

Swain, M., 246

Swann, W. B., 123

Swanson, D. L., 99

Syllogism, 23, 25, 75, 101, 159, 161, 162, 215, 246, 247, 248

Sypher, H., 166

Systems, 165, 196, 215, 241; cognitive, 218, 254–55; disciplines are not, 206, 209, 214, 219, 241; logical, 162

Systems theory, 124

Tagiuri, R. R., 22, 84

Tannenbaum, P. H., 133, 135

Tarsky, A., 111

Taubes, G., 6, 135

Taylor, D. A., 49

Taylor, S. E., 136

Taylorism (Taylor, F. A.), 248

Technique, 3, 158, 170

Teleology, 127, 138, 139, 161, 194, 251; of truth, 156–57

Tentativeness, 118–23. *See also* Good will

Text: milieu, 16, 40, 106–108, 209–12, 217, 239, 243, 244–45, 271; positions and MDLs related to, 268–71; object of analysis, 245, 250, 255, 256, 268–70; rationality a feature of, 159. *See also* Literatures

Textbook writing, 99, 114, 182, 254, 262

Textual: analysis, 94; studies, 23, 106–108

Theatrical (dramaturgical) metaphor, 16, 28, 34–35, 67, 107, 114–16

Theresa, Mother, 156

Thomas, D., 18

Thomas, W., 18

Thomism, 246

Thompson, W. N., 254

Thoreau, H. D., 197

Tocqueville, A. de., 23, 24, 25, 114, 144

Tolerance of disagreement, 11, 114, 121–23, 177. *See also* Dialectical motive; Opposition

Tomko, T. N., 8

Tonnies, F., 144

Topic and topical coherence, 89, 136

Topoi: and ethos, 136; and fallacies, 235–36

Torrence, E. P., 87

Toulmin, S. E., 2, 14, 15, 29, 37, 38, 74, 108, 132, 149, 159, 185, 186, 187, 188, 210, 214, 215, 217, 221, 225, 226, 230, 232, 247, 255, 268